Business Career College Life License Qualification Program Course

Version 14.08 - August, 2014

Business Career College (Edmonton) Corp

#206 Capilano Mall

5004 98 Ave NW

Edmonton AB  T6A 0A1

Telephone:  (780) 482-5990

Toll Free: (877) 934-5577

Fax:  (780) 482-6990

Toll Free Fax:  (866) 379-8025

E-mail:  sales@businesscareercollege.com

Web:  www.businesscareercollege.com

ISBN:  978-0-9809815-1-3

Distributed by:

Business Career College (Edmonton) Corp

#206 Capilano Mall

5004 98 Ave NW

Edmonton, AB  T6A 0A1

Printed and Bound in Canada

# TABLE OF CONTENTS

# Chapter 1 AN INTRODUCTION TO THE INSURANCE INDUSTRY

Welcome to a rewarding career in the insurance industry. In this career, you will help others to deal with a variety of risks. In order to prepare you for this industry, you will first be expected to complete your Life Insurance licensing exam. In order to be permitted to write your licensing exam, you will first need to pass a certification exam.

This text is designed to prepare you for your new career, while also preparing you for the exams that you will have to write.

The course is based on the Life License Qualification Program Design Document, which outlines exactly what every student obtaining a life insurance license is expected to know. Unlike many other courses, this course is based on practical application of the material. That is, you will be expected to recognize a client's potential needs and to know how to address those needs. Put another way, the student passing this exam is expected to be able to apply this information in a real-life scenario.

## RISK

In order to cover this material, we will first look at the idea of risk. Each of the products that you will learn about in this course is designed to help somebody (a family, an individual, a business, and others whom we will look at in this text) deal with one or more risks. What, then, is a risk? A risk is a chance for loss or, in some cases, gain. A loss could be a financial loss, an emotional loss, or a loss of health. A gain could be a financial gain, an emotional gain, or a gain of health.

An aspiring athlete who wants to be a star will have to take some risks in order to do so. First, she will have to train. Training is a risk; she stands to gain in that she could improve her physical conditioning and her skill at her chosen sport. However, she also risks injury each time she trains. She might choose to use performance-enhancing drugs in her training. This would be a further risk. If she does not get caught, she might excel and achieve success. However, the risk is that she might be caught and expelled from her sport. She could damage her body irreparably, and she also faces the risk of public humiliation. While these are extreme examples, each of us every day makes decisions about risk. Should I try and make that left turn? Should I take a shortcut through a residential neighborhood? Can I leave work early today?

## THREE PREDICTABLE RISKS

The risks that we will specifically deal with here are known as the three predictable risks. These are the risks that people may have to deal with in the course of their lifetime. These risks can have an impact on individuals, families, and businesses.

- The risk of premature death. Premature death means death that would happen before we expect it. If a person dies at 90 or 95 years of age, we are seldom shocked. This is not what we refer to when we discuss premature death. Rather, we're looking at the risk associated with death that would happen when it is unexpected. For example, the parent who is killed in an automobile collision on his way home from work is a premature death. We can see that this would have terrible and devastating consequences.

- The risk of disability and sickness. Disability and sickness can both have severe consequences. These can range from a loss of income due to inability to work, to medical expenses, to requiring family and friends to offer support and assistance.

- The risks associated with old age. In today's society, we typically equate old age with retirement. Retirement generally means a loss of income, but this can be a very expensive time. Money will be required for basic living expenses, possibly for fulfilling lifelong dreams such as travel, and for medical expenses. With no active sources of income, this can be a very expensive time, and the risk of running out of money is very real.

The products that we are going to look at in this course are all designed to deal with one or more of these costs in some way. When dealing with insurance, we are dealing with pure risks. Pure risks are risks where the risk involves only a chance for a loss by the risk-taker. This is opposed to speculative risk, where the risk-taker hopes to profit by taking a risk.

## RISK MANAGEMENT

In our day-to-day lives, each of us deals with risk. When we decide to hit the snooze button and get an extra 10 minutes of sleep, we risk that we are not going to get to work on time. In exchange for taking that risk, we get an extra 10 minutes of sleep. In the course of our day, we are constantly going through the process of assessing and dealing with risk. There are many different ways that we might deal with risk. We could broadly categorize those into:

- Risk Retention. This is the idea that we recognize that there is a risk, but choose to pursue a particular course of action anyways.

- Risk Avoidance. With this risk management technique, we take steps to ensure that we do not have to deal with a particular risk.

- Risk Mitigation.  In this case, we recognize that we take a risk, but we take steps to minimize or mitigate that risk or its consequences.  There are several different ways that we might control a risk:
    - Risk reduction:  We might employ safety measures to reduce the chance of suffering a loss;
    - Risk control:  We might take steps to reduce the severity of a loss; and
    - Segregation:  We might spread our risk around, so that one loss by itself will not be devastating.
- Risk Financing.  We might find ways to ensure that, even if a loss occurs, there will be funds available to offset the consequences of a loss.  This is sometimes called self-insurance.  This would involve setting aside enough funds that if a loss occurred, those funds could be accessed in order to offset the consequences of that loss.
- Risk Transfer.  We recognize that we face risks, and we look for others who are willing to help us deal with those risks.  We transfer some of that risk, typically by using insurance.  Insurance is a product designed to indemnify an insured in the case of a loss.  That is, the insured would receive some sort of financial compensation, ideally allowing them to minimize or negate the consequences of a loss.  Normally, there is some sort of financial consideration provided by the insured to the insurer in exchange for the insurer's willingness to take on that risk.

Working in the life insurance industry, you are going to have the opportunity to help families, individuals, and business owners deal with the three predictable risks.  The responsibility will fall on you to help these people recognize, prepare for, and deal with the three predictable risks.

In Canada, the insurance industry is subject to regulation.  At the federal level, that regulation comes in the form of the Uniform Life Insurance Act.  However, insurance is a provincially regulated industry, so the actual laws and regulations by which you do business do not flow from the Uniform Life Insurance Act, but from the Insurance Act in your respective province.  From the perspective of the agent, there are only minor differences in how the Act in each province applies to you.  Quebec, of course, has a separate set of laws governing the structure and sale of insurance in that province.  This course will prepare you to obtain a license to work in the insurance industry in any province except for Quebec.

As you read through this text, you will be introduced to a variety of products.  You will be expected to learn not just the basic structures of those products, but which of the risks they help to deal with and how they help to deal with those risks.  Ultimately, you will be tested in your ability to recognize which risks will be most significant for a client (be that client an individual, a family, or a business) and how you will help that family to deal with those risks.

# THE INSURANCE INDUSTRY IN CANADA

## HISTORY

The idea of insurance dates back several thousand years. The earliest historical evidence of insurance indicates that ship owners in ancient China and Egypt recognized that they faced risks - mostly financial - when their ships set sail. In order to prevent financial devastation in the event of the loss of a ship, they sought to transfer some of that risk. They would find like-minded ship owners, and those groups of like-minded ship owners would be prepared to cover off the losses of one of the members of their group. There is evidence of this happening as long ago as 6,500 years.

Life insurance is a slightly more recent innovation, with evidence of life insurance arrangements dating back some 4000 years. There is evidence that the ancient Babylonians, Turks, Romans, Indians, and Greeks all used life insurance in some form. Typically, these took on the form of burial societies - arrangements wherein, upon the premature death of a member of the society, funds would be made available to pay for a funeral for the deceased. In some cases, there were even additional funds made available to the survivors to help with their ongoing needs. We see similar arrangements in modern Fraternal Benefit Societies, which we will further discuss later on in this chapter.

It was the Romans who gave us the earliest Accident & Sickness (hereafter abbreviated as A&S) insurance. Roman military societies insured their members - serving and/or retired soldiers - for loss of life, imprisonment, and disability. These disability contracts were the ancient ancestors of a product that we will look at in great detail later on in this text.

With the fall of the Roman Empire, insurance in general fell out of favour in Western Civilization. Until the rise of the European merchant states in the 1400s, we did not see insurance used a great deal. In those merchant states, maritime insurance again became a common commercial arrangement. An unfortunate chapter in the history of life insurance saw all sorts of cargoes being insured in those times, including slaves in transit from one port to another.

The first modern life insurance contract that we are aware of was written in 1583 in London on William Gybbons. It was a one-year term insurance policy, and the reason we are aware of it is that there are court documents related to a dispute between the insurer and Gybbons' survivors as to the payment of the death benefit.

From those times on, we saw the evolution of life insurance products and annuities, and the eventual re-introduction of A&S insurance products. Whole life insurance was introduced in 1762; universal life came much later, in 1980. Disability insurance, health insurance, and travel insurance are all relatively new products in their present forms. It is only within the past few decades that critical illness and long-term care insurance were introduced.

In Canada, insurance dates back to the late 1800s. The biggest Canadian life insurers trace their roots back to these times. Sun Life was founded in 1865; Manulife in 1887 (with Sir John A Macdonald as its first President); Great West Life in 1891.

Today, the life insurance industry in Canada is a diverse, competitive market. As of 2012, there were 90 different insurers active in the life and health insurance industry. In that year, $83.3 billion dollars worth of premiums were collected. There were 94,700 life and health insurance agents active in Canada in 2012. The insurance industry is a major contributor to the Canadian economy. At the end of 2012, the life and health insurance industry represented $513 billion dollars worth of investment in the Canadian economy and directly employed more than 47,900 people in addition to the independent agents discussed above. A Statistics Canada survey of 20 different industries identified finance and insurance as the industry with the third highest average earnings for the years 2003-2007.

## STRUCTURE

While there is no one model for the structure of a Canadian insurance company, there are some common characteristics among Canadian insurers. We will have a look at the various entities involved in the operation of a typical Canadian insurer:

- Owners. Insurance companies, like other companies, have owners of some sort. Sometimes the owners of insurers doing business in this country are based right here in Canada; sometimes they are located elsewhere. The location of a company's owners has no bearing on how they do business here. All insurers doing business in Canada must adhere to the same sets of laws and regulations. There are, broadly, three types of ownership structures:

  - Stock Companies: Stock companies are owned by their shareholders. Sometimes these stock companies allow their stock to be publicly traded on the stock markets. In other cases, the stock in the company is closely held by a relatively small group. In either case, the shareholders control the direction, and ultimately, share in the profits, of the insurer. (examples: Manulife, Empire Life, and Great West Life.)

  - Mutual Companies: Mutual companies are owned by their policy owners. When a policy owner acquires an insurance policy from a mutual company, that policy owner also becomes an owner of the company. Like stock companies, corporate direction is typically set by a board of directors and carried out by the company's executives. (examples: State Farm, Assumption Life and Equitable Life.)

  - Fraternal Societies: Fraternal societies are not corporations in the traditional sense. Instead, they are organizations which have arisen to fulfill some goal common to their members. While they do offer insurance and investment products to their members, they typically have a broader goal of bettering the lives of their members or improving the communities in which they operate. They are normally organized into lodges or branches. (examples: Knights of Columbus and Independent Order of Foresters)

- Actuaries. These highly-educated individuals have a very good understanding of statistics and demographics. They combine these understandings to design insurance and investment products for insurance companies. It was only with advancements in actuarial science that we saw the insurance industry mature. When we look at the structure of premiums in Module 3, we will further discuss the role of the actuary.

- Underwriters. Underwriters are responsible for assessing risk. The agent (discussed below) gathers information from the client, and the underwriter uses that information to determine how the insurer will deal with the client. We will discuss in greater detail the role of the underwriter in Module 2.

- Claims Examiners. Claims examiners are responsible for the determination and payment of claims. When a claimant submits a request for benefits (called a claim), the claims examiners assess that claim to determine whether it meets the criteria laid out in the policy. If so, they will pay the claim as requested. If not, they may deny the claim, or arrange for a lesser amount of benefits to be paid. We will further examine how claims are paid in Module 3.

- Head Office. Insurance companies have head offices, sometimes centrally located, or sometimes distributed. This head office staff coordinates the activities of all the other parties involved in the operation of the insurer.

- Distribution and Support. It is most likely that you are obtaining your life insurance license because of your involvement in this aspect of the industry. It is through distribution and support that the products designed by actuaries, under the vision of the owners, and with the support of head office, get into the hands of the clients. There are three types of distributors of insurance products:

  - Agents: Agents work directly for an insurer. They will only distribute the products offered by that insurer. Their direct relationship with their insurer means that they will be hired, trained, and have their career managed by that insurer. At one time, the insurance industry distributed products nearly exclusively through the agency system. Through the rest of this text, we will refer to any distributor of insurance products as an agent, for ease of understanding. (examples: Sun Life, La Capitale.)

- Brokers: While there are still a large number of agents distributing products, brokers are responsible for a great deal of distribution in today's market. Brokers have no particular relationship with any one insurer. Instead, they may have contracts with several different insurers allowing them to distribute the products of those insurers. Those insurers will have no active role in the training or career management of the brokers. Brokers will usually have more independence than agents, but they will generally not have access to the same support structures as those offered to agents. Some brokers are owned by insurance companies, but they still operate as brokers. Some brokerages even provide a degree of support similar to that offered in the agency system. (examples: PPI, IDC/WIN and Hub Financial.)

- Benefits Consultants: Benefits consultants are a fairly new type of distributor. While at one time the range of benefits offered by employers was very straightforward, today we see that the very nature of employment has changed. Employers today use sessional workers, contract workers, and outsourcing. Workers are not likely to stay with their employer for more than a few years, and will switch careers several times in the course of their working lives. All this change has meant that the traditional set of employee benefits is not always the right match for an employer-employee relationship. In response to these changes, benefits consultants provide solutions to employers to help them manage their relationships with their employees, contractors, and whoever else does their work for them. Part of what these benefits consultants do is to offer access to certain types of insurance and investment products. (examples: Towers Watson, Mercer.)

- Clients. While not, strictly speaking, a part of the insurance company's structure, they are the focus of this whole process. Without clients, there would be no products, there would be no distribution, and there would be no premiums paid. There are three different types of clients that we will look at:

  - Insured: The insured, also known as the policy owner, is the party who takes out and controls the policy. The insured actually enters into a contract with an insurance company.

  - Life Insured: The life insured is the life which is being insured. It is the health of this party that we are concerned with in the insurance contract.

  - Beneficiary: The beneficiary is not a party to the insurance contract, but is a party named by the insured who will receive the benefits if a claim is honoured.

## REGULATION

The insurance industry in Canada is provincially regulated. The provincial regulations, which take the form of the Insurance Acts in each province, are based on a federal body of legislation, the Uniform Life Insurance Act. Because the Insurance Acts are based on the Uniform Life Insurance Act (except in Quebec, where legislation is unique to that province) there are not huge legislative differences from province to province.

Canadian insurers can be either federally or provincially chartered. The differences between the two are not normally of great consequence to the agent, but the agent would have to be aware if the company he represents is not chartered to do business in a particular province. Most insurers are federally chartered, but there are a few that only operate in one or two provinces.

# TYPES OF PRODUCTS

There are a wide variety of products offered by Canadian insurers today. We will break them down into three broad types:

### LIFE INSURANCE

Life insurance is designed to help protect against the costs associated with death. With life insurance products, the insured pays premiums into a pool (properly called the reserve). That pool is managed by an insurance company. When a life insured dies, some of the money in the reserve is used to pay a death benefit. Earlier in this chapter, we specifically discussed the risk of premature death. All the products we will look at here help to manage the risk of premature death, and some of them go beyond that. A life insurance license is required for an agent to sell and service these products.

- Term Insurance: The simplest, least expensive form of insurance. Term insurance offers the lowest initial premiums in most cases, and it is usually designed to fill a specific need for a specific period of time. Somebody taking out a mortgage will often acquire term insurance so that, if death occurs while there is still an amount owing, the mortgage will be paid off. Term insurance will be inexpensive at a young age, but it gets more costly with age, and normally becomes unavailable at a predetermined age. There is no cash value associated with term insurance; it's similar to renting an apartment. At the end of the term of your policy, assuming that no benefits have been paid, there is nothing concrete to show for having paid premiums. Most term insurance sold in Canada today is renewable. This means that at the end of a set term, it is possible for the client to renew coverage without evidence of insurability. These terms usually last 5, 10, or 20 years. Upon renewal, the client can retain their coverage, but will have to pay a higher premium based on their age. The last option to renew will usually come about around age 65 or 70. Many term insurance contracts are also convertible, which means they can be converted into permanent insurance without underwriting.

- Permanent Insurance: Permanent insurance is a more expensive and more versatile insurance product. It is designed to stay in force for as long as the life insured should live. Permanent insurance products are often used when there is a need for estate planning or estate preservation. The client who wishes to pass some sort of wealth on to a charity, a business, or their own family will use these products. There are, very broadly, three types of permanent insurance:

  - Whole Life: Whole life features guaranteed premiums which may be paid for a limited period, or for the whole life of the life insured. It is usually much more expensive at the policy's issue date than term insurance, but its cost will not increase. The insurance company manages the reserve, and, if a policy owner terminates the policy, there is the opportunity for that policy owner to access the cash values associated with the policy. Coverage is in force either until the policy is terminated by the insured or until the death of the life insured.

  - Universal Life: Universal life gives the policy owner great flexibility. It is still permanent insurance, but the policy owner is given flexibility to manage the policy reserve, the amount of premiums, and the coverage in force. It is somewhat more complex than whole life, and requires a degree of active management by the insured.

  - Term to 100: Term to 100, usually abbreviated as T-100, is permanent insurance with no, or very limited, cash values. Because it lacks the cash values associated with whole life or universal life, it is less expensive. At the same time, it is a more basic product and provides the policy owner with less flexibility.

## ACCIDENT & SICKNESS

Accident & sickness products are designed to help deal with the consequences of an accident or sickness. Sometimes this is simply a reimbursement of medical expenses; sometimes it involves income replacement, and sometimes it provides a lump sum of cash which can be used for whatever the beneficiary wishes.

- Disability Insurance: Disability insurance is designed to replace the income lost when an insured is unable to work because of a disability. Disability insurance can provide income replacement in the event of accident, sickness, or both. There is also a selection of disability insurance policies specifically designed for business owners. These policies do not necessarily replace lost income, but will help a business to deal with a disability of one of its owners or employees.

- Extended Health Care: We are fortunate in Canada to have a very good public health care system. However, not all health care costs are necessarily borne by the various provincial health care plans in place. In order to fill in the gap between publicly funded plans and the actual costs of receiving health care, one could acquire an extended health care policy. These policies reimburse a wide range of expenses, such as prescription drugs, eyeglasses, and dental care.

- Critical Illness Insurance: While cancer, heart conditions, and stroke are all leading causes of premature death today, advances in medical science have significantly increased the odds of surviving one of these conditions. Unfortunately, this does not always mean the problems have been addressed. A cancer survivor, for example, might have to undergo a regimen of chemotherapy, during which time that person would be unable to work, and would likely require significant support from loved ones. This carries a great financial burden. Critical illness insurance, which pays a lump sum benefit, is designed to assist with that burden.

- Long-Term Care Insurance: As old age sets in, it is likely that there will come a point at which one is no longer able to take care of oneself. While our health care system provides a basic level of health care at this point, there may be costs beyond what the health care system will help with. Long-term care insurance is designed to help with those costs.

- Travel Insurance: For somebody who is going to be spending time away from home, there is always a risk of becoming sick or injured while away. Travel insurance will help to deal with the costs associate with that risk. It may provide reimbursement for expenses incurred, or it might help to bring the sick or injured person home for treatment.

- Accidental Death and Dismemberment: Accidental death and dismemberment insurance provides a lump sum benefit in the event of death, or the loss, or loss of use of, limbs, or, in some cases, sight, hearing, or speech. This benefit is provided only in the event that the loss occurs as a result of an accident.

## INVESTMENT PRODUCTS

Insurers have developed a range of investment products in order to help insurance agents help their clients to deal with the risk of old age. These products do not see a large benefit paid in the event of a loss, unlike insurance products. Instead, these products provide ways to obtain a return on investments that will allow them to have a comfortable, risk-free retirement.

- Segregated Funds. Segregated funds allow a client to invest, be it a lump sum or a periodic investment of some sort. The investment is pooled with other like-minded investors. A professional manager will invest the funds and get returns based on some sort of underlying investment, such as bonds or equities. The insurer guarantees that if the investment loses value, or the client dies at the wrong time, the client (or the named beneficiaries) will still receive a portion of their investment back.  Ideally, though, the client would leave their money invested in the segregated fund for a period of time, and then be able to access the funds to accomplish some sort of objective, such as retirement.

- Annuities.  An annuity allows a client to use a lump sum of cash to purchase an income stream.  The income stream will be guaranteed either for a predetermined term, or for the life of the client.  This product is ideal for retirement, when a client might want to turn their life savings into a source of income.

## GROUP BENEFITS

It is worth noting that many of the products discussed in this section are also available through group contracts.  Employers, unions, associations, and creditors all acquire group plans to help their members or borrowers deal with the three predictable risks.

## SUMMARY

Having read module 1, you should now have a good understanding of the insurance industry in Canada.  Through the rest of the text, you will see these ideas amplified and you will learn the function and detail behind the various products introduced here.

# Chapter 2 THE APPLICATION FOR INSURANCE

In this module, we will examine the application for insurance. By understanding the application, we will learn how insurance contracts work, examine underwriting issues, and study the agent's role in this process.

## THE INSURANCE PROCESS

Before examining the application, we will briefly look at the three steps in the insurance process:

- **The Application**. Completion of the application is the first step in the insurance process. It is through the completed application that we know that the client has some interest in entering into a contractual relationship with the insurer.

- **The Policy**. If the insurer accepts the risk associated with insuring the client, based on the information provided in the application, then a policy will be issued.

- **A Claim**. A claim is the ultimate step in the insurance process. The claimant submits a claim for benefits, which the insurance company honours. In some contracts, the claim will terminate the contract. Some contracts, though, will continue even after claims have been submitted, allowing multiple claims on the same contract.

## PARTS OF THE APPLICATION

Insurance applications are broadly broken into four components. The components are:

- **Personal Information**. In this portion, we will gather information about the insured, the life insured, and the beneficiaries. This may include contact information, occupation, citizenship status, financial information, and lifestyle information.

- **Product Information**. This portion of the application will help the client to understand what product they are purchasing. It is common for insurers to insist that their agents create illustrations - projections of product performance and pricing - as part of the application process.

- **Medical Information**. It will be necessary in many cases to gather some degree of medical information about the client. This might be as simple as a few questions. When large amounts of insurance are sought, when clients are older, or when products are complex, medical information can be very detailed, and can include physician's statements, laboratory tests, and specialist appointments.

- **Agent's Comments**. The agent is the only representative of an insurer who normally has direct contact with the client. As a result, the responsibility falls on the agent to provide an assessment of the client. Sometimes this is very simple, but sometimes, detailed agent comments can make the difference between an insurer's decision to accept or deny an application.

## PERSONAL INFORMATION

There are a variety of reasons for collecting personal information about the client. We have already touched on the responsibility to Know Your Client, and we will discuss that further in Module 4, but the questions asked in the application process are basic to that process. While the agent should already have some familiarity with the client by the time the application process is started, the application gives an opportunity to make sure that all the relevant information has been collected.

There is a great variety of personal information that might be collected about the client at this point, and different companies will have different standards. Some of the information an agent might collect would be:

- **Contact Information**. Obviously it is necessary that the agent and insurer will be able to contact the client. It may also be necessary to see some sort of identification such as driver's license, passport, or citizenship documentation. This allows the insurer to know who the insured and life insured are.

- **Financial Information**. Depending on the type and amount of insurance being sought, it might be necessary to get pay stubs, old tax documents, or financial statements for the client's business.

- **Lifestyle Information**. Lifestyle choices can have a significant bearing on a client's insurability. Clients who have dangerous hobbies, who travel extensively, or who have a history of drug or alcohol abuse might find themselves treated differently than other clients. A poor driving record can also lead an insurer to treat a client differently.

- **Citizenship Status**. While Canadian citizenship is not a prerequisite for insuring somebody, insurers need to be aware of the risk they are entering into. Spending time abroad can be a source of additional risk. Also, the primary language spoken can be a concern if there are ever questions about the ability to read the contract or application.

- **Insurance in Force/Applied For**. Insurers do not wish to be placed in a position where somebody is planning to kill or harm themselves or somebody else for a benefit. Sometimes this can be revealed when somebody purchases an unusual amount of insurance relative to their net worth or income.

- **Occupation**. The job somebody does for a living can have a substantial bearing on their ability to acquire and justify the need for insurance. Disability insurance, especially, is structured around occupation.

- **Ownership**. At this point, it will have to be determined who the policy owner and life insured will be. Also, if multiple lives are being insured under the same policy, that will have to be indicated. Some of the information discussed will have to be gathered about the insured and all life insureds.

- **Beneficiaries**. For products that have a beneficiary, that will be identified in the application as well. There will be more discussion around beneficiaries in Module 3.

- **Business Information**. In cases where insurance is being acquired to deal with a business or corporate need, there can be significant additional information required. This can include financial statements and balance sheets, tax returns, articles of incorporation, and business plans.

For most of the information gathered, the client is taken at their word. Sometimes supporting documentation is required. For example, some insurers will ask potential clients to generate a motor vehicle report. The motor vehicle report shows a history of traffic infractions. However, for the most part, the client answers the question provided in the application, and they sign the application indicating that the information provided is true. We will deal with the consequences of false or misleading statements in Module 3

## PRODUCT INFORMATION

While the client likely already has some idea of what they are purchasing, this section of the application gives the client a written explanation of the products in question. This is also normally the point at which the client selects appropriate riders and benefits (to be discussed in Module 6).

Products that feature an investment component of some sort will typically require some supplemental documentation here. Agents are expected to prepare illustrations of future performance for such products. For example, a universal life insurance policy might require an illustration of how the coverage will change over time based on projected investment returns. Normally a software package of some sort will be made available to help agents prepare these illustrations.

Illustrations are not only necessary for investment-type products. Many other products require an illustration, which gives the client an idea as to what premiums will have to be paid, how coverage will work, and under what circumstances claims will be paid.

The illustration is not a contract, and is only designed to show how a product will most likely work. However, the illustration does create an expectation, and, as such, agents must be cautious when generating illustrations. Where a rate of return forms part of the illustration, the agent must use a realistic rate of return, and should also prepare an alternate illustration showing what will happen if the actual rate of return is less than what has been assumed.

## MEDICAL INFORMATION

Medical information will be collected about all lives insured. The amount of medical information collected varies depending on the type of product and amount of insurance in question. Other factors, such as age, occupation and previous medical history can lead to additional information being collected.

Normally the medical information process requires the greatest amount of underwriting. While the agent is not an underwriter, the agent is responsible for assisting in the underwriting process. Underwriting simply means assessing risk.

There are three levels of medical information that will be required:

- **Non-medical.** In many cases, the agent will be able to complete the medical portion of the underwriting process. This can consist of a few very short questions (smoking status, family history of certain conditions), or sometimes a more detailed set of questions. The agent might even be expected to take a swab test, having the client wipe a swab on the inside of their mouth. This swab kit ('spit kit') would then be sent in to the underwriting laboratory for further testing. Non-medical underwriting is normally done where a small amount of insurance is being sought, or the product in question is not overly complex, or the life insured is at a relatively young age.

- **Para-medical.** When larger amounts of insurance are being requested, or the client is older, or the situation is more complex, a medical professional will be involved in gathering medical information. The para-medical will normally be a nurse or paramedic who can take blood and other samples. When a para-medical is involved, there will normally be a more thorough set of medical questions asked, in addition to blood, urine, and saliva samples.

- **Full Medical.** For older clients seeking large amounts of life insurance, or where the client may not have seen a doctor in some time, or where there are specific medical concerns, a full medical will be required. The full medical is a complete medical exam conducted by a physician. Sometimes a specialist may also be involved in this process.

## AGENT'S COMMENTS AND RESPONSIBILITIES

While the client, a medical professional, and possible third party sources are all necessary providers of information, the agent has a vital role to play in this process. First, the application will be completed by the agent and the client(s) working together. The agent, who understands the insurance process, will help the client to understand the application. This process can be somewhat intimidating, and the client needs to understand the need for giving thorough and complete information in the application.

Wrong or misleading information provided during the application process can lead to significant problems during the underwriting process, or, worst of all, at the time a claim is submitted.

The agent has a responsibility during this process to act as a guide for the client. The insurance process is not necessarily transparent for most people, so anything the agent can do to make the process clear and easy to understand will be welcome. The agent is expected to present the questions and information in the application process in language that can be understood by the client. At the same time, the client must have a correct understanding of the insurance being offered.

The agent is not only responsible to the client. The agent also has a responsibility to the insurer. The insurer needs to understand exactly what sort of risk they are looking at so that they can deal appropriately with the client. The agent's responsibility to the insurer is twofold. First, the agent is expected to help the client to answer the questions in a truthful and accurate way. Second, the agent is expected to give the insurer some sort of opinion about the client. Keep in mind that the agent will, in most cases, be the only representative of the insurance company to have direct contact with the client. As somebody who understands the insurance process, the agent is expected to act as an intermediary between client and insurer.

In order to facilitate the agent's role, most insurance applications have a section where the agent would provide some sort of commentary. This is provided so that the agent can explain something that might not otherwise be clear in the application, or to provide information that there might not be an opportunity to provide in the application. For example, if a very large amount of insurance is being applied for, it might be good for the agent to explain why.

As the intermediary between insurance company and insurer, the agent must understand her dual responsibility. The responsibility to the insurance company is that the correct information is provided, and that the agent does not encourage the client to manipulate the facts in any way. The responsibility to the client is to ensure that the correct coverage is requested, taking into account the client's own situation.

Once all the relevant information has been gathered, the agent has some further responsibilities. The agent is expected to witness the signatures of the insured (owner/applicant) and the life insured. The agent also signs the application as an agent for the insurer.

The agent should not view the application as a form to be completed. Rather, it is an opportunity. It's an opportunity to explain the insurance process to the client. It's an opportunity to better understand the client's situation. It's an opportunity to explain fully to the insurer why this client is requesting this amount and type of insurance.

# THE COMPLETED APPLICATION

The agent's responsibilities do not end with the completed application. In many cases, the agent will also estimate (usually with the assistance of a software program) the first premium. The agent may collect the first premium as well. This creates what is, according to the law, known as consideration. Consideration simply means an exchange of value, and it is a necessary component of most contracts.

The completed application constitutes what is known as the offer. This is another legal component of a contract. The offer is the indication that there is some interest in doing business together.

Once the application is completed, the agent will deliver it to the insurer. The agent may also be required to arrange para-medical or medical underwriting. This is often done through independent contractors - often contacted directly by the agent.

It is not uncommon for the insurer to take more than a few weeks, and often some months, to decide on whether and how a policy will be issued. Because of this, the insurer might allow the agent to put some coverage in place. Before we discuss the underwriting process, we will learn about the temporary insurance agreement.

# THE TEMPORARY INSURANCE AGREEMENT

The Temporary Insurance Agreement (TIA) - also known as a Conditional Insurance Agreement - gives the agent the opportunity to put coverage in place for the client. This coverage is designed only to fill the void while the insurer assesses the risk and decides whether or not to issue a policy.

The TIA is not always available, but it is used frequently enough that the agent must understand it. Each insurer offers slightly different terms for their TIA, but it is fairly common to deal with the following:

- **The decision to issue.** The onus is on the agent to issue a TIA. Some insurers will place restrictions, so that if certain questions had an affirmative answer the agent will not be permitted to issue a TIA. Some insurers even have an 'application within the application' that must be completed in order for a TIA to be issued. For example, a client who has recently been declined for insurance coverage elsewhere might not receive a TIA. There is no requirement to issue a TIA. If an agent suspects that the client is not being honest, for example, she might decide not to issue a TIA.

- **Limits on the TIA.** While TIAs vary from company to company, they all have limits as to either how much coverage they provide, or how long the coverage will last for, or both. An agent should be familiar with the different terms and conditions for the TIAs offered.

- **Requirement for first premium**.  Normally it is necessary that the client pay the first month's premium in order to initiate the TIA.  There are a few insurers who waive this requirement.  However, for the purpose of contract law, it should be taken into account that consideration is required to have a valid contract.

- **Underwriting**.  TIAs will normally only be issued in cases where the agent is confident that the life insured does not present an unusual risk.  Some TIAs include an explicit list of questions that must be answered a particular way prior to issue.  In other cases, it is up to the agent's discretion.  It is important that the agent recognize that their activities in this matter bind the insurer.  The issuance of a TIA is not to be taken lightly.  Different insurers will treat the underwriting process differently.  The usual practice is to impose termination 90 days after the TIA is issued, or when the insurer either issues a policy or decides to decline coverage.

## UNDERWRITING

Now that the application has been completed and provided to the insurer, the underwriters will do their part.  Based on the completed application, and other information in some cases, the underwriters will make a decision.  The decision of the underwriters is based partly on guidelines generated by the insurer.  The underwriter, though, is also expected to exercise some judgment and discretion.  For that reason, an agent who understands the underwriting process can do a much better job of looking after the client's needs.  It is common during the underwriting process, as well, for the underwriter to seek more information.  An agent who understands the thought process that an underwriter goes through will generally have a much easier time getting their business approved and will minimize hassles for the client.  In addition to the application, there are other tools that an underwriter might use:

- **Medical Information Bureau (MIB).**  The MIB is a resource shared by all insurers in Canada.  Insurers give MIB access to information gathered in the application and claims process.  Then, when an underwriter — osiguravatelj receives an application for insurance, MIB can help to confirm the information in the application.  MIB does not keep detailed or confidential information on file; instead the MIB database is just a list of codes.  The codes are designed to allow the underwriter to recognize anything the client might have missed in the application process.  If the underwriter notices something at this stage, coverage will not necessarily be denied.  Instead, the underwriter will ask the agent to go back to the client and find out more details about the concern raised in the MIB report.

- **Inspection Report.** The inspection report is an investigation into a specific concern the underwriter might have. Inspection reports are often conducted where there is a particular risk posed by the applicant. Perhaps she has a dangerous hobby or a risky occupation. This will lead to the underwriter seeking further information in the form of an inspection report. The inspection report is basically a detailed interview with the client resulting in the insurer having an improved understanding of a particular risk.

At the conclusion of the underwriting process, the underwriter will have made one of three decisions:

- **The decision might be to deny coverage**. This can be very challenging for the agent. Often, for privacy reasons, the agent might not even be told why a client's application was denied. When this happens, the agent should consider that the client still faces some sort of risk, and the agent should help the client to find some other way to deal with this risk. Possible solutions for a denial of coverage might include using an insurer with less stringent underwriting standards, using a guaranteed issue product, or finding a non-insurance means of risk management.

- **The decision might be to issue a policy, or accept the risk**. In this case, the policy is issued. We will deal more thoroughly with this in Module 3.

- **The underwriter might issue a rated policy**. A policy can be rated one of two ways. The applicant might have to pay a higher premium, or the policy might be issued with exclusions. We will further discuss these two topics in Module 3.

## REINSURANCE

When assuming risk, insurers recognize the value of risk transfer. They will sometimes seek to transfer their risk to other insurers. The other insurers taking on this risk are known as reinsurers. Insurers will use reinsurers in several circumstances. This might be done because the risk associated with one particular policy is very large, and the original insurer (known as the ceding company) does not wish to expose itself to that much risk. It might be done because the insurer has many policies of one sort, and the insurer does not wish to expose itself to that many risks. Reinsurance sometimes is used where an insurer will not take on a risk on their own, but they recognize that a re-insurer might. This is known as facultative reinsurance.

The client generally has no idea that their risk is being reinsured. What it does mean, though, is that there might be additional underwriting considerations. When an insurer knows that they are going to reinsure a risk, the underwriting requirements of the reinsurer come into consideration in addition to the underwriting requirements of the ceding company.

The ceding company will pay a premium roughly proportional to the amount of risk being ceded to the reinsurer.

Reinsurers sometimes reinsure their own risk, and the company taking on that additional risk is known as a retrocessionaire.

## SUMMARY

With a good understanding of the application, which is the primary tool used by the insurer to place coverage and assess risk, you should be prepared to go on to Module 3.  In Module 3 you will see how the information gathered in the application process is used to put a contract for insurance in place.

# Chapter 3 THE CONTRACT FOR INSURANCE

Before we look at insurance contracts in particular, we will look at the system of law in Canada. Insurance contracts in Canada are governed by the laws of the land. All Canadian provinces, excepting Quebec, use a system of law called common-law. Common-law simply means the laws that apply throughout the land. The common-law set of laws is constantly evolving, as new laws are passed and the judiciary interpret those laws.

Within the common law system, there are four sets of laws we are concerned with for the purposes of this course:

- **Tort Law**. Tort law is the set of laws used when one party believes they have been wronged by another party. A tort arises when one party can identify a loss to the person, wealth, dignity, or property. As a result, the injured party will seek compensation from the other party. These attempts to gain compensation sometimes end up in the court system. In plain language, we would normally talk about suing somebody when we pursue a tort.

- **Criminal Law**. Criminal law is set of laws designed to protect members of society from one another. Criminal laws are supposed to discourage us from causing harm to others, or from committing acts that are detrimental to the functioning of society. When a criminal law is broken, the police will normally get involved, pressing criminal charges, and the matter will often end up before a judge and jury. The party who has violated the law might end up with financial penalties, or might end up forfeiting some of their freedoms.

- **Regulatory and Administrative Law**. Regulatory law refers to the broad set of regulations and rules that govern various activities. This can include anything from fishing, to hairstyling, to selling insurance. There are a vast array of organizations in Canada that have some responsibility for regulatory and administrative law. Several of the items discussed in this text flow directly from Insurance Acts, which are one example of regulatory and administrative law.

- **Contract Law**. Contract law concerns agreements between parties. Contract law is governed by a complex set of common-law rules. Insurance contracts, as a written agreement between two or more parties, are governed by contract law. Several of the items discussed in this module are specific concerns with respect to contract law.

# CALCULATION OF PREMIUMS

Once the underwriter has made the decision to issue a policy, the next matter to be dealt with is the calculation of premiums. There are some primary factors to consider when calculating premiums:

- **Mortality**. Mortality refers to the likelihood of dying at a given age. Mortality tables are drawn up by actuaries, and they are based on several factors. The two most important factors when calculating mortality are age and sex. Using a mortality table, an underwriter is able to estimate how many people out of a given group are expected to die in a given year. This allows for the accurate determination of premiums. It is noteworthy that mortality is not the same as life expectancy. Life expectancy simply refers to how long an individual should expect to live. It is considered when creating mortality tables, but the majority of the population will either die before or after their stated life expectancy.

- **Morbidity**. Morbidity, on the other hand, refers to the likelihood of becoming disabled in a given year. This calculation is much more complex than that done for mortality. Once mortality occurs, an individual is no longer represented on the mortality tables. With morbidity, though, disabilities of varying durations must be accounted for. There is even the possibility that an individual might suffer multiple disabilities in a lifetime. If the expected mortality or morbidity occurs in a given year, then the insurer will pay out all the premiums received for this portion of the calculation. When there are more losses than expected, the insurer must pay out those claims as well. When there are fewer losses than anticipated, then the insurer keeps the surplus. In this way, the insurer absorbs the risk for the members of the group.

- **Expenses**. The insurer must collect amounts to cover its expenses. Expenses include paying underwriters, actuaries, agents, administrative staff, and overhead. This amount is normally represented as a flat amount applied to each policy the insurer issues. It is referred to as a policy factor or policy fee. It is normally between $40 and $100 per year per policy issued. The insurer incurs significant costs in the first year that a policy is issued, and it normally takes several years to recover those costs. This is why financial underwriting is so important; the insurer needs to have confidence that premiums will be paid.

- **Investments**. With some types of policies, there is an investment component. Generally this results in a higher premium, but that higher initial premium is normally balanced out with lower premiums later on in the life of the policy. This is typically the case with universal life and whole life policies.

All of these factors are based on assumptions. There is no way for the insurer to know any of this information with absolute certainty before a policy is issued. Once these three factors have been taken into account, the underwriter will look at the characteristics of the life to be insured. If the underwriter has confidence in the health, financial situation, and lifestyle of the life insured, then the policy will be issued with a standard rating. (Some insurers have an above standard rating, where the premiums will actually be reduced based on underwriting considerations. This can also be referred to as a preferred or elite rating, depending on the company.)

If the life insured represents a substandard risk, the insurer will issue a rated policy. This can be done one of two ways:

- **Increased Premium.** If the insurer feels that the risk is worth taking on, but could result in earlier morbidity or mortality, then they will issue the policy with a higher premium. This higher premium can be applied one of two ways:

  o Table Rating. A table rating, or percentage increase, is the most frequently used method of increasing premiums. We might say that an insured represents a Table 1 risk, which might mean a 150% rating. That insured will pay a premium 50% higher than a standard risk would. Different degrees of risk are represented on different tables.

  o Flat Dollar Increase. A flat dollar increase is used less frequently. With a flat dollar increase, the premiums are increased by a flat dollar amount per $1000 of coverage. An insured who represents a higher risk might then pay an extra $5 of annual premiums per $1000 of coverage. This is normally only used when a condition is temporary and might be expected to subside over time, or when an event impacting the insured has recently happened and the insurer wants to reduce their risk while the full consequences of the event are discovered. If the condition does subside over time, the insurer might eliminate the higher premium. Underwriting will have to be done to make this determination.

- **Exclusions.** If the insurer feels that the insured represents an unusual type of risk (risky sports, hobbies, or pre-existing conditions that could lead to an early loss) then they might issue a policy with exclusions included. Exclusions might apply to an entire set of conditions or might limit the benefit payable. For example, a disability policy might be issued with an exclusion for foreign travel. In that case, any loss resulting during travel abroad will not be covered. The insurer might also issue the policy with a limitation. For example, if a disability occurs while travelling abroad, the insurer might limit the benefit period for the policy to 90 days. These exclusions mean that the insurer is not going to allow the client to fully transfer his risk.

When calculating premiums, the insurer will also take into account the frequency of premium payments. The insured can often choose to pay premiums monthly or annually, and sometimes will also be able to pay quarterly or semi-annually. Since premiums are calculated as if paid annually, choosing any mode of premium payment other than annually will result in the insurer applying a modal factor to the premiums. This is roughly equivalent to having the insurer pay the premium at the beginning of the year and then having the client repay that loan throughout the year. This application of a modal factor means that the total premium paid for the year for a client who chooses monthly premiums will be higher than it would for a client who pays annual premiums.

## DELIVERY OF THE POLICY

The delivery of the policy constitutes the insurer's acceptance of the contract. We now have the three elements of a valid contract:

- **Offer**. The completed application represented the offer, as discussed in Module 2.

- **Acceptance**. The policy document as provided by the insurer represents acceptance.

- **Consideration**. Consideration represents the exchange of value. Recall that in Module 2 we discussed the possibility that an agent might collect the first premium prior to issuing a temporary insurance agreement.

The agent has some responsibilities with regard to the delivery of the policy. In most cases, the insurer will provide the policy to the agent and the agent is expected to deliver the policy to the client. It is vital that the agent undertake this in such a way to protect both the insurer and the client from any future harm.

First, the agent should review the policy before delivery and make sure that the policy was written as expected. The agent must take care to look for any mistakes in the policy document. At the same time, the agent should understand very well the terms and conditions of the policy so that she can explain them to the client in a fair and easy to understand way. It is especially important to look at the exclusions included in the policy. This will help a client to understand the extent to which they are still responsible for their own risks.

Once the agent is comfortable with the policy, the agent should schedule a meeting with the client. There should be no unnecessary delays in scheduling this meeting. The agent has a responsibility to get the policy into the client's hands in a timely fashion.

At the meeting, the agent should clearly explain the coverage offered to the client. The client should also understand the premiums, any exclusions, and any additional riders and benefits offered by the policy.

At this time, the agent must also verify that there has been no change in the life insured's risk. If, for example, the life insured has recently signed up for flying lessons, or been diagnosed with high blood pressure, then the agent should not deliver the policy. Instead, the agent will write down the relevant details and provide them to the underwriters. Based on this new information, the underwriters will decide whether or not to re-write the policy.

The agent must obtain a signature from the insured. The agent will witness this signature, using a policy receipt. The policy receipt indicates the effective date of the policy, but it also marks the start of the client's right of rescission. Insurers offer a 10 day right of rescission, often known as a 'free look'. If, during this 10 day period, the client changes their mind, then they can notify the insurer and end the contract. This results in coverage being terminated and all premiums paid being refunded in full. The 10 days is normally based on 10 calendar days, as opposed to business days.

## CONTRACTUAL PROVISIONS:  GENERAL

In order to understand how insurance contracts work, there are several terms we should be familiar with. Each of these ideas relates to insurance contracts in some way:

- **Unilateral Contract.** An insurance contract is considered to be unilateral. This means that there is only one party bound by the terms of the contract. The insurer makes a promise that if a certain loss happens in a way covered by the contract, a benefit will be paid. The insured and life insured make no particular promise. If a life insured decides to start smoking, or is diagnosed with a life threatening condition, or has any other change in insurability, some months or years after a contract has become effective, coverage is not changed in any way, nor can the insurer deny a claim on this basis. The insured does not even make a promise about paying premiums. If the premium is missed, the policy will most likely lapse. Unlike other sorts of contracts (say, a cell phone contract, or an agreement to lease a car) the insurer will not pursue the insured to recover missed premiums. That's not to say that the insurer will happily let contracts lapse, but the insurer could not take the policy owner of a lapsed policy to collections for missed premiums. Instead, the coverage will simply lapse, in most cases.

- **Aleatory Contract**. An aleatory contract is a contract in which one party makes a promise to another party that will be fulfilled if a certain situation arises. Insurance contracts are aleatory in nature. An insurer will only pay a claim if the claim arises in relation to a specific situation mentioned in the contract for insurance.

- **Adhesion**. A contract of adhesion means that the contract document, as it is written, is unalterable. You may be familiar with other sorts of contracts, in which it is possible to cross out certain items and have both parties initial the contract indicating agreement. This is not possible with an insurance contract. Contracts for insurance will be enforced exactly as they are written. If a policy owner is not happy with a particular term or condition of the contract, then the agent could go back to the insurer and request that the entire contract be rewritten differently. This would not be a normal practice.

*Razotkrivanje*

- **Disclosure**. There is an expectation when entering into contracts that all parties have access to the same information. This is especially true of insurance contracts. In each province, the Insurance Act includes a provision which specifically indicates the consequences of non-disclosure. Non-disclosure of a material fact can render a contract voidable. It is because of the severe consequences of non-disclosure that the application for insurance and subsequent underwriting process tend to be very thorough. That is, the insurer wants to be absolutely certain that all information has been provided so that the policy will be honoured as issued. The consequences of non-disclosure can be very severe, resulting in a non-payment of benefits.

- **Mistakes**. A mistake is incorrect information, usually given by accident. If this incorrect information is fundamental to the intent of the contract, then it may cause the contract to have to be altered or voided. If this incorrect information is not fundamental to the intent of the contract, then the contract will simply be enforced as intended. A mistake would generally be the least serious type of non-disclosure.

  o Not Fundamental. An example of a mistake that would not be fundamental to the intent of the contract would be a misspelling of a name. The fact that the name is misspelled does not render the information collected in the application, nor the underwriting process, invalid. It does not change the nature of the insurance in any way. A mistake such as this would not affect the contract in any way. Mistakes concerning age and sex are also not considered fundamental to the intent of the contract. However, those mistakes could result in an incorrect premium being collected. As a result, insurance contracts typically include a provision called the Age and Sex Adjustment, which we will discuss later in this module.

  o Fundamental to the Intent. Some mistakes are more serious in nature, and may render a contract void or force an insurer to reconsider the whole contract in some way. An example of a mistake that would be fundamental to the intent of the contract would be if a client intended to purchase a disability policy with a $10,000 monthly benefit and the insurer issued a policy with a $1,000 monthly benefit. There is no universal standard for handling mistakes of this nature. There is no doubt that this is a fundamental mistake; if the insured were to become disabled, they would not receive what they thought they would receive. In these cases, different insurers will handle the situation differently. The scope and nature of the mistake, as well as the desire of the insurer to "make things right" will affect how the insurer treats these mistakes. There is no provision in the Insurance Act of any common-law province specifically pertaining to how mistakes of this nature will be treated.

- **Misrepresentation**. A misrepresentation tends to be a more serious form of non-disclosure than a mistake. A misrepresentation would involve incorrect information being given. Sometimes this is done deliberately, but it can often be an innocent misrepresentation. An

3-6

example of a misrepresentation in an insurance contract might involve a question about the medical history of a parent. Many insurers, during the underwriting process, will ask about the parents' history of cancer and other potentially genetic conditions. If a child is unaware of, for example, a parent's diagnosis and subsequent successful treatment for a mild cancer, this could lead to a misrepresentation. That is, it would be reasonable for the insurer to rate the policy or decline coverage based on this information, but the information was not available. We will come back to this idea of misrepresentation later in this module, when we discuss incontestability.

- **Fraud**. A fraud is the most severe form of non-disclosure. A fraud normally arises when one party deliberately provides incorrect information in order to gain some advantage. The best, and most frequent, examples of fraud in insurance contracts typically relate to smoking status. It is fairly common knowledge that smokers pay higher premiums than do non-smokers. As a result, somebody who thinks they can get away with lying about their smoking status will sometimes do so. We will deal with fraud in other parts of this module as well.

- **Parol Evidence Rule**. The parol evidence rule applies to insurance contracts. Basically, it means that the only evidence which can be brought into the courts concerning the insurance contract is written evidence. So, if there is some question later on as to whether or not an insurer should pay a claim, for example, it is only the policy and the application that can be referred to. A conversation with the agent would not be part of a court's decision as to whether a policy should pay its benefits. For that reason, the normal practice when delivering policies is to include a copy of the original application as part of the policy document.

- **Absolute Assignment**. An assignment of an insurance contract occurs when the policy owner changes ownership of the contract. The assignee becomes the new owner. The most frequent examples of assignment would occur when a parent purchases insurance on behalf of the child. Once the child becomes an adult, the parent might absolutely assign (a transfer of all ownership rights) the policy to the child. Other instances of assignment might occur when an employee leaves a company or when a couple divorces or separates. Insurers will request that a formal request be made, in writing, to effect the assignment. Once the assignment is complete, the former policy owner has no rights or control with respect to the policy. The new policy owner now has all the rights of ownership, including:

    - Assignment of the contract;
    - Termination of the contract;
    - Altering the contract, where possible;
    - Accessing cash values, where possible; and
    - Naming of beneficiaries.

- **Collateral Assignment**. The collateral assignment of a policy does not involve a change in ownership. Rather, this is done when a life insurance policy is being used to help secure financing for a business or investment loan. The lender might be concerned that, if the borrower dies with the loan outstanding, the debt might not be paid. To alleviate this concern, the borrower collaterally assigns to the lender a life insurance policy where she is the life insured. If the borrower dies with the loan outstanding, the lender has the first claim (before any named beneficiaries) to the death benefit up to the amount required to repay the outstanding loan amount. Any remaining amounts after the debt is paid would flow normally to the beneficiaries. Just like a beneficiary, the lender would receive this amount tax free.

# STRUCTURE OF INSURANCE CONTRACTS

There are several different ways that the ownership of an insurance contract can be structured. It may be necessary to review the section "Clients" in Module 1.

- **Personal Contract**. A personal contract is a contract for insurance in which there are only two parties. This would be the case where the insured seeks to insure her own life. Note that any other party could still be the beneficiary.

- **Third Party Contract**. A third party contract is a contract in which the insured takes out insurance on the life of another. A wife might take out insurance on the life of her husband, or a business owner on the life of an employee. In this case, the party entering into the contract is the insured - they are insured by the contract. The third party would be the life insured - it is their health that the insurer is most concerned with. In the event something happens to this person, a benefit should be paid.

- **Joint Contract**. A joint contract is normally issued for spouses. Joint contracts can be issued so that coverage is based on the last surviving spouse, the first spouse to suffer a loss, or some combination of the two.

- **Multi-Life Contract**. A multi-life contract is similar to a third party contract, except that we are now dealing with multiple lives being insured. Multi-life contracts can be issued on a joint-and-first basis, where the benefit will be paid upon the first loss occurring. A joint-and-last multi-life contract would see that a benefit is only paid when the last life insured is gone. There are variations available where some benefit is paid on each loss. It is possible within a multi-life contract for the insured to also be a life insured. Multi-life contracts are relatively rare in Accident & Sickness.

- **Group Contract**. Group contracts are very common in Canada. The majority of Canadians will most likely be familiar with Accident & Sickness insurance because of their dealings with group contracts. Group contracts see a plan sponsor enter into a contract for insurance in which the plan sponsor owns the contract and the plan members receive benefits. There are a great variety of different types of group contracts. The most common are employer plans, multi-employer plans, group creditor plans, association plans, and union plans. There is a relatively new set of arrangements available, often sold and administered by insurers, in which employers fund group insurance themselves. These include administrative services only contracts, third-party administered contracts, and health spending accounts. While these types of arrangements look similar to group insurance, they are not, strictly speaking, insurance contracts. We will deal with group insurance in more detail in Module 11. There can be significant differences between how group insurance contracts are enforced and individual contracts. Other than a brief section in Module 11, this course refers to individual insurance.

## CONTRACTUAL PROVISIONS: INSURANCE

Insurance contracts feature several contractual provisions. Not all insurance contracts feature the same contractual provisions, but if we are familiar with each of the following, it will help us to see how insurance contracts function.

- **Face Page**. The face page, or cover page, of the contract contains a summary of important details about the contract. Face pages all look very similar, and this allows a policy owner (or insured) to very quickly understand their insurance policy. The face page normally describes for us who the insured, life insured, and insurer are. We see what loss has to occur and to whom in order for a benefit to be paid. The amount and type of benefit will be described. The effective date of the policy will be indicated. There will be a breakdown of the premiums associated with the policy. This is normally laid out in point form, or in short paragraphs, taking no more than one page.

- **Insured.** The insured, also known as the policy owner, is the party who has entered into the contract. This party has all the rights of ownership associated with the policy.

- **Life Insured**. It is the life insured whose risks the insurance company is most concerned with. It is in the event of a loss related to this person that a benefit will be paid. Because of that, it is this person's medical and lifestyle information that the insurer is most concerned with.

- **Premium Payment**. The policy document will describe how premiums are paid. The policy owner will normally have the choice to pay premiums monthly or annually. Some insurers also give the option of paying quarterly or semi-annually. This will be described in the policy. If the insured chooses a method of premium other than annually, this will normally result in a modal factor being applied to the premiums. It should be noted that it is not necessarily the insured who will pay the premiums. There is no provision in the Insurance Acts that limits anyone else from paying the premiums.

- **Lapse**. You may recall that we have previously discussed the concept that an insurance contract is a unilateral contract. This means that the insured makes no particular promise about anything that they will do during the term of the contract. Only the insurer has a promise that they have to uphold. Students often fall under the misconception that there is a promise made to pay premiums. This is not the case. Unlike most other contracts, the only result of a missed premium is a lapse in coverage. If, for example, you have a cell phone contract, and you fail to make payments, the cell phone company will not only terminate your service, they will also come after you for the missed payments. Because of the unilateral nature of the insurance contract, the insurer cannot pursue missed premiums in this manner. Instead, the contract will simply lapse, meaning that no more claims will be honoured. Please note that a lapsed contract does not necessarily mean the contract is cancelled, just that claims will not be honoured during the lapse.

- **Grace Period**. Even when a premium is missed, the policy will not lapse right away. Insurance Acts state that a policy must provide at least a 30 day grace period. So, if a premium is missed, the insurer will still honour claims during that 30 days. Many insurers allow a more generous grace period than 30 days. It is not uncommon to find a grace period of 60 days. For exam purposes, though, it is best to consider a 30 day grace period. It is only at the end of this grace period that a policy will actually lapse.

- **Reinstatement**. We know that it is possible for a policy to lapse and that the contract is not terminated at this time. Insurance Acts contain a provision that insurers must allow a two year reinstatement period. If, during the two years after a policy has lapsed, the insured wishes to reinstate coverage, then the contract will allow that. However, there are several drawbacks to reinstatement. The life insured must provide evidence of insurability, usually to the same extent as what was required when the policy was originally acquired. This means the insurer will go through the underwriting process again, possibly leading to a decline or a rating on the policy. Also, any missed premiums must be paid. Finally, contractual provisions based on the issue date of the policy will reset. This means the suicide exclusion clause and the incontestability clause both reset from the date of reinstatement. It is only at the end of this two-year reinstatement period that the policy will terminate, if no application is successfully made for reinstatement.

- **Non-Forfeiture**. Related to the idea of lapse are provisions of non-forfeiture. Non-forfeiture provisions are designed to prevent a policy from lapsing in cases where premiums have not been paid:

  - Extended Term Insurance. This provision is only available with policies designed to last for the lifetime of the life insured. If an insured has paid premiums for a substantial amount of time, say 12 years or more, and a premium is missed, a policy carrying this provision will not lapse. Instead, it will turn into a term insurance policy. The term policy will be paid-up (no more premiums need be paid) for a number of years based on how long the policy has already been in force. In most cases, once the extended term option has been exercised (and this sometimes happens automatically) the policy cannot be returned to its original format. Extended term insurance is a far more preferable option to having the policy lapse.

- Reduced Paid Up Insurance. Reduced paid up means that a policy originally designed as permanent (having no expiry date, or staying in force throughout the life of the life insured) will retain that characteristic. However, the amount of coverage will be reduced. As with extended term insurance, no more premiums will be paid. Also, this option will only be available after the policy has been in force for a number of years.

- Automatic Premium Loan. The automatic premium loan provision allows for cash values accumulated in a policy to pay the premiums when the client has failed to do so. This is only possible in policies such as whole life and universal life, where some cash value has been accumulated. A missed premium will see the insurer automatically use cash values to pay the premiums, and treat it as a policy loan. This can be a very useful feature for helping the client to manage unexpected events, such as a job loss.

- **Cash Values and Policy Loans**. This provision gives the insured the opportunity to build a cash value within their insurance policy. Cash values within insurance policies generally grow on a tax-deferred basis, which we will discuss further in Module 8. There are a few different ways that the insured might access these cash values:

  - Cash Surrender Value. In some cases, when an insured surrenders a policy, the cash values might simply be made available to the insured. This is typically known as cash surrender value.

  - Policy Loan. It is possible for the insured to borrow a percentage of the cash surrender value of the policy from the insurer. Generally, this only happens in cases where there is a death benefit associated with the policy, because the insurer wants to be certain that, if the insured never pays the loan off, there will still be the opportunity at death to have outstanding debts repaid.

  - Return of Premium. We will discuss this concept in more detail when we look at riders, benefits, and waivers to insurance _odustajanje_ policies. Basically, though, return of premium means that at some pre-determined point, the insurer will return some or all of the insured's premiums paid. This sometimes results in a termination of coverage, but there are return of premium products that see coverage continue in some form after premiums have been returned.

- **Exclusions**. Exclusions are specific circumstances that will not be covered under the terms of the policy. The decision to exclude a loss or condition comes from the underwriting process. Some policies have broad exclusions that apply to all insureds. For example, it is very common in A&S contracts to find exclusions related to alcohol or drug use, or commission of a crime. Some exclusions will be particular to one insured. If a life insured has a family history of multiple sclerosis, for example, then a policy issued for that life insured might exclude multiple sclerosis and related conditions, such as blindness. We will discuss exclusions for each different type of policy as we go through the material. It is important to recognize that an exclusion has to be written into the policy to be effective. Exclusions not mentioned in a policy will not apply to that policy.

- **Incontestability**. The incontestability period refers to the period during which the insurer cannot contest the contract. If an insurer discovers a mistake in the first two years after the effective date (or reinstatement date) of the contract, they may alter or cancel the contract. After two years has passed, the contract becomes incontestable. At that point, the only way the insurer can not fulfill their contractual obligations is if they can demonstrate that the insured or life insured committed fraud in the application process. If that does happen, the insurer will render the contract void.

- **Age and Sex Adjustment**. As previously mentioned, mistakes around age and sex (gender) are not considered fundamental to the intent of the contract. However, they will result in an adjustment to the amount of benefit payable. Normally, when an insurer discovers that a mistake was made concerning either age or sex, the amount of benefit will be pro-rated based on the proportion of the overpayment or underpayment of premium. If, for example, an insured is paying a premium that is 80% of what should be paid, then the benefit paid would be 80% of the face amount. Conversely, if the premium is 120% of what it should be, the death benefit would be increased to 120% of the face amount. This works differently in a contract for group insurance, where the insurer will recover the amount not paid. If a group insurer had information showing that a client should be paying premiums of $100 per month, but the actual age meant that premiums should have been $110 per month, then at time of claim the group insurer will recover the missing $10 per month. For each month that the age has to be adjusted, the claim would be reduced by $10.

  - **Insurable Interest**. Insurable interest is a legal provision limiting who can take out insurance on the life of another. It also limits the amount of insurance that one could take out to the extent of the loss that would be suffered. Insurable interest means that there has to be a loss that would occur to the insured if something happens to the life insured. In the case of disability insurance, for example, insurable interest means that an insured could only take out enough insurance to replace their salary. If an employer is insuring an employee, the amount of insurance would be limited to what the employer would actually lose in the event of a loss of that employee. (Normally this is calculated as being two times the employee's annual salary.)  The Manitoba Insurance Act defines insurable interest as being present when the relationship of life insured to insured is:

- his child or grandchild;
- his spouse or common-law partner;
- any person upon whom he is wholly or in part dependent for, or from whom he is receiving, support or education;
- his employee; and
- any person in the duration of whose life he has a pecuniary (financial) interest.

- **Suicide Exclusion**.  Life insurance contracts normally carry an exclusion if the cause of death is suicide.  This exclusion normally only applies in the first two years of the contract.  No death benefit will be paid in this case, but premiums paid will be returned in full.

## CONTRACTUAL PROVISIONS:  ACCIDENT & SICKNESS

There are several contractual provisions specifically concerning contracts for Accident & Sickness insurance:

- **The contract**.  The insurer is limited to using the written documents associated with the contract to define the terms and conditions of the contract.  This normally includes the policy, the application, and other documents specifically designated as being part of the contract at the time the contract takes effect.

- **Material facts**.  The only facts that will be considered with respect to the contract for insurance are those specifically stated in the contract.

- **Changes in occupation**. Where the contract for insurance is based on the occupation of the life insured, a change in occupation can have some effect on the contract. If the insured changes to a more dangerous occupation, they should inform the insurer. The insurer might then adjust the policy accordingly.  If they fail to inform the insurer, then the amount of benefit might be reduced accordingly at the time of claim.  If the life insured enters into a less risky occupation, then the insurer must either reduce premiums or issue a new contract based on the reduced risk.

- **Relation of earnings to insurance**.  Where a disability policy is in force and a claim arises, if the amount of disability benefit that would be paid is greater than the loss that arises, then the insurer is only liable to the extent that there actually is a loss.  If the insurer does reduce the amount of benefit payable because of this provision, excess premiums must be returned.

- **Termination by insured**.  The insured may terminate the policy at any time by giving notice in writing.

- **Termination by insurer**.  The insurer may terminate the policy at any time by giving notice in writing and repaying premiums paid in advance.

- **Notice and proof of claim**. The insured has 30 days to notify the insurer of a claim and 90 days to provide proof in writing of a claim. If a delay should occur under reasonable circumstances, the insured cannot deny the claim based on this contractual provision.

- **Insurer to provide forms**. Once notice has been received of a claim, the insurer has 15 days to provide the forms to be used to submit the claim.

- **Rights of examination**. The insurer has the right to insist on a medical exam as part of the claims process.

- **Claims payable**. Other than in disability policies, claims must be paid within 60 days of receipt. In disability policies, the initial claim must be paid within 30 days of receipt of the proof of loss. After that, the insurer must pay subsequent claims within 60 days.

- **Limitation of actions**. The insurer need not honour a claim when it is submitted more than 1 year after benefits would have been payable.

- **Changes to the statutory conditions**. There are some circumstances under which insurers can issue policies with more or less favourable versions of these provisions. These circumstances are beyond what we need to be aware of here, but they are explicitly discussed in the Insurance Acts.

- **Travel insurance**. Most A&S policies must spell out the contractual provisions. However, travel insurance policies of less than 6 months duration can simply refer to the Insurance Act.

## CLAIMS

A claim will be paid when an insured loss has occurred and the claimant submits a claim for benefits. Normally the claim will be the beneficiary of the policy, but this is not always the case. In some instances, such as where the beneficiary is a minor, the claimant might be the insured. Upon receipt of a claim, the claims examiner will have to determine whether or not a claim is payable. The claims examiner will look at several considerations:

- **Coverage in effect**. Was insurance in effect when the loss occurred?

- **Insured loss**. Was the loss that occurred covered under the policy?

- **Exclusions**. Were there any exclusions in force that might apply?

- **The Contract**. Are there any contractual provisions that might apply?

- **Riders or Waivers**. Might there be any additional features of the policy that affect how the claim will be paid?

- **Proof of Loss**. Is there sufficient proof of loss for the claims examiner to be certain that a covered loss occurred? Further medical evidence or even an autopsy might be required. If further evidence is required, it might take the form of an Attending Physician's Statement (APS).

- **Claimant**. Is the claimant the proper person to be submitting a claim? To whom should the claim be paid?

- **Insurable interest**. Is the claim in this case greater than the insurable interest?

- **Underwriting**. Was the underwriting done correctly? Is there a possibility that a mistake, misrepresentation, or fraud might impact on the benefit payable?

Based on these considerations, the claims examiner will determine if a claim should be paid. If the claims examiner determines that a claim should be paid, the insurer will generally endeavour to pay the claim as quickly as possible. A claim can only be denied based on provisions present in the contract. For example, if a life insured is killed in a collision where he was driving while impaired, the instinct might be to deny the claim. However, if the policy was in effect and there was no exclusion for drinking and driving, alcohol use, or commission of a criminal act explicitly stated in the policy, then a claim will be paid.

- **Agent's responsibilities**. The agent has several responsibilities with respect to the claims process. If the claim is denied, the agent might choose to advocate on behalf of the client and try to get the insurer to reconsider. The agent must be cautious if this course of action is taken; there can be legitimate reasons for denial of a claim. There may be privacy concerns, for example, arising from the decision to deny a claim. If a claim will be paid, the agent generally has certain responsibilities:

  - Delivery of the claim. The agent will often deliver the first claim cheque. This is done so that the client receives a personal level of service, and has support from the agent at what might be a difficult time. Agents will often be aware of other issues that might be considered when a loss has occurred, such as access to government benefits and social programs.

  - Verification. The agent is expected to help confirm that the benefit is being delivered to the correct party based on the loss that was claimed. There have been instances in the past of insureds faking a loss in order to receive a claim.

  - Follow Up. It was the agent's recommendation that lead the insured to purchase this policy. The agent should have done a thorough needs analysis based on the anticipated needs of the insured in the event of a loss. Now, the agent should work with the insured or beneficiaries to make sure that the benefit amount is used as expected.

- **Settlement Options**. Some insurers provide the insured with a number of options as to how a life insurance death benefit will be paid:

  - **Lump Sum**. This is the most common settlement option. It is also the default, so if no other settlement option is selected, beneficiaries will receive the lump sum.  (Even if the insured has chosen a different option, insurers will generally allow the beneficiary to change it upon payment of the death benefit).  A lump sum payment is used when there are immediate needs for cash, or when the beneficiary is going to invest the funds after they are received to accomplish some objective.

- **Interest Only**.  The interest only option would see the insurer retain the death benefit.  Whatever interest accrues on the death benefit year after year would be paid to the beneficiary.  This would be useful if the beneficiary had a predictable set of needs year after year.

- **Instalment Option**.  The instalment option would see the insurer retain the death benefit, similar to the interest only option.  In this case, though, the insurer will pay out a combination of interest and principal year after year.  This option would not last as long as the interest only option, but it would provide a larger income.

- **Life Annuity**.  A life annuity is appropriate when the beneficiary is older and has a fixed need similar to the interest only option.  Because annuities are very expensive for younger people, this is not an appropriate settlement option until the retirement years.  Younger clients who have ongoing needs should choose the interest or instalment options.

# BENEFICIARY

The insured will normally name the beneficiary in the application process.  Almost anyone can be named as a beneficiary.  Normally, we might name any of the following as beneficiary:

- **A person or persons**.  An adult could be named as beneficiary, by name.

- **A minor**.  While some insurers will allow the designation of a minor as beneficiary, Insurance Acts prohibit paying benefits to minors.  Instead, insurers will hold benefits in trust until the minor reaches the age of majority.

- **A trustee**.  Because of the prohibition on paying benefits to minors, it is common to name a trustee as beneficiary.  This is also done in cases where the beneficiary might be infirm or incompetent.

- **A class of persons**.  It might be more practical to name a class of persons rather than naming specific people.  A grandparent looking to leave benefits for the grandchildren, for example, might name "My Grandchildren" as beneficiaries rather than naming each one by name.  Any grandchildren born after the fact would then be included in the benefits paid.

- **A business or charity**.  Either a business or charity can be named as beneficiary exactly as a person can.  We will discuss the naming of a business as beneficiary in more detail in Module 8.
- **The estate**. _property_  An insured could name their estate as beneficiary.  This is normally done for estate planning or estate preservation purposes, that is, to ensure that the maximum possible benefit is left for the heirs.  When the estate is named as beneficiary, several of the normal provisions of insurance benefits are changed.  There is no creditor protection of the death benefit, no freedom from probate taxes or fees, and whatever remains in the estate will be distributed according to the will rather than the insurance policy's beneficiary designations.  Note that the benefit would still be paid tax-free.

There are other considerations when naming a beneficiary.  First, it is possible to name beneficiaries in a variety of ways.  We might choose to simply name one beneficiary to receive the full benefit of the policy.  Or, we could name several beneficiaries to have the benefit divided amongst them at some pre-determined ratio.  We might name a contingent beneficiary in case the primary beneficiary is deceased at the time when a benefit is to be paid.  In the case where there is no surviving beneficiary, benefits are paid to the insured or, if they are deceased, to their estate.

In cases where there might be some doubt as to the willingness of the insured to keep a policy in effect, another beneficiary designation can be used.  In such cases, we can name an irrevocable beneficiary.  Where this has been done, the beneficiary designation cannot be changed without written permission from the irrevocable beneficiary.  This is normally done in cases such as a prenuptial agreement or a divorce settlement where the ex-spouses will be retaining each other as beneficiaries, often to take care of dependent children.

In virtually all cases, death benefits are paid to the beneficiary tax-free.  The same is true of most A&S claims.  There can be some exceptions to this, such as where an employer is paying for disability premiums on behalf of an employee.  Further, claims are protected from the claims of creditors and will bypass the processes normally associated with death, such as probate.  This means death benefits are normally paid out quite quickly and in the amount expected.

## ASSURIS & THE FINANCIAL HEALTH OF INSURERS

All of this assumes that when a claim is to be paid, the insurer is in good financial standing.  While it is relatively rare, it is possible for an insurer to experience financial difficulties.  The Office of the Superintendent of Financial Institutions (OSFI) conducts regular reviews of the reserves of insurers to make sure they are properly funded.  OSFI is a federal government body charged with regulating the solvency of all sorts of financial services companies, such as banks and insurers.

In addition to OSFI's role, private rating companies, such as Standard and Poors (S&P), Dominion Bond Rating Service (DBRS), and Moody's, rate the financial health of all kinds of companies, including insurers. Investors look to the ratings provided by these rating companies as an indication as to whether or not the company is a good place to invest. The insurers themselves aspire to high ratings, because it makes it easier to borrow money and raise capital. It also gives consumers a degree of confidence in the companies they deal with.

Even with these measures in place, it is still possible for an insurer to fail. Recognizing this, in 1990, the insurance industry in Canada got together and formed an insurer whose primary role is to deal with the bankruptcy of an insurer. Originally known as CompCorp, this entity is now known as Assuris. Four insurers have failed since Assuris' inception, the most notable being Confederation Life in 1994. On the failure of an insurer, Assuris steps in and makes every effort to make sure that beneficiaries who are owed benefits get what they are supposed to. Basically, Assuris pays benefits during the bankruptcy, when it is normally not possible for the bankrupt insurer to pay any benefits. Assuris works with other insurers, and organizations such as the Canadian Life and Health Insurance Association (CLHIA) to get other insurers to buy the business of the bankrupt insurer. The insurer who ultimately ends up buying that business also buys the responsibilities associated with those policies. Assuris makes certain minimum promises, so that clients know that they will receive something no matter what in the event of the failure of an insurer. The promises are structured as follows:

- **Death Benefits**. Assuris promises that a death benefit will be at least 85% of the promised amount. If the promised amount would be less than $200,000, then Assuris promises 100% protection. So, if an insurer declares bankruptcy, and a week later the life insured dies with a $150,000 death benefit owing, the beneficiary will receive $150,000 from Assuris. If the scheduled death benefit were $250,000, then the beneficiary could be assured of receiving at least $212,500 ($250,000 x 85%) from Assuris. There is no upper limit to Assuris' coverage.

- **Sickness Benefits**. Assuris guarantees sickness benefits as well, promising 100% coverage up to $60,000 and 85% when coverage exceeds $60,000. This would cover critical illness benefits and benefits paid from an accident and sickness policy. This would cover benefits from critical illness, vision care, extended health, dental, travel, dismemberment, and prescription drug plans.

- **Income Benefits**. Assuris also guarantees income-type benefits. The promise here is 100% coverage up to $2000 per month and 85% when coverage exceeds $2000 monthly. This would include benefits from long-term care, disability policies and annuities.

- **Cash Values**. The promise associated with cash values is 100% coverage up to $60,000, and 85% if the amount covered would exceed $60,000. This would include segregated fund contracts and the cash component of a UL or whole life policy. The guarantee for a segregated fund is based on the guaranteed amount as opposed to the market value.

- **Accumulation Annuities**. Accumulation annuities are insured differently than other insurance products. The coverage is 100% up to $100,000, but there is no coverage beyond that.

Every insurance company in Canada, with the exception of the fraternal benefit societies, belongs to Assuris. It is a member-funded organization, meaning the insurers fund Assuris directly. Assuris is an insurance company in its own right, but it does not sell insurance policies. Assuris' website, www.assuris.ca, provides excellent information, including brochures that can be printed and provided to clients.

## CONSUMER PROTECTION & DISPUTES

From time to time, a dispute might arise between a client and an insurer as to whether, or how, an insurance claim should be paid. There are a variety of mechanisms in place to handle these disputes. While the mechanisms vary slightly from province to province, any of the following mechanisms might be applied:

- **Informal Resolution**. It is generally desirable to handle such disputes at the lowest possible level, which will keep costs down and minimize frustration for all parties. Some disputes might be handled very simply by a visit from an agent, manager, or local representative of an insurer to explain to the client why a claim was handled a certain way. If this visit is done with the intent of understanding and working to resolve the client's concerns then it might work that the dispute ends at this level.

- **Provincial Insurance Regulator**. In some provinces, the regulatory body responsible for the insurance industry might entertain client concerns. Regulatory bodies normally have significant authority over those conducting insurance business, including the ability to suspend licenses or impose fines. Insurance regulators also issue warnings to the general public about people holding themselves out as agents despite a lack of proper credentials.

- **Insurance Ombudsman**. Some provinces employ the services of an insurance ombudsman to resolve disputes between insured and insurer. The ombudsman is typically a neutral third-party who can make non-binding suggestions to either party as to how a claim should be resolved.

- **Canadian Life and Health Insurance Association**. While the CLHIA does not provide dispute resolution services, they do publish a series of guidelines and codes of ethics by which insurers are expected to operate. There is some very useful information available from CLHIA for a consumer who is looking for information about a certain type of product, or information about the conduct of an insurer. CLHIA's website is www.clhia.ca

- **OmbudService for Life and Health Insurance**.  The OLHI provides an independent, national, bilingual ombudservice for disputes related to life and health insurance.  Their function is to assist consumers with complaints about their treatment by insurers.  OLHI's website is available at www.olhi.ca and provides a step-by-step guide for a consumer who has a complaint.

- **Courts**.  Unfortunately, disputes occasionally end up in the courts.  When disputes over insurance end up in the courts, the process is typically very expensive and time consuming.  Court disputes involving an agent will usually involve the agent's errors & omissions insurance, which we will discuss in Module 4.

## SUMMARY

There is a great deal to know about the contract and how it is applied.  Now that we are familiar with these concepts, we can go on to learn how the agent will conduct herself in her day to day affairs.

# Chapter 4 AGENT CONDUCT

## AGENT CONDUCT

While we have covered, at this point, a great deal concerning the structure of insurance contracts and applications, as well as an overview of the industry, we have only lightly touched on the role of the agent. In Module 1, we introduced the agent, broker, and benefits consultant. While we refer to the "Agent" in this Module, the concepts we will discuss here apply equally to all three.

Some of what is covered in this Module arises from legal considerations, some from moral considerations, and some from practical considerations. The point of all that we will discuss here is that the agent must put the client's concerns first while staying within the law. The agent does have a dual responsibility, though, to the client and the insurer. The agent must not conduct business in a way that will put the insurer at risk unduly. The agent's role in managing risk is sometimes referred to as 'field underwriting.'

## DEALING WITH THE CLIENT

- Know Your Client. The agent must respect the Know Your Client (often abbreviated simply as KYC) responsibility. The KYC responsibility means that the agent must place the client into appropriate products. This is not just a matter of knowing the technical details behind the products. In addition to knowing the technical details, the agent must be able to recognize when a product is appropriate for a client's needs. This means recognizing that it will pay benefits when required, that it will be affordable for the client, and that it will be in effect long enough to meet the client's needs. It also means not selling the client a more elaborate or expensive product than necessary. Note that it may not be the client's immediate needs that drive the need for insurance; the client also has long-term needs that must be met. The ultimate goal of the KYC responsibility for the insurance agent is to figure out which of the three predictable risks (discussed in Module 1) the client must deal with, and to put a plan into place to facilitate that process. The KYC responsibility arises at several points:
  - o Initial contact. Especially for new agents, the temptation is sometimes to try to do business with every client. This may not be appropriate. The agent should conduct a thorough KYC prior to entering into business with the client, making sure that the agent and advisor will be a good fit. You may not turn into best of friends with your client, but you should be able to work together comfortably. This initial KYC is sometimes done formally, perhaps through a letter of engagement, or sometimes done informally, simply by sitting down over coffee.

o  While conducting business.  Often a more formal KYC is required at this point.  Some insurers will require you to generate a thorough KYC form of some sort.  The application for insurance acts as a KYC in some ways.  It is at this point that we make sure that the product will meet the client's needs.

o  Ongoing reviews.  The agent should set a target of meeting with their clients on a regular basis after placing business.  The agent should review the client's circumstances and makes sure that plans and products in place are still meeting their objectives.  Meeting regularly with clients on an ongoing basis will build referrals and will prevent policies from lapsing and keep clients doing business with you.

o  Changing circumstances.  The client's circumstances may change from time to time.  By conducting ongoing reviews, the agent will stay abreast of these changes and will be ready to help the client deal with changing circumstances.  As the client gets older, gets married, has children, grows a business, and so on, the client's needs will change.  In response to these changing needs, the agent should always be updating the KYC.

- **KYC Information**.  There are many examples of KYC information.  It is important that the agent only collect the information that is required.  For example, it is probably not necessary to gather the same level of KYC information to sell a travel insurance policy as it would be to sell a disability policy.  The agent might collect information concerning:

o  Financial Status.  It might be necessary to learn the net worth (assets and liabilities) of the client, the income of the client, the client's debt ratios, and other financial information.  When insuring a business or business owner, it might also be necessary to gather financial statements for the business, and sometimes even a business plan.

o  Objectives.  What does the client wish to accomplish?  What are their priorities?  The agent should be aware of this information in order to properly meet the needs of the client.

o  Risk Tolerance.  Depending on the product being sold, it might be necessary to know the client's risk tolerance.  That is, how much money could they comfortably lose on an investment?  This is probably not necessary to know with most A&S products.

o  Family Situation.  Is the client married?  Divorced?  Do they have or are they planning to have children?  Grandchildren?  All of these factors will impact on how we deal with the client.

o  Health.  We must consider the health of the client.  It might also be significant to look at the health of their parents, spouse, and children.  These factors can all have a bearing on the client's approach to risk.

- ○ Time Horizon. How long does the client need protection for? Is the current level of protection enough to meet long-term needs? Have we put measures in place to deal with unexpected changes? It is important to balance immediate concerns with long-term objectives.

- **Client Monitoring**. The agent requires an effective client monitoring system. This is necessary so that the agent continues to respect the know your client responsibility. It will also help the agent to build referrals in the future. While client monitoring systems differ, some typical components of a system to maintain a relationship with the client are:

  - ○ Letter of Engagement. In order to initiate a relationship with a client, some agents will provide a letter of engagement. This letter of engagement can come in a variety of forms. Some agents will use a simple brochure, some will provide an actual letter, and some will enter into a contract for services with the client. These letters of engagement are useful in that they establish early on a set of expectations for the relationship.

  - ○ Policy Delivery. The agent's delivery of the policy is important. It is at delivery of the policy that the agent actually provides the client with a tool to manage risk. This gives the agent the opportunity to confirm all the details of the policy, and to have one more meeting with the client.

  - ○ Regular Visits. While there is no established frequency, agents have a responsibility for regular follow-up visits with the client. Visits might be semi-annual or annual, or might be done on an as-required basis. It is up to the client and agent to establish this. Responsibility rests with the agent, though, for making sure it happens. Regular visits are necessary for the client to make sure that the policy that was sold continues to meet its objective, and that the client has all their risk management needs met.

  - ○ Marketing. The agent might use other methods, such as mail-outs, e-mails, and client appreciation events to keep the client thinking about the agent's ability to help manage risk. These activities are a passive sort of client monitoring. The agent is basically making sure that the client always keeps risk management in mind.

  - ○ Record-Keeping. The agent should make sure to keep proper records of all dealings with clients and prospective clients. There have, unfortunately, been cases in the past where a client took action against an agent for failure to discharge her duties. By taking good notes of all client interactions, the agent can protect herself from such activities.

- **Privacy and Confidentiality**. The client will provide the agent with a great deal of information about their situation. The agent must be cautious to only use this information where appropriate. The client has provided this information with the expectation that the agent will use it to place the proper insurance coverage, and for no other reason.  It would be inappropriate to share this information with others, or to use to somehow further your own interests.  The only time when you might share it with others would be when it is required by law.

- **Fiduciary Duty**.  Fiduciary duty refers to the obligation we have to put client needs first.  Our fiduciary duty represents a legal, moral, and ethical obligation to our clients.  A fiduciary responsibility arises in cases where an agent receives financial compensation in exchange for his role as a trusted advisor.  This means that your client counts on you.  They are not the expert in matters of risk management; you are.  If you see that something should be done, and you fail to act on it, you have breached your fiduciary duty.

- **Constructive Notice**.  The concept of constructive notice means that when a client shares information with the agent, it is expected that the agent will share that information with the insurer.  The agent should not make the determination that the insurer 'doesn't need this information.'  We have already seen that a failure to disclose information can have serious consequences, up to and including the denial of a claim.  If the agent decides not to provide information provided by the client to the insurer, it might result in a policy not reacting as expected at the worst possible time.

- **Due Diligence**.  The insurance agent is expected to exercise due diligence.  This concept has very broad applications, but it basically comes down to asking yourself, at each step of the way, a couple of questions.  "Does this make sense?" and "Is this the right thing to do?"  If something a client is telling you does not make sense, it is generally worthwhile to have a second look.  If you are considering a recommendation for a client, and something about it seems in appropriate or awkward, rethink that recommendation.  There is usually a reason why we have these thoughts.  We should not take it for granted, either, that we have done this.  In all that we do, we must make a conscious effort to exercise our due diligence.  Sometimes it means conducting additional research, sometimes it means asking more questions, and sometimes it means getting a second opinion.  There are many instances of financial services professionals who have conducted activities that were not in their clients' best interests.  Sadly, many of these stories started off with just one small transgression by an agent.  In many of those cases, if the agent had just taken a few minutes to think through a course of action, that is, to conduct due diligence, an inappropriate activity might have been avoided.

- **Documentation**. The agent is required to document the relationship with the client. Proper documentation of the relationship with the client will prevent future problems. In the event that an agent ever ends up having to defend her actions, proper documentation will go a long ways. An agent who has a habit of proper record-keeping will generally be able to avoid problems that can sometimes arise with clients. This can be accomplished through the use of introductory letters, information sheets about clients, and retaining phone and e-mail records.

- **Claims**. The agent often fills a vital part of the claims role. The client will often be ill-equipped to handle a claim. A good agent will help their clients to understand the claims process. The agent might help to provide claims forms, give the client help filling out the claim form, and act as an intermediary between the client and the insurer. The agent might also work with the insurer to provide an element of verification, helping to confirm that an insured loss has occurred. Sometimes the agent will even be expected to deliver a death benefit cheque. An experienced agent will often know the tips and tricks that might get a claim expedited. It is still important that the agent remember the dual responsibility to both the client and the insurer. The agent should not do anything in the claims process that will cause a claim to be paid inappropriately.

- **Other Professionals**. The agent is often expected to interact with other professionals. Especially where clients have complicated tax or legal situations, the agent may have to deal with the client's lawyer, accountant, financial planner, and other advisers. The agent's role when dealing with these other professionals is to provide advice about risk and risk management.

## REGULATORY AND LEGAL CONCERNS

- **Errors & Omissions Insurance**. All insurance agents licensed in Canada are required to carry Errors & Omissions insurance. E&O requirements vary from province to province, but generally between $1,000,000 and $2,000,000 of coverage is required, and in some jurisdictions additional coverage is necessary to insure against fraudulent acts. E&O insurance is designed to pay legal defense costs and damages awarded through the legal system. In this way, it protects the agent, the client, and the insurer. The agent is protected because if a claim should arise, then the agent knows that she will not have to absorb all the costs herself. In these cases, the E&O insurer will subrogate; that is, step into the agent's shoes. At that point the E&O insurer will retain legal council, hire investigators, negotiate settlements, go to court, and do whatever else might be necessary within the limitations of the E&O coverage. Essentially, in the eyes of the law, the E&O carrier assumes the agent's liability. The client is protected because of the knowledge that the ability to resolve a dispute will not depend on the agent's ability to pay, but rather on the E&O insurer's ability to pay. The life insurer is protected because the E&O carrier will first come to the agent's defense. Because the E&O insurer will subrogate, they will normally require that, in the event that the agent suspects an E&O claim might arise, the E&O carrier will be the first point of contact. It is important to note that E&O insurance will only cover activities specifically related to the agent's conduct of her insurance business. For example, if an agent does a client's taxes and makes a mistake, this type of activity will likely not be covered by the agent's E&O carrier. Examples of situations where E&O normally will come to an agent's defense would be:

- An agent fails to comply with the client's instructions;
- An agent fails to explain a policy's coverages, exclusions, limitations, or waivers at the time of delivery;
- An insurer fails to pay a claim that should be paid according to the contract and the agent is held liable;
- An agent fails to submit a completed application in a timely manner;
- An agent fails to submit information related to a change in coverage to the insurer; or
- Errors are found in the application or policy documents that should have been noted by the agent.

- **Holding Out**. Holding Out refers to the manner in which an agent presents himself to the general public. Requirements around holding out typically indicate that an agent must present himself as an insurance agent. He must not indicate that he specializes in an area of which he has no particular knowledge. Promising rates of return or guarantees on investments, or giving the perception of making such promises, is forbidden. The rules around holding out govern what an agent's advertising, business cards, and presentations say. It also governs how an agent deals with prospective clients. In some jurisdictions, it is also necessary for the agent, as part of the holding out rules, to disclose how the agent will be compensated for doing business.

- **Disclosure**. Disclosure refers to the manner in which an agent deals with clients. A client is anybody who either is or might be engaged with the agent in order to put insurance coverage or investments in place. The regulations in force in many jurisdictions require that an agent disclose:

  o Conflicts of interest that might arise. This might occur, for example, where an agent could exercise some undue influence over the client. For example, an agent might be active in a local church, perhaps sitting on the board of a committee that doles out scholarships. If a client has a child who might be eligible for such a scholarship, a conflict of interest could arise. The client might be rewarded for doing business with the agent, or penalized for not doing so. Either way, a conflict of interest could arise. Often such issues are a matter of perception. Because of this, the agent must hold herself to a high standard. This will help to prevent any future problems from arising. The agent must also be sure to avoid conflicts arising from the dual responsibility to the client and the insurer. In order to prevent conflicts of interest from arising here, the agent must work early to ensure that the client understands the consequences of non-disclosure. As discussed in the previous section, the idea of constructive notice means that the agent must share all relevant information with the insurer. Also, the consequences of non-disclosure for the client mean that if all material information is not provided, the insurer may void a policy. By reinforcing these ideas early in the relationship, the agent will make sure that the proper coverage is put in place for the proper premium, and that claims will be paid when expected. This will reduce problems later on for all parties involved.

o    Referral fees. As discussed in the section on holding out, an agent may be required to disclose how compensation will be paid to the agent. In situations where a referral fee is being paid, it might also be necessary to explain this to the client. A referral fee is paid to somebody else who may or may not be licensed to sell insurance products. The referral fee should be paid for a referral, not based on the commission earned by the agent.

o    Commission splitting. In some jurisdictions splitting of commission with other licensed agents is also permitted. These commission splitting arrangements are sometimes a normal part of business. For example, an agent who is looking to sell a long-term care policy might bring in a specialist who understands these policies, and then split commission with that person. This assumes that both the agent and the specialist are licensed to sell the product.

o    Proper explanation of the product. The agent must explain the product to the client properly. At the time of presenting the product, the agent must offer a realistic and easily understood product illustration. The illustration must not indicate that guarantees are available, or that any values are guaranteed, unless there actually are guarantees in place. Upon delivery of the policy, the agent must disclose all features of the policy, including riders, waivers, and exclusions. Once the product is in force, the agent must inform the client of any changes that take place.

- **Criminal Activity**. An agent who takes care in her practice to conduct business as discussed so far in this chapter should avoid any serious difficulties. However, from time to time, financial services professionals in Canada have been found to conduct business on the wrong side of the law. When a fiduciary conducts business in an illegal manner, it can have dire consequences for the client, the insurer, and the agent. Some examples of illegal activity that occasionally might arise are:

o    Theft. Clients hold their agent in a position of trust. They will trust their agent to deal with their money, which can sometimes be in very large amounts. An unscrupulous agent might have the opportunity to abuse a client's trust and use the funds provided for purposes other than those intended. An agent who takes those funds and uses them for their own purposes would be guilty of theft. An agent must be very specifically aware of commingling of funds, which is not necessarily as obvious as theft, but is usually treated equally seriously. Commingling of funds arises when an agent fails to keep client's funds separate from the agent's own funds, or the agent's business' funds.

- o Fraud. So far we have discussed the consequences of fraud when committed by the client. It is also possible for the agent to commit fraud; this fraud might arise when an agent promises that a product will provide benefits that it will, in reality, not provide. The client might later on indicate that the product was sold under fraudulent pretenses.

- o Forgery. The insurer makes an assumption that when an application is received that all signatures were provided by the indicated party. Without those valid signatures, there is no offer & acceptance, and the contract will not be enforceable. Because of this, an agent who fails to obtain all required signatures will sometimes be tempted to forge a signature. This is a criminal act that also might void a contract.

- o Money laundering. Money laundering activity has received a good deal of attention in Canada in recent years. This activity can be related to a variety of criminal behaviours, such as the drug trade, financing of terrorist activity, and smuggling funds out of other countries. Usually there is an element of tax evasion to this, and sometimes money laundering can be done specifically with tax evasion as the goal. Insurance agents must be aware of their responsibilities with respect to money laundering. A commonly cited rule is that the Financial Transactions and Reports Analysis Centre of Canada (FINTRAC) must be made aware of any transaction involving over $10,000 in cash. However, agents must be aware of much more than just this $10,000 requirement. Today insurance agents have a legal responsibility to inform FINTRAC of suspicious transactions, or even suspicious attempted transactions. By conducting a thorough KYC process, the agent should be aware of what might be a suspicious transaction. For example, a young client who makes $50,000 per year and intends to invest $5000 per month should cause the agent to ask further questions. When the agent does believe that FINTRAC must be contacted, the agent does not have to be a detective and do a thorough investigation. In such cases, the agent's responsibility is simply to notify FINTRAC, plus whatever processes their own company might put in place.

- o Tax Evasion. Often related to money laundering, tax evasion is failing to disclose income or claiming false tax deductions or credits. The Canada Revenue Agency imposes harsh penalties on those who engage in tax evasion. Agents who knowingly assist clients with tax evasion can be fined the greater of $1,000 or the amount of tax savings falsely generated.

- **Licensing**. As you are studying this course, you are involved in the licensing process. The licensing process is essentially the same in all provinces except Quebec. The licensing process consists of completion of a qualifying exam, such as the one you are currently studying for. Upon successful completion of a qualifying exam, you will go on to write a provincial licensing exam, which will be of the same form, style, and content as the qualifying exam. In some jurisdictions, the sponsorship of an insurer is required in order to write the provincial licensing exam. In Saskatchewan only, it is also necessary to complete a supplementary Bylaws exam; information on that exam is available at http://www.insurancecouncils.sk.ca/lifbylaw.htm. Upon successful completion of your licensing exam, you will be able to apply for your insurance license, which will permit you to earn a living by selling and giving advice regarding insurance products. Application for this license normally requires application to the insurance regulator in your jurisdiction (for a complete list of regulators, see http://www.insurancecouncilofbc.com/PublicWeb/DisplayLinks2.aspx?CategoryCode=PRORE). In most cases, this will mean completing an application indicating that the applicant is seeking an insurance license for the purpose of gainful employment. Proof of errors and omissions insurance will also have to be provided. Normally a criminal record check is also required.

- **Licensed Agents.** Once the license is in place, the agent is subject to the rules and regulations of their respective insurance regulator. In some jurisdictions, this includes a requirement to obtain continuing education credits. This requirement varies significantly across jurisdictions, and you will have to become familiar with your own continuing education requirements upon completion of this course. Those authorized by their provincial insurance regulator to carry on insurance business can be subject to disciplinary measures, including suspension of a license, for certain activities. Some examples of those activities include:

  - Misrepresentation, fraud, deceit, or dishonesty;
  - A violation of the Insurance Act or related regulations;
  - Failure to pay amounts owed to an insurer;
  - Carrying on insurance business with unlicensed persons, unless specifically permitted to do so by the Insurance Act; or
  - Acts of incompetence or untrustworthiness.

- **Quebec**. Quebec is the only jurisdiction that uses a licensing regime significantly different from that used in other places. This course will likely not assist you significantly in obtaining a license to carry on insurance business in Quebec. For the Quebec rules, please see http://www.lautorite.qc.ca/clientele/futur-professionnel.en.html.

- **Replacement**. Replacement of a policy refers to taking a policy that is in effect and replacing it with another policy. There can be valid reasons for replacing a policy, such as:

  - The policy no longer meets the needs of the client;
  - The policy was set up poorly in the first place; or
  - The product is overpriced as compared to what is currently available.

Unfortunately, replacement has not always been done for these reasons. Often, replacement has been done specifically for the purpose of generating additional commissions for the agent. This unethical practice is known as churning. It is imperative that an agent who is considering replacing a policy conduct a thorough due diligence and be absolutely certain that the replacement is being done in the client's best interests. Most jurisdictions have a reporting requirement that must be met when a policy is being replaced. Normally, this reporting requirement must only be met when an individual contract for insurance is being replaced with another individual contract for insurance. It is important to note that an agent must respect the needs of the client first and foremost. Improperly done replacements can result in a client ending up without insurance at all.

- **Conflicts of Interest**. An agent has a responsibility to inform a client or prospective client of any potential conflicts of interest. It will not be uncommon for an agent to find clients within her circle of acquaintances. The agent must respect that, where she has the opportunity to exert some influence over the client, this should be fully disclosed.

- **Misrepresentation**. It is important for an agent to sell a policy based on its merits. The agent cannot indicate to the client that a product has benefits it does not have, nor that it will provide coverage that it will not provide. The agent's responsibility here is to make sure that the client fully understands the product being offered. The standard to which an agent is held is whether it would be considered reasonable by other agents to act in the manner that the agent in question did.

- **Premium Rebating**. In most jurisdictions, it is forbidden for an agent to provide a premium rebate to a client. This premium rebate might come in a direct form, in which an agent writes a cheque or provides cash to a client. It is also forbidden, though, where the agent provides some item of value that might be perceived as a rebate of client premiums. It is noteworthy that trinkets and gifts of nominal value are not considered a rebate of premiums.

- **Tied Selling**. Tied selling is a practice in which an agent compels a client to purchase one product in order that another can be acquired. The agent might offer homeowner's insurance, but tell a client that he will only sell the homeowner's policy if that client also buys a life insurance policy at the same time. This is an example of tied selling. It would be perfectly acceptable for the agent to encourage the client to purchase both types of insurance by offering, say, a 5% discount on each policy, assuming the insurer were supportive of this practice.

# DEALING WITH THE INSURER

- **Agency Agreement**. The agency agreement governs the relationship between the insurer and the agent. In this case, the insurer fills the role of principal. The principal enlists the agent to carry out certain activities. As an agent of the principal, the agent is bound to carry out the instructions of the insurer. The relationship between the two, though, is normally laid out in the agency agreement. The agency agreement will define and limit the authority which the insurer places in the agent's hands. A typical agency agreement will grant the agent authority to:

  o Solicit applications for insurance. Agency agreements always provide the agent the authority to solicit applications. This is the most basic duty of most agents, to go out and attempt to put insurance contracts in place.

  o Collect premiums. At one time, agents had a responsibility for the vast majority of premiums collected for their clients. Today, agency agreements will typically permit the agent to collect the initial premium. Subsequent premiums are normally collected directly by the insurer.

  o Delivery of policies. Most agency agreements place the responsibility on the agent to deliver policies. The agent must consider the consequences of misrepresentation and documentation (both discussed earlier in this module) when delivering the policy.

The agency agreement will normally limit the agent's authority. Agents will normally be limited from:

- Entering into a contract on behalf of the insurer, excepting conditional insurance contracts;
- Modifying existing contracts;
- Discharging contracts;
- Allowing the client a longer grace period than contractually permitted; or
- Exposing the insurer to any additional liability.

The authority granted to the agent is normally broken down into two distinct types. The agent is granted:

  o Actual Authority, which comprises:

  - Express Authority: Express authority comprises those things explicitly described in the agency agreement.
  - Implied Authority: Implied authority comprises any activities that would be implied by virtue of the express authority provided to the agent. For example, an agency agreement might expressly indicate that an agent can collect initial premiums. If no further details were provided, the agency agreement is also implying here that the agent could collect cash, cheque, or money order.

- o Apparent Authority: Apparent authority covers those things that the client would reasonably perceive the agent as being permitted to do by virtue of the agency agreement. There is significant opportunity for confusion here, which is what makes the agent's communication with the client so important. An agent should be very cautious as to how they hold out. For example, an agent who offers to prepare a client's tax returns might put themselves at risk. It is unlikely that the agency agreement either expresses or implies authority to carry out such activities. However, it might be perceived as reasonable for the client to believe that the agent is authorized to carry out these activities. Therefore, the agent is exercising apparent authority. A mistake made here might expose the insurer to liability. Technically, if something did go wrong, the insurer could pursue legal action against the agent.

The agency agreement must be adhered to, but more importantly, the agent must recognize that the client's perception can override the agency agreement.

## SUMMARY

In this module, we have looked at how the agent should conduct themselves. Agent conduct is vital because the agent provides the vital role of link between insurer and client. Both the insurer and the client expect that the agent is performing this role in an ethical manner. Failure to do so can cause problems for all parties, up to and including a denial by the insurer of a client's claim. An agent who has violated the rules discussed in this module subjects themselves to significant liability.

Having studied the workings of the insurance industry and the agent's role, we are now prepared to look at the products that are available to the client.

# Chapter 5 TAXATION

## OVERVIEW

For many Canadians, tax represents the single largest expense that we will have in our lifetime. Despite this, very few Canadians have a good understanding of the tax system. It would not be uncommon to find somebody who knows very well where to save $100 on a big-screen TV, but that same person might be wasting hundreds or thousands of dollars a year because they have not taken advantage of the efficiencies built into the tax system. As an insurance agent, you will end up dealing with questions around taxation. As you will see in later modules, several insurance products are designed to provide benefits in a very tax-efficient manner.

While this course is not intended to train you as a tax specialist, there are some basic taxation concepts that we have to be aware of in order to understand the functioning of the insurance and investment products that we will examine through the rest of this course. It is important to understand these concepts, but it is important to remember while studying that you are not training to be an accountant or tax preparer. So while we will see descriptions of marginal tax rates, amounts of tax credits, and other facts and figures, these pieces of information are provided to assist with understanding, not because you are expected to memorize them. For the most part, exam questions will provide you with marginal tax rates and other specific pieces of information where you require them. **To be perfectly clear, do not memorize the figures you see in this chapter.**

The information provided in this course is designed to help you understand taxation. We have chosen not to provide this information in its fullest complexity, only to provide a broad understanding. If you are already very comfortable with taxation concepts, you might recognize as you proceed with this chapter certain concepts missing or glossed over. (For example, we have chosen not to distinguish between deductions from total income and deductions from net income, which really have the same impact for our purposes, but would be different to an accountant.) We will also provide a very cursory look at corporate taxation, especially as it applies to small business.

This module is not intended as tax advice. Several of the provisions presented in this module are summarized for the purpose of understanding. Tax laws and administrative rules are in a constant state of change. Nothing in this module should be construed as tax advice, and you should seek professional advice early on when dealing with tax matters. It will be very useful for your career in the insurance industry if you develop relationships with competent tax professionals. You may look at fostering relationships with tax professionals specializing in:

- Estate tax;
- Personal income tax;
- Business tax;
- Business planning; and
- Cross-border taxation.

There are, unfortunately, common examples of people with no tax expertise holding themselves out as tax experts. These situations usually end with the taxpayer who was given bad advice paying significant penalties.

## BASICS OF PERSONAL TAXATION

The income tax system in Canada is based on taxation of worldwide income for Canadian residents. While taxation differs somewhat from province to province, the system is similar enough that provincial differences are not of great concern. (Quebec uses a separate tax system not administered by the Canada Revenue Agency and not dealt with in this course, but it is similar in many ways.) Canada Revenue Agency (CRA) has responsibility for the collection and administration of our taxes. Tax law is implemented by the Department of Finance, while the Department of Justice has responsibility for enforcement. For the purpose of this course, we are primarily concerned with CRA.

In this course, we are mainly concerned with personal income tax. Other sorts of tax such as the Goods and Services Tax will not be dealt with here. It is the personal income tax system that accounts for the majority of tax dollars that most of us pay. As a starting point, then, we will look at some of the concepts inherent in the personal income tax system:

- **Income**. In order to calculate the total tax owing, it is necessary to understand what income is. For an individual, income is calculated based on dollars earned during the tax year (Jan 1 to Dec 31 for individuals). In Canada, virtually all new dollars earned during the tax year are included in the income calculation. This includes salary, bonuses, taxable benefits, investment income, pension income, RRSP withdrawals, and business income. Very few sources of income are excluded from the calculation. Some examples of income that can be excluded from CRA's calculation of total income are winnings, income generated by within a Tax Free Savings Account (TFSA), inheritances, and, notably for our purposes, most benefits received from insurance policies.

- **Taxable benefits** (sometimes known as fringe benefits) form a part of the calculation for income. A taxable benefit arises when an employer makes some service of value available to an employee without the employee having paid for it. Examples of taxable benefits include vacations paid for by the employer, access to a company car, and, notably for our purposes, certain insurance benefits. We will cover this in more detail in Module 11, but an example comes about when an employer pays premiums for a life insurance policy on behalf of an employee. Imagining that an employer has a group insurance plan in which the premiums for the plan are $100 per year. If the employer pays that $100, then it's much the same as if the employer gave the employee $100 and the employee turned around and bought that same insurance policy. It is the employee (or, more accurately, their beneficiaries) who would benefit most from this policy. Therefore, at tax time, the employee would be assessed an extra $100 of income. This is a taxable benefit.

- **Family Income**. Family income is defined by CRA as being the income earned by a couple (married, common-law, or same sex) and their minor children. Once a minor child becomes an adult (age 18) then CRA considers that child to be part of their own family. Their family income would include their spouse and income of any minor children.

- **Deductions**. Once total income has been calculated, CRA allows deductions for certain amounts. Some notable deductions are based on Registered Retirement Savings Plan (RRSP) contributions, interest expenses related to borrowing to invest, and business expenses. These deductions directly reduce the amount of income on which tax will be paid. An understanding of deductions can help you to minimize your client's tax burden.

- **Credits**. Once deductions have been applied against earned income, the total tax bill for the taxpayer will be calculated. Any applicable tax credits, though, will reduce the tax bill. Most tax credits are non-refundable, which means they can reduce the tax bill to zero, but will not result in dollars beyond that being paid to the taxpayer. Examples of non-refundable credits include the medical expense tax credit, the disability tax credit, and the charitable contribution tax credit. The only refundable tax credit available in Canada today is the GST/HST tax credit. Most tax credits are automatically applied at the lowest marginal tax rate. As an example, all employed Canadians today receive a $1000 tax credit known as the Canada Employment Tax Credit. The actual value of this tax credit towards reducing a taxpayer's federal taxes owing is $1000 x 15% = $150. So our taxpayer would actually have $150 reduced from their total tax burden.

- **Withholding Tax and Refunds**. Many Canadians have received a tax refund at some point in their lifetime. For those who are newly learning about taxes, this can create some confusion. A tax refund is based on the fact that most people have some tax paid on their behalf throughout the year. For employed people, this is done when the employer withholds a portion of the paycheque and remits it directly to CRA. For the self-employed, the process involves a system of quarterly instalments. When the tax return is filed, CRA calculates the taxes owing based on income, deductions, and credits. This figure is then compared to the taxes already paid throughout the year. If the taxpayer has paid too much tax, a refund will be given. If the taxpayer has underpaid, there is a balance owing, and the taxpayer will have to pay this amount. This system of withholding tax is designed to prevent taxpayers from accumulating huge tax bills throughout the year and then not having the funds available to pay their taxes at tax time.

- **Attribution**. Attribution simply means assigning income to a certain taxpayer. If somebody earns an income, we attribute that income to that taxpayer on their tax return. Attribution can be somewhat complex in cases where there is lending between spouses, for instance. If a taxpayer lends their spouse money interest-free and the spouse invests that money, any returns would be attributed back to the lender. If, though, the lender charges the spouse a fair rate of interest, then returns would be attributed to the borrowing spouse. This is just one example of an attribution rule. You need not be familiar with the full consequences of attribution. However, where you are dealing with a loan or transfer of property, especially between related parties, it is necessary to consult a tax professional.

## MARGINAL TAX RATES

The federal tax system is progressive. This means as more income is earned, the taxpayer is expected to pay more taxes. At the same time, this system is set up so as not to be penalizing for higher income earners. The federal tax brackets (2014 figures provided) work like so:

- A taxpayer who earns up to and including $43,953 will pay 15% federal tax on that amount. This person would be said to fall in the lowest marginal tax rate. The term marginal tax rate refers to the rate at which the next dollar earned is taxed, or, put another way, the rate at which the last dollar earned is taxed.

- A taxpayer's income between $43,954 and $87,907 will have that income taxed at 22%, federally. So, a taxpayer who earns $60,000 would have the first $43,954 taxed at 15% and $16,903 ($60,000 - $43,907 = $16,903) taxed at 22%. There is a common misconception that this taxpayer would have all $60,000 taxed at the higher rate, that being 22%. However, this is not the case. It's only the income that fits in the higher tax bracket that is taxed at that higher rate.

- On income between $87.907 and $136,270, the taxpayer will pay federal tax at the rate of 26%.

- A taxpayer who earns more than $136,270 will be taxed at the highest marginal tax rate of 29%.

- **Provincial Tax Rates**. Each province has a different set of tax rates and tax brackets. For example, British Columbia has 5 marginal tax rates, with the lowest rate being 5.06% and the highest rate being 14.7%. Alberta, the only jurisdiction to use a flat tax system, imposes a 10% tax on all taxpayers regardless of income. In order to figure out the actual marginal tax rate, the provincial rate and the federal rate would be added together. So, a low income earner in BC would pay tax at 20.06% (15% federal plus 5.06% provincial) while a high income earner in

Alberta would pay tax at a rate of 39% (29% federal plus 10% provincial).  There are some variations in the tax system from province to province.  Ontario, for example, charges a surtax, meaning that once your provincial and federal tax have been calculated, if a certain threshold is exceeded, there is an additional tax added on top of what has already been calculated.  It is quite common to see industry literature assume a 50% marginal tax rate.  While this is not technically possible, high income earners in many provinces will see their top dollar taxed at 50%.  If you are provided with an exam question and no tax rate is given, and there is a significant amount of income at stake, it is probably safe to assume 50%.  A complete table of marginal tax rates is available at the excellent website www.taxtips.ca.

- **Average Tax Rates**.  The term average tax rate refers to the rate at which a taxpayer is taxed across all their income.  In order to figure out an average tax rate, it would be necessary to divide the total tax paid by the total income for the year.  So, carrying through with the example of our $60,000 taxpayer, let's imagine that the total tax bill at the end of the year is $10,311.  To figure out the average tax rate, divide $10,311 by $60,000, which indicates an average tax rate of 17.2%.

- **Exam Questions**.  As indicated above, there is no need to know all the tax rates.  When an exam question expects you to use a particular tax rate, that rate will be given.  You might, then, see wording in a question to the effect of, "John is taxed at a rate of 38%."  You should then use this rate throughout the question wherever a tax rate is needed.

## SPECIFIC DEDUCTIONS

While we do not have to know the consequences of each and every deduction, there are a few that are of particular concern to students in this course.  Each of these will come up again later in the course, but we will look at them here in brief detail.

- **RRSP Contributions**.  A taxpayer who makes a contribution to certain registered plans (RRSPs and Registered Pension Plans, or RPPs) will receive a tax deduction.  Working again with the example of our $60,000 income earner at a marginal tax rate of 22%, a contribution to an RRSP of, say $1000, will work as a deduction against income.  Effectively, this deduction against income would reduce taxable income from $60,000 to $59,000.  With $1000 less income, the taxpayer in this example would pay $220 less tax ($1000 x 22% = $220).  Making a $1000 RRSP contribution only cost this taxpayer $780.  All provinces also allow this tax deduction, so our taxpayer would also save a further $1000 times their provincial marginal tax rate.  However, in order to keep the math easy and straightforward, we are only going to use federal tax rates for this section of the course.

- **Borrowing to Invest**.  A taxpayer who borrows for the purpose of investing (a form of leveraging) can deduct the interest accrued.  In order to be able to claim this deduction, the investment has to be non-registered and the taxpayer has to have an expectation of profit. (This means investments that have a chance of producing income, such as a rental property or a stock that might pay dividends.) Our taxpayer who borrows $20,000 at a 5% rate of interest will have $1,000 in interest to pay ($20,000 x 5%). This would have exactly the same effect on that taxpayer's tax situation as in the RRSP example, above.

- **Business Expenses**. A taxpayer who spends their own money in order to go out and make money has incurred a business expense. Normally, business expenses are only available for the self-employed or those who work on commission. A self-employed person who spends, say, $500 on a training program would be able to deduct that $500 from their self-employment income. Again assuming a 22% marginal tax rate, the actual cost to our taxpayer in this case would only be $390 ($500 x 22% = $110, which would be the tax savings). Purchases of capital property such as rental property, business property, mutual funds, stocks, bonds, and segregated funds do not constitute a business expense.

## SPECIFIC CREDITS

There are dozens of different tax credits available to Canadian taxpayers, and each is applicable in different situations. It is not necessary to know each of them, but there are some tax credits that we should be aware of in order to help understand what comes later in this course. We will look at several of them (the dividend tax credit will be discussed in Module 6) here:

- **Medical Expense Tax Credit**. The medical expense tax credit is available to taxpayers who accumulate medical expenses for which no reimbursement is received. (If a claim is submitted against a group health insurance plan, for example, the portion paid by the group plan would not be eligible to be claimed by the taxpayer.) Like most tax credits, the medical expense tax credit is applied at 15%.

- **Basic Personal Amount**. The government chooses not to tax the first portion of our earnings. In 2014, the basic personal amount is $11,138. That means that a taxpayer can earn up to that amount and not pay any federal income tax. For somebody who earns more than that amount, it is basically like receiving a tax credit that will reduce the taxes owing by $11,138 x 15% = $1,670.70.

- **Disability Tax Credit**. The disability tax credit is available to taxpayers who cannot perform certain functions such as hearing, seeing, or the activities of daily living (to be discussed in Module 10). The disability tax credit form normally has to be completed by a qualified medical professional. The disability tax credit is notable for this course because it is a criterion for eligibility for the Registered Disability Savings Plan, which we will discuss in Module 14.

- **Pension Income Tax Credit**. The pension income tax credit is allows pensioners to claim up to $2000 in tax credits if they are earning pension income.  The pension income must come from a defined benefit or defined contribution plan if the pensioner is not yet 65.  Beyond age 65, the tax credit can be applied if the income comes from an RRSP, life income fund, life retirement income fund, pension, or the interest portion of an insurance company GIC (an annuity).  The $2000 tax credit translates into $300 in savings ($2000 x 15% = $300).  We will deal with this again in Module 14.

- **Charitable Donations**. Charitable donations have some slightly different rules than other tax credits.  Charitable contributions less than $200 are eligible for the same tax credit previously discussed, at 15%. Once charitable contributions exceed $200, though, the tax credit increases to the highest marginal tax rate, or 29%, regardless of what rate the taxpayer is actually taxed at. Charitable contributions can be combined between spouses as well, regardless of which spouse's name is on the charitable contribution receipt. It is usually better to give all charitable contributions to one spouse, because then it is easier to reach the $200 threshold at which point the tax advantage is greatly increased.

There are many rules specific to charitable contributions, most of which we will not cover here.  One point that is significant for the purpose of this course is that normally a charitable contribution can only reduce income by up to 75% (charitable contribution tax credits cannot reduce income to zero).  The exception to this is in the year of death, at which point a taxpayer can actually reduce their income to zero.  If there are still charitable contributions leftover after that, the taxpayer's income in the year prior to death can also be reduced to zero.

## TAX RETURNS

There are a few details around tax returns that are necessary for understanding this course. Normally, for an employed person, the filing deadline for tax returns is April 30 and for a self-employed person it is June 15.  This is all based on a tax year of Jan 1 to Dec 31. All living individual taxpayers use the same tax year. There are some circumstances which can change the tax year. Notably, on death, the taxpayer's estate will be expected to file a tax return for the period of the year that the taxpayer was alive, up to and including the date of death. This is known as a 'stub year'. The tax return filed upon the death of a taxpayer is known as the terminal tax return. There are several complex details around the terminal tax return, and a tax professional should be consulted for assistance with this return.

## CAPITAL GAINS SYSTEM

Since 1972, our government has chosen to tax capital gains.  Capital gains are most easily understood as the difference between the price you pay for a property or investment, and its value when you get rid of it. Only 50% of this gain is taxed, so the whole gain is not taxable, only half of it.  The taxpayer's marginal tax rate would be applied to half of the gain, and the other half is received tax free.  There are some concepts we need to understand in order to fully understand capital gains:

- **Adjusted Cost Base**.  Adjusted cost base refers to the purchase price of a piece of capital property.  The ACB is best thought of as after-tax dollars, or those that don't need to be taxed again.  This is where we can readily see the concept that dollars are not taxed twice in the same taxpayer's hands.  Let's imagine that a taxpayer paid $100,000 for a piece of rental property.  The $100,000 is the ACB, and this taxpayer will never again pay tax on those dollars.  It is important to note that the $100,000 paid for the rental property does not yield any tax advantage; it is neither a tax deduction nor a tax credit.  Now imagine that our taxpayer later adds an attached garage to the property at a cost of $50,000, which again yields neither a tax deduction nor a tax credit.  However, because our taxpayer has spent a total of $150,000 of after-tax dollars on this rental property, the ACB would be $150,000.

- **Disposition**.  A disposition occurs when capital property is sold, given away, donated, or destroyed (assuming insurance proceeds are received.)  Any disposition is taxable, and will result in a capital gain, as indicated by proceeds of disposition exceeding the ACB, the disposition is taxable.  Most important for those in the insurance industry is that the death of a taxpayer results in a disposition of assets.  That means that, on death, the taxpayer's estate would calculate, for each piece of property, the tax consequences of disposition, and then the estate would be responsible to pay those taxes.  A frequent estate planning strategy is to use life insurance to offset those gains that will arise on death.  We will revisit this concept in Module 8.

  The actual formula for calculating the capital gain on disposition is: Proceeds of disposition minus purchase and sale costs = capital gains.

  It is important to note that, while all property is considered disposed of on death, Canada does not have an estate tax (which would normally tax the full value of the estate on death) or an inheritance tax (which would impose taxes on the heirs of the property flowing out of the estate.)

- **Rollover**.  Certain situations allow property to be rolled over without immediate tax consequence on death.  We can roll property over to a surviving spouse without having to pay taxes on death.  The property is rolled over to a surviving spouse (or common-law spouse) retaining the original owner's ACB.  On the death of the surviving spouse, the property would be considered disposed of and taxed in that person hands.  This is an important form of tax deferral.  Note that this will not reduce the overall amount that will be taxed.  A good estate plan will make full use of rollover provisions.  It is because of rollover provisions that joint-and-last-to-die policies are useful in estate planning.  We will discuss some rollover provisions specifically relating to RRSPs (which are not capital property) in Module 14.

- **Principal Residence**. In Canada, the property designated as your principal residence (a residence which you customarily inhabit throughout the year) is disposed of tax-free. This tax-free disposition means that the principal residence can be sold or given away or deemed disposed of at death without tax consequence. A family can only have one principal residence at one time. This powerful rule means that the largest piece of property owned by many Canadian families will have no taxes associated with it when it is disposed of.

- **Inclusion Rate**. The inclusion rate for capital gains in Canada is currently 50%. This means that if a $100 capital gain is incurred, then 50% of that $100 will be taxed at the taxpayer's marginal tax rate. This means that $100 of capital gains is taxed at half the rate that other sources of income, such as interest or rental income, would be. You might also see reference to a 50% exclusion rate, which really means the same thing. At various times in the past, the inclusion rate has also been 66.67% and 75%.

- **Capital Losses**. When property is disposed of for less than its ACB, the investor can realize a capital loss. A capital loss allows the investor to offset capital gains, but cannot be used to offset other sources of income in most cases. Capital losses have the same inclusion rate as capital gains. If the investor has no capital gains in the year of the loss, the capital losses can be carried back up to three years, or forward indefinitely.

- **Life Insurance**. Insurance policies such as life, travel, critical illness and disability insurance all fall outside the capital gains system. We will examine the taxation of each of these in their respective Modules. Individual Variable Investment Contracts (or segregated funds) are subject to capital gains, and will be covered in more detail in Module 12.

## WILLS, DEATH AND TAXES

Because of the nature of this course, it is worth reviewing some of the concepts related to death and taxes. We know that on death, there is a deemed disposition of the taxpayer's capital property. A rollover to a spouse can allow a deferral of this disposition. Assuming, though, that there is no spouse, the estate will have to pay the taxes that arise because of the taxpayer's death. Once those taxes and any other debts owed by the estate are paid, the executor of the will can distribute assets to the heirs named in the will. One who dies without a valid will is deemed to have died intestate, which will give rise to a complex system of rules known as the laws of intestacy, in which the province enforces an inflexible set of rules designed to provide for those who depended on the deceased.

Only once the debts and taxes of the estate have been dealt with can the executor (ideally a party named in the will who will take responsibility for carrying out the wishes of the deceased) freely distribute the remaining assets. If there are not enough assets in the estate to resolve the debts, then those debts die with the deceased.  One's debts do not pass on to one's heirs, but those debts might prevent the heirs from receiving any assets.  There is no tax to pay for the heirs, but they might choose to pay the taxes that are owing by the estate.  They might do this if they wish to access a particular piece of property held by the estate, such as the family cottage.  The executor can be held personally liable if they fail to properly carry out their responsibilities.

In all provinces except Quebec the province assesses a fee or tax on death known as probate.  Probate is an amount charged to the estate by the province in exchange for the province's role in verifying the will and keeping records.  The will becomes a matter of public record upon death.  Probate varies from province to province.  Ontario has the highest probate fees, at as much as 1.5% of the value of the estate.  Alberta has the lowest probate fees, with a maximum of $400.

Life insurance is treated separately from this process.  If a beneficiary other than the estate is named in a life insurance policy, then the death benefit flows directly to the beneficiary regardless of claims against the estate or other considerations.  Life insurance death benefits are also not subject to probate, unless the estate is named as beneficiary.  It is possible to name a life insurance beneficiary in the will as well as in the policy.  Where there are discrepancies between the two, the valid document that was written most recently will be used to determine the beneficiary.

Especially in cases where a situation is complex, possibly due to custody issues, ongoing dependency, significant capital gains, business succession, or other issues, the agent may end up dealing with other professionals.  This might include lawyers, accountants, planners, or others.  These dealings, ideally, will come about prior to the client's death so that a proper risk management strategy can be implemented.

One example of a strategy that might be employed by a team (usually including the client, client's children and spouse, a lawyer, accountant, business valuator, and life insurance professional) is an estate freeze.  An estate freeze refers to any number of possible transactions in which the capital gains associated with a client's property are frozen at their current levels, with arrangements made to pass any future gains on to the next generation.  Estate freezes allow the insurance agent to build the estate planning portion of a life insurance needs analysis (to be discussed in Module 8) around a known need, rather than having to make assumptions and use guesswork.

Unfortunately, it is all too common to encounter situations in which the client has not done the appropriate planning prior to death.  In these situations, it is not uncommon to see the beneficiaries and heirs suffer for lack of planning.  Wherever possible, agents should work to make sure that their clients have taken care of planning issues as early as possible.  The agent should be comfortable working with these other professionals, and it might be prudent to have access to a network of professionals to whom the agent can refer clients with complex needs.

# PROVINCIAL PREMIUM TAX

Separate from income tax, each province charges a provincial premium tax on all life, disability, and A&S insurance. Provincial premium tax varies from province to province. The lowest tax is 2% (in Manitoba, Saskatchewan, New Brunswick, and Alberta), while the highest is 4% (in Newfoundland).

# TAXATION OF BUSINESS INCOME

Just as there is a system of taxation for individuals in Canada, so there is a tax system that applies to businesses. An unincorporated business such as a partnership or sole proprietorship, is taxed on its owner's tax returns each year. So if you personally run a business that has never incorporated, and that business has income and expenses, you would simply claim those on your own tax return.

Some business owners, though, will incorporate. The reasons for incorporating are complex and fall outside the scope of this course. Once a business has incorporated, the business will be taxed as a separate entity, a corporation. Corporations are taxed in a similar manner to individuals, except that there are no marginal tax rates. In order to best understand business income, we will put this in perspective using a simplified statement of earnings for a business:

| Item | Explanation |
|---|---|
| Revenue (or Sales) | This is the total amount of new dollars coming into the business. |
| - Expenses | The business pays expenses first |
| - Interest Payments | The business will have to service its debts, paying interest to its various lenders |
| - Taxation | Once all other expenses have been taken care of, the business will calculate its taxes |
| - Earnings or Net Income | What most of us would incorrectly call 'profit', this is the amount left for the business owner(s) to decide what to do with. It can be left in the company, or retained. Or the business owner(s) might choose to take it out of the business, which is what we call a dividend |

There are really two ways that a business owner can take income out of their business.  The first is to pay themselves a salary, which is tax deductible to the business but taxable in the owner's hands exactly as we discussed earlier in this module.  The second is to pay themselves in the form of dividends, which is taxable to the business (paid with the business' after tax dollars) but taxed favourably in the business owner's hands.  The tax system has set up the taxation of dividends in such a way that dividends received from a corporation should ultimately be taxed in about the same manner as if the business owner had chosen to pay himself a salary.  We will cover the taxation of dividends in greater detail later in this Module.

There are, broadly, three different sets of tax rates that might apply to a corporation:

- **Corporate General Tax Rate**.  In its basic form, corporate income is taxed at about 28%, depending on the province in which the corporation is resident.  There are slight variations, but this is the basic rate for active business income earned by corporations resident in Canada.

- **Small Business Tax Rate**.  Small businesses in Canada that meet certain criteria are taxed very favourably.  In order to be taxed in this manner, the corporation must be resident in Canada, must carry on the bulk of its business in Canada, and must be primarily owned by Canadians.  It must also not have shares trading on a public stock exchange.  If all of these factors apply, we have what is called a Canadian Controlled Private Corporation.  The first $500,000 of active business income earned by a CCPC is subject to tax at a rate of about 15%, again depending on the province.  This very low rate for this type of income is sometimes cited as a reason for incorporating a business.  Income over $500,000 is taxed at the general rate discussed in the previous paragraph.

- **Passive Corporate Income**.  When a corporation invests and earns income on that investment, it is taxed at a very high rate.  This passive, or investment, income is taxed in a corporation's hands at about 46%.  This is done to encourage the corporation to carry on active business, rather than just investing in other businesses.  This high rate of tax on investments in the corporation is a reason why corporations sometimes acquire permanent life insurance, the investment component of which is tax-deferred.

## DIVIDENDS

As discussed above, a business owner might, from time to time, decide that it is appropriate to pay dividends out of the corporation.  Dividends will be paid to shareholders, and there are legal requirements forcing business owners to treat shareholders equally according to their share of ownership.  If dividends are paid, they are taxed differently from other sorts of income.  The tax treatment of dividends is somewhat complex, but for exam purposes, in most cases it will be sufficient to be familiar with the rules, even if you do not memorize the math and formulas. We will look at two types of dividends:

- **Dividends paid by a CCPC**. When a business that is subject to the small business rate, as discussed above, pays dividends, those dividends will be subject to a 18% gross-up. The grossed-up amount is then subject to a 11% tax credit. Let's work with a business owner who has chosen to pay a $1000 dividend to himself. The business owner will be taxed as if he had received $1180 ($1000 plus the 18% gross-up). The gross-up is a notional amount applied by CRA; it does not mean that he actually receives $1180. Assuming a 29% tax rate for our business owner, that means $1180 x 29% = $342.20 of tax to pay. However, to help offset this, he will also receive a dividend tax credit. The dividend tax credit will be equal to the grossed-up amount, or $1180, times the 11% tax credit. Keeping in mind that a tax credit reduces the tax payable, our business owner's tax bill would be reduced by $1180 x 11% = $129.80. In total, then, our business owner ends up paying $342.20 less $129.80 = $212.40 of tax on $1000 of income. If he had chosen to take $1000 as salary, it would have been taxed at $1000 x 29% = $290. Keep in mind, though, that the salary would have been paid out of the corporation's before tax dollars, while the dividend was paid out of after-tax dollars.

  Until 2014, dividends were grossed up at 25% and credited at 13.33%. Revisions to the Income Tax Act in 2014 changed this. The changes reinforce the theory of dividend integration. This theory posits that, taking into account both personal and corporate tax paid, the same amount of tax should be paid in total regardless of whether a business owner takes his remuneration as dividends or salary.

- **Dividends paid by a Publicly Traded Company**. Larger companies, or those whose shares trade on a public stock exchange (we will discuss this in Module 6) have their dividends taxed differently. Let's say we have an investor who has purchased shares in Canadiana Life Insurance Ltd. In the current year, our investor receives $1000 of dividends as a result of ownership of those shares. This dividend will be grossed up by 38% and then credited at 15%. So this $1000 dividend will be taxed as if $1380 of income had been received ($1000 + 38%). Again, assuming our investor is taxed at 29%, this will result in a tax bill of $1380 x 29% = $400.20. However, as before, there will be a tax credit. That amount will be the grossed-up amount of $1380 x 15% = $207. Our investor's total tax bill is $400.20 less $207, or $193.20. Had the investor purchased a GIC paying $1000 interest for the year, that interest would resulted in $1000 x 29% = $290 of taxes payable. Dividends are significantly more favourably taxed than regular income.

# CAPITAL DIVIDEND ACCOUNT

In addition to the possibility for a business owner to take money out of the corporation as capital gains, there is one other method available. This is through the Capital Dividend Account. The Capital Dividend Account is a notional account (that is, it does not have any actual dollars in it). It represents a way for a business owner to take money out of the business tax-free. There are two primary ways that a business can build a credit in its capital dividend account:

- **Life Insurance**. A corporation which receives a death benefit from a life insurance policy will receive a credit to its capital dividend account. This credit is equal to the death benefit of the policy less the adjusted cost basis of the policy (ACB for life insurance will be discussed in Module 8). Say a business has one of its employees insured for $100,000. That employee dies and the $100,000 death benefit is paid to the beneficiary. The business might use the $100,000 for whatever purpose is appropriate. At any time after, though, the business has the opportunity to pay out up to $100,000 to its shareholders as before tax dollars from the corporation, and then that amount would also be tax-free in the shareholders hands.

- **Capital Gains**. When a corporation has capital gains, the corporation, like an individual, is only taxed on 50% of the gain. The 50% that is taxed will be taxed as passive income, as discussed above. The 50% that is not taxed will create a credit to the capital dividend account. This credit to the capital dividend account would be treated the same way as the capital dividend account discussed above.

## SUMMARY

While much of the information in this module will not be directly tested, it forms an important building block for almost every module that follows. We will look at tax and tax consequences in all modules going forward.

A successful agent, especially one who deals with business owners and high net worth clients, must have an awareness of the tax consequences of their dealings with those clients.

Having worked through the basics of taxation, we will now go on to deal with some fundamental concepts around investments and retirement.

# Chapter 6 INVESTMENTS AND RETIREMENT

## OVERVIEW

In Module 1 we looked at the three predictable risks. One of the risks we are expected clients to help manage is the risk of old age. In this module, we are going to examine some of the concepts related to investing, primarily with the aim of understanding retirement planning.

Most of the investment vehicles we will look at in this module cannot be sold based on a life insurance license. So why learn them? In most cases they provide the foundation for the insurance investments we will look at in Modules 8, 12, 13, 14, 15, and 16. Without understanding the concepts in this module, we are not going to understand the concepts discussed later in the course.

## MONEY

What is money? To many, this seems a simple question. In Canada, money is generally thought of as the multi-coloured bills that most of us carry around in our wallets and purses. In truth, though, money is much more complex. What about the funds in your savings account? What about the value of your investments? What about the worth of your home? We use money to represent all these concepts, yet none of them are the same as the money we carry around with us. It is increasingly common today to undertake financial transactions where no money physically changes hands. An economist would tell us that money has three purposes:

- It can be used to purchase goods and services;
- It is a store of wealth for future purposes; and
- It is used to measure the value of a good or service.

At one time, money was representative of an amount of precious metal held in a country's reserve banks. It was once the case that a government would only issue currency if they had gold to back it up. That system has evolved, and today we use a system known as fiat currency. Fiat currency has value because we collectively agree that it does. Our reasons for agreeing on this vary, but it normally boils down to some degree of faith in the economy of the country issuing the currency.

In today's system, central banks control the money supply for their countries. (For example, the Bank of Canada determines how much money to release into the money supply in Canada.) Central banks make money available to consumer banks (such as Scotiabank or Royal Bank in Canada) and those banks make the money available to individuals and corporations. Through a system of lending and saving known as the reserve system, banks fill an important role in supplying money to all of us. Contrary to the notion of printing presses printing new bills for circulation in the economy, almost all of this activity happens electronically. Only about 10% of the money supplied by the Bank of Canada actually shows up in the form of bills and coins.

What does all this mean for the individual investor? It means that there are a great deal more opportunities to create wealth than just saving dollars under your mattress.

## ECONOMIC CYCLE

Before investigating the individual investor, though, we will look at one more big-picture concept. Fundamental to the idea of investing is a basic understanding of the economic cycle, or the business cycle. Whether we recognize it or not, the economic cycle impacts all of us. Often we ignore this cycle when things are good, but when the economy is bad, the economic cycle gets a lot of attention.

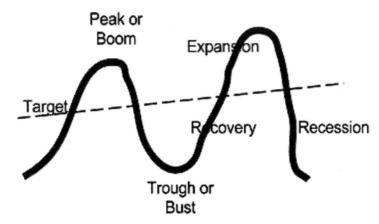

The picture above is a simplified version of the economic cycle. The curve shows how the cycle normally works. In a peak, businesses are doing well, there is plenty of money available, investment is at a high, and the government is able to collect lots of tax dollars. There is also normally high inflation during a peak. We will talk about inflation in more detail later in this module.

In a trough, there is high unemployment, businesses are suffering, investment is low, and the government has a tough time collecting enough tax dollars. Savings are normally high at this time because people do not have the confidence to spend or invest their money. (Savings refers to putting money in a bank account for safekeeping; investing refers to putting your money in the hands of a business or entrepreneur for growth.)

The ideal scenario for both business and the government is the line indicated on the chart with the word "Target." The target for growth in the economy is nice, even, predictable growth. This is easier for all parties to manage. In order to achieve this target, our government takes certain measures:

- **Monetary Policy**.  Monetary policy refers to the Bank of Canada's control over the money supply.  In order to create growth, the Bank will increase the money supply and decrease interest rates.  By increasing the money supply people are encouraged to spend more, which should help get the economy out of a trough.  Decreasing interest rates should make borrowing easier, encouraging people to borrow and therefore spend and invest more.  These are examples of expansionary monetary policy.

  When the economy is at a peak, the Bank will implement a contractionary monetary policy.  This involves attempts to slow spending and put the brakes on the economy.  Examples of contractionary policy include decreasing the money supply and increasing interest rates.  These measures should both discourage people from spending.

- **Fiscal Policy**.  While the Bank of Canada is responsible for implementing monetary policy, the government of the day is responsible for fiscal policy.  The two most obvious examples of fiscal policy are taxation and government spending.  A government should increase taxes in a boom to slow things down, while also decreasing government spending.

  When the economy is in a trough, the government should increase spending in order to stimulate the economy.  This is also the time when tax cuts are ideal, as they can be used to encourage consumers to spend more, spurring the economy on.

Certain types of investors will watch the economic cycle and look for opportunities to invest.  With your role helping your clients to manage their money, it is important that you recognize the effects of the economic cycle.  Sadly, it is common for investors to get very excited about investing when the markets are at or near their peak.  This can lead to poor decisions with potentially disastrous consequences.  By putting in place a sound risk management strategy, you can help your clients to avoid the highs and lows of the market.  This is a very real consideration, and it has an impact on more than just the market performance of investments.  Think of a client who purchased a home and invested a great deal during a peak, and then, a few short years later, lost their job as a result of a recession.  By educating clients about the economic cycle, we can help them to make sound decisions.

## KEY TERMS

There are some terms that we must be familiar with in order to understand investments.  We cannot properly discuss investment vehicles without an understanding of these concepts:

- **Principal**.  Principal refers to the amount invested.  If a client puts $100 into an investment, we would say that person had a principal amount of $100.

- **Interest**.  Interest refers to an amount paid by a borrower in exchange for the use of a lender's money.  Most banking arrangements involve interest payments of some sort.  A client taking out a mortgage knows that the bank will charge interest on the principal borrowed.  Conversely, a client who puts money into a savings account knows that some interest will be earned.  Interest can be accumulated one of two ways:

- **Simple Interest**.  Simple interest refers to a situation in which interest is paid for each period, and the interest is based only on the principal amount.  In a simple interest arrangement, the interest payment will remain consistent throughout the terms of the arrangement.  Bonds, which we will discuss later in this chapter, involve simple interest.  A properly managed credit card, in which full payment is made at the end of each month, also involves a simple interest arrangements.

- **Compound Interest**.  A compound interest arrangement involves the accumulating interest adding to the principal amount.  This means that, in the next period in which interest will be paid, the interest paid will result in a higher amount than in the previous period.  Compound interest arrangements can be very powerful.  Most Guaranteed Investment Certificates (GICs) involve compound interest arrangements.  A credit card holder who does not pay down the full balance in each month will end up paying compound interest to the credit card lender.

- **Capital**.  Capital is a term frequently referred to when investing.  Capital can be roughly equated to money.  A reference to the amount of capital held usually means how much cash could a person or business come up with.  Not all investments make capital available.  A real estate investor, for example, knows that her capital will not be easily accessible during the period of the investment.  An investor who uses a savings account will have easy access to capital during the term of their investment.

- **Maturity**.  Maturity refers to the time at which an investment will pay its investor the promised amount.  Not all investments have a maturity date.  Investments that do have a maturity date sometimes have a lack of liquidity, restricting the investor's ability to access funds.

- **Interest Rates**.  Interest rates refer to the rate at which a borrower will have to pay interest.  There are a variety of interest rates that we should be familiar with:

  - **Bank Rate**.  Earlier in this chapter we discussed monetary policy.  We mentioned that the Bank of Canada will raise or lower interest rates depending on the desired impact on the economy.  The interest rate that the Bank manipulates is the bank rate, the rate at which consumer banks borrow money from the Bank of Canada.  The lower this rate is, the less interest those consumer banks will have to charge to their customers in order to be able to make a profit.

  - **Overnight Rate**.  The overnight rate is the rate at which banks will lend each other money.  It is normally slightly (as much as .5%, or 50 basis points) lower than the bank rate.

○ **Prime Rate**.  The prime rate is used to determine the rate at which banks will lend to their customers (and the rate at which they will pay interest to their investors).  The prime rate is usually about 1% or 2% higher than the overnight rate, but this can change significantly.  A customer borrowing money might be told that their interest rate will be "Prime plus 1.5%".  This customer knows, then, that as the prime rate changes, so might the amount of interest that the customer has to pay.  Normally, the less secure the lender feels in the borrower, the greater the interest rate that the lender will charge.

- **Inflation**.  While we have already made brief reference to inflation, this concept is significant, and we must understand it.  Inflation refers to a reduction in the purchasing power of money.  We have all heard stories to the effect of, "When I was a kid, it cost a nickel for a soda."  Today we know this is not the case.  The price of a can of soda has increased significantly.  What has caused this?  The root cause is an increase in the supply of money, representing economic growth.  Because there are so many more dollars available today than there were when soda cost a nickel, the price has increased by about the same proportion as the increase in the money supply.  Inflation has very real effects.  Had somebody hidden away a dollar bill at the time when a can of soda cost a nickel, they would have given up the opportunity to buy a dozen sodas.  Were that person to pull out that dollar bill today, they would be very disappointed to learn that they could only buy one soda, or maybe even not that much!  When we help our clients with their investments, it is critical to consider the effects of inflation.  An investment that has a return that is less than inflation is losing purchasing power.  Inflation is measured based on the change in the cost of a 'basket' of goods essential to Canadian households from one year to the next.  The cost of this 'basket' of goods is called the Consumer Price Index.

- **Nominal Rate of Return**.  The rate of return stated on an investment is the nominal rate of return.  So a client who purchases a GIC earning 3.5% is earning a nominal rate of 3.5% per year.  (Most likely, this is also compounding.)

- **Real Rate of Return**.  The real rate of return takes into account the effects of inflation on an investment.  If we use the GIC from the previous example and assume a 3.5% rate of return, but inflation is 2%, then our investor would actually receive a return of 1.5% after taking inflation into account.  1.5% would be the real rate of return.  Investments that pay very little interest can actually provide a negative real rate of return.  (There is a more complex and precise formula for real rate of return, but we do not need to know that formula for our purposes.)

- **Time Value of Money**.  There is a well-known story about a Hollywood actress of the golden age of film who was offered $1,000,000 by a studio executive to make movies for that studio.  When given the choice between taking the $1,000,000 as cash or taking payments of $50,000 per year over 20 years, the actress chose the payment plan. This showed a lack of understanding of the time value of money. Had she understood this concept, she would have recognized that the $50,000 payment she would receive in the twentieth year would not have the same value as taking $50,000 today. The same would be true for all the payments she would have received after the first. This is the case because, had she taken the $50,000 at that time and invested for 20 years, allowing it to grow, it would have ended up being worth much more than $50,000. This idea, that a dollar is worth more today than at some point in the future, is known as time value of money. There are a number of complex calculations available to help us with time value of money, but you do not need to concern yourself with that for the purpose of this course.

- **Rule of 72**. One fairly simple way of calculating time value of money is by using the Rule of 72. The Rule of 72 is a quick way of measuring the consequences of a compounding investment over time. Take the return on the investment and divide it into 72. The answer will tell you how long it will take for an investment to double. This works best for investments with a return between about 3% and 12%. Let's imagine we invested $1000 at a rate of 7% for 20 years. The calculation is 72 ÷ 7 = 10. We know that the money will take about 10 years to double. Since the rule of 72 is just an approximation anyways, using 7 will serve us just fine in this case. So the money will double once in 10 years, growing from $1000 to $2000 ($1000 x 2 = $2000). Given another 10 years, the money will double one more time, growing to $4000 ($2,000 x 2 = $4,000). Note that, because this is a compounding investment, we use the amount from the end of the first ten years to calculate the consequences of growth over the next 10 years.

- We can also use the Rule of 72 to calculate the consequences of inflation. Let's say we're dealing with a can of soda that costs $1 today. We are wondering about what a can of soda will cost in the future. We will assume inflation of 3%, which is about what inflation has been over recent history. 72 ÷ 3 = 24. It should take about 24 years for the price of that can of soda to double to $2. In 48 years (24 x 2 = 48) it would be reasonable for that soda to cost $4. In 72 years, it might cost $8, and so on. The Rule of 72 provides a quick way to explain the consequences of growth to a client, but also to show the consequences of inflation.

- **Yield**. Yield, or return, is how the benefits of investing are normally measured. Yield refers to the change in the investor's financial position over a specified period of time. The terms yield and return are often used interchangeably. There are a number of ways of measuring yield:

  - **Current Yield**. Current yield refers to how much further ahead the investor is over a one-year period. If a client puts $1000 into a bond, and the bond pays $50 over the next year, we would say that the investor has achieved a 5% current yield ($50 ÷$1000 = .05, or 5%).  Current yield is most often measured where the investor is seeking cash flow.

- ○ **Yield to Maturity**.  Yield to maturity measures the investor's return for as long as the investment is in place.  The calculation for yield to maturity takes into account the time value of money, as discussed earlier in this module.  When calculating yield to maturity, we measure the difference between the initial investment and the value at the end of the investment.  The normal way of calculating yield to maturity would also see us take the passage of time into account.  This way, we recognize that an investment that grows from $1000 to $1500 over a period of one year is different from an investment that grows from $1000 to $1500 over a period of 5 years.  When we take into account the passage of time, we are calculating the time-weighted return of an investment.

- ○ **Discount Rate**.  Discount rate refers to a certain rate of return, depending on what type of investment we are discussing.  The discount rate is normally used as the benchmark for comparing other investment yields.  So if we make an investment, and we want to see if that investment was worthwhile, we would compare the performance of that investment to a discount rate.

- **Liquidity**.  Liquidity refers to the ease with which an investor can access funds.  The more liquid an investment, the easier it is for an investor to turn that investment into cash and spend it.  Liquidity is a double-edged sword.  An illiquid investment can prevent an investor from accessing funds when needed.  Conversely, a very liquid investment can allow an investor to access funds at the wrong time, giving the investor the ability to draw money from an investment when it is not really needed, reducing opportunities for future growth.

- **Index**.  This term has two separate but related meanings, but we will cover them both here.  For the purpose of investments, the term index refers to a tool that is used to track returns of some sorts of investments.  So a stock market index tracks a particular set of stocks.  Well-known stock market indices include the Dow Jones Industrial Average (which tracks the performance of 30 huge American companies) and the S&P/TSX (which tracks all stocks trading on the Toronto Stock Exchange).  Sometimes, then, we refer to an investment that is indexed to the market, or to one particular sector of the market.  This means that the investment is structured so as to provide a return based on the performance of that particular market.

The second application of the term index refers to inflation.  Some investments are designed to provide a degree of indexing that will see their returns or the income generated keep pace with inflation.  While this is often referred to simply as indexing, it should more accurately be called 'indexed to inflation'.

- **Redemption**.  Redemption refers to a decision by an investor to leave the investment.  Not all investments allow early redemption.  In some cases, the only way for an investor to end their investment is to dispose of it on a secondary market.  Other investments must be held to maturity.

- **Volatility**.  Volatility is a means of measuring investment risk.  Volatility refers to the extent to which an investment's returns might fluctuate over time.  Some investments, such as GICs, offer very low volatility.  A GIC investor can take some comfort in the fact that the returns she will receive will be consistent and predictable over time.  An investor who chooses to invest in the stock market, on the other hand, might face significant volatility.  In a good year, the investor might make a 25% return, but a bad year might cause a 35% loss.  This investor is hoping that the good years will outweigh the bad, resulting in a positive return over a long period of time.

- **Primary Market**.  The primary market is where investments are sold for the first time.  When an investment is sold on the primary market, that means that the investment has just been created.  It has been sold from the issuer to the investor, often through a broker, who is simply an intermediary.

- **Secondary Market**.  The secondary market is where investments that have previously been sold on a primary market can be transacted between interested parties.  The secondary market gives the opportunity to buy and sell investments that are already in existence.  Not all investments can be traded on a secondary market.

## BASIC INVESTMENT VEHICLES

Today's investor faces a spectacular array in investment choices.  We are going to look at some of those investment vehicles in the following sections.  Most investors will not be familiar with the full range of investment choices.  Some very sophisticated investors will have investments in their portfolio that are not discussed in this course.  It is incumbent on the agent to do their research in this case, and to consult with other professionals as required.  This course is designed as a starting point, and the concepts you learn here will serve you well.  There is, however, a whole world of investments out there that we will not explore here.

We will start by looking at some basic investment vehicles, then we will move on to securities, derivatives, and pooled investments.  The basic investment opportunities we need to be aware of are:

- **Bank Accounts**.  Strictly speaking, this is a savings vehicle rather than an investment.  Bank accounts are available in two broad forms.  We can use a savings account, in which case our funds are not designed to be easily accessible.  Those funds, though, will grow based on an interest rate, and because this growth is compounded, there can be good opportunities for growth. There are significant differences between different savings accounts available today. Some research into the most appropriate account for a client can make a difference.

The other type of savings account is a chequing account. A chequing account is designed for a customer who needs frequent access to funds. Most people use chequing accounts as the target for deposits for new funds coming in, such as their paycheque. The chequing account provides the necessary liquidity to deal with day-to-day expenses. These accounts do not normally offer any kind of meaningful interest rates. While chequing accounts are more liquid than savings accounts, both types of bank accounts offer significant liquidity.

- **Guaranteed Investment Certificates**. GICs are a commonly used investment vehicle for Canadians. GICs guarantee a minimum amount of growth and also guarantee the investor's principal. They are normally acquired from a bank, but other financial institutions, including insurers, do offer them. They normally feature a fixed term of between 90 days and 5 years. Generally, the longer the term of the GIC, the higher the interest rate offered. Because GICs feature guarantees of both interest and principal, they tend to offer lower returns than other sorts of investments. During the term of the GIC, the investor's liquidity is restricted. With some GICs it is impossible to access funds during this time. With others, it may be possible for the investor to access their funds under certain conditions, such as financial hardship. Accessing funds early normally results in a market value adjustment, which means the amount of interest paid is recalculated based on less favourable terms than those originally established.

A relatively recent innovation involves index-linked GICs. Index-linked GICs will offer a minimum guaranteed return (usually less than that offered by a conventional GIC of a similar maturity) but can provide greater returns if the underlying index performs well. All returns provided by GICs are taxed as interest. GICs usually have a very low minimum investment, usually $500 or $1000.

Term deposits are similar to GICs, but can have longer maturities. GICs normally have maturities of no more than 5 years, while term deposits can have much longer maturities. In other respects, term deposits are very similar. There are no index-linked term deposits.

- **Canada Savings Bonds**. Canada Savings Bonds (CSBs) are government-issued savings vehicles. Similar in many ways to a GIC, they can be purchased through almost any financial institution. CSBs are very secure, and they do offer investors the opportunity for early redemptions, which gives them more liquidity than a GIC. One of the attractive features of CSBs that sets them apart from other investments is that monthly payroll-deduction savings plans are available.

- **Annuities**. An annuity is a stream of income. We will discuss annuities in great detail in Module 13, but for the time being, it is important to recognize that an annuity is a guaranteed cash flow for the period of the annuity. Some annuities have an accumulation phase prior to paying an income. During the accumulation phase, annuities work very much like GICs. Other annuities are immediate, meaning their cash flow starts immediately after the investment is made. Because annuities provide guarantees, their returns are typically fairly low compared to riskier investments. Banks and insurers offer annuities, though life annuities can only be sold by insurers.

  Annuities offer a combination of interest and return of capital. Return of capital means that the income the investor receives is partially tax-free, because the annuity is paying the investor back his already-taxed dollars.

## SECURITIES

A security represents a claim to something. In this section, we will look at securities representing a claim against assets, debt, or cash flow. Investors use securities because they represent the opportunity to generate cash flow or achieve growth, or some combination of the two. Corporations and governments issue securities as a means to raise capital to take on new projects or grow their companies. The global securities market is massive, representing over $100 trillion dollars in value. In this section, we will look at the more commonly used securities:

- **Equities**. Equities, or shares, or stock represent ownership of the assets of a corporation. Equity ownership of a corporation gives the investor a claim against the assets of the corporation. In practical terms this gives the investor the opportunity to take advantage of future growth (capital appreciation) and income (paid as dividends). Some equities, usually those issued by new, unproven companies, represent an opportunity for significant growth. At the same time, these small, unproven companies may not succeed, and this opens our investor up to the possibility of losses. More mature companies will generally provide a more cash flow (dividends) and less growth, but they also generally represent less risk, as they have likely established themselves.

  We should recall from Module 6 that dividends are taxed favourably compared to other sources of income. Also note that an equity investment that grows in value over time will not be subject to taxation until it is disposed of. So an investor who buys a share in a company for $10 in 2010 and then sells it for $100 in 2020 does not have to pay any tax on the growth in value until disposition. Not only is this an effective form of tax deferral, but it also means that the investor will be taxed on a capital gain, which is only half taxed.

  Equities trade actively on a secondary market. In order to sell equities, an agent needs to hold a securities license. Equities must normally be purchased in blocks of 100, which can make the cost prohibitive for many investors.

- **Bonds**. Bonds represent a claim against the debt and cash flows of a company. Bonds are also secured by assets, so if a company that has issued bonds fails, the bond investors know there is some sort of asset backing their bond. This asset could be liquidated to help the investor recover her lost value. It is best to think of a bond as a sort of loan. Imagine a company came to you, asking to borrow $1000, and promised you repayment of that $1000 in some specified amount of time. You might lend them the money, but you would also recognize the time value of money means that your $1000 will not be worth as much when you receive your repayment as it is today. In exchange for this lost time value of money, you want something in exchange. The bond issuer - a company which needs your $1000 for some undertaking - will promise you a semi-annual flow of income. The bond market is extremely complex, but the student who wishes to improve their understanding of finance beyond what is dealt with in this course should learn about bonds.

  The semi-annual payments attached to bonds are known as coupons. As a result, bonds do not have an interest rate; instead they have a coupon rate attached. Bonds trade actively on a secondary market. Their price on the secondary market depends on the coupon rate attached to the bond. As interest rates fall, bonds issued at higher interest rates become more attractive, and their prices rise. On the other hand, as interest rates rise, bonds issued at lower interest rates become less attractive, and their prices fall. There is an inversely proportional relationship between bonds and interest rates.

  Bonds can be issued by corporations, or by governments. Corporate bonds normally represent a higher degree of risk. Government bonds are usually regarded as very safe. The federal government, provincial government, and even some municipal governments are regular bond issuers.

  The returns on bonds are taxed as interest. When a bond is sold at a higher or lower price than its purchase price, it generates a capital gain or loss for the investor. In order to sell bonds, a securities license is required. The minimum investment to acquire bonds is normally around $5000.
  Obveznice
- **Debentures**. Debentures are similar to bonds, but have no asset underlying them. Because they have no asset behind them, they represent greater risk for the investor. Because the risk is greater, the investor will also seek a higher return. In other ways, debentures and bonds are identical for our purposes.

- **Preferred Shares**. Preferred shares are a sort of hybrid between equity (common shares) and debt (bonds and debentures). Preferred shares offer the investor the opportunity for a stream of income like a bond, but they represent equity ownership, like a common share. Because they don't represent a claim against assets like a bond, they are generally considered riskier than bonds. Because the preferred shareholder is

6-11

entitled to dividends before the common shareholder (hence the name preferred share) the preferred shareholder faces less risk than the common shareholder. Preferred shares pay dividends, and can only be sold by an agent with a securities license.

- **Treasury Bills**. Treasury bills are issued by the government. They represent very short-term, low risk investments. An investor will often use treasury bills as a safe place, or a short-term investment. Treasury bills are sold at a discounted price, and then at maturity, which is normally 90, 180, or 360 days, the investor receives the par value of the t-bill. The yield on t-bills is very low, but it provides a risk-free investment vehicle. The investor will be taxed as if interest was received. There is an active secondary market for t-bills.

  Treasury bills form the basis of what is known as the money market. Most money market instruments, which include commercial paper and banker's acceptances, are safe, short-term investments similar to T-bills. In order to sell T-bills, an agent must be securities-licensed.

## DERIVATIVES

Unlike securities, derivatives do not have a claim against anything. Instead, they derive their value from some underlying investment. Derivatives are based on contracts between two parties. The original derivatives were forward contracts, contracts for delivery of a good at a specified time for a specified price. They were used by farmers to reduce the risk associated with fluctuations in the market for commodities. A farmer takes a risk when he brings in his harvest, knowing that the price he gets for that harvest will depend on what the market demands at harvest time. To reduce this risk (or hedge), the farmer enters into a contract with another party who commits to buy the commodity at a set price. Both parties now have some degree of certainty around what will happen at harvest time. From these forward contracts, the following types of derivatives have emerged:

- **Options**. An investor who purchases an option is buying the option to buy or sell a stock at a fixed price at a later date. The option buyer pays a fee to the option writer. In exchange, the option writer makes a promise to buy or sell at a fixed price. Essentially, this is a bet between the option writer and the option buyer as to which way the price of a stock will move. If an investor believes that the price of a stock will increase, the investor will buy an option in which the option writer promises to sell the option writer a certain amount of that stock at its current price at a later date. The option writer takes the buyer's money and hopes that the price does not go up. The option will have an expiry date, and if the price does not move by then, the option buyer has lost their option. If the price does go up, then the option buyer will exercise her option, and the option writer will have to sell the shares to the option writer at their original, lower price. The option buyer turns around and sells the shares immediately on the market at the new, higher price. This is known as a call option; a put option works if the share price falls below its current level. Options can be very lucrative, but they are incredibly risky. They are sometimes used for speculative purposes, when the investor is hoping to realize a very large gain in a short period. They can also be used to hedge, or reduce risk, against another position held by the investor. In this case, options are a form of insurance against an unexpected drop or rise in price. Gains realized on options are normally taxed as capital gains. A derivatives license is required for an agent to sell options contracts.

- **Rights**. Rights represent the ability to purchase a set number of shares in a company. The right itself derives its value from the value of the share that it gives the right holder the ability to purchase. Rights are normally issued to holders of existing shares when a company issues more shares. This gives the existing shareholders the opportunity to purchase the newly issued shares. This is sometimes referred to as right of first refusal. There is a secondary market for rights. Agents selling rights require a derivatives license.

- **Warrants**. Warrants are similar to rights in that they give the holder of the warrant the ability to acquire a set number of shares. They are normally issued in limited numbers. Warrants are normally issued to parties who have a business relationship, such as lender or supplier, to the company issuing the warrant. Warrants have a limited secondary market, and can often only be exercised by the party to whom the warrant was issued.

- **Futures**. Futures are similar to options, except that the underlying investment is some sort of commodity instead of a share. Futures contracts involve a promise to deliver a set amount of a commodity (such as oil, crops, or cattle) at a set date for a fixed price. Speculators trade futures contracts based on beliefs that the price of a commodity will rise or fall. Producers and consumers use futures in much the same way as the farmer in our forward contracts example at the beginning of this section, to hedge against the risk of a fluctuation in price.

# INVESTMENT RISKS

With each of the investments that we looked at above (excepting T-Bills, which are considered the risk-free investment) there will be risks associated with investing. While we still have one set of investments to examine, those being pooled investments, we will first take a few minutes to examine some specific risks associated with investing. We will then look at some strategies to manage those risks.

Risk, by itself, seems like a bad thing. We know that we should avoid risks. Why does anybody take a risk? We take risks because we expect some favourable outcome, whether it's a good time, extra money, or avoiding some difficult task. Risks in the world of investing are not much different.  If an investor takes very little risk, then the investor should expect very little return.  On the other hand, if the investor is looking for big returns, then the investor should take greater risks.  We generally say that risk equals return, though it might be accurate to say risk equals expected return.  The flip side of this is that greater risk equals greater potential loss. Let's look at this relationship between risk and reward.

Thinking back to some of the investments we have already examined, a bond investment usually represents relatively little risk.  The bond investor knows that there is some asset backing up the investment, so that even if the bond issuer fails, the bond investor still has some value.  The bond investor also knows that the bond investment is not likely to make him rich.  The principal amount will never appreciate, and the only source of returns for the bond investor is generally the regular coupon payments attached to a bond.

The equity investor takes on more risk.  The equity investor knows that if the company that issued the shares fails, there is no opportunity to recover the value of his investment.  On the other hand there is the potential for the equity investor to have both capital appreciation and a stream of cash flow from dividends.

The speculative derivatives investor takes on even more risk.  (Of course, we know that derivatives can actually be used as a hedge, to reduce risk as well.)  The derivatives investor is in an all-or-nothing situation, he will either make money or end up with a worthless investment.

We will look at some specific examples of investment risks:

- **Systematic Risk**. Systematic (or systemic) risks are the risks faced by all investors in all investments.  These risks are not unique to one company, one situation, or one asset class.  These risks would affect the value of a huge number of investments all at the same time.  For the most part, it is very difficult to reduce systematic risk through diversification.  That is, some events are so bad that they hurt all investors to some extent.  Keeping in mind that risk can be good, (risk = reward) investors take on systematic risk searching for returns.  Some examples of systematic risk include:

  - **Market Risk**. Market risk is the risk that the whole market will fall in value at one time.  There are some ways to hedge against this risk, but when a significant market risk event happens, every investor is likely to suffer some sort of losses.

  - **Inflation Risk**. As discussed earlier, all investors must contend with the effects of inflation.  Inflation risk arises when inflation outweighs the returns realized on an investment, resulting in a negative real rate of return.

  - **Political Risk**. From time to time, governments change the rules under which business is conducted. This activity, which is outside the control of most businesses, can have a great impact on the performance of investments.

- **Non-systematic Risk.** These are the risks that would only apply to one business, or one specific set of investments. Non-systematic risk is what investors look for when they look for an investment that will perform differently than the market as a whole. Examples of non-systematic risk include:

  - **Interest Rate Risk.** Interest rate risk refers to the possibility that an investor makes a particular investment choice with an interest component and then interest rates fluctuate. Bond, CSB, and GIC investors all face interest rate risk. A bond investor who purchases a bond and then watches interest rates rise will likely be disappointed, because she knows that, had she waited, she could have purchased a bond paying a higher yield. This same investor, though, who watches interest rates fall will be happy, as she is now making a return based on her bond that is not currently available to other investors.

  - **Business Risk.** Businesses come and go every day. This happens for a great number of reasons. It might be mismanagement, labour difficulties, supply issues, legal challenges, escalating costs, lack of consumer demand, or any of a number of other reasons. An investor who uses stocks or bonds is especially exposed to business risk. While the investor hopes that the business is well-run and operating in a favourable environment, this does not always happen. When a business fails or runs into problems, the investor can see the value of their investment wiped out.

  - **Liquidity Risk.** Investors sometimes make an investment decision based on the assumption that they will be able to sell at any time and then have access to their funds for saving, spending, or making other investments. This is not a safe assumption to make. In many cases the investor will not be able to readily access invested funds. GICs offer liquidity risk. Stocks and bonds have active secondary markets, but a decision to sell at a time when prices are depressed can subject the investor to liquidity risk.

  - **Currency Risk.** An investor who resides in Canada and invests in this country is not going to be greatly affected by fluctuations in Canadian currency. A decision to invest outside of our borders, though, can expose the investor to additional risk. An investor might choose an American company to invest in and see that company do very well. If at the same time the US dollar falls in value relative to the Canadian dollar, that will have a negative impact on the investment's value.

These are just a few of the risks inherent to investing. An agent recommending a particular investment should make sure that she is fully aware of all the risks associated with that investment, and that the client has a sufficient understanding of those risks to make an informed decision.

# COMPARING INVESTMENTS

The following chart compares the risk associated with the investments we have looked at so far in this module:

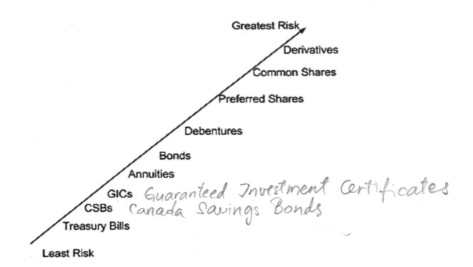

# INVESTMENT STRATEGIES

Now that we are comfortable with the risks associated with investing, we will look at some strategies used to help manage those risks. There can be significant overlap between these strategies. Some investors will choose one particular investment philosophy and always use that some philosophy. Other investors will pick and choose, and others will employ a number of different strategies at the same time, sometimes even employing opposing concepts concurrently so as to minimize risk. This is one form of diversification, which is the first investment strategy we will look at:

- **Diversification**. An investor who knows with certainty that some investment will experience spectacular growth in the near future would be foolish to do anything but commit fully to that investment. The investor would be richly rewarded for their commitment. The truth is, though, that it is nearly impossible to be certain about these types of growth opportunities. Most investors recognize the reality that we just cannot know what will happen in the future. In order to reduce risk around this uncertainty, investors will diversify. Diversification means using a variety of investment opportunities at the same time to reduce risk. A properly diversified portfolio of investments will overcome most non-systematic risks. It might still suffer the effects of systematic risks, however. For most investors of average net worth, the biggest problem with diversification is most likely the costs associated with building a diversified portfolio.

- **Timing Strategies**. The point at which an investment is made can have a great impact on the final results. There are three approaches to choosing the point in time to invest:

  - **Market Timing**. Market timing is the most difficult of the three strategies to implement successfully. A market timer will attempt to invest when an investment is at its lowest, and then hang on to it until a high point is reached, at which time the timer will sell. This buy-low sell-high strategy seems very straightforward. In truth, though, it can be very difficult to choose the low points and the high points. Some market timers are very successful, but many others have been burned by their inability to predict the future.

  - **Buy and Hold**. A buy and hold investor will choose an investment based on the merits of that investment. The investment will be held for a long time, without the investor being concerned about fluctuations in price. Buy and hold investors are generally patient investors with very long time horizons. Buy and hold can be effective, but some investors get caught when they are not paying attention to investments that once looked attractive, but then run into some sort of difficulty.

  - **Dollar Cost Averaging**. Dollar cost averaging strategies are an alternative to market timing. While the market timer believes that he can beat the market, the investor using dollar cost averaging is going to follow the market. Dollar cost averaging means that the investor is going to make a commitment to putting a certain amount into their investments at certain intervals, such as $500 per month, or $50 per paycheque. Sometimes the investor is going to buy at a high point, and sometimes at a low point. The investor does not concern himself with the price of the investment. Dollar cost averaging strategies assume that the chosen investment is going to grow over time, and that swings in price are normal and not a cause for concern. Investments such as stocks, bonds, and treasury bills normally require large lump-sum investments, and as such, cannot normally be purchased with dollar-cost averaging plans. GICs and CSBs do have features that allow investors to buy them in this way.

- **Asset Allocation**. Asset allocation refers to the mix of investment types that an investor has selected. A proper asset allocation is a form of diversification, in which the investor has chosen a variety of different types of investments (asset classes) in which to invest. There are a number of reasons for asset allocation, and a number of different possible mixes. Asset allocation is normally based on three classes of investment:

  - **Cash**. Cash includes savings accounts, CSBs, chequing accounts, money market investments, and, yes, actual cash. Cash is generally used for short-term requirements. It is also often used as a form of insulation against a loss in the market. Imagine an investor has experienced significant gains with their equity investments, and wants to lock in some of those gains.  The investor could sell some of their equities and turn the proceeds into cash.  While there will not be meaningful growth and any gains will be taxed as interest, the investor knows that the cash component will be safe.  Cash is an especially attractive component for older investors who have built up enough net worth to meet retirement objectives.  Younger investors will use cash as an emergency fund and to meet short term objectives, such as paying tuition, buying a car, or making a down payment on a house.  Most investors should hold between 5% and 40% of their total investments as cash.

- ○ **Income**.  Income investments includes bonds, GICs, annuities, and preferred shares.  The income component is used for income generation, such as for a retired person who can no longer rely on employment income.  Income assets are also a way to generate some growth, usually enough to beat inflation, while taking relatively little risk.  Usually as an investor gets closer to retirement, asset allocation will shift more and more towards income.  Younger investors tend to hold relatively little income in their portfolio, while an investor approaching retirement will often have 40% to 70% of their assets in income.

- ○ **Growth**.  The growth component of a portfolio comprises equities, or common shares.  These are the investments that should provide an investor with the opportunity to generate additional wealth.  At the same time, these normally represent the riskiest investments.  A common rule of thumb for the equity mix of a portfolio is 100 - Client's Age = Target percent of equities.  So, a client aged 40 might have 60% of their portfolio invested in equities.  A less risk tolerant client might use 90 - Client's Age = Target percent of equities.  These formulas are only intended as a starting point, and are not firm rules.

- **Leveraging**.  Leveraging refers to borrowing to invest.  Leveraging strategies are attractive because the give the client the opportunity to realize additional gains beyond what they would have made had they only invested their own money.  This increased opportunity, however, requires the client to take on additional risk.  Leveraging strategies amplify the results of both gains and losses.  There are a great number of leveraging strategies out there, and an agent who is helping clients to implement leveraged investments must make themselves familiar with the good and bad points of leveraging.  It is important when pursuing this to consider the reasons why.  A client who has done a good job of saving and investing and is on target to meet their financial objectives might not need to take the additional risk associated with a leveraged investment.  Leveraging is most appropriately used in situations where a client is not going to meet their financial objectives, but has the risk tolerance to take on more risk than they are currently taking.  As discussed in Module 5, leveraging strategies have certain tax advantages.

# GENERAL CHARACTERISTICS OF INVESTMENT FUNDS

The average Canadian investor has never been exposed to many of the concepts we have discussed so far in this module. It is likely that most investors never want to educate themselves about these ideas. Many investors do not have the time or the willingness to manage a portfolio of investments. The cost of investing on one's own can be prohibitive. As a result, investors have the opportunity to invest in a variety of pooled investments, or funds. These funds allow the average investor to overcome many of the challenges to investing. Some features common to these investments are:

- **Professional Management**. A professional manager selects the investments that will give the pooled investment value. Depending on the objectives of the investor, the professional manager (who usually has a strong understanding of finance, including carrying the Chartered Financial Analyst designation) selects stocks, bonds, money market instruments, and derivatives to help the investors meet their objectives. This professional management takes the burden of appropriate securities selection off of the investor. A well managed fund will help the investor to meet their objectives. A criticism commonly levelled against these funds is that this management is not free. Fund managers will charge fees annually in exchange for their services.

- **Diversification**. We have previously discussed the advantages of diversification. Most funds have built-in diversification. The fund manager will choose a variety of investments. The investor should be able to meet their objectives without facing the risk of investing in just one or two securities. Instead, because of the structure of the fund, the investor will end up with fractional ownership of dozens or even hundreds of different securities. The upside of this diversification should be reasonable and steady investment returns. At the same time, it is not likely that investors using these funds are going to realize spectacular returns over a short time frame.

- **Liquidity**. Most funds allow the investor excellent liquidity. This liquidity comes in two forms. It is usually easy to get money into the funds, and then usually easy to get money out of the funds. Most funds allow investors to make a purchase using some sort of dollar cost averaging plan, often committing as little as $25 or $50 per month. Then, when the investor wants their invested amounts plus their growth back, most funds allow the investor to exercise the right of redemption. There can be costs associated with redemption; these costs are typically higher the shorter the holding period has been. An investor who stays invested for the long term will normally not have to deal with redemption charges. Also, most funds do not guarantee the value of an investment, so an investor who wants to get their money out when the investment has lost value will be able to do so, but may not get all of their original principal back.

- **Record Keeping**. The investor also does not have to worry about tracking the value of their investments, nor the tax consequences of investing, as the fund will take care of all the record-keeping and client notification.

- **Flexibility**. As we proceed through this module, we will learn about a number of different fund types. An investor can find a fund to help with almost any investment objective. Most fund companies allow investors to move their money around within that company's family of funds.

## TYPES OF FUNDS

Now that we have explored some of the characteristics of funds, we will look at some commonly used types of funds.

- **Mutual Funds**. Probably the most well-known of the types of funds are mutual funds. Mutual funds are sold by a broker who carries a specific mutual funds license, issued by the provincial securities commission in each province. They cannot be directly sold with an insurance license. Mutual funds come in a variety of forms, which we will examine in the next section. For the time being, we will look at some of the characteristics of mutual funds:

  - **Net Asset Value**. The net asset value of a mutual fund refers to the total value of all the stocks, bonds, money market instruments, and cash held by the fund. This is expressed to the individual investor as a net asset value per unit. Basically, each investor owns a number of units of ownership determined by the net asset value divided by the number of units in distribution. Let's imagine that we have a fund with net assets of $128,000,000 and 18,000,000 units in distribution. We know that each unit is worth (or has a net asset value per unit of) $7.11 ($128,000,000 ÷ 18,000,000 = $7.11). An investor who puts, say, $25 into this fund, will end up buying 3.52 units ($25 ÷ $7.11 = 3.52). The fund manager will take that $25 and pool it with other investors' money, purchasing new investments which are then owned by the fund.

    It is important to recognize that new investments do not increase the net asset value per unit of the fund. The net assets would be increased by new investments, but so would the number of units in distribution. Following through with our example, once our investor has put their $25 into the fund, the fund would have $128,000,025 in it, but there would be 18,000,003.52 units in distribution. The net asset value per unit remains the same. What would change the net asset value would be changes in the value of the stocks and bonds held by the fund. So our investor in our example might be pleased if the fund manager selected good securities and the net asset value rose to $130,000,000. This would increase the net asset value per unit to ($130,000,000 ÷ 18,000,003.52 =) $7.22. The value of the investment would now be (3.52 units x $7.22 per unit) $25.41.

- ○ **Open-Ended**. Mutual funds are said to be open-ended. This is because every time an investor wishes to invest, new units of ownership are created. When an investor wants to leave, those units are redeemed (they cease to exist). There is no need for mutual fund investors to seek buyers or sellers when they are investing in mutual funds. The fund manager simply takes their funds and invests on their behalf. When the investor leaves, it is known as a redemption.

- ○ **Distributions**. From time to time, the holdings of the fund will generate dividends, coupon payments, and capital gains. This means that the fund manager will be holding cash, which may not meet with the intent of the investors. In order to do something useful with this cash, the fund will pay a distribution. Distributions occur on a regular basis, sometimes monthly, quarterly, or semi-annually. The fund manager will take the built-up cash and pay it out to the unit holders. Unit holders who are seeking income will be happy to receive the cash, as they will use it to meet their current financial objectives. Unit holders who are seeking growth or other long-term objectives will not want cash; the fund manager will take the distributed amount and automatically reinvest it on their behalf. The result of this will be a reduction in the net asset value per unit as the fund takes the cash out. Investors who choose to reinvest their distributions, which is automatic with most mutual funds, will end up automatically acquiring more units. The end result is that even though the value of each unit will decrease, the investor will end up with more units. The distribution does not directly affect the total value of the investor's holdings, only how the value is distributed.

- ○ **Taxation**. Because a mutual fund owns a variety of securities, and those securities can pay a combination of interest, dividends, and capital gains, a mutual fund investor can face tax consequences. If a security held by the fund generates, for example, a dividend, that dividend will be taxed in the unit holder's hands, on a proportional basis. This is done as part of the distribution process, as described above. As discussed in Module 5, the ACB of the mutual fund is equal to the amount invested at the time of purchase. When an investor pays tax on distributions, the ACB is increased accordingly. The result of this is that the investor originally acquires the fund at an ACB equal to the purchase price (sales charges also contribute to the ACB). While the fund is owned, the investor will pay tax on the distributions, increasing the ACB. At the point when the investor exercises her right of redemption, there may still be taxes to pay, only if the fund has gains that have not yet been realized. Just as if an individual purchases a stock and then holds it for a long period of time before selling it, the fund can do the same thing.

- ○ **Redemptions**. At the time when the investor determines that she wants her money out of the fund, she exercises her right of redemption. The fund manager will sell the proportional chunks out whatever securities are held and then facilitate the flow of funds from the fund to the client. The units that the client owned cease to exist at that point.

- ○ **Fund Company**. The fund company is the entity that is responsible for the structure of the fund. The fund company makes sure that the agent who deals with the client is compensated and has the necessary information for dealing with the client. The fund company hires the fund manager and makes sure that the fund is run properly.

- ○ **Investor Protection**. The mutual fund industry in Canada is heavily regulated. Because of this heavy regulation, consumers can count on the fact that the mutual funds they invest in are sold in a structured regime. Mutual fund companies are required to produce a Simplified Prospectus, which provides a client with a disclosure document explaining the structure of the fund.

  In the rare event that a mutual fund does fail, investors are protected by the Mutual Fund Dealers' Association's Investor Protection Corporation (IPC). IPC promises clients who suffer losses because of the failure of a fund company up to $1,000,000. This protection does not cover market events, such as a decline in value. It is only designed to compensate investors in the event that a mutual fund company ends up in bankruptcy.

- **Individual Variable Investment Contracts**. We will cover Individual Variable Investment Contracts (IVICs) in detail in Module 12. IVICs are normally referred to as segregated funds. A segregated fund is basically the insurance industry's answer to mutual funds. With the exception of the investor protection available, some tax differences, and some terminology changes, everything we have learned about mutual funds applies to segregated funds. They offer professional management, diversification, liquidity, and flexibility just like mutual funds do. In addition, they also offer investors guarantees of a return of a portion of the original investment on death of the investor or maturity of the contract. We will examine these features in greater detail in Module 12.

- **Life Insurance Investments**. We will examine life insurance in greater detail in Module 8. For the time being, it is sufficient to understand that universal life insurance contracts feature an investment component. That investment component will hold investments that are based on either mutual funds, GICs, or savings accounts.

- **Labour-Sponsored Funds**. Labour-sponsored funds are similar to mutual funds in some ways, but they have notable differences. The federal government provides a tax credit for investment into labour-sponsored funds. These funds invest primarily in unproven companies, often companies that have only just started into business. Usually the focus of these companies is high-tech. The government provides the tax credit because it gives investors some incentive to invest into these companies, which creates growth in the economy. In order to receive the tax credit, though, an investor cannot redeem their investment within the first 8 years. Also, because these companies tend to be small, unproven companies, these tend to be very high risk investments. They lack the regulation that mutual funds benefit from, so there is a chance for an investor to suffer a loss because of risks that were never disclosed to the investor. Some provinces match the tax credit offered by the federal government, but many do not. The licensing requirements for these funds vary, but some of them can be sold without any license whatsoever. Recent budget changes have seen the government take away some of the tax advantages for labour-sponsored funds.

## INVESTMENT OBJECTIVES

It is not only for the purpose of retirement that we need to understand the concepts in this module. In reality, a client might have a number of reasons to invest. The client might wish to fund a child's education, purchase a new home, start a business, or any number of other objectives. The agent must understand why the client is investing in order to be able to make proper recommendations for the client.

In some cases, the agent will be able to help the client with the suite of products available. From time to time, though, the agent must recognize that the client's needs go beyond what the agent can provide. When this is the case, the agent should have access to investment specialists whom he is comfortable recommending.

We are going to look at some concepts here that are fundamental to helping a client make good investment choices:

- **Time Horizon**. Different clients will have different points in time when they may need to access funds from their investments. Some clients will have a time horizon far out into the future, maybe too far away to know for certain exactly when they will need access. Other clients will have very explicit goals that will require them to access a known amount of money at a known time.

- **Stability**. Some investors cannot tolerate volatility. These investors might watch their investments fall for a few consecutive months, and end up wondering if they will ever be able to retire on their investments. An investor who cannot handle this volatility should likely choose more stable investments. They will likely earn lower returns than an investor who is willing to take a risk. However, leaving an investor like this in high-risk investments will see them make a bad decision, selling off their investments at a low point.

- **Liquidity**. Investors require varying degrees of liquidity. This is closely related to the investor's time horizon. An investor seeking liquidity should not select investments that will lock them in for extended periods.

- **Guarantees**. Some investments offer certain guarantees. This can be very attractive for the risk averse investor. Offering products that feature guarantees will allow the client to invest and reduce their worries about their investments.

- **Growth**. Having discussed the effects of inflation earlier, we can see that some investors need to realize capital appreciation. Investors seeking growth will normally have to take greater risks.

- **Income**. Especially in retirement, many investors will require additional income. Several of the investments we have looked at provide income in one form or another. In addition to considering income, we should also consider the tax consequences of the various investments. Investments that provide an interest component are taxed more heavily than those that provide a dividend component.

- **Risk Tolerance**. When gathering the know your client information for a client who will be investing, risk tolerance becomes vital. Risk tolerance basically measures how much a client would be comfortable losing in a worst case scenario. An agent must be certain that a client fully understands the consequences of an investment gone wrong. It can be very challenging to accurately assess risk tolerance. The same client might appear to have great risk tolerance in good markets, but then might demonstrate risk aversion when the markets are at a low point. It is important that clients understand the cyclical nature of the economy.

- **Investment Knowledge**. When deciding which investments are appropriate, we must take the investor's understanding of investments into account. More sophisticated investors might choose riskier or more complex investments. Investors who do not have a great understanding of the markets should likely stick to fairly straightforward types of investments. This is especially important when considering investment strategies like market timing and leveraging. Setting a client who does not understand investments up with these types of strategies might seem a good way to help that person accomplish an objective, but it might not be sustainable.

- **Investment Performance**. Clients will often compare their investments to other investments, whether it's something they read about in the paper, something their neighbour has done, or something they have seen in the past. In order to compare an investment fairly, it should be compared to a similar sort of investment. It is also fair to compare the investment to a benchmark. Benchmarks are available from a variety of sources; they are very similar to the index discussed earlier in this module. Making fair comparisons of investment performance can help to manage client expectations.

# RETIREMENT OVERVIEW

Having looked at investments in some detail, we will look briefly at retirement. Many, if not all, of your clients will require assistance with retirement planning and saving for retirement. There are numerous software packages that can help you to estimate how much a client will need to save in order to retire, but an agent should understand the concepts that go into developing a retirement plan.

Before we look at those concepts, we should consider that, as Canadians, we are not on our own in retirement. Our government has put into place three systems, generally called the three pillars of retirement, to help us. The three pillars are:

- **Old Age Security**. The Old Age Security (OAS) program will be discussed in detail in Module 7. Old Age Security is designed to guarantee a minimum level of retirement income to all Canadians. It does not provide a great amount of money, but it does provide a basic level of income.

- **Canada Pension Plan**. Canada Pension Plan is the second pillar of retirement savings. This is a contributory plan, which means it is only available to those who have paid into it. For the most part, all working Canadians are required to pay into it. It provides something more than OAS, but even somebody earning the maximum CPP and OAS will be limited to about $1500 of monthly income.

- **Registered Retirement Savings Plan**. The RRSP is the third pillar. The RRSP puts the responsibility on the individual to invest wisely, using the tax advantages offered by this plan. The RRSP is designed to allow Canadians to put enough money away on their own so as to maintain their lifestyle in retirement. We will examine the RRSP in detail in Module 14. Most of the investments we have looked it in this module can be placed into a RRSP.

While OAS and CPP do provide a basic level of retirement income, we need to figure out how much more will be required. This will vary significantly from client to client. There are some basic guidelines, though, and in most cases we assume that we want the client to retire on an income that is somewhere between 50% and 70% of their working income. This will vary based on lifestyle choices and monthly expenses. As part of the risk management process, the agent should work with the client to assess how much retirement income will be required.

Once we have an idea about how much retirement income will be required, we have to figure out how we are going to get there. The agent should work with the client to put a plan together to start investing to meet the retirement objective. The agent and client are going to have to work together to estimate investment returns, inflation, and how much the client will have available to save.

This process can be repeated for any sort of investment objective; it is not unique to retirement planning. A client who is saving to buy a house or a car or tuition for the kids has to go through the same steps. You will not have to do this math for the purpose of this course. In practice, you will be able to use a financial calculator (also not employed in this course) or a software package to do this for you. For very complex retirement scenarios, it would be appropriate to enlist the services of a Certified Financial Planner[tm].

## THE RETIREMENT PLANNING PROCESS

In order to help the client prepare for retirement, we will go through a six-step process with the client. The steps in the retirement planning process are:

- **Establish the relationship**. Prior to developing a retirement plan, the agent and client should be aware of what each expects from the other. The agent should inform the client of exactly what services will be offered, how the agent will be compensated, and what level of commitment will be required from the client. By establishing the boundaries of the relationship at the beginning, the agent will ensure a smooth process through the next 5 steps.

- **Gather and analyze information**. The agent will gather a variety of client information. This might include any of the following:

    - Statement of Net Worth;
    - Income Statement;
    - Business Financial Statements;
    - Investment Statements:
    - Tax Returns or Notices of Assessment;
    - Pension Statements; and
    - Other information specific to the client's situation.

  The agent will use this information to generate a comprehensive picture of the client's current financial situation.

- **Determine objectives**. The agent will now work with the client to determine exactly what the client's plan for retirement is. The agent may have to help the client to understand the realities of retirement. Factors such as health, activity levels, elderly parents, and dependent children may complicate retirement planning.

- **Create the plan**. The agent will create a retirement plan for the client. The plan should take into account the client's objectives and the agent's expertise. The agent may have to work with other experts to create a comprehensive plan.

- **Implement the plan**. The agent and client will work together to implement the plan. This will often require a re-allocation of the client's resources. It may even be necessary to educate the client about certain financial matters in order to change a behaviour.

- **Monitor and modify the plan**.  The plan is only as good as the will to follow through with it.  The agent must make a habit of following up with the client to see that the plan is being adhered to.  Failure to adhere to the plan will render it useless and all the effort of both the agent and client will have been wasted.  At the same time, the agent must be aware of any material changes in the client's circumstances so that the plan can be adjusted if necessary.

## SUMMARY

Now that you have a good understanding of investments, we will go on to learn about the various government programs that Canadians have access to.  We will come back to the ideas discussed in this module throughout the rest of the course.

# Chapter 7 GOVERNMENT PROGRAMS

In this module, we will examine the basic protection afforded most Canadians. While these are not specifically insurance products, they do use many of the concepts inherent in insurance. For many Canadians, these will be the only programs available when certain of the predictable risks are encountered. The programs are not intended as such; they are intended to provide the first level of protection. As we go through the various programs, you will see that they do provide very broad coverage, but each of the programs has its own particular limitations.

For exam purposes, it is important that you recognize when the benefits would be available, and who would be eligible to collect these benefits. For practical purposes, as an agent selling insurance products, you must consider the government benefits available to all Canadians when structuring a risk management strategy for your client.

## OVERVIEW OF GOVERNMENT PROTECTION

- **Canada Health Act**. The Canada Health Act applies to residents of Canada. While there are some variations in how the act is applied based on the province or territory of residence, there are some elements that apply in all jurisdictions. The Canada Health Act provides free access to medically necessary services to residents. While the Canada Health Act is a federal body of legislation, it is up to the provinces to implement it. However, there are four criteria to the Act that have a direct bearing on this course:

  - Comprehensiveness. The Act requires that each resident can access all medically necessary services offered by doctors, dentists, hospitals, and other health care providers.

  - Universality. All residents must have access to health care. For new residents, the provinces cannot impose a waiting period of greater than three months.

  - Portability. While this provision is somewhat complex, it basically means that residents have access to health care while out of province. The provinces are expected to cover the costs of health care up to the amount they would have provided had health care been accessed in the province of residency. It is noteworthy that there are some limitations here. What one province covers may not be covered by another, so residents can incur some health care costs while receiving health care out of province. This same principle generally applies to out-of-country health care.

  - Accessibility. Provinces are discouraged from the application of additional charges or fees.

- **Provincial Health Insurance Coverage**. As previously discussed, the Canada Health Act describes the obligations of the provinces to provide medically necessary health care. The definition of medically necessary varies from province to province, but there are a variety of services that are normally included. The list of services included is far too broad to include here. There are, however, some types of services that are often not included. Examples of services that would be excluded in some provinces are:

- Ambulance services;
- Prosthetics;
- Elective surgery;
- Prescription drugs;
- Certain diagnostic services;
- Non-medically necessary cosmetic surgery;
- Experimental treatments;
- Some dental services;
- Vision care; and
- Non-medically necessary hospital services, such as private rooms.

- **Retirement Plans**. In Module 6 we were introduced to the idea of government-sponsored retirement plans. In this module, we will look at Canada Pension Plan retirement benefits as well as the Old Age Security program. There are certain benefits specific to each province, but you do not need to be familiar with those for the purpose of this course. Once you are working as an agent, it would benefit you and your clients for you to understand the particular benefits available in the jurisdictions in which you operate.

# GOVERNMENT PLANS

There are several programs at both the federal and provincial levels which can provide some disability coverage. We will examine some of these programs here.

- **Canada Pension Plan**. Canada Pension Plan (CPP) is best known for providing retirement benefits. It also provides a death benefit and survivor's pensions. (Quebec administers its own version of this program, Quebec Pension Plan. For the purposes of this course, QPP and CPP are identical.)

Canada Pension Plan is a contributory plan. Benefits are only available to those who have contributed. Employees aged at least 18 who have not yet begun CPP retirement benefits contribute to the plan. Employer contributions mirror employee contributions. All Canadians who earn a salary (with some exceptions, such as clergy who have taken a vow of poverty) are required to contribute. Contributions are not optional. A self-employed person is also required to contribute, but that person would provide both the employer and employee contributions. Currently, contributions to CPP are based on 4.95% of income earned, starting at $3500 of annual income. Contributions are not made on income above $52,500 for 2014. The bottom end ($3500) of this bracket is known as the Year's Basic Exemption. The top end is known as the Year's Maximum

Pensionable Earnings (YMPE). We will revisit the concept of YMPE in Module 14. Note that contributions to CPP, as well as CPP benefits, are based on residency, and not on citizenship.

Contributions to CPP are tax-favoured. Employee contributions generate a tax credit, and employer contributions are tax deductible. This means that any contributions made are made with pre-tax dollars. For this reason, any benefits received from CPP are taxable as regular income. This becomes an important consideration when we deal with offsets against CPP income later in this section.

Based on the level of contributions, a CPP contributor can expect to receive the following benefits:

- Starting at age 65, a CPP contributor can apply for and receive a retirement benefit based on that person's contributions throughout their working years (ages 18 to 65). The calculation for the actual benefit amount is quite complex, and beyond the scope of this course. Basically, though, the calculation is based on a maximum retirement income ($1,038.33 for 2014) times the average level of contributions over the working years. So somebody who earned YMPE or close to it from age 18 to 65 can count on receiving the maximum retirement benefit. On the other hand, somebody who only worked periodically, or did not earn as much as YMPE for most of their working life, will not receive the maximum benefit. When performing this calculation, CPP excludes the lowest 15% of years, certain child-rearing years, and any period during which the CPP contributor was collecting CPP disability benefits.

- Not all CPP contributors elect to receive CPP starting at age 65. It is possible to receive it earlier or later. Many Canadians will opt to receive it earlier; taking it late is quite rare. Taking it early will result in a reduced benefit, while taking it late will increase the benefit. The benefit amount will be adjusted by .6% per month, or 7.2% per year, for early election and by .7% per month, 8.4% per year for late election. So a contributor who would have been eligible for a $900 per month CPP retirement benefit at age 65 who elects instead to start CPP at age 62 years, 4 months, will have their CPP benefit reduced. This is a common exam question. The reduction in benefits would be for the number of months prior to the 65th birthday (32 months, in this case) times .6% (32 x .6% = 19.2%). So what would have been a $900 benefit will instead be a ($900 - 19.2% =) $727.20 benefit. This decision will permanently affect the value of CPP benefits received. That is, this contributor will not end up receiving a $900 benefit at age 65 once the decision to take early CPP has been made. The earliest that early CPP can be taken is age 60, and the latest it can be delayed to is age 70. A late election will increase the benefit.

  In order to be eligible to receive early CPP, the contributor must demonstrate reduced income. That would be the case if total income were less than the CPP benefit for two consecutive months. Contributors sometimes elect early CPP because they are having trouble meeting all their expenses, and the extra dollars in their pocket will be welcome. Sometimes the decision to take early CPP is related to a desire to halt contributions. A CPP collector is no longer able to make the 4.95% (9.9% for self-employed) contributions otherwise required of working Canadians. Some people are going to invest the dollars they collect, taking advantage of the time value of money.

○ Indexing. All CPP benefits (retirement pension, survivor's benefits, and disability income) are indexed. That means that a CPP collector can count on their benefits increasing at a rate roughly equivalent to inflation. This is a very powerful feature of these government benefits. It is rare to find private benefits that guarantee this full indexing to inflation.

○ CPP also provides survivor's benefits. These survivor's benefits are available for the spouse and certain children of a deceased CPP contributor. Survivor's benefits are available as follows:

■ The spouse of a deceased contributor can expect to receive benefits based on what the contributor would have received as a retirement benefit. The amount of this benefit varies. It will be quite small for a survivor who is younger and has no kids. If there are kids involved, and as the survivor approaches retirement age, the amount of survivor's benefit will also increase. The definition of spouse includes same-sex and common-law couples.

■ Children who are dependent on the deceased contributor can also receive a survivor's benefit. These children have to be dependent and either under 18, or under 25 and attending school full-time. They do not have to live at home; only be dependent. The benefit is also payable to the disabled child of a deceased CPP contributor, as long as that child was disabled and dependent on the CPP contributor prior to reaching age 18. The amount of the orphan's benefit is $230.72 for 2014. This amount is taxed in the child's hands. For minors, it will be paid to the parent, and for adults it will be paid directly to the adult.
Canada Pension Plan also provides a lump sum death benefit. This amount is $2500 or 6 times the monthly retirement benefit, whichever is less. It can be paid to the estate of the deceased or to the survivors, whichever is selected when the death benefit is applied for.

• CPP can provide disability benefits. These benefits can be quite difficult to access, as they require the following:

○ The disabled person must have been a CPP contributor in 4 of the past 6 years. This requirement can be reduced for a long-term contributor to CPP who has only contributed in 3 of the past 5 years;

○ The disabled person must be under 65 years of age. Beyond that age, the disabled person should be collecting CPP retirement benefits;

○ The disabled person cannot be receiving CPP retirement benefits. Note

that it is possible to start collecting CPP retirement benefits as early as age 60 in some cases;
o The disability must be severe and prolonged. Severe and prolonged basically means that the disabled person will likely never again be well enough to work. It is important to note that the disability need not be related to work. It could be a disability resulting from a sickness, or from an off-the-job accident, or from something that happens in the workplace.

There is a waiting period (or elimination period) of four months from the time it is determined that there is an eligible disability before benefits will be received. The benefit amount varies based on the level of contributions. As of 2014, the maximum benefit is $1,236.35 per month; the average benefit is slightly less than $800 per month. Benefits are paid monthly. An advantage of this benefit, as with most government benefits, is that it is fully indexed to inflation. That means a recipient of CPP benefits can expect to see their benefit increase each year to keep pace with inflation. As discussed earlier, the benefit would be fully taxable as regular income.

In addition to the contributor receiving a benefit, it is also possible for the contributor's children to receive a small benefit. If the contributor has dependent children who are either under 18 years of age, then a benefit will be paid to the contributor and taxed in the child's hands. If the contributor has dependent children who are under 25 years of age, but 18 or older, and attending school full-time, then a benefit will normally be paid to the child. Unlike for the child of a deceased CPP contributor, no benefits are payable based on a child of a disabled CPP contributor being disabled themselves. The amount of the benefit is slightly over $230 per month. There are no benefits paid to the spouse of a disabled person.

Although we have not yet discussed disability insurance, we have to note that disability insurers have specific considerations around CPP income. If a client is eligible for and receiving benefits from a disability policy (whether group or individual) and becomes eligible for CPP disability benefits at the same time, there will be an offset applied. In practice, this means that the amount of disability income will be reduced. We will see in the next chapter that disability benefits are normally paid tax-free. This creates a situation in which the tax-free benefits from a disability policy can be replaced by taxable benefits from CPP. Let's say that we have a client who is receiving a $2,600 monthly disability benefit from an insurance policy and that person applies for and receives CPP disability benefits of $800. The disability benefit would be reduced to $1,800 (2600 - 800). Insurers who are paying benefits to clients and estimate that the client may be eligible to receive CPP disability benefits will assist that client in applying for such benefits. In cases where benefits are paid in arrears, the insurer will subrogate (assume the position held by the client in the eyes of the law) and collect those benefits instead of having them paid to the client. Going forward, the client's disability benefit will be offset by the CPP benefit being paid. Because of these considerations, CPP is considered first payor when compared to individual disability insurance.

- **Canada Pension Plan Splitting**. Canada Pension Plan can be split between a couple, whether married or common-law. This form of income splitting can be used to reduce the tax burden for a couple. If both are eligible for and collecting CPP, then they can split their CPP benefits. If one or the other is at least age 60 and not eligible, then splitting is also possible. If however, one of the couple is eligible for but not yet collecting CPP, then splitting is not possible.

  When CPP is split, each spouse is deemed to have provided 50% of their CPP benefit to the other. The easiest way to calculate this is to add up the CPP benefits of each spouse, and divide by two. This will indicate the amount of CPP each spouse is going to be taxed on. This would be advantageous in a situation where one spouse collects $900 per month in benefits and is taxed at a rate of 40%. Say the other spouse collects $500 per month and is taxed at a rate of 25%. In this case, the higher income earning spouse is taxed at a fairly high rate. Moving some of that income to the lower income earning spouse will generate tax savings for this couple.

  Before utilizing any split, this couple is paying ($900 x 40% =) $360 plus ($500 x 25% =) $125, for a total of $485 in taxes. If they were to split their CPP benefit, each of them would be taxed on ($900 + $500 = $1400 ÷ 2 =) $700. The higher income earning spouse now pays just ($700 x 40% =) $280 in taxes, while the lower income earner pays ($700 x 25% =) $175 in taxes, for a total of ($280 + $175 =) $455 in taxes owing. This generates a tax savings of ($485 - $455 =) $30 in tax savings. While it is not a great deal of money saved ($360 for the year) it is a very easy process to take advantage of, and only requires the spouses to elect for the CPP split on their tax returns.

- **Old Age Security**. Old Age Security (OAS) benefits are available to all residents of Canada, based on a minimum residency requirement. In order to collect OAS, one must meet a minimum residency requirement. There is no citizenship requirement; only residency. OAS is non-contributory, meaning that we do not contribute specifically to OAS. Instead, OAS programs are funded out of general revenues. In order to collect OAS, one must be age 65 and have applied for it. OAS is not available prior to age 65. OAS benefits are taxable as regular income.

  The residency requirement for OAS is based on a minimum of 10 years of residency between the ages of 18 and 65. With only 10 years of residency, though, the OAS benefit will be quite limited. The maximum OAS benefit ($551.54 in January of 2014) can only be received with 40 years of residency between those ages. If the total Canadian residency (it need not be consecutive, only cumulative) is less than 40 years, the OAS benefit will be reduced by 2.5% per year.

  OAS is subject to an income test. If an OAS recipient earns more than $71,952 (for 2014) in taxable income, the OAS amount will start to be reduced. This reduction is $.15 for every dollar earned over the $71,952 threshold. Once an OAS recipient earns more than $115,716, the OAS will stop completely. This is normally referred to as the clawback. It is because of this clawback that many seniors will look for ways to split income between spouses, or keep taxable income low in retirement. We will look at these concepts in greater detail in Module 14.

For an easy example of the OAS clawback at work, let's imagine that the threshold for the OAS clawback is $70,000 of annual income. At age 65, our OAS-eligible person has $90,000 of income. That is $20,000 of income over the threshold, resulting in a ($20,000 x 15% =) $3,000 clawback of annual OAS benefits at age 66. That works out to ($3,000/12 =) $250 of OAS benefits per month that would not be received. At age 66, this calculation would be done again with respect to the age 67 benefits, and again at age 67, and so on.

In addition to the basic OAS benefits, OAS also has two further programs designed specifically to assist low-income seniors. Those programs are the Guaranteed Income Supplement and the Allowance. You need not know these in great detail. The Guaranteed Income Supplement is designed for those age 65 who earn below $16,728 (for 2014) excluding their OAS benefits. (The amounts are slightly different for couples.) It will provide as much as $747.86 (for 2014) to low-income seniors.

The Allowance is designed to help people starting at age 60 and up to age 64 who are living on low incomes, but are not yet old enough to receive OAS. The Allowance will not be paid to somebody who has reached age 65. The Allowance provides $1,047.86 (2014 figures) for those aged 60-64 whose income is less than $30,912.

- **Employment Insurance Sickness Benefits**. Employment insurance can be applied in a variety of situations. Regular EI benefits are paid to somebody who has lost a job. Parental and maternity benefits are paid to somebody who is having or in some cases adopting a baby. Other benefits are available, such as retraining benefits. For the purpose of this course, however, we are concerned with EI sickness benefits. EI sickness benefits are paid to somebody whose income has been reduced because of injury or sickness.

In order to be eligible to receive EI sickness benefits, earnings must be decreased more than 40%. An applicant for sickness benefits must have worked at least 600 insured hours in the previous year. An application for sickness benefits must include a note from a doctor or dentist indicating that the applicant is unable to work and estimating how long it will be until the applicant will return to work. This note must be received at the applicant's own expense. This is not a cost normally borne by provincial health care plans.

As of the time of this writing, the EI program is taking 28 days to process claims for sickness benefits. Once a claim is accepted, there is a two-week waiting period. At the end of the two-week waiting period, benefits can be received for up to 15 weeks. An employee must have been unable to work for 7 days before starting the claims process.

EI premiums are paid by both employers and employees. Both are paid with pre-tax dollars, so employees receive a tax credit when paying EI premiums. As a result, any benefits received will be taxed.

The amount of the EI sickness benefit is currently $501 per week, up to a maximum of 55% of the previous salary earned. The benefit is reduced dollar for dollar if any income is earned while collecting sickness benefits. Income from an individual disability policy will not reduce EI benefits, but EI is reduced by group disability benefits. EI benefits are indexed, so this amount will change every year.

The EI program is primarily designed for employees. The self-employed and business owners are largely restricted from using these programs.

- **Worker's Compensation**. Workers' compensation programs (known in Ontario as the Workplace Safety and Insurance Board - WSIB) vary from province to province. A basic knowledge of these programs is required, but the student need not be familiar with the details for each province. WCB premiums are paid by employers; employees do not contribute.

  An employee who becomes sick or is injured as a result of something that happens in the workplace can submit a claim. Waiting periods for WCB benefits are normally very short; usually 1 day for accidents and 8 days for sickness. The benefit amount varies, but is normally between 75% and 90% of the employee's after-tax income. There is usually a maximum based on an annual pre-tax income of between $60,000 and $75,000. WCB benefits are not taxable. In most cases, WCB benefits will normally be paid up until age 65 or until a return to work is possible.

  In addition to an income benefit, WCB can provide a variety of other benefits, including retraining and rehabilitation benefits.

  While the majority of Canadian employees are covered by WCB, there are some industries that are not covered. Salespeople and the self-employed often are exempt from WCB. The greatest limitation of WCB, though, is that an injury or illness must be work-related.

- **Veteran's Affairs Benefits**. Veteran's Affairs benefits are only available to members of the Canadian Armed Forces, the Royal Canadian Mounted Police, and, in some instances, other federal government departments. The primary purpose of Veteran's Affairs programs is to provide services to veterans. Those services can take on a variety of forms. For our purposes in this course we are primarily concerned with disability benefits. Veteran's Affairs pays a tax-free lump sum benefit to those injured on duty. It also pays death benefits to the families of those killed on duty. A variety of other services and benefits are available.

- **Provincial Programs**. In most jurisdictions, there is some sort of program designed to provide a minimum level of income to somebody who is seriously disabled. Ontario, for example, has the Ontario Disability Supports Program; Alberta provides Assured Income for the Severely Handicapped. These programs vary significantly across the provinces. No knowledge of these programs is expected of students in this course. Most provinces also have programs to assist the elderly financially. Sometimes this comes in the form of direct income; sometimes it comes in the form of increased access to medical care.

## CHARACTERISTICS OF GOVERNMENT DISABILITY PROGRAMS

- **Financial**. The programs discussed in this Module are designed to provide a basic level of protection. Especially with EI and CPP, the financial benefits offered are not great. Somebody relying on those benefits for all their financial requirements will likely encounter challenges.

- **24/7 Coverage**. The EI and CPP programs both offer coverage for both work-related and non-work-related conditions. WCB on the other hand, provides coverage only in limited circumstances.

- **Changing Situations**. These programs generally work well for somebody who enjoys long-term employment with the same employer. In today's world, however, this is not a common reality. Many of us in the workforce today find ourselves changing careers regularly, sometimes being self-employed, with periods of unemployment as well. The days of the long-standing employee are, for the most part, behind us.

- **Time Limits**. While WCB can provide benefits quickly and for a long time, EI and CPP both have significant limitations which makes them unreliable as means of risk management. EI will normally only pay sickness benefits for 15 weeks, while CPP takes 4 months to start paying benefits.

- **Discretion**. With each of these programs, there is no clear definition of disability or sickness. In each case, the determination to pay benefits is made by a bureaucrat or committee, based on the input of medical professionals. This can lead to frustration occasionally for claimants.

## CHARACTERISTICS OF GOVERNMENT RETIREMENT PROGRAMS

- **Financial**. The financial benefits offered by these plans are limited. Most people will not be able to live the retirement of their dreams on these benefits. These benefits are designed to provide a minimum level of coverage and nothing more. Some people insist that the government should offer greater benefits, but we must consider that somebody would have to pay for those higher benefits. So higher benefits may be possible, but we could count on paying more taxes or contributing more of our own money. CPP benefits are indexed every January 1st. OAS benefits are indexed 4 times per year, in January, April, July and October.

- **Widely Available**. These programs are designed to be available to all retirees. While CPP is contributory, OAS is not. Nearly everybody has something they can rely on.

- **Taxable**. OAS and CPP are both taxable sources of income. GIS and the Allowance are received tax-free.

## SUMMARY

Now that we have covered the building blocks of understanding financial services in Canada, we will go on to look at the specific products that you will offer with a life insurance license. As you explore the next 8 modules, you may have to come back from time to time and reacquaint yourself with some of the concepts in these earlier modules.

# GOVERNMENT DISABILITY BENEFITS SUMMARY TABLE

| Program | Benefit Amount | Taxable? | Who Contributes | Who is Eligible | Other Benefits | Waiting Period | Benefit Period | Notes |
|---------|---------------|----------|-----------------|-----------------|----------------|----------------|----------------|-------|
| CPP | Average: $882/mo Maximum: $1236/mo | Yes | Employees and Employers | Severe and prolonged disability; must have contributed. | Children of a disability recipient or deceased contributor. CPP also provides retirement, death, and survivor's benefits. | 4 months | To Age 65 | Indexed |
| EI | Max $501 per week or 55% of salary. | Yes | Employees and Employers | Sickness prevents claimant from working. | For unemployment, maternity, parental leave, retraining, and others. | 2 weeks (after processing period | 15 weeks (longer in some cases) | Indexed |
| WCB | Varies; usually 75% to 90% of after-tax salary. | No | Employers only | Job-related injury or illness | Retraining, rehabilitation death benefits, and others. | 1 day for accident; 8 days for sickness | To age 65, but normally ends upon recovery | Lightly tested |

# GOVERNMENT RETIREMENT BENEFITS SUMMARY TABLE

| Program | Benefit Amount | Taxable? | Who Contributes | Who is Eligible | Can it be split? | Other considerations |
|---------|----------------|----------|-----------------|-----------------|------------------|----------------------|
| CPP | Depends on contributions; average is $594/mo; Max is $1038/mo (at age 65) | Yes | Employees and Employers | Age 65, but can be taken as early as 60 or as late as 70 | Yes, as long as both spouses are 65 or both have opted to collect early. | Indexed to inflation; amount is reduced if taken early; increased if taken late. Heavily tested. |
| OAS | Max is $546.07/mo | Yes | All taxpayers, through general revenues. | Age 65 and have met residency requirement of 10 years between the ages of 18 and 65. | No. | Indexed to inflation; Subject to a clawback for high income earners |
| GIS | Max is $747.86/mo | No | Funded through the OAS program. | Must be eligible for OAS benefits and have low income. | No. | Only designed for very low income earners. |

# Chapter 8 LIFE INSURANCE

Having now covered some of the basics of risk management, we will move on to learn about life insurance. Life insurance is specifically designed to deal with the risk of premature death. In this module, though, we will also explore methods of using life insurance to manage the risk of old age and the risk of disability. Prior to reading this module, it will be worthwhile for you to review Modules 2 and 3, both of which contain many concepts fundamental to understanding life insurance. We will also touch on taxation (especially the Wills, Death, and Taxes section) and investments in this module.

We will start this module with a discussion around assessing the need for insurance. Once we have determined the need for insurance, we will explore some basic concepts relating to the structure of insurance policies. We will then examine each type of policy in some detail. Once we have explored the types of policies, we can learn about the riders, additional features that we add on to a life insurance policy to better suit a client's particular circumstances. Finally, we will cover some technical details, such as taxation of insurance policies.

As discussed in Module 1, insurance is not a new concept. The idea of a large number of people each contributing a small amount of dollars in exchange for a larger promised amount at death dates back thousands of years. We have seen evolutions in the actuarial science, which has allowed insurers to become much more precise in calculating how much premium to collect in exchange for the promise of a death benefit. The basic concept, though, has not changed.

## NEEDS ANALYSIS

Every insurance agent will, over the course of their career, hear from a prospective client that, "I don't need insurance." There are a number of reasons for this argument (group insurance coverage, mortgage insurance, counting on the government, saving on our own) and the prospective client might even be correct. It is foolish and potentially disastrous, though, to take it for granted that there is no need for insurance.

Some of the financial considerations that a client's family might have to deal with on death include:

- **Unpaid Debts**. While it is true that our creditors cannot legally pursue our heirs for our unpaid debts, it is also true that the value of our estate cannot pass to our heirs until all debts have been settled. This means, for instance, that a couple with a mortgage on their home might find that, in the event of the death of one of that couple, the bank will insist that the mortgage be paid off. Failure to deal with the mortgage on the death of the first spouse might result in the bank taking ownership of the home in order to pay off the outstanding mortgage. This is a worst-case scenario, but it does happen. When calculating the need for life insurance, we must take into account all unpaid debts. This can include business debts, consumer loans, and mortgage.

- **Final Expenses**. On death, a client will normally leave certain final expenses. This can include legal and accounting fees, especially where there is a business or a large amount of property to deal with. The funeral expense must be considered. Even a relatively inexpensive funeral will cost between $6,000 and $10,000. Very elaborate funerals can cost $25,000 or more.

- **Taxes**. As discussed in Module 5, there is a requirement to file a terminal tax return on the death of a taxpayer. The terminal tax return must take into account all unpaid taxes. There is also the possibility of capital gains taxes to be paid, as the death of a taxpayer is considered a deemed disposition of assets. Keep in mind, though, that assets can roll over to a spouse tax-free, so this capital gain can be deferred until the death of the last spouse.

- **Ongoing Family Expenses**. Especially where a survivor earned an income and supported a family, there is a requirement for income replacement. We must assess how much of that income will be required (around 70% is a common estimate) for the surviving spouse and kids to get by. An alternate, and more accurate method of assessment, is to look at the actual expenses that the family will have to deal with. We would then put enough insurance in place to make sure the family will be able to meet those expenses. This exercise can be somewhat emotional, but it is probably necessary. Think of a couple with two young kids. As with many couples today, imagine that both of the parents work outside the home and earn an income. For the sake of argument, let's say that they both earn $50,000 per year. The temptation might be to say, "Our annual expenses are $72,000 per year, so as long as we still have that amount after the death of one of us, we will be okay." This is not, however, the reality. Put yourself in the shoes of one of the surviving spouse, having just lost your husband or wife. There used to be two of you to take care of the household, help the kids with homework, shuttle the kids around, and all the other trappings of family life. Now, with only one person to do all this, is it realistic to assume that the expenses will stay the same? The remaining parent might have to work less hours or hire outside help to keep the family functioning the same way it did prior to the loss of the other spouse. By performing a realistic calculation and putting the appropriate amount of insurance in place, we can help this family to maintain the standard of living they were used to.

In order to perform this calculation, we are going to use a formula called capitalization of income. Let's say we have a family that estimates their annual unpaid expenses upon the death of a first spouse to be $2,000 per month, or $24,000 per year. We now need to make a realistic projection as to interest rates. Taking into account the know your client information and the fact that any investments made here will be income-focused rather than growth-focused, we should use a fairly conservative interest rate projection. It is probably best to use something between 2% and 4%. For the sake of argument, let's use 3% here. So what we really need to know is, how much capital will the family need to invest to generate $24,000 per year of income? This math is actually fairly simple using a basic calculator. Take the $24,000 and divide it by 3%. (The keystrokes are 24000 ÷ 3 %).  You should see an answer of $800,000 on your screen.  If you are using an accounting calculator, it will not use the % function the same way; you should then run 24000 ÷ decimal 03, or .03.  .03 is exactly the same as 3% in math terms.  Some financial calculators will require you to enter 24000 ÷ 3 % = to get this figure.

We recommend that students acquire a basic Staples or Office Depot type calculator, which should cost about $8.  Scientific, accounting, and financial calculators can react in ways that you will not expect, especially if you are not comfortable with the model of calculator you have chosen.)  So, for this family, we can see that there is a requirement for $800,000 of life insurance if they are going to continue to live the way they are used to after the death of a spouse.

An alternative, and often simpler, method of putting insurance in place to cover family expenses is to use a simple multiple of income.  For example, the Canadian Life and Health Insurance Association recommends 5 to 7 times annual income for this purpose.  Many insurance agents use a multiple of 10 to 20 times annual income for the same purpose.  Families with younger children should generally use a higher multiple.  It is probably safe, where this method is appropriate for exam purposes, to use a multiple of 10 times annual income.  Using this method, an income earner with $60,000 of annual income should have about $600,000 of life insurance in place in order to help meet family expenses.

- **Family Assets**.  Some families will have access to assets that they can liquidate in the event of death.  If these assets will not be needed by the survivors and will be able to be liquidated fairly easily on death then we can plan to use those assets to help the family deal with this death.  We would not include, for example, the family home in this calculation because it will be needed by the survivors.  We might also not use potentially illiquid investments like real estate, which might not necessarily be easily turned into much-needed cash for the survivors.

- **Family Income**.  It would be unrealistic to consider the family expenses without also taking into account the family income.  In most families today, whichever spouse were to die, it is most likely that the surviving spouse would have some income to rely on.  As discussed previously, we must be realistic about how much income will be available with only one income earner in the family.

- **Estate Preservation**.  There are a number of sales concepts that focus on using life insurance as a tool to create wealth for a later generation.  Parents or grandparents might acquire a large amount of insurance with the intent of leaving some wealth for their heirs.  This is not a need so much as a desire for insurance.

- **Charitable Giving**.  Many charities today rely on generous donations from the estates of their deceased patrons.  Life insurance has become a very popular way of funding these donations.  A gift of life insurance can be very attractive, because it allows the donor to donate an amount that otherwise might not have been available.  Done properly, a gift of life insurance can also reduce taxes owing on death, so it can have a financial benefit for the estate of the deceased. Not every client will want to pursue charitable giving strategies, but an agent who asks this question can give clients the opportunity to do some good. Adding an extra $50,000 or $100,000 to the face value of a life insurance policy can be quite inexpensive, but the impact of those dollars for a favourite cause can be huge.

- **The Calculation**. Once we have gathered all this information, it is time to figure out how much insurance will be required. We recommend a simple table to calculate the need for insurance. The table might look something like this:

| Immediate Haves | Immediate Needs | Ongoing Haves | Ongoing Needs |
|---|---|---|---|
| Liquid Assets | Funeral | Surviving Spouse's Income | Family Expenses |
| Emergency Funds | Taxes | CPP Survivor's Benefits | Household Expenses |
| Cash | Final Expenses | Investment Income | Children's Education |
| Life Insurance Benefits | Debts | Rental Income | Retirement Savings |

Once the table is created, we need to subtract the haves from the needs on the immediate side, which will give a lump sum figure. If this amount is negative, no insurance is needed. If the figure is positive (they need more than they have) then insurance is needed for the immediate period. On the ongoing side, we subtract the haves from the needs. If this figure is positive then we would run a capitalization of income calculation to figure out how much they need. Once we are done with the two sides, add the two figures together, and we know how much insurance is required! (If the immediate haves outweigh the immediate needs, we could use that amount to reduce what is required in the capitalization of income on the ongoing side. However, excess income cannot be used to offset the immediate needs, because the excess income would not be immediately available.) Practice this for yourself. Do you have enough insurance? To see a practical demonstration of the needs analysis, go to http://www.youtube.com/watch?v=_57o8UdYu8.

# UNDERSTANDING LIFE INSURANCE

Before looking at the different types of life insurance, we will look at some concepts that we need to understand in order for life insurance to make sense. We have already looked at many of these concepts, such as beneficiary designations and underwriting, in previous modules. Some ideas we must be familiar with are:

- **Taxation of Premiums**. Premiums paid for life insurance policies are paid with after-tax dollars. That is, there is no tax deduction or tax credit available based on premiums paid for a life insurance policy.

- **Taxation of Death Benefits**. In almost all cases, the death benefit from a life insurance policy is paid tax-free. The exceptions to this are rare, and we will deal with both of them later in this module. Most Canadians can safely assume that their personally owned life insurance policies are going to pay a tax-free death benefit. Those policies that will pay a tax-free death benefit are known as exempt life insurance policies, meaning that they are exempt from the regular accrual taxation to which most investments are subject.

- **Cost of Insurance**. Insurance companies are companies in the business of making money. As such, they are not going to sell products that will see them generate losses. Insurance companies employ actuaries to design products that will allow them to collect enough premiums to pay out the promised death benefits. Underwriters make sure that the insurance company is not taking on risks that will see it have to pay out more death benefits than it can reasonably afford. When an insurance policy is sold, the insurance company will calculate a cost of insurance (COI) that will allow the insurer to collect enough premiums to make sure that the policies sold will work as planned. There are two basic ways that COI can be calculated:

  - **Term**. Term COI requires less immediate cash outlay by the client. Under a term premium structure, the client pays the cost of insurance for the year in which the policy is acquired. If the client still has the same insurance policy next year, the premiums will be slightly higher. A client who has purchased a policy with a term premium structure can count on the premiums increasing each and every year. Generally, younger clients will see fairly small increases in their premiums. Older clients will see substantial and sometimes prohibitive increases in their premiums. This premium structure is often known as annual renewable term (ART) or yearly renewable term (YRT). Within the last sixty years or so, it has become quite common to offer terms other than one year. Most insurance policies sold today are not sold with annually increasing premiums; instead insurers will average out the term costs over, say, 5 year terms. This means a client can be assured of a level premium for five years, but at the end of 5 years, the premium will increase. It will then stay at that level for 5 years, and so forth. This can also be done with 10 year, 20 year, and even 30 year terms. The longer the term, the higher the initial premium will be, but the longer the policy will stay at its original price. A term premium structure should not be confused with a term insurance policy.

  - **Level or T-100**. Level premium structures are designed to give the client a predictable cost for as long as they own the policy. With a level premium structure, the insurer figures out the average cost of insurance for a pre-determined number of years (85 or 100 are common, depending on the exact type of policy). That sets the premium then, for as long as the policy is in force. A client who chooses this premium structure is going to have a higher initial cost than a client who chooses a term premium structure. However, this client can count on their premiums staying level throughout the life of the policy. T-100 COI should not be confused with T-100 life insurance policies.

- **Net Cost of Pure Insurance**. Net cost of pure insurance (NCPI) is a Canada Revenue Agency calculation used when determining the tax consequences of certain activities associated with life insurance policies. NCPI is calculated based on a Term COI, so it is very low in the younger years, but increases sharply later on in life. For comprehension purposes, it is best to equate NCPI with the cost of the cheapest possible YRT Term policy that could be acquired without having to pay a policy fee or a modal factor.

- **Guaranteed Cost of Insurance**. Most life insurance policies sold in Canada today feature guaranteed premiums, which come about because the cost of insurance is guaranteed. With a guaranteed premium structure, the client knows that premiums will never increase, except because of a scheduled increase, such as the increase in premiums that will happen five years after a policy with a 5 year term is acquired. In the past, some life insurance policies did feature non-guaranteed premiums. With a non-guaranteed premium, the premiums could increase based on the insurer having more claims than expected, or, in some cases, if the health of the life insured deteriorated. Term and T-100 premium structures can both feature both guaranteed and non-guaranteed premiums.

- **Term Insurance**. Term insurance is the most basic type of life insurance. In a term insurance policy, coverage lasts for as long as premiums are paid, up to a pre-determined date, such as the life insured's 75th birthday. With most term insurance policies, at the end of the term, the client has nothing to show for it, except for having been insured throughout the term, providing peace of mind.

- **Permanent Insurance**. Permanent insurance is more complicated, and comes in a variety of forms. Permanent insurance is normally more expensive than term insurance, but the client cannot outlive it. The insurance is designed to stay in force for as long as necessary. Clients will sometimes own both term and permanent insurance at the same time. Plenty of Canadians have multiple policies on their lives to cover their varying needs. Permanent insurance can help to manage the risk of old age, as there are many premium structures and funding options that allow a policy to be paid up prior to retirement.

- **Death Benefit**. When a life insured dies while insurance is in force, this results in a death benefit being paid. As previously discussed, this also normally results in the end of the contract. The death benefit is paid tax-free in most cases. If beneficiaries are named in the policy, then the death benefit will be paid directly to them, bypassing the will and probate. Death benefits are normally paid very quickly after claims are submitted, meaning that beneficiaries can count on having good access to cash.

- **Face Value**. The face value is the amount of insurance sold, as identified on the face page of the insurance contract. Note that there are some circumstances, such as where a policy is sold with an increasing death benefit, where the death benefit might exceed the face value. It is rare, but possible, to sell a policy with a reducing death benefit. Otherwise, it is only because the client has an outstanding debt to the insurer (because of a policy loan or unpaid premiums) that the death benefit could be less than the face value.

- **Renewable**. Renewable contracts will allow a client to go from one term to the next without having to re-apply for insurance or provide evidence of insurability. Almost all life insurance sold in Canada today is renewable to a certain point. The term policy discussed earlier in this section could be said to be renewable to age 75.

  Renewable policies renew automatically at the end of their term. The usual mechanism for this is that, about 90 days before the end of a term, the policy owner will receive a reminder that their premiums will increase. This should not come as a surprise, since the policy was originally sold as a renewable term policy. A policy owner purchasing, for example, a five year renewable term policy, will receive an illustration showing the annual premium each year between the acquisition of the policy and its expiry date. As long as the policy owner does not take any action to cause their policy to lapse, it will automatically renew at the end of each five year term.

- **Cash Surrender Value**. Certain permanent insurance policies will start to accumulate a cash surrender value (CSV) based on premiums paid. This CSV is an amount of money that the client can access if the policy is surrendered, or to take a policy loan (as discussed in Module 3), or if the client needs to use the policy's non-forfeiture provisions (also in Module 3). In almost all cases, growth in the CSV will not be taxed.

- **Adjusted Cost Basis**. You will recall that in Module 5, we discussed adjusted cost base as being the amount of after-tax dollars we put into an investment. It was important there because it meant that, on disposition of a piece of property, that amount need not be taxed again. Life insurance has similar considerations. We will further define and explore ACB of a life insurance policy at the end of this module.

- **Convertible**. Many term policies issued in Canada today feature a conversion privilege. This conversion feature allows a client to convert their policy from one form to another, without having to provide evidence of insurability. This is often offered as a feature of a term policy, to allow the client to later convert that policy into permanent insurance. Conversion can be done for an amount up to or equal to the face value of the existing policy.

  Recently, insurance companies have introduced much more flexibility into conversion options for life insurance policies. It is possible to convert only a portion of an existing term policy into permanent insurance. For example, an $800,000 term insurance policy might undergo a conversion from $800,000 of term insurance into $200,000 of permanent and $600,000 of term insurance. Sometime later, the policy owner might again elect to convert a portion of the policy. They might then have the $200,000 of permanent insurance, possibly another $100,000 of newly purchased permanent insurance, and $500,000 remaining on the original term policy. Conversion is even possible from one sort of term to another, such as conversion from ten year term to twenty year term.

- **Endowment**. Strictly speaking, endowment means that the policy will pay out its death benefit despite the life insured not having died. This was once a common feature of certain types of permanent insurance. A client would have known that if she lived to a certain age, she would receive an endowment equal to the death benefit, because that would have been the point at which the CSV of the policy was equal to the death benefit. If she died early, a death benefit would be paid. These policies are no longer sold in Canada today. However, we still use this term 'endowment' occasionally to refer to the situation when the CSV is the same as the death benefit.

- **Creditor Protection**. When the beneficiary of a life insurance policy is the parent, spouse, child, or grandchild of the life insured, the CSV of the policy and the policy itself are protected from the claims of the insured's creditors. This provision also applies when the beneficiary is irrevocable. Amounts deposited in the policy in the 12 months up to a claim arising by a creditor may not be protected.

  When an irrevocable beneficiary has been named, this also creates creditor protection during the lifetime of the life insured.

  On death of the life insured, death benefits are considered separate from the estate. As such, they are protected from the claims of creditors. (The parent, spouse, child, and grandchild are sometimes referred to as the preferred class of beneficiaries.)

- **Living Benefits**. Some insurance policies can provide living benefits. Living benefits mean that the policy will pay some portion of its death benefit to a client who has become terminally ill or developed a critical illness. This can be done in a variety of ways; we will look at one when we examine riders, and another when we cover taxation of life insurance. Living benefits from life insurance policies are paid tax-free, much the same as life insurance death benefits are.

- **Exclusions**. While we discussed this in Module 3, it is worth noting that the only exclusion to a conventional life insurance policy is for suicide in the first two years after the policy is issued or reinstated. Life insurance does not have exclusions for drinking and driving, commission of a crime, service in the armed forces, acts of war, or anything else.

# TYPES OF LIFE INSURANCE

While life insurance has taken on a number of forms since it first came to Canada in the late 1800's, there are four types of life insurance policies that are widely available in Canada today. We will look at each of those four types of policies in some detail here.

## TERM LIFE INSURANCE

Term life is the most basic type of life insurance sold in Canada today.  It is also the most frequently sold type of life insurance.  With a term insurance policy, the insurance company structures the premiums to pay for the costs of mortality plus the expenses associated with the policy, just as discussed in Module 3.  There is little or no investment component with a term policy.  The cost of the policy is basically equal to the life insured's estimate of how much death benefit they will have to pay if the expected number of people within that certain mortality class die in the year in which the policy is purchased, plus the expenses of the insurer.  Term insurance is normally designed to expire right about the time when insurance starts to get very expensive, around 75 or 80.  Because the very expensive years of insurability are not built into this policy, and because the client is only paying for insurance and not investments, the policy will be inexpensive compared to other forms of insurance.

Term policies almost always have term premium structures; 10 and 20 year renewable term policies are the most frequently sold in Canada today.  While relatively rare, there are some non-renewable term policies sold today.  This product is usually slightly cheaper than its renewable counterpart, but the insured knows that the coverage will end at the end of the set term.  This might be done where there is a specific need for a certain period with no chance of the need extending beyond the term.

Death benefits for term policies can be set according to one of three models.  Most individually sold term insurance is sold with a level death benefit.  This is straightforward.  A client buys a policy with a $100,000 death benefit; that will be the death benefit for as long as the client continues to pay premiums.

The second way that a death benefit can be structured is on an increasing basis.  This is quite rare, but it is possible to offer a term policy that will increase its death benefit to keep pace with inflation.  The premiums for this policy would increase at the same pace as the death benefit would.

The third way is a decreasing death benefit.  A decreasing death benefit is usually attached to some sort of financial obligation, such as a mortgage (mortgage life insurance will be discussed later in this module).  In this case, the death benefit will decrease as the mortgage is paid off.  Premiums for a decreasing death benefit are usually level, but some insurers have started offering policies with decreasing death benefits and decreasing premiums.

Term policies are ideal for a client with a short term need, such as when a client takes out a mortgage.  The client knows that the mortgage will be paid off eventually, but if he dies with the mortgage outstanding, he wants to make sure that the mortgage will be paid.  A term policy is the least expensive way to accomplish this.  Term policies are also well-suited to families with limited disposable income.  If there is a recognized need for insurance, but limited financial resources, a term policy is a good solution.

A common sales practice with term insurance is to offer convertible policies. Convertible term insurance, which is only marginally more expensive than non-convertible, can later be converted into permanent insurance (either whole life or universal life, depending on the insurer). This conversion happens without underwriting. Premiums will increase significantly. The advantage here is that the insured has the flexibility to switch later to permanent insurance, but the initial cost of the term policy is still manageable. This can be good for a young couple or a business with an insurance need but not a lot of cash.

The low cost of term insurance has a downside. Coverage will run out at some point. There is no CSV associated with a term policy. The lack of CSV also means that there is no opportunity to take advantage of non-forfeiture provisions. There is little flexibility with a term policy; the client acquires the product, and pays premiums for as long as insurance is required.

- **Mortgage Insurance**. Mortgage insurance is a separate product from life insurance. Mortgage insurance is a form of group insurance, which we will discuss in Module 11. We are referring here to the product offered by banks (and underwritten by insurers) which most mortgage lenders offer at the time a mortgage product is purchased. This product, on the surface, looks very much like decreasing term insurance. However, there is no life insurance policy in place. The life insured enters into an agreement with the mortgage lender to be covered under that lender's contract of group insurance. As such, there is no contract of insurance, and the insured lacks the protection normally available to an insured who purchases a contract from an insurer. These policies are often sold with no underwriting done at time of purchase. This can mean that underwriting is done at the time of claim, which can create a situation in which it is shocking when no death benefit is paid. This is not to say that all mortgage insurance is bad. However, as with any important purchase, it is incumbent on the customer to understand the product being purchased.

## WHOLE LIFE INSURANCE

Whole life insurance is the oldest form of permanent insurance. In a whole life insurance policy, the insured enters into an insurance contract which features level premiums based on a need for permanent insurance. The premiums will be based on a level structure, but abbreviated premiums schedules are available with whole life policies. Some whole life policies are sold with a pay-to-age-65 premium structure; others with a 10-pay or 20-pay premium structure. This would mean that the premiums are paid for just 10 or 20 years, at which point the policy is considered to be paid up, and no more premiums have to be paid.

A whole life policy has three components. There is an investment component, a protection component, and the insurer's expenses. The investment component is used by the insurer to generate a policy reserve. The policy reserve is used to fund the death benefit. Because the policy reserve is based on a guaranteed set of investments, the reserve will grow over time, reducing the need for the protection component. In the early years of the policy, the policy reserve will be quite small, so the protection component will be quite large. As the policy reserve builds, the protection component will decrease. The portion of a whole life policy that is required to pay for protection is referred to as the net amount at risk. At the point at which the policy reserve has grown enough to fund the death benefit by itself, the policy is considered paid up, as discussed in the previous paragraph.

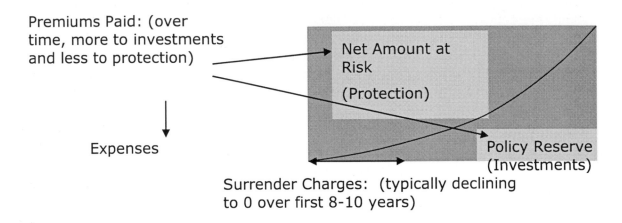

A client purchasing a whole life policy knows that there is going to be very little thought given to the policy once it is in force. The client pays premiums; the insurance company takes care of the management of the policy. There is an investment component. This investment component will normally attain growth at rates similar to long-term GICs. As with a GIC, the growth within a whole life policy is guaranteed. As with any investment in a life insurance policy, the growth will not be taxed in most circumstances. In some whole life contracts, additional deposits are possible, which would generate additional CSV. There are usually heavy surrender charges in a whole life policy over the first 8 or so years of the contract, so a client may not be able to access the full CSV until they have paid premiums for a number of years. The CSV can be accessed as a policy loan, using the non-forfeiture provisions, at the surrender of a policy, or, in some cases, as a withdrawal from the policy (a partial surrender).
Death benefits paid from whole life policies are level. There are not increasing or decreasing death benefits available, although we will look in a few minutes at a couple of ways to increase the death benefit on a whole life policy. The death benefit of a whole life policy does not increase as the CSV increases. A whole life policy with a $50,000 face value will pay a $50,000 death benefit at time of claim (reduced by any outstanding policy loans) regardless of what the CSV is at that time.

Whole life insurance requires a higher (usually much higher) initial premium than does term insurance. The reason for this is that there are many years of insurability being averaged together, instead of just paying for the current year. The investment component of whole life also creates additional costs. However, it is not necessarily true that whole life costs more than term insurance. When the full costs of a term policy carried to maturity are compared to the premiums paid for a whole life policy over the life of the policy, the two amounts are often very similar.

There are two types of whole life insurance. The basic whole life policy is a non-participating policy. A non-participating policy works exactly as we have seen so far. The more expensive version of the whole life policy, a participating whole life policy, has additional features and flexibility not available in non-participating (non-par) policies. A participating whole life policy is so called because it allows the policy owner to participate in the profits associated with the pool of whole life policy owners. As with other forms of insurance, the premiums for a whole life policy are based on three factors: investments, mortality, and expenses. Whenever any of these perform better than expected, the participating policy owners will be rewarded with policy dividends. Policy dividends, while they have similar origins, are not the same as stock dividends discussed in Modules 5 and 6. Note that, of all the different types of insurance we will look at, only participating whole life policies pay policy dividends. Policy dividends can be used seven ways, which we will break down into three categories:

- **Cash or Savings**. The insured has the opportunity to take the policy dividend out of the policy as cash, or to invest it in a non-insurance investment with the insurer. The three specific opportunities normally available are:

  o **Cash**. The policy owner simply takes the dividend in the form of cash.

  o **Accumulation or Savings**. The policy owner might choose to leave the dividends on deposit with the insurer. This works very much like attaching a savings account to the life insurance policy. This dividend option is often called 'dividends on deposit'. Extra savings are attractive for clients who are looking for a liquid investment with stability.

  o **Invested in an Individual Variable Insurance Contract**. Some insurers give the option of investing the dividends in an IVIC offered by that insurer. We will discuss IVICs in more detail in Module 12. Even though an IVIC has certain insurance characteristics, this is not a purchase of additional insurance. This is an investment supplemental to the participating whole life policy. The IVIC option is useful for clients who are looking for growth beyond what the whole life contract will provide.

- **Purchase More Insurance**. Alternately, the insured could use the policy dividend to buy more insurance. This is one way to have a whole life policy pay more death benefit than the original face value of the policy. When dividends are used to buy more insurance, no underwriting is required and no application need be completed. The insurer simply takes the dividends and uses them to acquire more insurance on behalf of the client.

  o **Term Additions**. Using term additions, the client takes the dividend paid and purchases a one-year non-renewable term policy. This effectively increases the amount of insurance in force without increasing the premium. Because term insurance requires a smaller premium than whole life, the amount of insurance that can be added is normally quite large relative to the face value of the participating whole life policy. Some insurers offer an option in which the client can be guaranteed a certain amount of term insurance every year; this amount is normally smaller than what the current dividend scale would provide. Term additions would normally be used by a client who is looking for extra coverage at a low cost.

- ○ **Special Term Additions**. Special term additions are a hybrid between term additions and cash. The dividend is used to buy a one year, non-renewable term policy with a face value equal to the current CSV of the par whole life policy. Any excess amount is paid to the client as cash. Special term additions are purchased when clients are looking for an increasing death benefit, which is effectively what will happen here. Special term additions are sometimes referred to as the 5th Dividend Option; they were traditionally 5th on the list of dividend options from which the client could choose.

- ○ **Paid Up Additions**. This dividend option allows the client to buy more permanent insurance. The dividend is used to buy a tiny participating whole life policy with its own face value and its own CSV. While in the early years, these additions will be quite small, over time, there will grow to be a large number of paid-up policies, each producing its own dividends. This compounding can be quite powerful, and will result in significant additional whole life coverage being acquired. Paid up additions are normally purchased when the client has a very long time to allow the compounding power of the paid up additions to accumulate.

- • **Reduce Premiums**. Dividends can be used to reduce premiums as well. Basically, the insurance company keeps the dividend and the client is freed from a month or two (approximately, depending on the dividend scale) of premium payments.

Normally, once an insured makes a decision as to which dividend option to use, there is no opportunity to change that decision. Some insurers will allow a change under certain circumstances, but the client should consider whichever dividend option they choose at the time of application as being a permanent choice.

Dividends are not guaranteed. Canadian insurers have a fantastic history of paying regular dividends, but the agent must not indicate in any way that dividends are guaranteed. Normally, whole life policy illustrations will show three sets of figures. They will show the policy performance if the dividends continue to be paid as they currently are. They will show the policy performance if the dividends are paid at a reduced level, and they will show the policy performance if dividends are no longer paid. The formula for determining how much dividend will be paid in a given year is referred to as the dividend scale.

- **Premium Offset**.  In the early 1980s a sales technique around whole life insurance involving using the dividends to allow premiums to stop being paid became very popular.  At the time, bond yields were in the mid-teens.  These bond yields allowed insurers to offer policies with very generous dividend scales.  These policies often featured schemes in which the dividends would grow by such an extent that within 8 or 10 years the dividends would be able to pay the premiums.  These were called premium-offset or vanishing premium policies.

  Unfortunately, as bond yields fell through the late 1980s and into the 1990s, insurers cut their dividend scales.  The cuts in dividend scales meant that the illustrations for these vanishing premium policies were no longer valid.  Many insurers ended up settling large torts related to these types of policies.  This is why it is so important today for the agent to generate realistic projections about how a policy might perform over time, accompanied by worst-case scenario illustrations.

  Whole life insurance policies are attractive because of their permanent nature.  The client acquiring a whole life policy knows exactly what their costs will be for as long as premiums have to be paid.  The non-forfeiture provisions provide the client with some flexibility in the event that premiums cannot be paid as planned.  Participating whole life policies provide some flexibility for clients who are willing to pay extra premiums.  The client need not worry about the CSV; it will grow according to the promises made by the insurer when the policy was sold.  The greatest downside of whole life insurance is the fairly high cost.  At the same time, the policy is not very flexible (outside of the dividend options, if available) so clients who might have changing needs over time might not like this policy.

  In summary, whole life is sold to clients who have a permanent need and can afford it.  It is a great estate planning tool.  Where there are needs such as capital gains on death, estate preservation, or charitable giving, the whole life policy is an ideal product.

- **Adjustable Whole Life Insurance**. Prior to universal life becoming a major part of the market for life insurance in Canada, there was a product called adjustable whole life insurance. Adjustable whole life insurance gave the client the opportunity to have some exposure to the ups and downs of the markets within a whole life policy. If the investments associated with the policy did very well, the policy might have increased its death benefit, or the client could decrease premiums. If the investments did poorly, the death benefit might have decreased, or the client could increase premiums and keep the death benefit at its original level. Adjustable whole life is not sold in Canada today, but you might still run into these policies from time to time.

## TERM TO 100

Term to 100 is a form of permanent insurance, but is best thought of as a hybrid between term and permanent. Basically, a T-100 policy takes the cost of a term policy for every year between the time of purchase and age 100 and averages that cost out. That average cost becomes the premium. The only additional cost is the policy factor. There is no investment component with a T-100 policy. (Though some T-100 policies do start to build CSV after 20 years or so of premium payments.)

With a T-100 policy, the client is only buying life insurance. There is no opportunity for policy loans, no access to non-forfeiture provisions, and no cash available if the policy is surrendered. This is a very basic insurance product. In fact, one of its major appeals is its simplicity.

T-100 will feature level death benefits in almost all cases. At one time, T-100 death policies worked like the endowment policies discussed earlier in this module; if the client reached age 100, the policy would pay its benefit at that time even though the client was still alive. Modern T-100 policies are simply considered paid-up (no more premiums) at age 100.

T-100 is often used where there is an estate planning need identified late in life. Perhaps a couple in their late 60s or early 70s realizes that the family cottage (which is capital property) will end up with a capital gain of $200,000 on their death. They don't have the $50,000 or so that will be required to pay the taxes that will be owed. Term insurance will not work in this case, because the couple could easily outlive the 75 or 80 year age limit that most insurers place on pure term policies. Whole life will be costly, and the couple is not going to have time to build any meaningful CSV. So they acquire a T-100 policy (probably on a joint-and-last-to-die basis) planning to use the death benefit to pay the taxes they anticipate will come due when the last of them dies. This policy will have premiums about 10-15% less than if they had purchased a comparable whole life policy.

T-100 is sold to clients who have a need for permanent insurance, but do not require any of the features available with whole life or universal life insurance. Younger clients should be cautious when acquiring T-100, because the lack of non-forfeiture provisions means that a missed premium will cause the policy to lapse. Missed premiums in a whole life policy will trigger the automatic premium loan provision.

## UNIVERSAL LIFE

Universal life insurance is a more complex product than any of the life insurance products we have looked at so far. This complexity comes about because it offers great flexibility. The flexibility, though, comes at a cost, as the client does have to take some steps to manage a universal life insurance contract. Universal life, developed in the early 1980s for the North American market, allows the client to manage investments within a life insurance contract.

In order to understand universal life insurance, it is best to consider it as having two components:

- **Life Insurance**. This is a life insurance product. There will be a life insurance policy document, an application, underwriting, and a death benefit. All of these components will work in the same manner as any other life insurance product. The premiums for the product, as with all insurance will be based on mortality plus investments plus expenses. Universal life provides protection from the risk of premature death, and can help with estate planning, just as with other types of life insurance.

- **Investments**. While we recognize that life insurance is not an investment product, it does have an investment component. This investment component can feature several of the types of investments discussed in Module 6. This can include mutual funds, GICs, Term Deposits, and Savings Accounts. Unlike most of the investments discussed in Module 6, the investments held in a life insurance contract will grow on a tax-deferred basis.

Understanding these two components lets us see the big picture with universal life. The real flexibility, though, comes in the details. In order to understand this flexibility, we are going to look at five characteristics of universal life insurance:

- **Flexible Premiums**. With the three types of life insurance policies we have looked at so far, the premium is set when the policy is acquired. The policy owner knows that those are the premiums he will pay throughout the term of the policy. Universal life insurance is much more flexible in this regard. When a universal life insurance policy is purchased, a minimum premium is set, based on the mortality costs plus the expenses of the policy. The mortality costs can be based on either T-100 or YRT pricing. The choice of T-100 or YRT pricing depends on the client's circumstances. A client who is looking to maximize their investments might want to keep the COI low, and might choose a YRT structure. A client who is looking for certainty in their insurance costs will choose a T-100 or level COI. Some agents have sold Universal Life insurance with a YRT cost where clients could not afford a T-100 premium structure. This is a dangerous practice. We know that, under a YRT premium structure, the client's costs will increase over time. If a client cannot afford T-100 premiums today, it will likely not be long until the client's YRT costs increase to a point where the policy is too expensive. This will result in a policy lapse. It is unethical for agents to sell policies in situations where there is a good chance that the policy will lapse.

  In addition to the choice between YRT and T-100 COI, the policy owner has great flexibility in the actual amount of premium paid. There has to be enough money in the policy to cover the cost of insurance plus the insurer's expenses. Any excess amounts deposited into the policy will go to fund the policy's investment component. Unlike a whole life policy, the universal life policy gives the policy owner the opportunity to decide exactly how much to invest in the policy year over year. The amounts paid into a universal life policy are sometimes referred to as premiums (as we have done in this text) or sometimes referred to as deposits. This ability to determine the amount of premiums gives the policy owner good flexibility. The policy owner could choose to just pay the minimum premium (COI plus expenses). The policy owner could put in extra funds and build up the investments. If there is an excess pool of investments based on the policy owner's earlier premiums paid, the policy owner could choose not to pay any premiums, and just allow the insurer to access the investments in order to cover off the COI and expenses. There is a tax rule limiting how much excess premium can be paid; we will cover this rule later in this module.

- **Flexible Investments**. Many of the investments discussed in Module 6 are available within universal life insurance policies. The investments available include mutual funds, GICs, term deposits, indexed accounts, and daily interest accounts. The client has the opportunity to choose not just one investment, but to allocate investments within their policy. So, a client might choose to invest 50% of their universal life investments in mutual funds, 30% in a GIC, and 20% in an account indexed to the Toronto Stock Exchange. The client can generally change their allocation over time as well. So, later on, if this same client decides that he would rather have 80% invested in a GIC and 20% in a mutual fund, the insurer will make that change. Clients who seek to change their allocation more than about once per year will normally be charged fees for frequent trading.

  Many clients favour universal life over other forms of insurance because of the opportunity to invest on a tax deferred basis. A policy owner who uses a universal life policy as an investment vehicle can benefit from tax deferred, or possibly even tax-free, growth.

  The investment component of universal life insurance can be useful when other investment vehicles, such as registered retirement savings plans or tax free savings accounts, are not sufficient to meet an investor's needs. We will see in Module 14 that both of these types of investments have limitations as to the dollar amount that can be contributed. Universal life insurance, on the other hand, offers great flexibility as to the amount of money that can be invested.

- **Flexible Coverage**. Universal life insurance policies are available with two death benefit structures. A level death benefit can be used. In a level death benefit, the client who acquires a policy with, for example, a $100,000 face value, knows that the death benefit will always be $100,000. This policy structure looks similar to the diagram of the whole life policy we looked at earlier in this module. The only time that the death benefit would exceed $100,000 would be if the client had invested heavily in the policy and done well with their investments. This might see the investment component grow to exceed $100,000. If a life insured dies with an investment component that exceeds the face value, the higher amount will be paid as the death benefit. The advantage of the level death benefit is that it has the lowest COI of all the UL coverage options. The net amount at risk will decrease over time.

The second death benefit option is an increasing death benefit. With an increasing death benefit structure, the policy owner can count on the death benefit growing on a regular basis. There are three ways to structure an increasing death benefit:

- **Level Plus Account Value**. This is the death benefit option that carries the highest COI. In most cases, it will also result in the highest death benefit. In this situation, the death benefit paid is equal to the face value of the policy plus whatever value the investments have grown to. So a policy with a $100,000 face value and a $10,000 account value would have a $110,000 death benefit, if the life insured were to die. A policy with a $100,000 face value and a $100,000 account value would generate a $200,000 death benefit. There is some risk for the client, as their death benefit will be tied to the investments. A client who has strong equity exposure within their UL contract might see their death benefit fluctuate. This can create some uncertainty, and is not appropriate for all clients. A client who has a long time horizon and an estate (business, investments, real estate) that is growing in value might need an increasing death benefit to accommodate their growing needs over time. The level plus account value structure offers this flexibility.

- **Level Plus Cumulative Gross Premiums**. This is the death benefit option that we find students have the most trouble understanding. In this death benefit option, the death benefit will increase with every premium dollar paid. So a policy with a face value of $100,000 in which the client is paying premiums of $1000 per year would have a death benefit of $101,000 in the first year; $102,000 in the second year; $103,000 in the third year, and so forth. The death benefit will grow in this linear manner. This option has the second highest COI. This option will see the death benefit grow in a way that the client can manipulate directly. Not all universal life contracts offer this option.

- **Indexed**. With an indexed death benefit, the death benefit will grow every year based on inflation. Some such policies would feature a fixed increase (such as 3% per year). Some would offer an increase equal to inflation for that year, up to a maximum (up to 4% per year, for example). This option has a COI only slightly higher than what a level death benefit would carry. It is useful for a client who is only expecting the value of their estate to grow in accordance with normal inflation. Relatively few insurers offer this option.

- **Consumer Accountable**. There is great flexibility available within a universal life contract. This is a good thing in many cases, but it also means that the consumer is going to have to make decisions about how the contract will work. It is up to the consumer to decide on the asset allocation within the investment component. The consumer can increase or reduce the premiums, as long as the minimum premium gets paid. A poor decision made at the wrong time can cause the policy not to work as planned. For that reason, the agent must be careful when selling this policy. The consumer has to understand the consequences of decisions made at a later date. An uninformed client or one who is prone to rash decisions might not be the best candidate for a universal life contract.

- **Transparent or 'Unbundled'.** Unlike in a term policy, T100, or whole life, in a universal life contract the client can see exactly what is happening within the policy. The client will be provided an annual policy statement which will indicate exactly how the investments have performed, what the account value is, how much surrender charge there would be on a withdrawal, and other information needed to be informed about the policy. These statements can be quite detailed. They need to be, because the client will make decisions based on these statements.

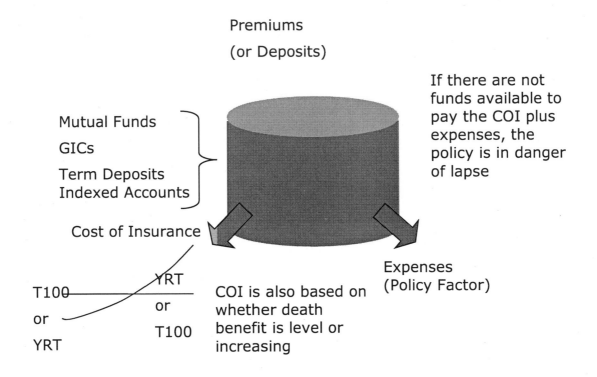

The picture above provides a representation of how a universal life policy works.

Universal life insurance is a complicated, versatile product. You will be tested on it, and you will be exposed to it during your career in the insurance industry. You will be expected to know who buys a universal life policy, the advantages of it, and how it will react to various circumstances.

The client who buys universal life insurance normally has disposable income available to afford it. They are usually looking for the investment component, including the tax deferred growth. The flexibility in the policy, including the ability to increase the death benefit, is attractive. Creditor protection of the cash values is especially useful for business owners, contractors, and the self-employed.

# RIDERS, WAIVERS, AND BENEFITS

Riders, waivers, and benefits are features added to an insurance policy. These are additional provisions within the contract that provide the insured with the flexibility to build a policy to fit his own individual needs. Normally there will be an increased cost and sometimes additional underwriting is required as well. Not all insurers offer all the riders we will look at it in this section. Sometimes if a particular rider is being sought, it might be necessary to deal with a particular insurer. Riders are available with all types of life insurance, but there are some limitations. It would not be practical, for example, to offer a term rider on a term life insurance policy.

Because the addition of riders can significantly increase the policy premium, it is necessary to be judicious when adding riders to a policy. There is a trade off between what will be useful for the client and what the client can afford. We will see several of these riders again in the following modules.

While there are others, the following are the riders that you must be familiar with for the purposes of this course:

- **Guaranteed Insurability Benefit**. GIB (also known as guaranteed insurability rider or guaranteed insurability option) allows the policy owner to increase the amount of insurance after the policy is in force without underwriting. There are normally fixed options to increase the amount of insurance in set amounts at fixed intervals. (For example, a $50,000 option at each of ages 18, 21, 24, 27, 30, 33, 36, 39, and 42.) Options cannot normally be carried back; if no option to increase the amount of insurance is exercised at, say, age 21, that option is lost. Because no underwriting is done to add the extra insurance, the premium is based on the amount of insurance acquired at the attained age, but using the underwriting information that was gathered when the policy was first sold.

  This premium is quite attractive for a client who anticipates that their circumstances might change later on in life. Parents often purchase this rider when buying insurance for their minor children. The effectiveness of GIB is reduced as the client gets older. Using the information provided above, a client who is 35 would only have three options left to increase the amount of insurance. It might be more economical and more practical for this person to just purchase the anticipated amount of insurance at age 35 and not add this rider.

- **Accidental Death Benefit**. Accidental death benefit is designed to increase the death benefit if the insured is killed in an accident. The benefit will sometimes pay double the death benefit, or sometimes increase it by an amount purchased, such as $500,000. In order for the benefit to be paid, the death must occur within 365 days of the incident that causes the death. Accidents would include events such as an automobile collision, an industrial accident, or a loss resulting from being the bystander in a violent crime. There can be exclusions to this rider, such as driving under the influence of alcohol, self-inflicted injuries, or piloting an aircraft. For a more detailed list of possible exclusions, see the next rider (Accidental Death &

Dismemberment). So the beneficiaries of a life insured with a $500,000 term policy and a $250,000 accidental death benefit would receive, if he drowned after falling off a boat, $750,000. If he died of cancer, though, they would not receive the accidental death benefit, and the death benefit would only be $500,000. Accidental death benefits are relatively inexpensive. They are most often sold when the life insured works in a dangerous occupation. When performing a needs analysis for life insurance, it is not safe to include amounts associated with accidental death benefits, because there is no certainty that this is how the client will die. Normally accidental death benefits are not available to clients aged 55 and older.

- **Accidental Death & Dismemberment**. Accidental Death & Dismemberment is often sold as a stand-alone product, and we will look at it as such in Module 10. It can also be sold as a rider to a life insurance policy. AD&D riders will have a benefits schedule, which will show that if the insured suffers a loss, there will be a lump sum benefit paid. The loss has to occur as a direct result of an accident. The loss must also occur within 365 days of the occurrence of the accident. The schedule of benefits will normally be very comprehensive. It will indicate exactly what the benefit payable will be. An excerpt from the schedule of benefits might look like so:

| Loss | Benefit Payable |
|------|-----------------|
| Death | 100% |
| Loss of both legs | 100% |
| Loss of one leg above the knee | 60% |
| Loss of one leg below the knee | 40% |
| Loss of one foot | 25% |

Many other losses would also be covered, this is just a brief sample. The actual amount of the AD&D benefit depends on the amount chosen when the policy is purchased. AD&D benefits vary widely. It is possible to see AD&D policies as small as $1000 and others ranging into the millions of dollars.

In most cases, there are exclusions to AD&D benefits. As previously stated, the loss must directly relate to an accident. There are certain types of accidents that will not be covered under some contracts. Some common exclusions are:

- An accident caused by impaired driving;
- Acts of war;
- Self-inflicted injuries;
- Suicide;
- Inhalation of poisonous gas;
- Illness, whether mental or physical;
- Under the influence of non-prescription drugs;
- Participation in illegal activities;
- Aviation accidents not occurring on a commercial flight;
- Ingestion of a poisonous substance;

- A loss resulting from dental or medical treatment; or
- An infection not directly resulting from an accident.

Certain types of losses might cause an insurer to deny the AD&D benefit but still pay the disability benefit or other benefits promised in the policy. Each set of benefits must be considered with its own applicable exclusions.

AD&D riders are normally relatively inexpensive. They are often used by insureds who perform dangerous jobs or have dangerous hobbies. Many insurers will not offer AD&D to an insured beyond the age of 55.

- **Disability Waiver of Premium**. An insured who becomes disabled may have trouble making premium payments during the period of disability. As such, insurers offer a disability waiver of premium rider. This rider will see that, if a policy owner becomes disabled, the insurer will pay premiums during the period of disability. There is normally a 90-day waiting period, and many of the same exclusions as in the previous section (AD&D) can apply to waiver of premium riders. This rider is available in two forms. The more common variety is used in two-party contracts (personal contracts) and the waiver begins when the life insured becomes disabled. There is another version available in third-party contracts, a disability waiver of premium for payor, which sees the premiums waived when the party who normally pays the premiums becomes disabled. There is some limited disability underwriting done when a disability waiver of premium is applied for.

- **Living Benefits**. As previously mentioned, it is possible for insurers to pay living benefits as a result of provisions in a life insurance contract. There are a number of ways this can be done, but one common way is for insurers to offer an Accelerated Death Benefit rider. The accelerated death benefit rider will allow the life insured (or the insured, in some third party contracts) to access up to 50% of the face value of the policy in certain situations. As this is considered an advance on the death benefit, it is paid tax-free, like a death benefit. The most common provisions include:

  - **Critical Illness**. Some policies will make a portion of the death benefit available when the life insured is diagnosed with a critical illness. This is discussed in greater detail in Module 10.

  - **Terminal Illness**. A fairly common rider allows 50% of the death benefit to be paid in the event that the life insured is diagnosed as terminally ill, usually defined as having less than 12 months to live.

  - **Long-Term Care Benefits**. This will also be discussed in greater detail in Module 10. A few insurers will allow a portion of the life insurance policy to be converted into long-term care benefits when the client meets criteria, such as an inability to perform certain Activities of Daily Living.

- **Term Insurance Riders**. In some situations, a client will have a need for both permanent and term insurance. The permanent insurance might be required for an estate planning or charitable giving need, while the term insurance might be needed to cover a temporary need, such as a mortgage. The impulse here might be to sell two separate policies and many clients will have two or more policies to cover off varying needs that arose in different circumstances. In a case, though, where an agent identifies multiple needs at one time, it will usually be more cost effective to put just a permanent policy in place and to attach a term insurance rider to that policy. The biggest advantage is that this will save the client from having to pay a policy factor every year. A secondary advantage is the flexibility. The client could convert the term rider into permanent insurance later, or could simply drop the term rider when it is no longer required.

- **Spousal Rider**. A variation on the term insurance rider is to add a spousal rider to a policy. This will allow a policy owner to acquire insurance in the form of a two-party contract, and then to add some term insurance for the spouse as a rider. This again saves on the policy factor associated with purchasing two separate policies. Normally the spousal rider is convertible into individual insurance (either term or permanent, depending on the insurer) for the spouse. This can be useful for keeping costs down. In the event of divorce or separation, these riders can be awkward to deal with, but the ability to convert into individual coverage can reduce this awkwardness.

- **Child Rider**. Yet another variation on the term rider is to add a child rider. Child riders are an inexpensive and easy way to get the children insured early. Normally, child riders are limited to about $20,000 or $30,000 of insurance. For a low cost, all children of the insured under the age of 25 are insured. The child rider can normally be converted into individual insurance for the child later on without additional underwriting. This conversion can sometimes be done at as much as five times the original face value of the child rider. While the child rider is inexpensive and easy, parents who can afford it should be encouraged to buy life insurance for their children at as early an age as possible. Because mortality costs are incredibly low for children, even permanent insurance policies are relatively inexpensive at a young age. Further, starting a cash value policy (such as universal life or whole life) at a young age gives the child a very long time horizon in which to accumulate large cash values.

- **Parent Waiver**. The parent waiver is a rider that is sometimes added when parents are acquiring life insurance on the life of a child. The parent waiver will ensure that a policy will stay in force if a parent dies, or in some cases, becomes totally disabled. The benefit will begin after the death of the parent, and premiums for the policy will be paid until the child reaches the age of majority.

# TAXATION OF LIFE INSURANCE

We will spend some time now discussing the taxation of life insurance. There are certain details that you will have to be familiar with for the purposes of this course. However, it is important not to allow the most important consideration to get lost in the shuffle. One of the wonderful things about life insurance is its simplicity, and for the most part, this applies to taxation of life insurance as well. A client pays premiums (not tax deductible). The life insured dies. A non-taxable death benefit is paid. Simple.

Prior to reading this section, it might be worthwhile to go back and review Module 5. Once you have done so, these concepts will be much easier to understand. In order to understand the taxation of life insurance, we will first look at the Adjusted Cost Basis of a life insurance policy.

- **Adjusted Cost Basis**. The ACB of a life insurance policy varies depending on when the policy was last acquired (issued, absolutely assigned, or allowed to lapse and then reinstated). For policies issued since December 1st, 1982, the ACB is equal to:

> Premiums Paid excluding riders and benefits, but including term riders. Costs for substandard risks (ratings) are not included.
>
> Less Dividends Received (from Par Whole Life policies providing cash or savings components)
>
> Less Net Cost of Pure Insurance
> (basically, the cost of a term insurance policy less any policy fees)

In practical terms, then, the ACB of a life insurance policy is equal to any amounts that were put into the contract beyond the COI. ACB is only of concern for life insurance policies when dealing with the relatively rare circumstances that might see a policy owner have to pay tax. Term insurance policies have no ACB.

For older policies - issued prior to December 2nd, 1982 (and not allowed to lapse or absolutely assigned since) - the ACB is:

> Premiums Paid
>
> Less Dividends Received (from Par Whole Life policies providing cash or savings components)

- **Disposition**. The disposition of a life insurance policy is similar to the disposition of other property in that it can have tax consequences. Unlike other dispositions, there are no capital gains on disposition of life insurance! Life insurance gains are taxed as regular income. Gains from life insurance policies are referred to as taxable policy gains, and are not eligible for the 50% capital gains treatment. We will look at some of the dispositions, and the tax consequences of each. For the sake of argument, we will assume that we are dealing with a life insurance policy with a face value of $250,000, a cash value of $60,000, and an ACB of $25,000. Dispositions of life insurance occur in the event of:

- **Policy Loan**. Insurers will allow a policy loan for up to 90% of the cash value of the insurance policy. Not all insurers permit loans of as much as 90%; some will limit loans to 50% or 75% of the cash value. In a policy loan, the insured does not apply for a loan in the traditional sense. Instead, this is treated as an advance on the death benefit taken at the insured's choice (unlike the tax-free accelerated death benefit, which is tied to an uncertain event). Because it is an advance, it has tax consequences. In the case of the life insurance policy in this section, our policy owner could borrow up to $25,000 without paying taxes. A loan of more than $25,000 would reduce the ACB to zero and render the excess amount taxable. So, a loan of $30,000 would mean (Loan of $30,000 - ACB of $25,000 =) $5,000 of taxable income. If the policy owner chooses to repay the loan, there will be a tax deduction for any previously taxed amounts. If the policy owner never repays the loan, the insurer will take repayment out of the death benefit on death of the life insured.

  As this is a loan, there will be interest owing. How the interest is treated depends on the purpose of the loan:

  - **Personal Use**. If the loan is for personal use (buying a car, living expenses, etc.) then interest payments made will increase the ACB of the policy. Note that interest payments do not reduce the actual amount of the loan.
  - **Business or Investment Use**. As with other loans made for investment purposes, the interest in this situation would be tax deductible. These interest payments will not increase the ACB of the policy.

- **Complete Surrender**. A complete surrender of a life insurance policy will result in taxation of the policy. This is a simple calculation. A policy with a $60,000 cash value (proceeds of disposition) and a $25,000 ACB would generate ($60,000 - $25,000) = $35,000 in taxable income. This $35,000 would be taxed as regular income.

- **Partial Surrender**. A partial surrender of a life insurance policy is somewhat more complicated. In a partial surrender, the policy owner will only be taxed on the proportion of the value withdrawn. The easiest way to look at this is to do the calculation as in the previous section (the complete surrender). Then determine what percentage of the cash value has actually been accessed. This will tell you how much taxable income there will be. If our policy owner determined that he wanted $20,000 out of this policy, we can see that would represent ($20,000 ÷ $60,000 =) 33.33% of the cash value, still using the values from the previous section. So, the policy owner would have taxable income of ($35,000 (from the previous paragraph) x 33.33% (the percentage of the policy disposed of) =) $11,667. Again, this would be taxed as regular income. The new ACB of the policy would be reduced by 33.33%, reducing it to $16,668.

- ○ **Absolute Assignment**. An absolute assignment of a policy is a taxable event. This is taxed exactly as a complete surrender is. There are some exceptions. A spouse receiving an absolute assignment of a life insurance policy can elect to receive the policy at the original owner's ACB, which would allow taxes to be deferred. A parent absolutely assigning a policy to a child, where the child is the life insured, can do so without tax consequence.

- ○ **Annuitization**. A policy owner who chooses to annuitize the policy surrenders the policy in exchange for a cash flow based on the account value of the policy. This is normally taxed as a complete surrender. The one exception to this is where the life insured has suffered a permanent and severe disability, in which case the annuity stream would be taxed as a series of partial surrenders.

- ○ **Lapse**. A policy that is lapsed and not reinstated is considered disposed of for income tax purposes. This is almost never a concern, as the cash values would have been reduced to zero by automatic premium loan provisions before the policy would have been allowed to lapse. So there should be no real tax consequences for a policy owner on the lapse of a permanent life insurance policy.

- • **Events that are not Dispositions**. There are a couple of circumstances that we must cover that do not constitute a taxable disposition of a life insurance policy. These are:

  - ○ **Collateral Assignment**. A collateral assignment of a life insurance policy, as discussed in Module 3, is not a tax-triggering event. The policy owner can make a collateral assignment without it being considered a disposition. If the following conditions are met:

    - ■ The loan is made for business or investment purposes;
    - ■ The loan is from an insurer, a trust company, a bank, credit union, or other recognized institution in the business of lending; and
    - ■ The lender has set a condition that there must be life insurance in place;

  - ○ then the policy owner will be able to deduct premiums, or a portion of the premiums. The limit to what can be deducted is the lesser of the net cost of pure insurance (NCPI) or the actual premium paid. Further, the amount that can be deducted must be proportional to the amount of the loan. So, a policy owner who owns a $200,000 life insurance policy and pays $500 per year in premiums borrows $100,000 to invest. The lender, a bank, sets a condition that there must be life insurance in place. The borrower collaterally assigns the policy to the bank.

  - ○ The borrower can take a tax deduction for 50% of the premium paid or the NCPI, whichever is less. (The loan is equal to 50% of the death benefit.) If the borrower dies with the loan outstanding, the first $100,000 (or whatever the amount of the loan at the time of death is) is paid to the bank tax-free. Whatever is left is paid to the named beneficiaries. Note that the only way the life insurance policy becomes meaningful to the lender is if the life insured dies. The borrower will have to qualify for the loan based on more than just the fact that there is a life insurance policy in force.

- o **Loan Using Cash Values as Collateral**. This is different from a collateral assignment. Let's imagine that our policy owner has the same policy discussed in the disposition section of this module ($250,000 face value; $60,000 cash value; $25,000 ACB). The policy owner needs $10,000 to help with living expenses for this year. The policy owner approaches her banker and offers the cash value in the policy as collateral in exchange for a loan. The banker is happy to lend this money; the life insurance investment is fairly secure. The banker knows that the loan will be paid, whether by accessing the cash value, or possibly by waiting until the life insured dies and then collecting the death benefit through a collateral assignment. This loan, because it is separate from the policy, is not a disposition of the policy, unlike the policy loan discussed earlier.

- **Charitable Giving and Taxation of Life Insurance**. Earlier in this chapter we discussed the opportunity to use a life insurance policy to help fund a charitable donation. There are some tax considerations we need to be aware of:

  - o **Naming a Charity as Beneficiary**. When a two-party contract is in place and the insured has named the charity as beneficiary, then, on death, the death benefit will flow directly to the charity. This results in a charitable donation tax credit for the estate of the deceased. This tax credit can be used to reduce income to zero for that year. If there is an excess after that, it can also be used to reduce the previous year's income to zero. Clients who see this opportunity might choose to name a charity as beneficiary to reduce or wipe out their taxes due on death rather than leave their money to the government. If there is a third-party contract in place and a charity is named as beneficiary, there is no charitable donation tax credit. Instead the death benefit should be left to a person who would then make the donation, or an absolute assignment of the policy should be made to the life insured (which would make the policy a two-party contract).

  - o **Assigning a Policy to a Charity**. Instead of naming a charity as beneficiary, it is possible to absolutely assign the policy to the charity during lifetime. This is a taxable disposition, and will be taxed in the hands of the donor. At the same time, the donor will receive a charitable donation tax credit equal to the cash value of the policy. Assuming the donor continues to pay the premiums, those premium dollars will also qualify for a charitable donation tax credit. There will be no tax advantage to the donor or the donor's estate on death.

- **Exempt and Non-Exempt Life Insurance**. We have mentioned several times throughout this module that the investment component of a life insurance policy is not normally subject to taxation. This is true as long as the policy remains an exempt policy. Policies that fit into the pre-Dec 2, 1982 tax rules are always considered exempt. Newer policies, though, must be tested to ensure they are exempt. This exemption test occurs at every policy anniversary and when the policy is first issued. The exemption test basically measures whether the amount of money going into the policy is appropriate, given the death benefit of the policy.

Canada Revenue Agency and the insurers run this test; the agent need not know the exact details. So a policy owner with a $250,000 death benefit paying premiums of $5000 per year would likely not have a problem. CRA would test that policy and say that is well within the bounds of what is reasonable. However, a policy owner with a $250,000 death benefit who is paying premiums of $50,000 per year might not be considered reasonable.

In that case, CRA might question why so much money is being put into the policy. Their assumption would be that it is being done for the sole purpose of minimizing or avoiding tax. This would cause CRA to deem the policy as non-exempt. When a policy is deemed non-exempt, that is considered a disposition for tax purposes, and taxed as a complete surrender. Any future growth would be taxed as regular income. Insurers will work with clients to make sure that policies do not fail the exemption test. In mid-2014, the language used by CRA will change, and non-exempt policies will start to be considered as 'avoidance policies.'

CRA's rules allow the insurer to move funds out of the account within 60 days of failing the exemption test, or to increase the death benefit by up to 8% per year. If either of these actions are taken the policy should remain exempt. The line against which policies are tested is based on maximum allowable deposits made for 8 years after the policy is issued, with a 3.5% growth rate, and the policy values continuing to grow until the life insured reaches age 90. If that projection ever suggests a value exceeding the death benefit payable from the policy, then the policy would be non-exempt, creating a deemed disposition of the policy. The line against which policies are measured to determine their tax-exempt status is referred to as the Maximum Tax Actuarial Reserve (MTAR).

## SUMMARY

Now that you are familiar with life insurance, we will go on to examine some other types of insurance that can be offered with a life insurance license. This module will be very heavily tested. It is not realistic to pass your exams without an excellent understanding of the need for and different types of life insurance

# Chapter 9 INDIVIDUAL DISABILITY INSURANCE

Individual disability income insurance is a complex product. There is a great deal to be aware of when selling and servicing disability policies. In this chapter, we will break the construction of disability policies down into a six-step process, and then we will look at the claims and servicing process. The 6 steps involved in the construction of a disability policy are:

1. **Assess the Need**. A needs analysis is always the first step in placing insurance coverage. In the case of disability insurance, the needs analysis is based on the income that would be lost to the insured in the event of a disability.
2. **Morbidity**. Morbidity refers to the likelihood that one becomes disabled at some point.
3. **Definition of Disability**. Different policies will define disability differently. The definition of disability is important because it describes when benefits would begin.
4. **Types of Contracts**. The disability contract can vary in its structure. More elaborate contracts pass all the risk on to the insurer, while simpler contracts see some risk retained by the insured.
5. **Benefit Structure**. Disability contracts will pay benefits out at different points, depending on how the contract was originally set up.
6. **Riders, Waivers, and Benefits**. Additional features can be added to disability policies to make them suit a particular need.

## ASSESS NEED

The need for disability insurance is based on the pre-tax income of the insured. The concept is to put roughly the same amount of disposable income in the insured's hands when the insured becomes disabled as the insured was earning prior to a disability. An important consideration here is that income earned is normally subject to taxation. The average Canadian income earner can count on losing somewhere between 20% and 50% of income to income taxes. Disability benefits are not normally taxable, so the disability benefit is calculated as a percentage (usually 50% to 70%) of pre-tax income. The idea behind this is that there should be only a small reduction in disposable income for the recipient of a disability benefit.

The factors that we must consider when assessing the need for disability insurance are discussed in this section.

- **Passive vs Active Income**. A variety of sources of income are available. Some sources of income would continue to be available in the event of a disability, but for most people, the majority of income would be lost in the event of disability. Let's have a look at some of these possible sources of income:

| Active Income | Passive Income |
|---|---|
| Salary | Investment |
| Bonus | Rental |
| Commission | Trust |
| Net Research Grants | Inheritance |
| | Royalty |
| | Trailer |
| Business | Business |

Business income, of course, shows up on both sides of the chart. When a client has income from a business, a determination must be made as to whether that income is active or passive income. The owner of a large robust business with significant support structures would normally have this income considered as passive. The owner of a smaller business would likely have their income considered as active. This decision is normally made at the underwriting level. An excessive amount of passive income may render somebody uninsurable. Insurers generally will not insure somebody who would have a substantial amount of income even while disabled. Those who, for example, earn over 50% of their income from a trust or from rent, may not be able to purchase disability insurance.

When assessing the need for disability insurance, the only income that will normally be considered will be active income. Each source of income earned should be looked at, and an assessment made as to whether that income stream would continue despite a disability.

- **Taxation of Benefits**. As already discussed, disability benefits from an individual disability policy are normally received tax-free. An exception would be made in cases where an employer pays premiums on behalf of an employee. When the employer pays the premiums, the benefit becomes a taxable source of income should the employee become disabled. (This would also be the case for group disability coverage.) The tax-free nature of individual disability benefits is critical to a correct understanding of the functioning of disability insurance.

- **Benefit Calculation**. The actual amount of benefit will vary from insurer to insurer, and from situation to situation. Some insurers, for example, would always offer a benefit of 60% of active income. Other insurers might offer a benefit as high as 70% for lower income earners and maybe a 50% benefit for higher income earners. Disability benefits are normally expressed as a monthly benefit. Let's look a client who earns a salary of $70,000 per year and is purchasing a disability policy from a company with a 60% disability benefit. $70,000 of annual income translates into $5,833 of monthly income. 60% of $5,833 is $3,500, which would be the monthly disability benefit in the event that this client becomes disabled. This is the amount that would be expressed on the face page of the policy, as discussed in Module 3.

- **Integration with Government Benefits**. When structuring a disability policy, it is not normally appropriate to take into account any government benefits. Keep in mind that if a client becomes eligible for CPP disability, the individual disability benefit would be directly reduced by that amount. EI sickness benefits are available for only 15 weeks. EI benefits will not be impacted by income from an individual disability policy. Worker's Compensation benefits only apply if an injury or illness occurs in the workplace. Worker's Compensation benefits are normally considered first payor against individual disability policies, meaning that the disability benefit would be reduced by the WCB benefit received. Some insurers offer disability policies that will not offset their benefit if CPP or WCB benefits are received.

- **Issue and Participation Limits**. Insurers will generally impose a limit on the amount of benefit that can be received. They will not issue coverage such that the client would be overinsured. As part of the underwriting process, most disability insurers will inquire as to what other disability coverage is in place. A client who, for example, already has a disability policy in force will normally not be able to acquire more disability insurance that would exceed their need for disability coverage. Once a client becomes disabled, insurers will normally restrict the client's ability to collect benefits. Most insurers will not allow a disability claimant to receive income from all sources in excess of 85% of the client's pre-disability income.

## MORBIDITY

Morbidity will determine the cost and availability of disability coverage. The most important factor is the occupation of the applicant. Generally speaking, somebody who works in a relatively safe office job will have access to much better coverage - at a cheaper price - than somebody who works in a dangerous and physically demanding job.

- **Age, Gender, Smoking Status**. Generally speaking, older clients pay more for their disability coverage than younger clients. Policies are normally only issued to those up to age 55, with coverage usually ending at age 65. Women are, generally, more likely to become disabled than men are. Smokers are more likely to suffer a disability than are non-smokers. All of these factors will be considered when calculating premiums for disability insurance.

- **Occupation Classification**. The most important factor when underwriting disability insurance is occupation. Most insurers have specific lists of occupations that they will offer coverage to. We will have a look at different occupation classifications and the factors behind them:

| Occupation Class | Sample Definition | Sample Occupations | Degree of Risk | Likely Duration of Absence | Motivation | Stability |
|---|---|---|---|---|---|---|
| 5 or 4A | University degree; no physical work | Physician, Senior executive, Chartered Accountant | Very Low | Short | Very High | Very High |
| 4 or 3A | Post-secondary diploma; no physical work | Hospital administrator, Outside sales | Very Low | Short | High | High |
| 3 or 2A | Less than 20% physical work | Retail sales, Lab technician Utilities industry site supervisor | Low | Short to Medium | Moderate | Moderate |
| 2 or A | More than 20% physical work; low risk of accidents | Tradespeople, Painters | Moderate | Medium to Long | Moderate | Moderate |
| 1 or B | More than 20% physical work; high risk | Agricultural workers, Landscaper | High | Medium to Long | Low | Low |

Different insurers use different numbering systems for occupation classifications. The two most common numbering systems are represented on this chart. The sample occupations provided will not be representative of all insurers. Some insurers will specialize in one section of this chart. Certain insurers use 6 occupation classes, breaking the top occupation class into two further subcategories.

- **Other Underwriting Concerns**. The chart shown above is useful for an understanding of disability insurance. There are some factors that can move somebody one way or another on the chart. Engineers will often be an occupation class 4 or 5. However, an engineer who spends a great deal of time on risky job sites may be reduced to a 3. Ownership can also have an influence. An owner would typically have greater motivation and stability than an employee. As a result, ownership can bump an insured up an occupation class. A record of stability can also have some influence. A pipefitter would normally be at an occupation class 2, but a journeyman pipefitter would, in many cases, be considered an occupation class 3. The occupation class is determined during the underwriting process; it generally cannot be changed once a policy is in force.

- **Availability of Disability Insurance**. Disability insurance is not always available. Dangerous occupations such as police, military, and emergency services cannot normally acquire individual disability insurance. Those occupations normally rely on association insurance and organizations such as Veterans' Affairs. Also, because disability insurance is based on active income, people in situations where there is no regular full-time income do not have disability insurance available. This would include, for example, a parent who stays home to raise children.

- **Motivation and Stability**. Motivation and stability are significant concerns for disability underwriters. Motivation refers to the likelihood that somebody will take advantage of a situation to stay away from work. Underwriters will look at claims experience to assess motivation. The occupation classification, though, determines the basic level of motivation. Stability refers to the likelihood that an insured will stay in their present occupation. Where a prospective insured has shown a pattern of switching jobs on a regular basis, this is a concern for underwriters. Insurers do not want to insure clients who will make inappropriate use of disability insurance. By properly assessing motivation and stability from the beginning, the insurer can avoid a situation in which the client ends up filing superfluous claims.

- **Premiums**. The occupation classification provides the basis for determining premiums. The highest occupation classifications will pay the least premium per dollar of coverage, usually paying a base premium of about 1% of salary for their coverage. The lowest occupation classifications will pay the highest premiums, usually paying about 2% of their salary for a basic disability plan. As with most insurance, other underwriting concerns will affect this base premium, as described in Modules 2 and 3.

## DEFINITIONS OF DISABILITY

While the definitions of disability will vary from policy to policy, there are two conditions that must be met for a disability policy to be put in place. The disabled person must be **unable to work** and must be **under the care of a medical professional**. It is the question of being unable to work that we will deal with in greatest detail here. The care of a medical professional is harder to look at from the perspective of the insurance agent. This process generally consists of the claimant being told by their doctor that they can no longer work. Paperwork based on this decision is provided to the claims department at the insurer, who may enlist medical professionals to help assess the validity of the claim.

The disability policy, when it is written, will define exactly what is considered to be a disability. The definition of disability will depend on what duties the insured is able to perform. We will look at four different definitions of disability in this course:

- **Total**: The total definition of disability means that the insured is unable to work. This would also mean unable to earn active income. However, the definition of disability included in the policy has some bearing on exactly what unable to work means for the insured.

    o **Own Occupation**. The most generous definition of disability is the own occupation definition. Own occupation means the insured is considered totally disabled when he is unable to perform the duties of his own occupation. That means the insured is considered totally disabled purely by reason of not being able to perform his own occupation. It might be possible in some circumstances for an insured to continue working, but not in his own occupation. For example, a surgeon who has a disability policy and can no longer perform surgery will be considered totally disabled. It might still be possible for this surgeon to work as a professor, for example. This situation is rare in disability insurance, because it gives an insured the opportunity to collect income beyond the normal 85% participation limit. In the example of the disabled surgeon, income will be received from both the disability policy and employment as a professor. Underwriting for own occupation policies is very strict because insurers do not wish to take a risk where there might be some question about motivation or stability. The own occupation definition of disability is normally only available to insureds in the top occupation class. It is normally offered as a rider, so the insured has to decide to pay a higher premium to have this definition apply to his policy. In industry slang, this is normally referred to as an 'own occ' definition.

    o **Regular Occupation**. Most individual disability policies sold in Canada today feature the regular occupation definition. Under the regular occupation, the client receives benefits when unable to perform the duties of her regular occupation. This is normally defined as unable to perform the duties of an occupation that falls within the skills, education, or experience of the client. Basically, the insurer will not expect the client to do a job that she would be unfamiliar with. If the insured does end up suffering a disability that prevents her from doing her own job, but she can still do the duties of a regular occupation, then no benefit will be paid. However, if the insured ends up earning less than her policy's disability benefit as a result, the insurer will normally pay enough benefits to bring her up to her pre-disability level of income. The actual application of this concept varies, so the student will not be expected to calculate such benefits. The regular occupation definition of disability is normally used for insureds in the 2, 3, and 4 occupation classes. This is normally referred to as a 'regular occ' definition. Group insurance policies often use this definition of disability for the short-term portion of policy.

    o **Any Occupation**. The most restrictive definition of disability is the any occupation definition. When the any occupation definition applies, the insured will only be able to collect benefits when she cannot perform any occupation at all. This definition normally applies to those in occupation class 1 or sometimes 2. Normally policies with an any occupation definition will also be restrictive in other ways, such as shorter benefit periods and less riders available. Group insurance policies often use this definition of disability for the long-term portion of the policy.

- **Presumptive Benefits**. The presumptive definition of disability is an extra feature that is often added to disability policies. Today most disability policies sold automatically carry the presumptive definition of disability. The presumptive definition means that the insured will receive benefits if any of the following occur:

  - Loss of sight in both eyes;
  - Loss of hearing in both ears;
  - Loss of speech; or
  - Loss of use of both hands, both feet, or the hand and foot on the same side of the body.

  Even if the insured is able to return to work after having suffered this loss, it is possible to continue receiving this benefit. The benefit would continue until the insured has regained whatever capacity was lost, if that ever happens, or until the end of the benefit period for the policy.

- **Residual and Partial Benefits**. It would not be uncommon for an insured to spend a period of time on total disability and then find himself able to return to work in a limited capacity. Insurers offer residual and partial benefits to help accommodate these situations. Residual and partial benefits are often included in modern disability policies. They must be chosen as a feature at the time of application, and they will cause an increase in premiums. We will look at each of residual and partial benefits separately:

  - **Partial Benefits**. Partial benefits are normally paid as 50% of the benefit available in the disability policy. This would be available in cases where the insured has been totally disabled and returns to work, usually less than 80% of the normal hours worked. An insured doing this is said to be partially disabled. It is likely in this situation that the employer will not pay a full salary. Therefore, the insurer will provide the partial disability benefit. Partial disability benefits normally have a benefit period that is shorter than that offered in the policy, usually no more than two years. Partial benefits are useful because they will allow the insured to return to work in a manner that will allow effective disability management. The pressure is reduced on the insured to force a full return to work. Partial benefits are normally used by salaried employees and those in the bottom three occupation classes.

    Some insurers offer a modified form of partial disability benefits with a schedule where a 50% benefit would be paid for the first year, 40% in the second year, and 25% in the third, fourth, and fifth years.

○ **Residual Benefits**. Residual benefits allow more flexibility than partial benefits. When an insured returns to work and is earning more than 20% of their pre-disability income and less than 80% then residual benefits will apply. (If an insured is earning 20% or less, then the insured is considered totally disabled. If earning more than 80%, then the insured is not considered disabled at all.) In the case that the insured is capable of a limited return to work, and the income is reduced, the insurer will provide a residual benefit. The residual benefit is calculated as a percentage of the total disability benefit. The math behind this, which a student in the LLQP program might have to calculate, would look like so:

(Healthy (non-disabled) income less new (disabled) income) divided by (Healthy (non-disabled) income)

So, carrying on with the situation discussed in the needs analysis (at the beginning of this module) where we dealt with an insured who was eligible for a $3,500 monthly disability income benefit based on a healthy income of $5,833 per month, let's look at an application of residual disability benefits. Let's imagine that this insured becomes disabled and spends a period of time collecting total disability benefits. After some time has passed, the insured returns to work, but is only able to earn $3,000 per month because of her disability. Obviously she doesn't need a total disability benefit. She would receive a residual benefit, calculated as ($5,833 - $3,000) ÷ $5,833. This becomes $2,833 ÷ $5,833 = 48.6%, which means she is missing 48.6% of her regular income. She needs only 48.6% of her disability benefit. She would receive a residual disability benefit of $3,500(her total disability benefit) x 48.6% = $1,701. The $1,701 residual disability benefit would not be taxed, but the $3,000 income would be taxed, as it is regular income.

Residual benefits are normally used by clients who earn some sort of flexible income, such as commissions or active business income. It is often associated with occupation classes 3, 4, and 5. Some insurers refer to this as proportional disability. Note, however, that if a benefit was calculated based on business income, and the insured continues to earn business income through the period of disability, this can hinder the ability to actually collect a residual disability benefit.

It is often said that partial disability replaces an insured's income based on loss of time, while residual benefits provide income replacement based on a loss of income. This is because the inability to work full-time results in a partial disability claim, while a reduction in income results in a residual disability claim.

## TYPES OF DISABILITY CONTRACTS

When looking at the structure of individual disability contracts, it is easiest to think of them as one-year contracts. A client who purchases a disability policy will have coverage for at least one year from the date of purchase. After the first year is up, what happens to the coverage depends on what type of contract was purchased. It may be possible for the insurer to change the contract at that point. Changes can be made to the premiums or to the benefit offered. Contracts which allow such changes to be made must spell out explicitly in the contract the circumstances and rationale for such changes.

In practical terms, the insured does not have to do anything year after year to continue to have coverage in place. No additional medical underwriting is required. Underwriting for an occupation change may be necessary. If premiums are going to increase, or coverage will be somehow limited, the insurer will notify the insured of those changes in advance.

Generally speaking, as the insurer offers more guarantees, the premium increases. The lower cost contracts are normally chosen by insureds in higher risk categories as a cost control measure. Higher occupation classes normally acquire disability contracts with more guarantees built in. While there are several types of disability contracts available, we are going to look at three of the more commonly available types of contracts in this course:

- **Non-Cancellable Guaranteed Renewable**. This is the most elaborate (and most expensive) type of disability contract available. With this coverage, the insurer cannot change the coverage on any basis. The insured knows that the contract will be renewed each and every year at rates that are set out when the contract is acquired. The contract is normally renewable up until age 65. Some of these contracts will allow an insured who continues working beyond age 65 to carry their coverage beyond that age, though coverage will usually continue as a guaranteed renewable contract after age 65. With a non-cancellable guaranteed renewable contract, the insured knows that nothing that she does during the term of the contract will affect coverage.

- **Guaranteed Renewable**. Guaranteed renewable contracts are slightly less favourable for the client than Non-cancellable guaranteed renewable contracts. With this type of contract in place, the client knows that he will be able to renew year after year, normally until age 65. However, if the client's circumstances change, especially in the case of a career change, the client will have to inform the insurer. The insurer may change the policy based on the client's changing circumstances. Also, the insurer may change the coverage based on the experience of the occupation class that the insured belongs to. This can only happen if there has been an increase in claims, or severity of claims, for that particular occupation class. Changes in coverage can show up in the form of increased premiums, restrictive riders, or reduced benefits.

- **Cancellable**. Cancellable contracts (also known as Commercial contracts) are normally offered to the lowest occupation classes. With a cancellable contract, the insurer can change or cancel the coverage. As with guaranteed renewable contracts, these decisions will be based on experience for the occupation class or a change in the client's circumstances. The insurer can only make changes based on circumstances explicitly set out in the contract. Note that the insurer will not cancel the contract without cause; insurers are in business to collect premiums, and a cancelled contract means no more premiums will be collected. Cancellable contracts will normally have no renewal possible after age 55. These are the least costly types of contracts. Changes in coverage can show up in the form of increased premiums, restrictive riders, reduced benefits, or a cancellation of the policy.

## BENEFIT STRUCTURE

Policies are issued today with varying types of benefits in place. Clients will select policies that have benefit periods that fit their particular needs. In some cases, a disability policy is purchased to accommodate a short-term need. Some disability policies are purchased to take care of a long-term need. Normally, the sooner benefits begin, and the longer they last, the higher the premiums will be.

- **Elimination Period**. The elimination period refers to the period that an insured will have to wait before benefits can be collected. This is also often referred to as the waiting period. Some insurers start the elimination period from the date that a claim is submitted, and some insurers start it from the date that the disabled begins. For exam purposes, it is best to consider a disability as starting from the date that the client is told by their doctor that they are disabled.

  The elimination period is important because it represents a period of self-insurance for the client. A long elimination period will make a policy more affordable, but it will mean that the insured will have to take care of themselves in some way while waiting for disability benefits to begin. It is common to plan to use Employment Insurance sickness benefits to help manage the elimination period, although this does not work in all cases. As discussed in Module 7, the dollar amount of EI benefits is limited, and this may not be enough to help an insured meet her living expenses.

  Common elimination periods are 30, 90, 120, or 180 days. In cases where there might be some other benefits in place, an elimination period of 1 or 2 years might be used. This can also be done where the insured's primary concern is about a long-term disability. A shorter elimination period will result in a higher premium.

  The elimination period can be met under the non-consecutive period of disability provision. This allows a claim based on meeting the elimination period even though an attempt was made to return to work. As long as the insured is not able to return to work for longer than 6 months, the elimination period can be met using non-consecutive periods of disability.

  Most important to note is the fact that disability benefits, like a paycheque, are paid one month in arrears. So, a 90 day elimination period means that no benefits are received until the 120th day.

- **Benefit Period**. The benefit period indicates how long an insured will expect to receive benefits. Common benefit periods are 2 years, 5 years, 10 years, or to age 65. A 5 year benefit period would mean that, from the date the insurer starts to pay benefits, the insured will receive 5 years of benefit payments.

A longer benefit period will normally result in a higher premium than a shorter benefit period would. Some insurers will limit their benefits payable, so that somebody in an occupation class 1 or 2 might only have access to a 2 year or 5 year benefit period.

Once the benefit period has been met, the benefit is paid in arrears, like a paycheque. (An employee does not get paid until after they have put in their work.) So, a policy with a 90 day waiting period would actually not pay its first benefit until the 120th day.

- **Qualification Period.** Qualification period is an idea that is not always used in newer disability policies, but was once common. Insurers who offered residual or partial benefits often implemented a qualification period. The qualification period was put in place to prevent abuse of residual or partial benefits. The basic idea is that the insured had to be have been on total disability benefits for a period of, say, 90 days, before residual or partial benefits could be accessed. The concern was that an insured might look to take advantage of those benefits.

  Most newer disabilities policies no longer use a qualification period, and simply require that an insured has spent some time on total benefits prior to using residual or partial benefits. However, as an agent working in the field, it is likely that you will encounter older policies with a qualification period built in.

- **Recurring Disabilities.** The recurring disability clause is included in most disability policies sold today. The purpose of the recurring disability clause is to not penalize a client who attempts to return to work. It would not be uncommon for an insured to believe that a disability finished and return to work. Upon returning to work, there is the risk that the insured might re-injure themselves. If the insured returns to work, and their disability recurs, or a related situation arises, within 6 months of the return to work, then the insurer will not make the client wait through the elimination period again. Instead, the insurer will simply allow the claim to continue from where it left off.

  Most disability insurance sold today automatically includes a recurring disability clause.

- **Lump Sum.** In the event that a disability claim is likely to last for a very long time, the insurer will often pay out a lump sum benefit. This is routinely done in cases where the insured is diagnosed with a condition that will render them permanently disabled. Examples would be diagnoses of conditions that will create a disability, but are likely not fatal, such as multiple sclerosis. In these situations, the insurer will negotiate with the insured to pay a lump sum benefit that will be roughly equal to the present value of all benefits that would have been paid out if a lump sum were not being paid. Insurers will normally start looking at a lump sum offer after a disability claim has gone on for more than a year with little opportunity for a return to work.  Unless the contract indicates otherwise, the insured is not required to take the lump sum offer.

## RIDERS, WAIVERS, AND BENEFITS

Riders, waivers, and benefits are features added to an insurance policy.  These are additional provisions within the contract that provide the insured with the flexibility to build a policy to fit his own individual needs.  Normally there will be an increased cost and sometimes additional underwriting is required as well.  Not all insurers offer all the riders we will look at it in this section.  Sometimes if a particular rider is being sought, it might be necessary to deal with a particular insurer.

Because the addition of riders can significantly increase the policy premium, it is necessary to be judicious when adding riders to a policy. There is a trade off between what will be useful for the client and what the client can afford. Sometimes the temptation when offering disability insurance is to add several riders, but this can cause the policy premium to move out of the client's reach. We will look in this section at some of the more commonly used riders. While riders in this form are only available in individual disability insurance, group disability plans sometimes have features that mirror some of these riders. Several of these riders are also available with the other Accident & Sickness products that we will look at in the next module.

- **FIO/FPO**.  The future income option, future insurability option, or future purchase option, allows the insured to increase the amount of insurance at pre-determined periods later on in the life of the policy.  This rider is ideal for a client who is starting out in a new career, such as a lawyer just establishing herself in a law firm.  The starting income for that lawyer will likely be comfortable, but there will be significant opportunity for future increases.  Without this rider in place, every time this lawyer tried to increase her disability coverage she would have to purchase a new policy and go through underwriting again.

  With FIO in place, though, this lawyer would be able to increase her disability coverage on an ongoing basis. She might be permitted to increase her coverage by up to twice the amount she started with, usually in increments of 20% per year, on her policy anniversary. Probably the greatest advantage is that she will not have to go through underwriting to initiate these increases. The insurer will ask for proof of her increased income, but that will be all. So even if her health has deteriorated, the insurer cannot deny her the increased amount of insurance, and nor can they increase her premiums based on new evidence. Her premiums will increase simply because she will have more insurance in force. These increases will be based on her health when she originally purchased the policy and her age when she elects to increase her amount of insurance. FIO options will have to be exercised while the client is not disabled. Once the client becomes disabled, she would not be able to increase her amount of insurance using this rider.

Increases in coverage are normally not permitted beyond age 55. The cost of an FIO rider would normally increase premiums by about 15% to 25% of the base policy premium. This rider is most useful for young professionals or business owners who are just starting out. Keep in mind, though, that insurers prefer to deal with clients who have demonstrated stability, and this can make it challenging sometimes for somebody who is just starting a business to acquire disability insurance. Some insurers offer a variation on this rider that provides automatic increases each year without proof of income, but the amount of the increase might be just 5% per year.

- **COLA**. Cost of living adjustment, or cost of living rider, allows a client to increase the amount of insurance after a disability has occurred. Increases in the amount of coverage are normally designed to keep pace with inflation. The policy will normally indicate a maximum annual increase of 3% or 4%, often up to the limit of consumer price index. The rider is designed so that a client's disability benefit should keep pace with inflation. He should not, then, suffer a loss in purchasing power as his benefit will increase at the same pace as inflation does. Without COLA in place, the insured who suffers a long-term disability takes the risk that inflation could reduce the purchasing power of his benefit. This would cause significant concern to the insured who requires the full disability benefit to cover living expenses.

  COLA is normally used for younger clients, as a long-term disability would mean inflation could have a significant impact on their disability benefit. An older client is less likely to have to deal with a very long-term disability, simply because their benefits will most likely expire no later than age 65. COLA normally increases the premiums on a policy by about 10%.

- **Waiver of Premium**. Waiver of premium is often included automatically with disability policies. With a waiver of premium in place, if the insured becomes disabled, the insurer will pay the premiums on her behalf. Normally there is a 90-day waiting period associated with this benefit, during which time the insured will be responsible to pay her own premiums. Once the waiting period has been met, the insurer will start paying the premiums. In most cases, the insurer will also retroactively pay (in effect reimbursing) the client for the premiums she paid during the waiting period. The reason that insurers will normally include this in all policies sold is because it will prevent a policy from lapsing during a period of disability. The insurer would like to see the insured recover from her disability and start paying her own premiums again.

- **Rehabilitation Benefits**. Rehabilitation benefits are normally included in most disability policies sold today. This will include a benefit designed to assist the insured in getting back to work. It might cover the costs associated with medical expenses for rehabilitation, or it might cover job retraining, or some combination of the two. The insurer will include this coverage automatically in most cases because it means the insured is more likely to get back to work sooner and therefore off of the disability claim.

- **Accidental Death & Dismemberment**. Accidental Death & Dismemberment is often sold as a stand-alone product, and we will look at it as such in Module 10. It can also be sold as a rider to an individual disability policy. AD&D riders will have a benefits schedule, which will show that if the insured suffers a loss, there will be a lump sum benefit paid. The loss has to occur as a direct result of an accident. The loss must also occur within 365 days of the occurrence of the accident. The schedule of benefits will normally be very comprehensive. It will indicate exactly what the benefit payable will be. An excerpt from the schedule of benefits might look like so:

| Loss | Benefit Payable |
|---|---|
| Death | 100% |
| Loss of both legs | 100% |
| Loss of one leg above the knee | 60% |
| Loss of one leg below the knee | 40% |
| Loss of one foot | 25% |

Many other losses would also be covered, this is just a brief sample. The actual amount of the AD&D benefit depends on the amount chosen when the policy is purchased. AD&D benefits vary widely. It is possible to see AD&D policies as small as $1000 and others ranging into the millions of dollars.

In most cases, there are exclusions to AD&D benefits. As previously stated, the loss must directly relate to an accident. There are certain types of accidents that will not be covered under some contracts. Some common exclusions are:

- An accident caused by impaired driving;
- Acts of war;
- Self-inflicted injuries;
- Suicide;
- Inhalation of poisonous gas;
- Aviation accidents not occurring on a commercial flight;
- Illness, whether mental or physical;
- Under the influence of non-prescription drugs;
- Participation in illegal activities;
- Ingestion of a poisonous substance;
- A loss resulting from dental or medical treatment; or
- An infection not directly resulting from an accident.

Certain types of losses might cause an insurer to deny the AD&D benefit but still pay the disability benefit or other benefits promised in the policy. Each set of benefits must be considered with its own applicable exclusions. AD&D riders are normally relatively inexpensive. They are often used by insureds who perform dangerous jobs or have dangerous hobbies. Many insurers will not offer AD&D to an insured beyond the age of 55.

- **Return of Premium**. A return of premium rider will see some or all of an insured's premiums paid back to him at a certain point. The original return of premium riders would normally have seen 100% of the insureds premiums returned to him at age 65. This is a linear calculation, so if he paid a $1000 annual premium for 30 years starting at age 35, at age 65, he would receive a $30,000 return of premium. Today there are a variety of return of premium riders. Many of these riders today provide a 50% return of premium, some every 7 years, some every 10 years, and some at the expiry date of the policy (ie. age 55 or 65).

  Premiums are only returned if the policy owner purchased this rider and did not suffer a serious disability during the term of the disability coverage. A typical clause might see an insured not receive their return of premium if total claims were greater than 20% of the amount of premium paid.

  Return of premium does not specifically help with the management of disability risk. Instead, it can make the policy more attractive to the client, because there is certainty of receiving some sort of benefit no matter what. Return of premium is used where the client wants to make sure that he will be guaranteed some sort of return on his investment. This rider will normally increase premiums by about 20%.

- **Zero-Day Hospital Coverage**. This rider will waive the policy's elimination period if a disability is severe enough that it forces the insured into hospital care. Benefits would then start immediately, with no waiting period.

  This is an attractive rider for a client who might be concerned about her ability to manage financially through the policy's waiting period.

- **Business Overhead Expense.** In Module 15, we will examine the Business Overhead Expense insurance disability contract. This type of coverage is available not just as a standalone policy, but also as a rider to a disability policy. This rider would normally be offered where the amount of BOE required is smaller, typically less than $1000 per month of benefit. This would be appropriate for many smaller, unincorporated, and home-based businesses.

- **Restrictive Riders**. There are some situations where an insurer might place a rider that imposes restrictions on the coverage. An example of a restrictive rider is used when the insured already has group benefits in place. Some insurers, in this case, will impose a rider that will reduce the individual disability benefit by one dollar for every dollar of group benefits received. This rider will reduce the premium that would be paid on this policy, usually by about 10%. Other restrictive riders can be added as a result of an underwriting decision, as discussed below.

## EXCLUSIONS

Disability insurers will choose to exclude certain conditions or situations. Exclusions are normally put in place so that the insurer can limit their exposure to risk. Insurers are comfortable dealing with the risk of insuring a reasonably healthy person who engages in normal day-to-day activities. When an insured represents risks beyond these, though, the insurer will normally offer exclusions. Exclusions are sometimes offered as riders to the policy, or are sometimes built right into the policy.

- **Standard Exclusions**. There are several conditions that most insurers will exclude from disability insurance. Standard exclusions to disability coverage include:

  o A loss resulting from war. This exclusion can be quite broad, and generally extends to include anything that results from war or war-like activities. The insured need not be a participant for this exclusion to apply.

  o Situations where the insured chooses to receive surgery. Examples of this would include:

    ▪ Elective surgery; or
    ▪ The insured has chosen to donate an organ and surgery is required.

  o A normal pregnancy or childbirth. Complicated pregnancies or childbirth causing a disability normally will be covered.

  o A disability resulting from time spent in a penal institution.

  o A disability resulting from service in the armed forces.

- **Pre-Existing Conditions**. Pre-existing conditions will normally result in some sort of limitation to the coverage. This is an underwriting decision. The information about the pre-existing condition will be collected during the application process. Based on the information collected, the underwriter will approach a pre-existing condition in one of the following ways:

  o **Issue the policy as requested**. Some pre-existing conditions are limited in severity and do not require any amendments to the coverage. This might be done for a sports injury which occurred a number of years ago and has not recurred.

  o **Deny coverage**. A recent diagnosis of cancer, or an instance of cancer which has recurred, is an example of a condition that will normally lead an underwriter to deny coverage. In some cases when coverage has been declined, the insurer will indicate that they will reconsider their decision after some period of time has elapsed. For example, a client who has had surgery recently for a back problem might get declined. At the some time, the insurer might provide that if, in the next 5 years, the applicant has experienced no problems, they will issue a policy then.

  o **Increased premiums**. Conditions that have not yet caused a disability but could do so will usually lead to an increased premium. Hypertension, which can lead to a variety of problems, is an example of such a condition. It is relatively rare to increase premiums on disability insurance policies.

o **Exclusion riders**. A rider excluding the condition will be added where there is a specific concern that may lead to future problems. A history of lower back problems will likely lead to an exclusion for any future disability related to the lower back. This exclusion would be in addition to exclusions discussed in the "Standard Exclusions" section of this module.

o **Extended elimination period**. Pre-existing conditions that could lead to a series of short-term disabilities will often cause the insurer to issue a policy with an extended elimination period. If, for example, an insured applied for a policy with a 30 day elimination period, but that insured suffers from mild asthma, the insurer might consider that a possible source of short-term disabilities. As a result, the policy might be issued with a longer 90-day elimination period.

o **Reduced benefit period**. A client who has a pre-existing condition that the insurer believes might lead to long-term disabilities could have coverage issued. However, the insurer might limit the benefit period. This might happen where an applicant for insurance is overweight. This condition can lead to a variety of disabilities. The insurer might choose to issue a policy, but the insurer wants to limit their risk. In a case like this, if a benefit period to age 65 is requested, the insurer might issue the policy, but will only permit a 5 year benefit period.

- **Soft Tissue Injuries.** Many disability policies carry limitations for soft tissue injuries such as strains and sprains. Hernias and degenerative disc disease are typically subject to limitations as well. These soft tissue limitations normally reduce the benefit period for such an injury to 15 days (typical for a sprain) up to 180 days (common for a degenerative disc disease). These limitations are very common to disability policies issued to higher risk occupations (As and Bs, for example). It is important that the client be made aware at the time of purchase, and reminded again at policy delivery, of these limitations. This is sometimes referred to as the Standard Limitations section of a policy.

The use of the items discussed above in a policy might also limit the availability of riders and waivers. Some of these underwriting considerations might also be applied for non-medical reasons. An insured who participates in dangerous hobbies (insurers refer to a hobby as an avocation) might have an exclusion applied, exactly as discussed above.

Regardless of what is written in this chapter, no exclusions apply unless they are expressly stated in the policy. Policy documents must clearly express the exclusions and explain exactly how they would apply. Ambiguity in the exclusions can create difficulties for the insurer, agent, and insured.

## CLAIMS CONSIDERATIONS

We have already discussed claims in Module 3. Those considerations would all apply to disability insurance, but there are some additional considerations specifically dealing with disability insurance.

- **Issue and Participation Limits**. We have already discussed issue and participation limits in this module. At the time of claim one of the jobs of the claims examiner will be to make sure the insured is not receiving disability income in excess of the issue and participation limits expressed in the policy.

- **Medical**. As discussed at the beginning of this module, in order to be considered, an insured must be under the care of a medical professional. For short-term disabilities, this is generally not a challenge, as the insured will most likely have to visit various medical professionals to get whatever help is required. As a claim persists, though, the insured might not have a medical necessity to continue visiting medical professionals on a regular basis. The claims examiner can insist, in this case, that the insured continue to deal with medical professionals to demonstrate that the disability is ongoing. It has been established in case law that the insurer can reasonably ask for this every six months.

- **First Payor Status**. While not every insurer approaches this in the same way, there are some general principles that apply to help us determine which benefits are considered paid in what order. We will review how each disability source of income views other sources of income using the following table.

| Source of Income | Normally Reduced By: |
|---|---|
| EI | Employment Income, Group Disability Benefits, WCB |
| WCB | CPP; WCB is normally first payor against all other benefits |
| CPP | CPP is normally first payor |
| Individual Disability Benefits | Employment Income |
| Group Disability Benefits | CPP, WCB, EI |

- **Coordination of Benefits.** The process of determining which benefit pays first is sometimes referred to as the coordination of benefits. Coordination of benefits for Health and Dental policies is dealt with in detail in Module 10. With disability insurance, coordination of benefits is quite complex, and depends on the wordings of the particular policy. For example, some individual disability policies allow the full benefit to be collected even if the insured is collecting CPP disability benefits. Other policies might allow up to $1000 of CPP disability, and others yet might provide for a dollar-for-dollar offset of disability benefits based on the amount of CPP disability benefit being paid. The only way to know in a particular scenario is to read the contract.

- **Proper Underwriting and Claims**. With disability insurance more than with any other type of insurance, a mistake or misrepresentation in the underwriting process can lead to problems at time of claim. For this reason, the agent must understand very well the application process, the product being sold, the needs of the client, and the expectations of the insurer. A properly constructed disability policy can help a client to manage the risk of disability, which can otherwise be financially devastating.

- **Subrogation.** Especially in the early days of a disability claim, it is common for a disabled person to apply for a number of disability benefits. In order to respect the concept of proper indemnification (restoring somebody to their proper position, but not allowing them to benefit from a claim), disability insurers may subrogate. This means they will step into the shoes of the disabled person and accept one or more disability benefits on that person's behalf. In some cases, for example, a disability insurer will require a disability claimant to subrogate their CPP disability benefits. This means the insurer will pay the regular disability benefit to the insured person, but the insured person's CPP disability benefit will be paid to the insurer. In practice, the actual application of subrogation provisions varies substantially from situation to situation.

## OTHER CONSIDERATIONS

- **Accident Only Policies**. There are some insurers who offer an accident-only disability policy. These policies will normally require less underwriting than a comprehensive disability policy. Sometimes they are even offered on a guaranteed issue basis, requiring no underwriting at all. These policies are useful for a client who would have medical concerns that would render them uninsurable. An accident only policy will not provide benefits in the event of sickness, but will serve a client well who has concerns about a disability that might result from a dangerous occupation or avocation.

- **Guaranteed Issue Policies**. In some cases, an applicant for insurance might not be an ideal candidate. An agent who is familiar with the underwriting process will learn to recognize in the application process items that will likely lead to a decline. In such cases, it may be appropriate to seek out guaranteed issue coverage. A guaranteed issue policy will be issued with little or no underwriting. The trade-off for this limited amount of underwriting is a higher cost. At the same time, a policy holder of a guaranteed issue policy may have to provide evidence at the time of claim that a conventional policy holder would not have to provide. This might include proof of lost income or evidence that the condition was not pre-existing. Guaranteed issue policies are not likely to be tested, but an agent should be aware of the opportunity they provide.

- **Policies for the Difficult to Insure**. The nature of employment has changed over the past generation. People move freely between jobs, work on a contract basis, and move across borders more readily than ever. Several insurers have introduced innovative products designed to cover people in a variety of ways that were not previously insurable. Examples include insuring short-term employment, insuring somebody with no income, and insuring somebody whose primary employment will be outside of Canada. There is almost no disability risk that cannot be insured today, if the policy owner is willing to pay the premium.

# TARGET MARKET

The target market for disability insurance is normally the self-employed, or employed without group benefits. The self-employed especially will have limited or no access to benefits such as EI or WCB. Employees who lack group benefits but have access to EI and WCB might still be concerned about a non-work related disability or about the amount of income they would have to survive on if they have access only to government benefits. Even where there are group benefits in place, it is not safe to assume that those benefits will fully meet the needs of the insured. Group benefits are sometimes subject to limits to the amount of benefit payable, or to the benefit period.

Unfortunately, disability insurance is often overlooked as a risk management tool. There are situations, such as a sole income earner in a family, where disability insurance should be looked at as the most important type of insurance. There are many agents active in the insurance industry today who do not sell any disability insurance at all, or sell it only in very limited amounts. An agent entering into the industry with a good understanding of disability insurance will find great opportunities, as the disability market is underserviced today. Using the information provided in this module and educating yourself on the particular product or products that you will sell will help you to provide excellent services to your clients.

# SUMMARY

Disability insurance is a complex product, but using the information learned in this module, you should now have a good understanding of it. You will certainly see exam questions that expect you to know how to build a disability policy and how a disability policy will react to the client's needs over time. Using the information we have, we will now go on to look at some other, less complicated insurance products. We will see many of the concepts we have discussed in this module revisited in the next two modules.

# Chapter 10 OTHER ACCIDENT & SICKNESS PRODUCTS

There are a variety of accident & sickness (A&S) products available today. This is an expanding market. At one time, insurers offered fairly straightforward health and dental plans. In the past twenty years, insurers have begun offering long-term care insurance and critical illness insurance. Recently, insurers have begun offering medical access insurance. There have been many innovations in products such as extended health care and travel insurance.

Whether through group plans (which will be covered in Module 11) or through individual coverage, most Canadians rely to some extent on the coverages discussed in this module. A good understanding of these products will allow you to sell the products where appropriate, and will allow you to provide excellent service to your clients.

In the following section, we will examine each of the A&S products available in the Canadian marketplace today. It is important to understand under what conditions the insured will be able to receive benefits. It is also necessary to recognize when a client has a need for each of the products discussed here. That is, when does the risk faced by the client match the benefits that the product will offer?

## EXTENDED HEALTH CARE

In Module 7, we looked at the Canada Health Act and the benefits offered by provincial health care plans. While the services offered are fairly comprehensive, there are some gaps in provincial health plans. Gaps left by provincial health plans can include:

- Ambulance services;
- Prosthetics;
- Elective surgery;
- Prescription drugs;
- Certain diagnostic services;
- Non-medically necessary cosmetic surgery;
- Experimental treatments;
- Some dental services;
- Vision care; and
- Non-medically necessary hospital services, such as private rooms.

Extended health care plans are designed to fill these gaps. The following is a list of some of the types of services typically offered by extended health care plans:

- Orthotics and specialized footwear;
- Massage;
- Chiropractic;
- In-home medical care;
- Hearing aids;

- Certain prostheses;
- Naturopathic medicine;
- Psychologist's services;
- Physiotherapy;
- Ambulance services;
- Semi-private and private hospital rooms; and
- Diagnostic and imaging services.

This is just a sampling of what these plans might offer. The services described in the list above may be covered to a limited extent by provincial health plans, but it is not uncommon for a patient in the health care system to incur out-of-pocket expenses when accessing those services. Each plan will be slightly different in the levels and type of coverage that it offers. In order to know exactly what is covered, the policy document would have to be examined.

- **Exclusions**. There are certain types of health care that will be excluded. Common exclusions to extended health care plans are:
  - Elective treatments;
  - Treatments needed as a result of an act of war;
  - Cosmetic surgery;
  - Treatment required as a result of self-inflicted injuries; and
  - Anything that would normally be covered by a provincial health care plan.

- **Benefits and Claims**. Extended health care plans normally offer a reimbursement benefit. The reimbursement is based on a claim submitted by the insured. Sometimes this is done directly by the health care practitioner's office, and sometimes the insured sends a receipt to the insurer with a completed claims form. In some cases, reimbursement will be for the full amount of the claim. We will see later on in this module that this is not always the case.

  There are some plans that will provide benefits in addition to a reimbursement for medical expenses. This sometimes comes in the form of a hospitalization benefit of, for example, $100 per day spent in the hospital. Similar benefits might be available for a fracture, for example.

  Some insurers will impose a restriction that certain types of claims cannot be submitted until coverage has been in force for a number of days or months. It is very common today for service providers to directly bill insurers for the amount of a claim. Dentists, pharmacists, and providers of paramedical services subscribe to electronic services that facilitate this process.

- **Taxation**. Benefits paid from an extended health care policy are paid to the insured tax-free. We will discuss the taxation of premiums later on in this module.

- **Underwriting**. When extended health care policies are sold on an individual basis, the insurer will normally collect medical evidence of insurability. Pre-existing conditions can result in a modified policy being issued, much as described in Module 9 concerning disability insurance. Where there are significant pre-existing conditions in place, it may be preferable to use a guaranteed issue product. This will remove any underwriting requirements, but normally demands a higher premium for a product that will provide limited coverage.

- **Target market**. At one time, most Canadian households could count on coverage of this sort coming from a group benefits plan. This is less common today than it once was. The self-employed, contractors, short-term employees, and retirees all face uncertainty about how they would deal with medical expenses. An individual extended health care plan can help to reduce or remove this uncertainty. Even for employees who have group benefits, the ability to rely on those group benefits is changing. At one time, it would have been very common for an employee to work for the same employer for their whole working life, and possibly even have benefits that carried through into retirement. Today, though, it is much more common for the employed to find themselves in a more fluid employment situation, where it might not be possible to count on having medical insurance. Because of this, there is an increasing trend towards the employed acquiring individual health care.

  In considering the need for extended health care insurance, the family situation should also be considered. A self-employed person who has young children, for example, might seek extended health care not just for her own benefit, but might also require coverage for her whole family. Family plans can usually extend coverage to children up to age 18 or up to age 25 if they are still students. Spouses and common-law spouses can also normally be covered.

- **Summary**. Extended health care policies are useful for managing the costs related to health care. For routine, predictable expenses, they make costs predictable, which can help with budgeting. For catastrophic expenses, these policies can reduce costs in a situation that could otherwise be very expensive for the insured. This is a growing market, providing significant opportunity for the agent who understands it.

## DENTAL CARE

Dental coverage is generally designed to add an element of certainty to what could otherwise be an uncertain set of costs. Dental coverage can be very basic, covering only routine preventative services, or it can be quite comprehensive, covering surgery and orthodontics.

Dental plans look fairly similar to extended health care plans in their structure. The plan will define exactly what sort of services will be covered and to what extent. Reimbursement will be based on all or a portion of the claim submitted.

Dental plans are generally available in three forms, or three levels of coverage:

- **Preventive (or Preventative) or Basic services**. This covers routine dental care. Broadly this means work done on the original teeth. Any dental plan will include preventative services at the very minimum. Services covered under the preventative portion of the plan will usually include:

  - X-rays, fillings, check-ups, and cleaning;
  - Periodontics (routine scaling of the teeth and gums); and
  - Certain extractions.

- **Restorative**. A client willing to pay a higher premium will be able to receive reimbursement for certain restorative procedures. Restorative benefits will normally be limited in the amount of reimbursement available. The restorative procedures covered will normally include:

  - crowns;
  - dentures;
  - repair and adjustments to dentures;
  - bridgework;
  - surgical services;
  - major surgery;
  - anaesthesia - when oral surgery is required;
  - drug injections;
  - laboratory procedures; and
  - root canal.

- **Orthodontic**. Also at an additional cost, coverage for orthodontic procedures is available. As with restorative benefits, there is normally a limited amount of reimbursement available. This normally covers braces and other appliances as well as the procedures, anaesthetic, and laboratory work associated with them. In order to avoid anti-selection, insurers normally place restrictions on the amount of orthodontic benefits available in the first one or two years of coverage. An insured might not, for example, be able to submit a claim for braces until the third year of coverage. Note that this does not mean that one could have the work done in the first year and then save the receipt for two years. Claims for orthodontic work in the first two years would simply be ineligible.

- **Fee Guide**. In most provinces a fee guide is used to determine what the reasonable and customary expense would be. For example, a dentist might charge $150 for a routine cleaning but the fee guide for the province might indicate that a cleaning should cost only $135. In such a situation, the insurer will base reimbursement on what the fee guide indicates. In this example, the client would be responsible for the $15 ($150 - $135 = $15) beyond the amount authorized by the fee guide. It is up to the discretion of the dentist to assess the actual amount charged; the fee guide is only a guide.

- **Claims**. It is common to see claims for the restorative and orthodontic portions of dental plans subject to an elimination period. It might be the case that premiums have to have been paid for up to two years before claims can be made. Dental plans do not always use a calendar year to calculate when benefits are paid. Some dental plans might pay benefits based on getting certain services every 6 or 9 months, rather than every year.

- **Dental Emergency**. In cases where a medical trauma causes a dental emergency, claims will be borne by an extended health care plan rather than a dental plan. Dental plans are designed to cover routine dental procedures as opposed to medical traumas.

- **Taxation**. As with health plans, dental plans provide a tax-free benefit.

- **Target Market**. The target market for dental plans is much the same as the target market for extended health plans. Again, family coverage is an important consideration. Dental plans are often sold as a package with extended health care.

- **Summary**. Dental plans are useful for helping an insured to have a predictable set of costs associated with dental care.

## PRESCRIPTION DRUG PLANS

Prescription drug plans are designed to provide reimbursement for expenses related to the purchase of prescription drugs. Prescribed medication can be an expensive component of a family's health care expenses. Putting a prescription drug plan in place is a way to manage those expenses.

At one time prescription drug plan claims were normally handled in the same manner as health and dental claims, as described above. Today it is more common for insurers to provide a pay-direct card, which the insured can use to have a claim handled directly between the dispensing pharmacy and insurer.

Reimbursement is normally provided for some or all of the costs of the actual prescription. There is also normally an allowance to claim a dispensing fee, up to a set limit. Not all costs will necessarily be covered. Some examples of drugs that may or may not be covered are:

- Birth control;
- Smoking cessation;
- Fertility drugs;
- Over-the-counter medications; and
- Dietary supplements.

- **Taxation**. Benefits are paid tax-free from prescription drug plans.

- **Target Market**. Prescription drug plans are available as stand-alone plans, but are also often bundled with health and dental plans.

## ACCIDENTAL DEATH AND DISMEMBERMENT

Accidental death and dismemberment (AD&D) plans operate differently from health, dental, and drug plans, all of which provide reimbursement for medical expenses. Instead, AD&D plans provide a lump sum benefit in the event that a covered loss should occur.

AD&D benefits are normally based on a lump sum benefit, as described in Module 9. A schedule of benefits will be described in the AD&D policy. It is very common to see AD&D used as a rider or bundled with other benefits.

For a complete review of AD&D policies, see the riders section of Module 9.

- **Taxation**. AD&D benefits are paid tax-free.

- **Limitations**. Exclusions are thoroughly discussed in Module 9. It is important, also, to remember that in order for benefits to be paid, the covered loss must occur within one year of the event.

- **Underwriting**. AD&D policies are almost always sold without any underwriting.

- **Target Market**. AD&D policies tend to be relatively inexpensive compared to the amount of benefit offered. Because of this, they are widely available and frequently sold. Because of the lack of underwriting, they are useful in situations where the potential insured works in a dangerous occupation or has dangerous hobbies. It is vital to keep the exclusions for these policies in mind when selling and servicing the product.

## VISION CARE

Vision care policies are almost never sold as stand-alone products, but are sometimes sold as a package with other types of coverage. Within prescribed limits, a vision care policy will provide tax-free benefits on a regular basis for the purchase of corrective eyewear (glasses and sometimes contact lenses) and the services of an optometrist or ophthalmologist.

## TRAVEL INSURANCE

Travel insurance policies vary significantly and have undergone a great deal of recent evolution. In their most basic form, travel insurance policies are designed to provide reimbursement for medical expenses incurred while travelling outside of Canada. However, travel insurance policies offered today can provide a great range of benefits. Benefits offered by travel insurance policies can include:

- Emergency medical;
- Routine medical expenses;
- Medical services such as chiropractics;
- Ambulance services;
- Emergency dental services;
- Travel expenses to send the insured to Canada;
- Travel expenses to bring a loved one to a hospitalized insured's location;
- Transportation of insured when deceased;
- Trip cancellation insurance;

- Trip interruption insurance;
- Lost luggage;
- Accidental death and dismemberment benefits for events that happen while travelling; and
- Other possible coverages depending on the insurer and policy in force.

- **Exclusions**. It is quite common to see exclusions included in travel insurance. Common exclusions can include:

  - Pre-existing conditions. Insurers will not normally cover pre-existing conditions. The actual definition of pre-existing conditions can vary significantly between policies. It is important that the insured understand exactly what will be covered and what will be excluded;
  - Acts of war;
  - Travel in countries where a travel advisory is in effect;
  - Health care that should reasonably have been sought in the insured's home location;
  - Self-inflicted injuries;
  - Commission of a criminal act by the insured;
  - Conditions caused by drugs or alcohol; and
  - Other exclusions that may be written into the policy.

- **Taxation**. Benefits paid from a travel insurance policy are normally paid tax-free.

- **Underwriting.** Most travel insurance is sold without any underwriting done at the time of sale. More comprehensive policies, such as those designed to cover multiple trips or extended trips may require some underwriting. The disadvantage of not having underwriting done at time of sale is that pre-existing conditions will not be defined until a claim is submitted. There have been instances where travel insurers have denied a claim based on a pre-existing condition, where the insured believed the condition would be covered. Insureds tend not to read the policy documents that they are provided. This is where a good agent can help an insured to understand what will and will not be covered, preventing future challenges.

- **Target market.** The target market for travel insurance is anyone who spends time away from their province of residence. While nobody plans to have something go wrong while travelling, it can be very expensive and stressful if something does go wrong. Having good travel insurance in place can help manage these issues. Basic travel insurance policies can be sold directly by travel agents. More comprehensive types of policies require an insurance license for sales and service. Even if you do not sell travel insurance, you can take good care of your clients by helping them to understand their needs around travel insurance.

## MEDICAL ACCESS INSURANCE  *NOT TESTED*

Medical access insurance is a very new innovation in A&S insurance. It is specifically designed to allow somebody who has received a referral from a physician to access health care ahead of waiting lines. This can be done by accessing private health care, often directly accessing the American health care system. Medical access insurance is designed to reimburse the costs associated with doing so.

As a fairly new product, medical access insurance is not a frequently offered product. You do not need to be aware of it for exam purposes.

## CLAIMS AND COST SHARING IN A&S PLANS

The plans discussed so far in this module are primarily designed to provide reimbursement for medical expenses. If we consider that the insurer is in the business of offering these plans to make a profit, and that the client needs to purchase an affordable product, we can start to understand the funding model for these plans. The insurer must structure a plan that will allow it to generally collect premiums beyond the average amount of claims that will be paid. The product must be attractive enough that it is worth the client paying these premiums.

Routine expenses (which the insurer would refer to as prospectively rated) would include items such as regular prescriptions, basic dental services, and vision care. These types of claims would most often be submitted in similar, predictable amounts year after year. Generally the insurer will charge a slightly higher premium than what they would anticipate those expenses adding up to. If that were the only benefit to the insured, the only benefit of A&S policies would be to aid in budgeting. The greater benefit offered by most of these policies comes from the fact that they help a client to claim extraordinary expenses. Those extraordinary expenses can cause a client great difficulty.

In order to keep the costs of the plan manageable, the insurer will impose restrictions on how much of a particular expense they will reimburse. The measures put in place, referred to as cost sharing, can consist of any of the following:

- **Deductibles**. A deductible refers to an amount the insured will have to pay before the insurer will pay any benefits. Normally, a deductible will be applied to the first claim or claims submitted. Deductibles can be set up a number of ways. Some plans include an individual deductible and a family deductible (only if the plan has coverage for family members), some use just one deductible. Deductibles can vary in their dollar amount. Normally the deductible is reset at a regular interval. Some deductibles might reset each year, some every two years, some every nine months. Once the deductible is reset, the insured will have to start over again and pay the deductible if any claims are submitted.

  For exam purposes, deductibles are normally applied on an individual and family basis. You should consider that plans will generally feature an individual deductible of $25 or $50 per family member, with a family deductible normally set at $75, but sometimes higher. This means that, for each individual, deductibles will be applied until the $25 deductible is reached. For the whole family, once the $25 deductible has been applied three times, the family deductible of $75 has been reached. No more deductibles will be applied at that time.

Within prescription drug plans that use a pay-direct card, there is often a deductible applied to each claim. This is usually $5 or $7.50. There is no annual limit or family deductible applicable with these deductibles.

- **Co-Insurance (or co-pay)**. Co-Insurance is the portion of the claim (after the deductible has been applied) that the insurer will pay. Common co-insurance factors are 50%, 80%, and 90%. An 80% co-insurance would mean that the insurer will pay 80% of the claim while the insured will be responsible for the remaining 20%. Some insurers would refer to this as a 20% co-pay. Most covered services, such as basic dental and prescription drug plans, use 80% or 90% co-insurance. Certain restorative and orthodontic dental procedures will use a 50% co-insurance factor.

- **Maximums**. Depending on the plan structure, certain covered items will be subject to a maximum. These maximums can be applied a number of different ways. Orthodontic plans almost always have a maximum, and the maximum might look like any of the following:

  - Annual maximum for the entire plan. For example, the plan might have a $2000 annual maximum for orthodontics;
  - Annual maximum per person covered by the plan. The plan might limit a parent and each child to $1500 per year for orthodontics; or
  - Lifetime maximum. The plan might carry a $5000 lifetime maximum. As with annual maximums, a lifetime maximum might apply to either the entire plan or to each person covered by the plan.

These cost sharing measures are put in place to keep plan costs in check, which should also keep premiums affordable. The idea is to put some responsibility for costs into the insured's hands, which should make them consider whether they need to submit a claim. Cost sharing measures are not legislated or regulated. Instead, the Canadian Life and Health Insurance Association (CLHIA) has produced guidelines to indicate how claims will be handled. Because these are guidelines and not rules, there can be some variation between insurers as to how claims will be handled.

- **Coordination of Benefits**. In cases where a claim might be covered by more than one plan, the CLHIA has introduced guidelines to limit the amount of benefit that will be paid. The guidelines are referred to as the Coordination of Benefits guidelines, and insurers use them to prevent insureds from benefiting from claims that are submitted. The Coordination of Benefits guidelines work by first indicating who the primary carrier will be. We then determine how much that carrier will pay. Once that amount is determined, we go to the secondary carrier to assess how they will treat the remaining amounts.

Let's say that we have a scenario in which a couple, Rebecca and Mark, go to the pharmacist to fill a prescription for their young son, Ethan. Rebecca was born January 15, 1979. Mark was born March 12, 1978. Rebecca's plan has a $25 deductible and 80% co-insurance. Mark's plan has a $60 deductible and 90% co-insurance. The amount of the claim is $320, and we will assume that this falls within the maximum allowed under each plan. These charts show the process in detail:

| Order of Priority for Determining Primary Carrier |
| --- |
| 1. The plan under which the claimant is a member. |
| 2. The plan of the parent who celebrates their birthday earlier in the year. (**Note:  Not necessarily the oldest parent**. A parent with a June birthday would be primary to a parent with a November birthday) |
| 3. If the same birthday, the one whose name is first alphabetically. |
| Claims for Children where Mom and Dad are not together: |
| 1. Parent with single custody first. |
| 2. Spouse of the parent with single custody. |
| 3. Parent who does not have custody. |
| 1. If there is joint custody, we revert back to the earliest birthday. |
| Note that this only matters where both parents have a plan that would cover the child. |

| Step | Input |
| --- | --- |
| 1. Determine the Primary Carrier | Rebecca |
| 2. Send the Claim to the Primary Carrier | $320 |
| 3. The Primary Carrier applies the deductible | -$25 |
| | $295 |
| 4. The Primary Carrier applies the co-insurance | x 80% |
| 5. The amount remaining will be paid by the Primary Carrier | $236 |
| 6. We take the original amount of claim to Secondary Carrier | $320 |
| 7. The Secondary Carrier applies the deductible | -$60 |
| | $260 |
| 8. The Secondary Carrier applies the co-insurance | x 90% |
| 9. The amount remaining is the maximum the Secondary carrier will pay | $234 |
| 10.  We compare the amount from Step 9 ($234) to the amount that the Primary Carrier would not pay ($84) | $320 - $236 $84 |
| 11.  The Secondary Carrier will pay the lesser of the two amounts.  $84 is less than $234. | $84. |
| 12.  The total reimbursement is equal to the sum of step 12 and step 5. The claimants have to pay the rest. In this case, they will have their full claim reimbursed, between the two plans. | $236 +$84 $320 |

In practice, this is all done by the insurers. When a claim is submitted to one carrier, it is normal to provide information about who the other carrier is. The insurers will then coordinate benefits. You will almost certainly see questions on this 2-3 times on each exam you write.

- **Premiums**. Because insurers will be unable to exactly predict the extent to which plans will be used, many A&S plans feature non-guaranteed premiums. That is, the insurer might alter premiums based on claims experience. Insureds whose usage of the plan is greater than anticipated will sometimes increase the insured's premiums. This is not always the case, and a reading of the policy document is necessary to understand the conditions under which the insurer might take such action.

## TAXATION OF ACCIDENT AND SICKNESS POLICIES

Where A&S policies are designed to fill a gap left in the provincial health care system, the premiums are normally eligible for the medical expense tax credit. This is the case with extended health care, prescription drug, vision care, dental plans, and travel insurance. Even though this can mean that premiums are paid with untaxed (or before tax) dollars, the benefits are still received tax-free. Self-employed people have a further ability to take a tax deduction for a portion of these premiums. In most cases, a tax deduction is more favourable than a tax credit.

## STRUCTURE OF ACCIDENT AND SICKNESS POLICIES

For the purpose of understanding, this module breaks the various A&S coverages out into their individual components. In reality, though, it is very common to see A&S policies included several of these components within one policy. For example, we might find an A&S policy that includes health, drug, dental, and vision care. Another policy might just offer health and drug coverage together.

## CRITICAL ILLNESS INSURANCE

Critical illness insurance is a relatively new product, having been originally developed in the 1970s. It is not a traditional A&S product, in that it does not provide reimbursement for medical expenses. Instead, critical illness insurance pays a tax-free lump sum benefit in the event that an insured is diagnosed with certain conditions. Normally the insured must also survive for a set number of days before a benefit will be paid. The benefit is based on the amount purchased in the policy, and can be used for whatever the insured wishes. The intent is to alleviate the financial stress that is often associated with a serious illness.

- **Covered Conditions**. Critical illness policies vary in exactly what conditions they cover. Most critical illness policies cover, as a minimum, what are considered the four dread conditions. These are:

| Conditions normally covered under a "Basic" CI Policy | | | |
|---|---|---|---|
| Cancer | Coronary Bypass Surgery | Heart Attack | Stroke |

In addition to these four conditions, it is common for CI policies to cover a range of other conditions, including:

| Conditions normally covered under a "Comprehensive" CI Policy | | | |
|---|---|---|---|
| Alzheimer's | Coma | Loss of Speech | Occupational HIV |
| Anemia | Aortic surgery | Organ Transplant | Paralysis |
| Brain Tumour | Deafness | Organ Failure | Parkinson's |
| Meningitis | Kidney Failure | Motor Neuron Disease | Severe Burns |
| Blindness | Loss of Limbs | Multiple Sclerosis | Brain Injury |

CI policies specifically designed to cover children will normally cover the conditions listed above, plus:

| Conditions normally covered under a Children's CI Policy | | | | |
|---|---|---|---|---|
| Cerebral Palsy | Congenital Heart Disease | Cystic Fibrosis | Muscular Dystrophy | Type 1 Diabetes |

Some CI policies will pay a limited benefit in case of certain diagnoses. Examples of conditions that may result in a limited benefit payment are:

| Conditions normally paying a limited CI Benefit | | | |
|---|---|---|---|
| Early stage breast cancer | Early stage prostate cancer | Early stage skin cancer | Coronary Angioplasty |

The lists above are not necessarily the case with every critical illness policy. Some CI policies will cover exactly these conditions; others will cover more or fewer conditions. In order to know for certain, it would be necessary to examine the policy. Further, the policy will very explicitly define the condition covered. The definitions are written in such a manner that they would correspond to a doctor's diagnosis. Almost all CI policies will cover the four dread conditions.

- **Elimination Period**. In order to receive the benefit, it is normally necessary for the insured to survive for 30 days after diagnosis. At the end of the elimination period, if the insured has survived, the benefit will be paid.

- **Policy Structures**. CI policies can be purchased as either term or permanent insurance. Terms can vary, but it is common to find critical illness policies sold as term to 65 or term to 75 policies. Terms are usually 10 or 20 years, with the policy renewable without evidence of insurability. Permanent CI policies can be purchased with pay-for-life structures, or with paid-up premiums. A paid-up policy might be fully paid for once premiums have been paid for 10 years, 20 years, or to a certain age.

- **Benefits and Claims**. Benefits will be received once a diagnosis has been received for a condition as described above, and the insured has survived for the elimination period expressed in the policy. Some policies will terminate once a claim has been paid. Some will continue and allow further claims to be submitted if necessary. The amount of claim is determined by the benefit purchased. Let's say an insured purchases a policy with a $50,000 benefit. Four years later that insured is diagnosed with multiple sclerosis. 30 days after diagnosis, the insured receives a $50,000 cheque from the insurer. The policy may terminate at that point, or may carry on, depending on what type of policy it is.

- **Taxation**. CI benefits are paid tax-free. Premiums are paid with after-tax dollars.

- **Underwriting**. Underwriting for CI policies is done much as described in Module 3. Information is collected at time of application, and a policy is issued if the insurer believes the risk is good. Policies can be issued with exclusions, or increased premiums, also as described in Module 3. There are guaranteed issue policies available as well, with no underwriting done. These guaranteed issue policies are normally relatively expensive.

  A history of the covered conditions, or a family history indicating a propensity to these conditions, can lead to a decline of coverage or exclusions in the policy. For that reason, it is important to place CI coverage as early as possible, before anything has gone wrong.

- **Exclusions**. Each condition covered by the policy will be very explicitly described. Most CI policies include a provision that no benefits will be paid in the event of a diagnosis of cancer within the first 90 days after the policy is first issued. The concern being that the insured had something arise that led them to believe they might have cancer and, before going to their doctor to get it checked, they acquired a CI policy. In addition to the requirement for very specific definitions, CI policies normally exclude some of the same causes that are excluded from disability policies. This can include self-inflicted injuries, acts of war, or condition caused by driving while impaired.

- **Riders, Waivers, and Benefits**. There are some riders available for CI policies. The following riders are often sold with, or automatically included with, CI policies:

  - **Disability waiver of premium**. This is exactly as described in Modules 8 and 9.

  - **Return of premium**. Return of premium can be structured a number of ways. The return of premium can happen on death (if no benefit has been paid), at the termination of the policy, or at certain intervals throughout the policy.

  - **Medical consults**. There are programs available as part of CI policies that give the insured preferential access to medical advice regarding their particular condition.

- **Conversion**. Some CI policies feature a conversion option, which allows the insured to decide to convert to a long-term care policy. This conversion can be done without underwriting, and is normally only available between ages 60 and 65. This is a very new feature of CI policies, and not all insurers offer it.

- **Target market.** The target market for CI policies would be anybody who might have a concern about being diagnosed with the conditions mentioned in this section. The likelihood of developing cancer, for example, is quite high. Any of these conditions can be devastating for a family. The recognition that this could 'happen to me' often leads somebody to consider CI. Unfortunately, most people do not purchase CI before something does happen. Insurance agents can prevent problems by placing this insurance on clients who are relatively young and healthy. CI policies should be considered both for single people and people with families.

Recently many insurers have begun introducing CI policies specifically focussed on children. The cost of insurance for children is very low. Underwriting is generally easier for children than it is for adults. Placing insurance at a young age guarantees that the child will have coverage in place later in life.

- **Summary**. CI insurance is a relatively new product. Because it is relatively new, there is an ample market of potential clients who have never been exposed to this product. CI benefits can be very useful when a critical illness arises.

# LONG TERM CARE INSURANCE

Long-term care insurance is another new innovation in the Canadian insurance market. Long-term care will provide benefits at the point when an insured is no longer able to care for themselves. It is normally sold to help a client deal with the risk of old age, to make sure that the client will be able to obtain sufficient health care in retirement.

At one time, long-term care policies provided simple reimbursement of the expenses associated with checking into a long-term care facility. Today, though, long-term care policies can provide coverage in a wide variety of forms, including reimbursement and income benefits.

- **Coverage**. Long-term care policies can provide a wide range of benefits, depending on the actual policy. Coverage from long-term care policies can include:

  o **Long-term care facilities**. The cost of spending time in a long-term care facility can be high. While there are provincially and federally-funded long-term beds available in Canada, these public facilities are often far from home and not available without using a waiting list. It is common to see seniors accepted to facilities which are far from their home, requiring the person using the facility and their families to travel. Even with all these limitations, there are still normally costs associated with using these facilities. Private long-term care facilities are often readily available, but at a high cost.

- o **Palliative care (or Hospice care)**. These facilities are designed to allow a terminally ill patient to spend their final days in a comfortable location with access to excellent medical care.

- o **In-Home care**. Elderly people may not necessarily want to seek care in a facility. Many people might wish to remain in their homes, or to move in with their children or grandchildren. Costs associated with such a decision can include having medical professionals come into the home, medical devices, and lost income for family who are taking care of elderly relatives. While not all long-term care policies will cover all these expenses, some policies will.

- o **Respite care**. In situations such as those described above, it sometimes becomes necessary for the family caring for a loved one to put that person in a facility on a temporary basis. This is known as respite care, and it often comes at a cost.

- o **Adult day care**. Similar to respite care, which normally involves stays of a few weeks, adult day care allows caregivers to put a loved one in a facility. In this case, though, the stay is just for a day at a time. This is done in a similar manner to day care for children, with the cared for person spending their days in a place where there are social activities as well as access to medical care. This normally comes at a cost.

- o **Other benefits**. This list is a representation of the types of care offered by a long-term care policy. Other benefits might also be available.

- • **Claims**. Claims for a long-term care policy are generally based on one of two situations. The criteria for claiming benefits are:

  - o **Activities of Daily Living**. Once an insured is unable to perform the activities of daily living, benefits can be claimed. Most insurers require that the insured be unable to perform two ADLs. Some insurers use a list of 5 ADLs, some 6, and some 7. The list of ADLs includes:

    - ■ Bathing;
    - ■ Continence;
    - ■ Toileting (Some insurers combine this with continence);
    - ■ Transferring positions of the body (also known as mobility);
    - ■ Dressing;
    - ■ Feeding; and
    - ■ Hearing (Not all insurers use this ADL).

  - o **Cognitive Impairment**. Once the insured is diagnosed by a medical professional as being unable to think, perceive, reason, or remember, a claim for benefits can be submitted.

- • **Elimination period**. Elimination periods for LTC policies vary. Once a claim is submitted, the insured might have to wait 0, 30, 60, 90, or as long as 180 days to receive benefits.

- **Policy Structures**. LTC policies are sold in a variety of forms.  The most common in Canada today is either a 20-pay policy, if purchased at age 35 or later, or a policy that is paid-up at age 55, if purchased before age 35.  Other structures, such as pay-for-life, are available.  Premiums are normally level for five-year terms.  Because LTC is a relatively new product and has not been sold a great deal yet, insurers don't have a clear picture as to how often claims will be submitted.  In order to make up for this lack of certainty, LTC policies normally feature non-guaranteed premiums.  They are normally sold in five-year level amounts, but that means that an insured's premiums could increase, up to a pre-defined limit, every 5 years, based on the claims experience of the insurer.  LTC policies are not normally available before age 31, but some insurers make them available at a younger age.

  Some insurers offer joint-LTC policies.  Normally designed for spouses, these policies might provide benefits only for the last spouse to need coverage.  They might provide a limited benefit for the first spouse.  More elaborate joint-LTC policies will provide benefits for both spouses.

- **Benefits**.  Benefits for LTC policies can be paid three different ways:

  - **Reimbursement**.  The original LTC policies paid a reimbursement benefit, meaning that they only paid benefits based on receipts submitted for care covered under the LTC policy.  Many policies still provide benefits under this structure.  Reimbursement policies generally have the most affordable premiums.

  - **Indemnification**.  Under an indemnification plan, the insurer estimates the cost of long-term care, based on known factors, and provides a benefit in that amount each month.  This removes the requirement for the insured to submit claims and wait for benefits to be paid.

  - **Income**.  The most elaborate type of disability policies provide a regular income, similar to a disability policy.  This income can be used for LTC needs, or other needs as they arise.  Income-type policies are generally the most expensive, but they offer the greatest flexibility.  Income will only be paid while the insured is actually eligible for LTC benefits.  Because they offer the most flexible benefit, income policies are usually the most expensive.

- **Benefit Period**.  The benefit periods for LTC policies greatly influence their cost.  There are three different ways that a benefit period or benefit amount can be structured:

  - **Recurring Amounts**.  Some LTC policies provide a benefit based on a dollar amount per period.  For example, a policy might provide benefits of $2000 per month.  A higher monthly benefit will be more expensive than a lower monthly benefit.  Benefits are sometimes expressed in daily or weekly figures as well.

  - **Time Limit**.  The method discussed, above, is sometimes used hand-in-hand with a time limit on benefits.  Similar to a disability policy, some

LTC policies will provide benefits for up to a fixed amount of time. Common benefit periods are 3, 5, 7, 10 years, and lifetime benefits.

   o **Cumulative Dollar Amount**. This limitation on benefits is sometimes present in LTC policies along with the previous two. The result of this limitation is that once a total amount of benefits received reaches a certain limit, that no more benefits would be paid. LTC policies might limit benefits to $100,000, $300,000, $500,000, or maybe $1,000,000 of benefits. Other amounts are available, but these are typical.

Taking all this into account, then, a LTC policy might offer a $2000 per month benefit for 5 years and to a cumulative total of $100,000 of benefits. It is important to note that a LTC policy will only pay benefits for as long as the insured continues to be unable to perform activities of daily living or demonstrates a cognitive impairment. An insured who recovers will no longer be able to receive benefits, even if there is still some benefit payable from the policy.

- **Taxation**. LTC benefits are received tax-free. Premiums are paid for with after-tax dollars, and do not qualify for the medical expense tax credit.

- **Underwriting**. Underwriting for LTC policies is based on a separate set of factors from what we are normally concerned with for other insurance products. In the underwriting process, we will normally look for anything in the insured's history that might indicate a likelihood to need long term care. This would often be indicated by an inability to perform what are known as the Instrumental Activities of Daily Living (IADLs). These IADLs are distinct from the ADLs discussed above, but an inability to perform IADLs is a good indicator that the applicant is going to have trouble with the ADLs. This would normally lead to a decline. Age, sex, and smoking status are also important when assessing the risk for an LTC product. Some of the IADLs (actual lists vary) include:

      ▪ shopping for groceries;
      ▪ taking care of others;
      ▪ using medication;
      ▪ using the telephone; and
      ▪ meal preparation.

- **Exclusions**. LTC policies normally exclude self-inflicted conditions. Treatment required for drug and alcohol dependency is excluded. Policies will generally not provide coverage where there is no identifiable organic reason for the requirement for long-term care. Ratings and additional exclusions for substandard risks are relatively rare with LTC policies. Most insurers, when a problem is identified in underwriting, will decline coverage.

- **Riders, Waiver, and Benefits**. There is a limited selection of riders available with LTC policies. Riders that are offered by some insurers include:

- o **Cost of Living Adjustment**. This rider will allow regular, automatic increases in the benefit amount to match inflation. This rider is normally quite expensive, but the benefits can be enormous.

- o **Return of Premium at Death**. If an insured ends up dying because of an accident, or an illness that claims his life suddenly, then this rider could be useful. It will see some or all of the premiums paid by the insured paid as a death benefit to a named beneficiary.

- **Non-forfeiture Provisions**. A problem that can arise with LTC policies is that at the point when a client starts to need LTC, their ability to do things like pay premiums will be limited. We might find somebody in the early stages of a cognitive impairment who has a LTC policy in place already, but fails to pay premiums because of the cognitive impairment. The danger here is that the policy lapses and once the cognitive impairment has taken hold, there is no coverage in place. To prevent this from happening, some insurers offer non-forfeiture provisions (as discussed in Module 3) within LTC policies.

- **Target Market**. LTC has not been sold in significant amounts in Canada to this point. Part of the problem is that many people wait until very late in life to try to acquire LTC. Unfortunately, late in life these policies become very difficult to underwrite. Ideally, LTC should be offered at a younger age in anticipation of future needs. Even up to the mid-60s, LTC products can generally be put in force at an affordable price. After that, though, LTC becomes costly and difficult to underwrite. LTC should be considered in situations where there is some risk that the client might have to take care of themselves or seek professional medical attention in old age.

  A discussion around LTC should be initiated with clients at the same time as the discussion around other risk management, such as disability, medical expenses, and critical illness. Adding LTC to the discussion early, even if the product is not sold at that time, will make the client aware and help them to plan for this need. As the client matures and has access to more disposable income, some of that income should be put towards premiums for an LTC policy.

  As part of the effort to better service the LTC market, many insurers who offer this product have LTC specialists. These LTC specialists will work with an agent to help put appropriate coverage in place, and to show an agent how to discuss LTC with a client.

- **Summary**. LTC insurance, because so little of it is in force today, represents a market rife with opportunity. The agent who understands this product will find ample opportunity to help clients plan for and deal with the risks associated with old age.

## SUMMARY

You should now have a good understanding of what the various A&S products are, when they would be sold, and how their benefits would be paid.  This will help you to sell and service A&S insurance.
Having now learned all the individual insurance products, we are now going to move on to group insurance.

# Chapter 11 GROUP INSURANCE

A common way in Canada for people to have insurance coverage is through employer sponsored, union, or association group insurance plans. There are other variations of group policies in existence which provide protection to Canadians. Up until this point most of our discussion has concerned individuals seeking out and purchasing individual insurance protection for losses arising from premature death, disability, health and dental expenses, and the risk of aging. Each time an individual seeks protection, an application for insurance of whatever type is made with that application being subjected to the risk assessment/ underwriting process. At the end of the process the insured has a contract that binds the insurer to pay when a claim comes due. We have already talked about the various components of that process.

Let's take the example of 50 individuals of roughly 50/50 gender split and of various ages ranging in age from 18 to 65. Each one of these individuals are approached by an insurance professional and sold on the need for protection in some area of their lives. Each one of those individuals makes application and is underwritten, receives a contract and makes payment directly to the insurer.

Now let's take those same 50 people and lump them together under a common umbrella. They all work for the same employer or belong to the same union or association or they all borrow money from the same creditor. Each of those entities has a vested interest in the health and well-being of the employee, association or union member or borrower. Unhealthy people are less productive than healthy people. Sadly, in many cases, when it is left to the individual's discretion, adequate protection will not be sought.

## STRUCTURE OF GROUP CONTRACTS

Most of our discussion here focuses on employer/employee arrangements. Employers want healthy productive people showing up for work each day. Employers want employees to be able to afford to provide basic and sometimes enhanced medical and dental services for themselves and their families.

Imagine the 37 year old technologist in a business, making about $80,000 per year with a spouse making $35,000. There is a mortgage, 2 cars financed and 3 children ages 7, 10 and 12. The 12 year old has just returned from the dentist with the news that he needs orthodontic work on his teeth which may result in very expensive treatment over a 3 or 4 year period. Of course this could be ignored but the dental professional can well justify proper jaw and teeth alignment and that there will likely be a negative impact on future health if the need is ignored. We probably would see that the entire process of visiting and being treated by the orthodontist would stretch out over about 3 years requiring special appliances and numerous visits and over that time it will cost somewhere in the neighborhood of $10,000. The stress that puts on the employee who has to pay that bill is enormous especially considering that 2 more children are coming up to that age. Or consider someone who has just been diagnosed with cancer and needs expensive drugs and other treatments. One can quickly see the impact of these health concerns on both the employee and employer.

- **Master Contract**. The entity under which these people come together or exist enters into a contractual arrangement with an insurer to provide benefits to their employees or plan members. That contract is known as the Master Contract and is not made available to the plan members. The plan members receive a Certificate of Insurance as a requirement and perhaps even an employee booklet. The Certificate of Insurance, or employee benefits booklet, will describe the benefits available, but it is not a contract for insurance.

There are a variety of ways that group insurance contracts can be funded. We will look at some different funding and administrative models here:

- **Fully-Insured Plans**. It has been most common until recently to have group insurance plans structured as a fully-insured plan. That means that an insurer would be used to offer the benefits. The insurer would collect the premiums and would pay all claims and at the end of the year, keep all the profits. Nothing would be refunded to the plan owner hence this is referred to as the non-refund accounting method. Likewise if the insurer experienced a loss, in other words paid out more claims than premiums collected, the insurer does not go back and re-assess the plan owner. The shortfall would be reflected in premiums for the following year.

  For larger groups, it might be proper to establish a retrospective rating arrangement in which the insurer collects all the premiums, perhaps earns some interest on the funds collected and pays all the claims and covers administration costs. The difference in the income (premiums and interest) in excess of expenses (admin charges and claims) is deposited into the claims fluctuation reserve (CFR). Once that reserve exceeds 10% of premiums that amount is refunded to the plan owner. The purpose of the CFR is to smooth out the premiums from year to year. This plan structure is referred to as refund accounting.

- **Self-insured Plans**. Unlike a conventional fully-insured plan, in a self-insured plan, the employer will take on responsibility for paying claims. The employer, instead of paying premiums to an insurer, keeps the premiums they would have paid. Then, when employees submit claims, the employer pays out the benefits instead of having an insurer do it. This is a very common structure today. Keeping an insurer out reduces the employer's costs, but it increases the risk. If there are an unexpected number of claims, the employer might end up with a financial problem. For that reason, employers will usually be very careful what self-insured plans they offer. A smaller employer might choose to self-insure only its basic dental coverage, while a larger employer might self-insure everything except its life and AD&D coverage. Two other measures often incorporated into group plans are:

- ○ **Administrative Services Only**. ASO contracts see the employer self-insure, but bring in an insurer for its expertise in claims adjudication and to respect employee privacy. Insurers perform these administrative services for a fee. Virtually all self-insured plans use an ASO structure to some extent. For that reason, the terms ASO and self-insured plan are used interchangeably.

- ○ **Stop-Loss Insurance**. Employers using self-insured plans will limit their risk by purchasing stop-loss insurance. With this type of insurance, if claims exceed a pre-determined amount, the insurer will start to pay them.

- • **Third Party Administrator**. While not specifically a funding model, third party administration of plans has become increasingly popular of late. In a TPA plan, the employer engages a third party (a service often offered by group insurance agents) to take care of all plan administration. This includes designing and shopping for a plan, handling employee enrolment and departures, and providing administrative information to the insurers involved.

## CHARACTERISTICS OF GROUP INSURANCE

As previously discussed, there are different group insurance arrangements. Employers will provide group insurance for employees. Associations will seek group insurance as a benefit for their members. Creditors will arrange group insurance contracts for their borrowers (a specific example of this was discussed in Module 8 under mortgage insurance.) From this point forward, we will concentrate on employer-sponsored group insurance plans. Association insurance often follows some of the same structures.

Creditor insurance tends to be focused on the ability to repay a specific debt, such as a mortgage, credit card, or car loan. There are certain tax advantages for an employer acquiring a group benefits plan. Insurers have certain requirements that they need to meet in order to decide to take on the risk associated with a group. Human rights legislation compels employers to provide certain types of benefits to certain employees. When we combine these sets of ideas, we arrive at five concepts that generally apply to most group insurance contracts. These five principles are:

- • **Full-time Employment**. Group plans are typically designed for people who are considered full-time employees or are at the very least permanent part-time employees. Generally to be on a group plan one must work a minimum number of hours per week, such as 21, 25, or 28, depending on the insurer and the type of plan.

  The day that coverage is to begin, which will either be the day that the plan takes effect for a new plan or the day when the probationary period ends for a new employee joining an existing plan, all full-time employees (according to the master contract's definition of full time) who are actively at work will be covered. This leads to another crucial issue referred to as the eligibility period.  When the group exceeds a certain size (ie. 5 or 10 lives depending on the insurer's rules) there is no requirement for individual underwriting because of the benefits of pooling a group of generally healthy, productive people.  If a plan member is actively at work on a full-time basis on the day coverage is to begin then there will be no underwriting requirements and the eligibility period begins. The employee may also have to wait for a probationary period to expire. If the employee decides to join the plan after the eligibility period they will then need to be individually underwritten to be granted coverage. That requirement extends as well to any dependants covered on that employee's plan.

Insurers consider groups to be standard when they have either 25 or 50 members.  With these standard-sized groups, insurers offer a full range of benefits.  For smaller groups insurers create package plans with limits, referred to as Non-Evidence Maximums (NEMs) on each benefit based on their own assessment of what is considered a reasonable and cost-effective risk.  If employees wish to have coverage in excess of the NEM, but within the range of what is available within the plan, they will then have to qualify medically for that coverage.  This situation can arise, for example, where a group disability plan offers a benefit of 66.67% of salary, but the NEM is just $2000/month.  Any employee earning more than $3000 per month would have to qualify medically to have disability insurance that would offer protection up to the amount of their salary.

- **Limited Availability of Benefits**.  Group insurance contracts can be quite robust, but in order to prevent anti-selection, group insurers will limit the available benefits.  Because group insurance is sold with little or, in most cases, no underwriting, there would otherwise be a concern that the only reason for acquiring the group insurance is to deal with an already known condition.  For example, a business owner who has several employees who have recently been told that their children need braces might go looking for a group insurance plan that covers orthodontic work.  This is an example of anti-selection, in that we know already that there is a problem and that there will be claims.  For this reason, insurers do not typically offer plans that feature unlimited orthodontic coverage.  Instead, the orthodontic benefits might not begin until the plan has been in place for two full years.  The limited availability of this specific benefit will prevent anti-selection.

The availability of benefits can vary by class of employees.  The benefit schedule is laid out in the master contract either stating what all plan members are covered for as a group or broken down by classifications. These classifications must be based on real circumstances, and cannot be artificial only for the purpose of group insurance.  The granting of benefits or the creation of classes cannot be done on a discriminatory basis.  That is, it must be based on job duties, and cannot be based on age, sex, or other discriminatory factors.

Back to our 50 life group plan, it might be that 3 of those are owner/employees and even though they enter into the contract as representatives of the business, they are also covered as employees and thus receive benefits for themselves and their dependents. This group might be referred to as class 1 and would be defined as such in the master contract. They would each receive the same basic benefits. Class 2 might be office workers and middle managers and class 3 might be the plant and field workers. Each class represents different levels of risk for the insurers so it is obvious that class 3 would have more limitations and lower benefit limits than class 1, in our example. Some people think that the creation of the different classes by itself is a form of discrimination but under current group insurance practices and guidelines this is perfectly acceptable.

- **Payroll Deduction**. When a group is established the insurer only deals directly with the plan owner on contractual issues such as plan design and premium payments. Many plans are what we refer to as contributory plans where the employee contributes to the cost of the plan. Instead of having the employee submit the payment for their portion directly to the insurer, the employer collects through payroll deduction the employee portion and submits payment to the insurer. This reduces the possibility of lapse that becomes such a significant cost factor for individual insurance. In some cases the plan is set up on a non-contributory basis. In this case the employer funds the entire plan cost.

- **Minimum Employer Contributions**. The employer must fund at least 50% of the costs of any employer/employee group plan. If the employer does not fund at least that portion of the group plan, the employer will not have access to the tax deductions permitted by CRA under most group plans. Some insurers have recently introduced innovative funding models that allow employers to circumvent this regulation, but these plans are relatively rare. (Keeping in mind that these are principles and not rules, some insurers today require only a 25% contribution by the employer.)

- **Minimum Participation Limits**. In order to take full advantage of pooling and effectively spreading the risk amongst the healthy and slightly less healthy and the young and the old it will be written into most master contracts that a minimum percentage of employees must participate in the plan. This would vary from plan to plan. For instance a small group of 15 employees might have a requirement to have all employees take the life and disability benefits but allow people to opt out of health and dental. Insurers have basic plan sizes that allow them to maintain cost effectiveness. They are at liberty to require that a certain number of employees (usually 75% or 85%) must enroll in each benefit in order to maintain that benefit as part of the plan.

## GROUP INSURANCE PREMIUMS

Group insurance is priced on an annual basis, similar to a non-guaranteed yearly renewable term contract. If the plan is large enough, usually 50 lives or more, the new carrier (insurer) being proposed will obtain a claims and premium report based on the existing carrier's experience for the previous 2 or 3 years and use those numbers to forecast rates for the next 12 month period. The plan owner will agree to pay premiums in advance each month until the following year's renewal. About 2 months prior to the contract anniversary (or in some cases the first year is actually stretched out to 15 months) the insurer examines the experience and claims for the current year and perhaps still using one or 2 years from the previous carrier and uses that to set the rates for next 12 months. That process is repeated annually.

The group insurance market is highly competitive and most insurers will say that margins are slim therefore rates are adjusted accordingly to fit marketplace trends. Health and dental benefits are a significant part of most group plans today and the fluctuating and ever-increasing nature of those expenses creates constant pressure to keep rates moving upward. The process of using previous claims and premiums is called experience rating. When an insurer is determining the rates for the next year, they will look at the group's credibility. Larger groups will have more credibility than smaller groups, and credibility increases as a group has been covered under the same benefits for a number of years.

A 5 life group does not carry the same credibility as would a 50 or 75 life group. When pricing insurance today for smaller groups, less than 20 lives typically, insurers manually borrow from the experience of a pool of similar groups in the same or similar industry and in the same geographic area. For mid-size groups, 20 to 50 lives perhaps, the insurer will likely use what is known as a blended rating - a combination of experience and manual rating. Sometimes it is possible that an insurer will use manual rating for certain benefits and experience rating for others.

When calculating premiums, the insurer will look at the group's experience for benefits that are measurable within the group. This includes health and dental and short-term disability claims. For other benefits, such as life insurance and long-term disability, the insurer will consider the claims experience of all their insureds. With this in mind, a group will not be penalized if they suffer a catastrophic loss, such as the death of two employees at the same time. Such a loss will not affect the group's premiums. However, if all the employees seek expensive dental and prescription drug treatments at the same time, the group's premiums will increase significantly.

## THE SALES PROCESS

An advisor would approach the owner or key decision maker of a company that had gained the attention of the advisor. Perhaps the advisor had been dealing with an employee of that company doing a thorough insurance analysis and had discovered that the person had coverage through their employer. It would be beneficial then to ask the employee how they felt about the coverage and the plan, to see if the plan was properly being serviced and if the claims paying experience was favorable. The advisor could then contact the owner/decision maker and ask for an appointment to discuss their employee benefit package. The owner's concern is that the employees have good coverage and that plan hassles are kept to a minimum, but the bottom line is that having a benefit package in place helps the employer to **attract and retain employees**. Costs absorbed by the employer are a tax deductible business expense to the employer.

In order to facilitate a successful meeting with the employer, the advisor would obtain from the insurers that she represents a Request for Quote (RFQ) form. That form would require the gathering of information as follows:

- Business name and structure;
- Business address and locations;
- Number of employees;
- A complete listing by name, date of birth, gender, income (hourly, monthly or annual), marital status and dependent details, and job classification of each employee;
- Benefits requested;
- Name of current carrier (insurer) if applicable;
- Length of time with current carrier;
- Number of carriers in previous 5 years. Note that it is common for insurers to approach with caution those business owners who have more than 2 carriers in a previous 5 year period;
- The employer's willingness to absorb a portion of the premium costs; and
- Plan effective date.

Having gathered all of this information, the RFQ would then be submitted to a carrier or numerous carriers along with the desired plan design and benefit schedule and a quote would be prepared. It is not always the case that the whole group plan is placed with one carrier. Especially for larger groups, it is common for different carriers to take on different parts of the plan.

The advisor takes the quote to the business owner and asks for the buying decision. If agreed then the advisor would complete an application and collect payment for the 1st monthly premium. The insurer/carrier would then underwrite where necessary and subsequently create the master contract for delivery to and signing by the employer/plan owner. The plan owner would be subsequently billed for ongoing premiums. The rates would be established based on incomes, age, dependent status and benefits selected and would be adjusted annually or when changes in employee's incomes and new employees were reported to the insurer.

Even though the rates are established on an annual basis the contract is based on monthly commitments. The employer can cancel the plan at any time. As long as the monthly premiums are paid on time the plan will stay in effect.

Based on the full-time employee requirements as outlined in the master contract, all employees actively at work on a full-time basis on the effective date and who have completed the enrollment paperwork are covered on that date. For larger groups where no evidence of insurability or underwriting is required, coverage begins on that date. For smaller groups where Non-Evidence Maximums are set, coverage is granted up to that limit.

Any employees who are not actively at work on a full-time basis on the plan effective date will have a probationary period applied. The plan member is not covered during the probationary period. Probationary periods vary, but 30 day to 6 months are common, with 90 days being the most common. Some employers will request that the insurer waive the probationary period in certain circumstances.

Near the end of the probationary period, the employee will enter the eligibility period. During this 30 day period if the employee shows up for work full-time, signs their enrolment or otherwise chooses to join the plan, coverage begins. If the employee waits until after the eligibility period to join the plan, they can still join the plan but medical evidence would be required for themselves and each of their insured dependents. Underwriting of individual plan members would only be required when the employees sought coverage in excess of the Non-Evidence maximums.

# PLAN BENEFITS

Having looked at the structure of group insurance, we will now look at the benefits available through group plans. Not all plans feature all these benefits. A typical employer/employee plan will include all the coverages we see below. There are examples of plans, though, that only cover certain items. Automobile associations often offer membership in a group plan that features only accidental death & dismemberment benefits. Students' unions sometimes put plans into place for the sole purpose of offering health and dental benefits. As mentioned in Module 10, some group plans even feature critical illness insurance, which is not covered in this section.

## LIFE INSURANCE

Most employee-benefit plans offer group life insurance. For a considerable segment of the Canadian market-place, group life insurance is the only coverage that most families have. The Benefit Schedule found in the master contract outlines how much life insurance each plan member is provided with. The amounts provided are sometimes a flat amount, typically $100,000 or $50,000 for each insured employee. The minimum amount for a plan member is $10,000. Some plans are established with different classes, each class created based on job description.

Going back to our original group of 50 lives, there could be one class of all 50 lives and all employees would get the same benefits. Or it could be set up with multiple classes, say Class 1 being owners and executives, Class 2 being office workers and middle management, and Class 3 being plant and field workers. Each class represents different level of risk. Class 1 could be offered a flat rate of $100,000 life insurance, Class 2 could be offered $75,000 and Class 3 $50,000. More commonly one will see group plans with the life insurance coverage based on a multiple of earnings. If there is only one class it might be 2 times annual income. But with multiple classes like our earlier example, Class 1 could have 5 times annual income to a maximum of $400,000 (an executive earning $90,000/year would not have $450,000 coverage but rather $400,000).

Group life insurance is not portable. It only is in effect as long as the master contract is in place and as long as the employee is working for that particular employer. A standard provision of group insurance contracts is the conversion option. Upon termination from the plan where the employee actually terminates employment with that employer, the coverage for an amount up to and including the total amount covered under the group plan can be converted to a plan of personal insurance at the attained age and smoking status of the coverage being converted to. The conversion options may be a 1-year renewal and convertible term policy, a term to 65 policy or any permanent insurance policy being offered by the carrier at that time. That conversion option must be exercised within 31 days of coverage, which normally coincides with termination of employment. It is not uncommon for group insurers to limit the amount that can be converted to a maximum sum; $200,000 for example.

Another variation of the conversion privilege is that if the plan itself is terminated by the employer or plan owner, the life insurance component can be converted by employees/plan members who have been on the plan for 5 years.

A recent development with conversion options is that some plans now allow for conversion of the long term disability and others allow for the conversion of the health and dental plans. That would be dependent entirely on the options and structure established by each carrier. In those cases where one is converting the long term disability, all that would have to be proven would be income.

Currently, group life insurance comes in the form of yearly renewable term insurance.  The rate is based on a per thousand basis and is calculated based on a blending of all ages.  The insurance company would establish a rate for each 5 year age band; ie. 20-24; 25-29; 30-34; 35-39 right up to 60-64.  The average would then be set for all plan members. Larger groups with enough people in the plan might have different rates for each age band but some smaller groups would use the same cost per thousand for all plan members.  It would seem from this practice that the younger people on the plan would be paying a higher premium than what they would pay if they purchased individual coverage. This might be true, but the reality is that most of the group plan members in the 18 to 25 age range would not have likely have any coverage other than what they would get on a group plan. The older people, aged 55 plus, would benefit from this blending process as they would likely pay less per thousand for group coverage than they would if they were paying for individual coverage.  The other issue is that if the group size is big enough, there would be no underwriting required thus allowing people to obtain coverage where otherwise they might be unable to do so.  As agents become more skilled in this area, they spend much time talking with plan owners about cost containment.  Ideally to have a plan become very cost effective there must be the right mix of younger and older employees or plan members.

Note that with most groups, life insurance benefits would drop to 50% at age 65, terminating at age 70.  In the contemporary workplace there is a movement away from mandatory age 65 retirement, therefore group plan structures are being adjusted to keep up with societal changes.

In some cases it may be that group plans offer lifetime benefits for retired employees. Of course that would only include life, dependent life and health and dental coverage. If the life insurance is offered for retired employees, then it is likely that the coverage offered will be some form of paid-up permanent insurance. That is likely the only time that permanent insurance will exist with group insurance.

In Module 8, we learned about calculating the correct amount of insurance. In that process we learned about immediate and ongoing needs. Forcing people to make significant investment decisions during the period immediately after death may not be in the beneficiary's best interests. Therefore an option, though rarely used, with group life insurance is to have the proceeds paid out as part of a survivor income plan. Take, for example, the 36 year old employee earning $75,000 per year with a benefit package that offers 2 times annual income. Upon his death his beneficiary would receive a tax-free death benefit of $150,000. It might be better to have that amount paid out over 2 years in equal monthly installments. That would certainly allow the survivors to get comfortably through the re-adjustment period without the financial stress that comes from the death of a loved one.

Group life insurance carries a waiver of premium benefit that allows for the premium for the life insurance benefit to be paid should the employee meet the definition of disability as outlined in the master contract. The benefit would commence once the claim for Long Term Disability was approved. The waiver of premium would cease at the end of the benefit period or at age 65 or when the recipient recovered and returned to work. The waiver of premium portion is not convertible into individual coverage.

## DEPENDENT LIFE

Most plans also include dependent life coverage. This would cover the legally-married spouse; common-law partner or same-sex partner for a basic amount of life insurance. The amount is usually quite low, in the range of $10,000 to $20,000 but in some case perhaps as high as $50,000. Unmarried children up to age 21 or 25 if full-time students would be covered for half the spousal amount. There is usually no conversion option with the dependent life coverage. This insurance is always in the form of yearly renewable term.

## ACCIDENTAL DEATH AND DISMEMBERMENT

Almost all group insurance plans include accidental death & dismemberment. AD&D benefits within group plans work in a manner virtually identical to what we saw in Modules 9 and 10. This is a very inexpensive benefit to include in a group plan. Many group plans feature a basic amount of AD&D coverage for all members, and then optional amounts if the plan members so choose. Of course, if members choose optional benefits, they are expected to bear the whole cost of those optional benefits.

## GROUP DISABILITY

Most employers who have group insurance include some disability benefits. Group disability benefits are normally broken into short term and long term benefits. Short term is typically described as covering a period of disability of less than 2 years. Group insurance plans most often include both short term disability (STD) - otherwise known as Weekly Indemnity (WI) - and long term disability (LTD). In some cases it may be that the employer chooses to offer either one or the other.

In addition to a disability income benefit, group insurance contracts normally include a disability waiver of premium. This allows benefits such as life insurance, critical illness, and health and dental insurance to continue through the period of an employee's disability, without a requirement for premiums to be paid. Disability waiver of premium does not apply during an employee's parental or maternity leave. These special circumstances must be dealt with by the employer's own internal policies, and often require the assistance of a human resources professional, or possibly an employment or labour lawyer.

## SHORT TERM DISABILITY

Also known as Weekly Income or Weekly Indemnity, short term disability is in place to cover those absences from work due to illness or injury that would not be considered long term. The risk of loss of income, although still financially devastating to most families, would not be as great as someone suffering a long term or permanent disability.

It should be noted that in the process of underwriting and insuring income replacement it is important to note that it is not beneficial to individuals, families, employers and society in general to create scenarios where one could profit financially from being on disability. The loss of income is considered a pure risk and as we learned in Module 1, one cannot profit from a pure risk. This becomes a guiding principle in the world of insuring against the three predictable risks.

As with all forms of disability insurance there is a waiting period, otherwise known as the elimination period. That period is typically 0 days for disabilities resulting in hospitalization, usually requiring an overnight stay in a recognized medical facility. Most plans also have an 8$^{th}$ day sickness benefit so that disabilities resulting from sickness require one to be away from work for 7 full days before benefits begin. This would help to reduce the number of claims for people who are off work due to a cold or the flu. An illness would have to be quite severe to require someone to be off work for more than 7 days. The risk of insuring those shorter periods of absence from work is shifted back to the employer through a relatively standard practice of granting 1.25 days per month of paid sick leave to employees. This is very common with large employers.

After the elimination period ends and the claim has been approved based on providing a doctor's report, usually obtained from the claimant's personal physician, benefits are paid based on a percentage of regular weekly earnings.  This is exclusive of overtime and bonuses. That percentage is typically 66.67% or 75% of the regular weekly earnings.  The benefit period could be 13 weeks, 15 weeks, 17 weeks, 26 weeks, 52 weeks and in some cases an employer will offer a two-year benefit period for the STD portion of the plan.  The elimination period for STD benefits is normally very short, usually less than two weeks, and often as short as one day.

The most common benefit period is 17 weeks.  One reason for this choice is that it allows for the employer to apply for a reduction on the amounts paid to Employment Insurance by the employer on behalf of the employees.  In some cases employers choose not to offer short term disability benefits and simply rely on their employees to utilize the EI disability benefits to cover their short term loss of income.  Recall from Module 7 that EI offers an income benefit after a 14-day waiting period.  Note that for every dollar that is deducted from an employee's pay through payroll deduction and submitted to EI, the employer submits $1.40.  Under the EI Premium Reduction Plan an employer who offers short-term disability benefits that exceed what EI sickness benefit would provide can apply to have the EI premiums reduced.  The amount of the reduction varies, but it is normally about an 8-10% reduction off the employer's EI premiums.  While this might not seem like a lot, on a plan of 50 lives it could result in a savings of about $7,000 per year.  Of that savings, 5/12 must be refunded in some manner back to the employee. That could be achieved through enhanced benefits, cash payments, or to fund some sort of employee function.  In order to be a qualified wage loss replacement plan the benefit period cannot be less than 15 weeks, the elimination period cannot be more than 14 days and the minimum benefit cannot be less than the EI minimum currently in place.

The definition of disability used for short term disability is "Own Occupation". That is if the insured employee was unable to perform the important or normal duties of his or her own occupation based on a doctor's certificate, the employee would be eligible to receive benefits. Group insurance is usually own occupation for the first 2 years of the disability and then switches to any occupation thereafter.  The adjudication of own occupation group claims requires the insurer to use sound reasoning to determine the person's ability to perform other duties.  It would be unreasonable to force a company executive or business owner to take a job in a call centre because their education, training or experience qualified them to do so.

Group insurance also uses the process of subrogation.  In its simplest form subrogation is the right of the insurer to recover the losses paid out on a claim from the at-fault party.  An example of this is someone visiting a relative for dinner on a Sunday afternoon and upon leaving late in the day, the person slips on the icy steps and badly injures their back.  That person might require extensive medical treatment and perhaps even be off work for an extended period of time.  That person, if employed with a company that offered disability would receive benefits based on the inability to go to work because of accidental injury. Subrogation is the legal process that allows the insurer paying those benefits to recover those costs from the homeowner with the icy steps.  Even if that homeowner was a close family member the process cannot be stopped because it is fundamental to the process of insuring risk and written into the master contract.  Reference to this clause also appears in the employee's group benefit handbook.

## LONG TERM DISABILITY

If the insured employee is still disabled at the end of the short term disability, and if the employer offers a long term disability benefit, the employee would then apply for that benefit.  If the claim was approved that employee would receive a benefit equal to 66 ⅔ of their regular monthly income, not including overtime and bonuses.  A small proportion of plans pay a 75% disability benefit.  Many LTD plans carry a rehabilitation or partial disability clause which allows the insurer to financially assist the injured employee to re-train for work that is more suitable to the person's new reality. With partial disability, the employee might be expected to return to their job on a reduced basis or be integrated back into the place of employment into a lesser paying, perhaps less demanding job.  A good example of this might be someone working in a car dealership as a mechanic and suffering a disability that left her/him with a partially paralyzed arm, limiting its use.  That person could be rehabilitated to perhaps learn how to do administrative duties within the dealership.  If that new job paid less, under the partial disability clause, the LTD benefit would top-up to the benefit amount as entitled to under the benefit schedule for the duration of disability as defined by the benefit period.

We learned in Module 7 that the Government of Canada offers basic disability to all working Canadians between the ages of 18 to 65 through the Canada Pension Plan disability benefit.  A person would be required to apply for that benefit at the same time as applying for the LTD benefit and if approved the group plan would offset the amount it paid to the injured or sick employee by what that person was entitled to receive from the CPP disability.

The benefit period for LTD is typically 2 years, 5 years or to age 65. There are rare plans with a 10 year benefit period. Some also offer benefits to employees over 65 but under 70 of 50% of what their normal coverage would have been. Plans are generally designed so that a disabled employee would go straight from the STD portion of the plan to an LTD claim with no gap in between.

## DISABILITY EXCLUSIONS AND LIMITATIONS

For both LTD and STD, an employee must be under the care of a physician. Benefits will not be paid if one refuses to participate in a rehabilitation or partial disability program. Other common exclusions to group disability include:

- Attempted suicide or self-inflicted injury;
- Service in the armed forces;
- Committing or attempting to commit a criminal offense;
- Injuries resulting from an accident while impaired;
- Flying in a non-scheduled aircraft, either commercial or private as a crew member or pilot; and
- When housed in a jail or correctional institute.

One of the great advantages of all group benefits is the lack of underwriting.  Plan members can join a plan and know with certainty that they will be covered despite any pre-existing conditions or other factors that would be a concern in individual insurance.  With group LTD, though, there is normally a specific exclusion for pre-existing conditions.  This exclusion only applies to LTD, and it normally indicates that for the member to receive LTD benefits, the member cannot have received treatment in the 90 days prior to the start of coverage if the LTD claim starts in the first year after the member joined the plan.  So a diabetic who receives regular treatments and has a disability claim resulting from diabetes 6 months after joining the plan will have his claim denied.  If the claim didn't arise for a year and half, though, the claim could not be denied based on it being a pre-existing condition.  If the diabetic became disabled in an automobile crash not related to his diabetes 6 months after joining the plan, that claim also could not be denied based on a pre-existing condition.

## HEALTH AND DENTAL

Most group plans include health and dental benefits.  Many employees regard this as the most valuable component of a group plan.  This perception is common because employees will use this portion of the plan regularly, while many employees will never have an LTD claim and very few will have a life insurance claim.

Health and dental plans within group insurance work exactly as described in Module 10.  Cost sharing measures (deductibles, co-insurance, and plan maximums) become even more important with group insurance, where the employer will often look for ways to keep premiums manageable.

## EMPLOYEE ASSISTANCE PROGRAMS

A very new innovation within group insurance is the offering of Employee Assistance Programs (EAPs).  EAPs take a more preventative approach to the well-being of employees than other group benefits.  EAPs are not really an insurance benefit, because they do not provide indemnification for a loss.  Instead, EAPs allow an employee to access a service to deal with a problem before it affects the employee's performance or family life.  EAPs are included with many group plans today, and the cost is still quite low.  The low cost is attributed largely to employees not utilizing available services to the extent that they could.

EAP services are accessed anonymously in most cases.  The employee recognizes a need and calls a referral service, who locates the appropriate service for the employee.  As with other sorts of group benefits, this information is kept confidential from the employer.  The employer will find out that an employee accessed a service, but they will not know which employee accessed which particular service.  A reverse EAP allows the employer to have discretion as to when employees can access the EAP.

Services commonly offered by EAPs include:

- Crisis counselling;
- Psychological and social counselling;
- Financial counselling;
- Elder care information;
- Legal advice;
- Teen/Parent hotlines; and
- Childcare information.

# TAXATION OF GROUP INSURANCE

The taxation of group insurance can be quite complex, but there are some basic principles that we need to be aware of. We will look at taxation as it applies to each type of benefit:

- **Life Insurance Benefits**. If the employer pays the premiums, the employee will be assessed a taxable benefit (see Module 5) based on the amount of premium paid. Any death benefits paid would then be tax-free. In this case, the employer would deduct the premium payments as a business expense. If the employee pays the premiums, there is no tax deduction, no taxable benefit, and death benefits would be paid tax-free.

- **Critical Illness Benefits.** These are treated exactly the same way as life insurance for tax purposes.

- **Accidental Death & Dismemberment Benefits**. These are treated exactly the same way as life insurance for tax purposes.

- **Health and Dental Benefits**. If the employer pays the premiums, the employer will receive a tax deduction. The employee will not be assessed a taxable benefit. Any benefits received will be tax-free to the plan member. If the employee pays the premiums, then there is no tax deduction, and benefits will be tax-free. It is clearly more advantageous for the employer to pay the premiums, because it allows the employer to deduct the cost while the employee receives a tax-free benefit.

- **Disability Benefits**. If the employer pays the premiums, those premiums are deductible for the employer. The employee will not be assessed a taxable benefit. However, if the employee ends up disabled and collecting disability income, that disability income will be taxed. This is not ideal, given that disability income normally represents only 66.67% of regular income. As a result, when structuring plans, it is common to recommend to employers who plan to pay this benefit that they offer a 75% disability benefit instead of the usual 66.67%.

If the employee pays the premiums, then any disability benefits will be tax free. The premium payments are not deductible for the employee. Smaller companies will normally structure their benefits so that the employer pays the life insurance and health and dental portions of the plan, while the employee pays the disability portions. Larger companies sometimes need more tax deductions, and might pay the costs of all benefits themselves (ie. a non-contributory plan).

When employers set up group plans, they are sometimes careless about indicating who is paying for what component of a contributory plan. This can result in an employee unexpectedly being informed that their disability income benefit is taxable. For this reason, agents should work with their group clients and their accountants to make sure that group benefits are taxed in the most efficient manner possible, and that this is all documented.

## SUMMARY

A great many Canadians rely on their group insurance benefits for much of their risk management. Whether or not you sell and service group insurance, it is likely that you will end up advising your clients about it to some extent. We have learned the basics of group insurance here. The group insurance market in Canada is a vibrant and dynamic market. It presents opportunities to the agent who understands it.

Now that we have covered group insurance, we will go on to examine, in greater detail, some investment products particular to the insurance industry.

# Chapter 12 INDIVIDUAL VARIABLE INSURANCE CONTRACTS

You may recall from Module 6 that Individual Variable Insurance Contracts (IVICs) are the insurance industry's answer to mutual funds. When IVICs, or segregated funds, were first introduced, they were primarily sold as a vehicle for pension funds to invest in with relatively little risk. Today, though, IVICs are widely sold to individual investors. IVICs go by a variety of names. You will see them offered today as Guaranteed Income Funds (GIFs), Seg Funds, IVICs, and IVACs (Individual Variable Annuity Contracts). A life insurance license is required to sell IVICs.

IVICs differ from other investments in that they offer certain guarantees to investors. These guarantees are associated with the death or maturity of the contract. Investors can use IVICs with peace of mind, knowing that the losses they can suffer will be limited because of the associated guarantees.

Prior to reading this module, it will be worthwhile to go back and re-read Module 6, especially paying attention to the sections dealing with funds, and mutual funds in particular. We will recall that funds, including segregated funds, offer the following advantages for investors:

- Professional Management;
- Diversification;
- Liquidity;
- Small Investments;
- Record Keeping; and
- Flexibility.

In addition, segregated funds share the following characteristics with mutual funds:

- **Net Asset Value**. Although the ownership structure is somewhat different than a mutual fund's, a segregated fund still expresses its value in terms of net asset value per unit. The IVIC still holds a pool of equities, bonds, or money market instruments, depending on the investment objectives of the investors.

- **Open-Ended**. Segregated funds are open-ended. Investors do not have to deal on a secondary market; they simply provide funds for the fund manager to invest, and redeem their investments when they see fit. This is one of the greatest misconceptions that students have when learning IVICs for the first time. Because of the guarantees and maturity dates associated with IVICs, some students believe that this investment has limited liquidity. This is simply not the case. An IVIC is as liquid as a mutual fund. An investor can invest any time and get their funds out anytime, except for very rare suspensions of redemptions. (Another common misconception is that IVICs are insurance. While IVICs have insurance characteristics, they are not life insurance policies in the sense of paying a relatively small premium in exchange for a potentially large death benefit.)

- **Redemptions**. As mentioned in the previous section, the IVIC investor can exercise the right of redemption at any time.

## PARTIES TO THE IVIC

An IVIC differs from a mutual fund in its basic ownership structure. While the end result is very similar, an IVIC investor does not invest directly into a fund. Instead, the IVIC investor enters into a contract which entitles the investor to a share of the ownership of the units in the fund. Because this ownership is not direct, it is referred to as notional ownership. The IVIC investor has their ownership represented as a number of notional units. The notional units represent an investment in a segregated fund. An investor might enter into an IVIC and choose to invest in multiple segregated funds under the same contract. The segregated fund is so named because it is a pool of investments that is separate (or segregated) from the general assets of the insurer. Because of this requirement to separate the segregated fund assets from their general assets, insurers must maintain at least $10,000,000 in unencumbered capital in order to start into the business of offering IVICs. While we have dealt briefly with the investor and the insurer, there are actually as many as four parties involved in an Individual Variable Investment Contract:

- **Contract Holder**. The contract holder, or policy owner, is the party we have so far identified as the investor. This is the party (normally a person, though it can be a corporation) who chooses to invest. It is this person's objectives, risk tolerance, and investment knowledge that we will take into account when selling the IVIC. It is common to name a successor owner to a seg fund contract, in case the owner dies while the annuitant is still alive.

- **Annuitant**. The annuitant is roughly the equivalent of the life insured in a life insurance contract. When we deal with the death benefit guarantee, it is the annuitant's life that we are concerned with. In the case of an IVIC held within a registered plan (RRSP) the annuitant and contract holder must be the same person. In a non-registered plan, it is possible to name multiple annuitants; this is often done for spouses.

- **Beneficiary**. The beneficiary is the party named by the contract holder who will receive the death benefit on death of the annuitant. The death benefit of an IVIC is based on the amount invested. It is paid out free from probate and creditor protected, in a manner similar to life insurance death benefits. Unlike a life insurance death benefit, it is not tax-free. Instead, the policy owner (or the policy owner's estate) must pay tax based on a disposition of the IVIC. The beneficiary, as with life insurance contracts, is not actually a party to the contract. Instead, they are named within the contract, possibly without their knowledge.

- **Insurer**. The insurer is the party offering the IVIC. The insurer's responsibility is to coordinate the relationship between the fund manager, the agent, and the client. The insurer must provide disclosure to the client in the form of an information folder, which we will discuss in more detail later on in this module.

# GUARANTEES

Probably the feature of IVICs that most sets them apart from other investments is their range of guarantees. Contract holders can be assured of, at the very least, a minimum return of their invested principal. The investor has exposure to bonds, equities, or whichever investments she chooses, but has the security of knowing that even if those investments do very poorly, a portion of the original investment is safe. The guarantees are normally based on 75%, 90%, or 100% of the invested amount. 75% is the minimum allowed for an IVIC. The guarantees are based either of two circumstances. The guarantees need not be the same. Some contracts might, for example, feature a 75/100 guarantee, meaning 75% in the event of maturity and 100% in the event of death. All IVICs must offer death benefit and maturity guarantees. We will examine here how these guarantees work:

- **Death Benefit**. If the annuitant dies and the market value of the fund is less than the guaranteed amount, the beneficiary will receive the guaranteed amount. If, when the annuitant dies, the market value is more than the guaranteed amount, the beneficiary will receive the market value. The death benefit guarantee only has an impact when the annuitant dies while the investment is at less than the guaranteed amount. We will look at three scenarios:

  - **Annuitant dies when market is down**. Our contract owner has invested $1000 into an IVIC with a 75% death benefit guarantee. The investment falls to $600. This is less than the guarantee of ($1000 x 75% =) $750. The beneficiary will receive $750. Of the $750, $600 is paid from the original investment, while the remaining $150 must be made up by the insurer. We could say, then, that the guarantee had a value of $150 in this case. This amount is free from probate and is creditor protected. The $150 is taxed in the hands of the contract owner as a capital gain.

  - **Annuitant dies when market is slightly down**. Our contract owner has invested the same $1000 as in the previous scenario, with the same guarantees. The investment falls to $900. This is more than the guarantee of $750. The beneficiary receives the market value of $900. In this case, the guarantee is not invoked. Any tax consequences would flow to the contract owner.

  - **Annuitant dies when market is up**. Again using the same information, our annuitant dies when the investment has grown to $1200. The $1200 is paid to the beneficiary as a death benefit. Any tax consequences would flow to the contract owner.

- **Maturity Guarantee**. The maturity date is the date at which the contract will pay its value to the annuitant if the annuitant has not died and a death benefit already been paid. If the annuitant dies prior to maturity, the death benefit is paid to the beneficiary and the contract ends. In order to understand the maturity guarantee, we must understand the maturity date for the contract. IVICs will have a maturity date when issued. The maturity date will be at least 10 years from the date the Contract Date (the date the policy owner entered into the contract). In many cases maturity will be much longer than that, possibly the annuitant's 65th, 69th, or 71st birthday, for example. In some cases, the amount will be paid as a lump sum, but many IVICs allow for the market value to be paid as an annuity, which we will discuss in Module 13. The Information Folder for the IVIC in question will indicate how long maturity is and what happens at maturity.

As discussed in Module 6, the IVIC investor has the opportunity to make either regular investments or to add lump sum deposits into the contract. Additional deposits to an IVIC can change the maturity date. There are two different ways that an additional deposit can move the maturity date, and it depends on the contract that was entered into. The Information Folder will indicate which of the methods the insurer will use:

o   **Policy Based Guarantees**. A policy based guarantee treats the whole policy as one entity for the purpose of determining the maturity date. Any additional deposits made to the contract will affect the maturity date of the entire contract. In a policy based guarantee, the maturity date will always be December 31st of the year of maturity. Policy based guarantees are often used where clients are going to be paying regular amounts into their contract. In practice, a policy based guarantee (assuming a 10 year maturity) might look like so:

| Action | Date of Action | Result of Action | New Maturity Date |
|---|---|---|---|
| Client invests $100 | April 30, 2010 | Maturity Date is 10 years later | Dec 31, 2020 |
| Client invests $25 | Jan 31, 2011 | Maturity Date is pushed back; old maturity date is now lost | Dec 31, 2021 |
| Client invests $25 | Feb 28, 2011 | Maturity date is not affected | Dec 31, 2021 |
| Client invests $25 | Jan 31, 2012 | Maturity date is pushed back; old maturity date is now lost | Dec 31, 2022 |
| Client invests $25 | Feb 28, 2012 | Maturity date is not affected | Dec 31, 2022 |

A policy based maturity guarantee is easy to administer, and makes the most sense for a client making regular investments. In the situation above, the client would likely not want a series of $25 deposits maturing one at a time 10 years after each deposit is made.

o   **Deposit Based Guarantees**. Deposit based guarantees treat each deposit as its own entity for the purpose of calculating maturity. With a deposit based guarantee, the maturity date will be 10 years after the date the actual deposit was made. Each deposit will retain its own maturity date. Deposit based guarantees are more often used when a client is making lump sum deposits.

| Action | Date of Action | Result of Action | Maturity Date |
|---|---|---|---|
| Client invests $1000 | April 30, 2010 | $1000 deposit matures 10 years later | Apr 30, 2020 |
| Client invests $1500 | Feb 28, 2011 | $1500 deposit matures 10 years later; Apr 30, 2010 deposit is not affected | Feb 28, 2021 |
| Client invests $1200 | Jan 15, 2012 | $1200 deposit matures 10 years later; Previous deposits are not affected | Jan 15, 2022 |

- **Resets**. In addition to offering valuable guarantees, many IVICs allow an investor to reset their guarantees. Resets allow the investor to lock in gains, increasing guarantees based on growth in the investment. Not all insurers offer resets. Some insurers provide automatic resets; some insurers allow resets upon request; some insurers would have their client pay a fee to use the reset feature. When the reset feature is used, the guarantees (death benefit and maturity) are recalculated based on the current value of the investment. At the same time, the maturity date is reset. Let's look at an IVIC with an initial deposit of $1000, no further deposits, death benefit and maturity guarantees of 75%, and a 10 year maturity date using a deposit based guarantee:

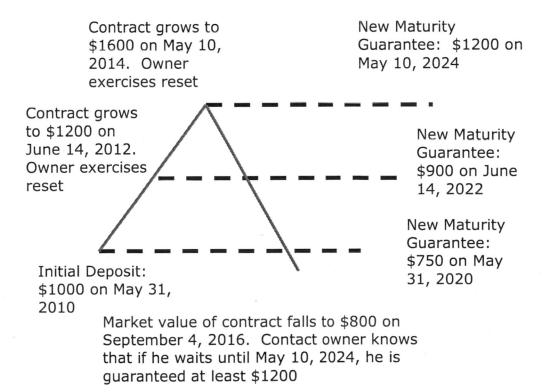

Contract grows to $1600 on May 10, 2014. Owner exercises reset

New Maturity Guarantee: $1200 on May 10, 2024

Contract grows to $1200 on June 14, 2012. Owner exercises reset

New Maturity Guarantee: $900 on June 14, 2022

New Maturity Guarantee: $750 on May 31, 2020

Initial Deposit: $1000 on May 31, 2010

Market value of contract falls to $800 on September 4, 2016. Contact owner knows that if he waits until May 10, 2024, he is guaranteed at least $1200

# WITHDRAWALS AND UNIT VALUES

In order to understand withdrawals, we must have an understanding of the unit values of the fund. In a manner similar to mutual funds, the total assets of the segregated fund are added up. The unit holders have their ownership represented in the form of notional units. When an investor acquires new units of the fund, those new units are purchased at the current net asset value per unit. Redemptions are done at the same price. An investor who invested when the net asset value per unit was $100 and redeemed when the net asset value per unit was $110 has made a positive return.

When the fund manager has cash in the fund to reinvest (from the proceeds of dividends, interest payments, or capital gains) those reinvestments are done in the form of an allocation. With an allocation, the fund manager simply allocates the cash back into the fund. Through this process, the IVIC investor is exposed to compound growth; she knows that the fund's future growth will be amplified by the effects of past growth.

As previously mentioned, the contract holder can choose to withdraw funds at any time. The value of the withdrawal is simply the number of units withdrawn times the notional value of those units. There may be surrender charges, as we will see later on in this module.

The decision to withdraw funds does have consequences. We already know that the guaranteed values are based on the original amount invested (or on a reset, if one has been used). If a client decides to withdraw funds at some point, this is going to have a negative impact on the guarantees. There are two ways that a reduction in the guarantee can be calculated. Again, the exact handling of the reduction will be discussed in the Information Folder. Let's assume that we have a segregated fund with guarantees of 75% on maturity and death, an initial investment of $1000, a deposit-based guarantee, the investment has grown to $1200, and no resets have been exercised:

- **Linear Reduction Method.** In the linear reduction method, the guarantees will be reduced based on the dollar amount withdrawn. Let's look at a linear reduction in practice, using a withdrawal of $200. We can see from the figures provided above that this fund will have guarantees of $750 in the event of death or maturity. If the client withdraws $200, the guarantees will be impacted as follows:

| Original Guarantee | Withdrawal | New Guarantee |
|---|---|---|
| $1000 | - $200 | $800 |
| x 75% | | x 75% |
| $750 | | $600 |

Using the linear reduction method simply means we are applying a dollar for dollar reduction to the amount used to determine the guarantees.

- **Proportional Reduction Method**. The proportional reduction method will use a percentage reduction to the amount used to determine the guarantees. Using the same figures as in the last example, the proportional reduction method would work like so:

| Original Guarantee | Withdrawal | Withdrawal Proportion (based on current market value) | New Guarantee (Step 1) | New Guarantee (Step 2) |
|---|---|---|---|---|
| $1000 | $200 | $200 | $1000 | $833.33 |
| x 75% | | ÷ $1200 | - 16.67% | x 75% |
| $750 | | 16.67% of value was withdrawn | $833.33 | $624.98 |

When the market value of the investments has increased, the proportional reduction method is more favourable. However, when the market value has decreased, the linear reduction method is more favourable. Note that in both examples, the actual value remaining in the fund after withdrawal will be ($1200 - $200 =) $1000. The examples show the guaranteed values as a consequence of these withdrawals. If the contract holder had resets available, she could exercise them at this point and the guarantees would then be ($1000 x 75% =) $750.

# FEES AND CHARGES

Nobody is in this business for free. The fund manager, insurance company, and agent all need to get paid. In order to facilitate payment to all the parties involves, there are two sets of costs. One is sales charges, which are paid by the client to the agent (although indirectly, as the amounts will flow from client to insurer and back to the agent) and the other is an annual management fee, which will be taken directly from the fund. The management fee is designed to compensate all those involved in the management of the fund and cover the costs of operating the fund. These fees work the same way for mutual funds as they do for IVICs. We will look at these two sets of charges:

- **Sales Charges**. Sales charges vary from fund to fund and agent to agent. At one time, every agent charged these the same way, as a front-end load. Over time, the industry evolved, and agents started using more deferred sales charges. Today, there are a number of ways that agents charge sales charges. We will look at the four most common, broken into two categories:

  - **Acquisition Charges**. An acquisition charge is a sales charge applied when the client makes their purchase. There are two types of acquisition charges:

    - **Front Load**. Front load sales charges vary, but they are normally around 2-3% of the value invested. This can be negotiated between agent and client. A client who invests $1000 with an agent who charges a 3% front load (also called a front-end load) will actually have ($1000 x 3%) = $30 paid directly to the agent, meaning that only $970 will actually flow to the fund. Front load charges are often used when the agent is helping the client to invest in a non-registered investment.

- **No Load**. A no load transaction sees the client charge no sales charge at all. There will not be any costs at the back end, and there are none at the front end. The client who writes a cheque for $1000 will actually see the whole $1000 invested. No load investments are sometimes offered to clients who have very large amounts to invest, or who have short-term objectives where it would not be practical to pay a sales charge because it would actually become more difficult to meet that short-term objective.

- **Redemption Charges**. If the agent does not apply an acquisition charge then a redemption charge will be applied. The redemption charge will see the client pay a sales charge at the point of redemption. Sometimes redemption charges are based on the initial amount invested; sometimes they are based on the current market value. The Information Folder would provide that detail. The two types of redemption charges are:

- **Back Load**. A back load is basically the opposite of a front load. The amount will be negotiated at the point of sale, but will not be applied until the client withdraws funds. Back loads are quite rare today.

- **Deferred Sales Charge**. The deferred sales charge (DSC) would see the client pay a large sales charge if they withdrew funds early, but that sales charge would decrease over time, eventually ending up at zero. The idea here is that the agent and insurer can be compensated properly if the client invests for the long-term, but short-term investments do not give the agent and insurer time to be compensated, so the client must make this up. A DSC schedule might look like so:

| Years since Contract Date | Sales Charge |
|---|---|
| 1 | 4.5% |
| 2 | 4% |
| 3 | 4% |
| 4 | 3.5% |
| 5 | 3% |
| 6 | 2% |
| 7 and on | 0% |

DSCs tend to be used when clients are investing for the long-term, such as a leveraged investment or a registered investment. Agents must be careful not to apply a DSC in situations where the client might need their money in the first three or four years. A DSC is the most popular sales charge when a client is investing in a registered account.

DSCs are normally waived at death. Also, they are structured to permit minimum withdrawals, such as those required under a registered retirement income fund (RRIF) or life income fund (LIF) – both of which will be discussed in Module 14 – to occur without a DSC being assessed.

- **Management Fees**. Funds will assess a management fee every year. The insurer adds up all the costs associated with operating the fund (paying the fund manager, client servicing, administration, regulatory costs, etc.) and applies those costs to the fund. So a fund with $128,000,000 in assets might have $3,500,000 in operating costs. We would say this fund has a management expense ratio (MER) of ($3,500,000 ÷ $128,000,000 =) 2.7%. IVICs usually (but not always) have an MER that is about .5% higher than a comparable mutual fund. The reason is that the IVIC has more features, and requires more management. MERs tend to be lower for funds that hold primarily fixed income investments (in the .5% to 2% range), and higher for funds that hold primarily equities (2% to 4%, usually).

The MER will directly affect the investment return that the client receives. Continuing with our previously calculated MER of 2.7%, let's imagine our fund manager did a good job investing this year and made a return of 9.8%. The 2.7% MER would reduce that to (9.8% - 2.7% =) 7.1%. The client's return is 7.1%. Any time that a return is disclosed to a client, it is always net of MER (has already taken the MER into account.) It would be deceptive to tell this client that they obtained a 9.8% rate of return. The idea is that the benefits of investing in the fund should outweigh the costs associated with investing.

## TAXATION OF AN IVIC

As with all investments, the IVIC investor is going to have to deal with tax considerations. These considerations do not apply when dealing with IVICs held within registered accounts, which we will examine in Module 14.

There will be certain considerations during the lifetime of the annuitant, and a few extra factors to consider on death. The following are concepts we must deal with as far as taxation of the IVIC:

- **Adjusted Cost Base**. The adjusted cost base for the IVIC is equal to any amounts invested plus any allocations and minus any capital losses. The ACB for the IVIC, as with any property, is important on disposition of the IVIC.

- **Allocations**. On a regular basis, the fund manager will take the gains accumulated in the fund in the form of interest, dividends, and capital gains, and reinvest those back into the fund. The interest, dividends, and capital gains do incur tax, just as we learned in Module 5. It is the investor who must pay the tax accruing within the fund. This is assessed on an annual basis, and the insurer will provide the investor with a T3 statement of investment income which the investor will then file with Canada Revenue Agency. When an allocation is reported and the resulting tax is paid, the investor's ACB is increased. That is, the investor will never again have to pay tax on that same growth. Note that not all gains will generate an allocation. If the fund manager purchases an equity and never sells it, no capital gain is realized. If the investor chooses to redeem while this investment is held, that capital gain will need to be taxed at that time. So funds that have frequent turnovers of their assets will generate a lot of immediate tax consequences for their investors. Funds that use a buy and hold philosophy will subject their investors to more capital gains at the time of disposition. Agents should take their client's circumstances into account when selecting the fund in which to invest.

- **Capital Losses.** An advantage that IVIC investors have that mutual fund investors do not is that in a year when the fund experiences a loss, the IVIC investor will receive a T3 showing a capital loss. As mentioned in Module 5, the IVIC investor could use that capital loss to offset the effects of any capital gains in the previous three years, or going forward indefinitely. The IVIC's ACB would be decreased based on this capital loss.

- **Disposition.** The disposition of an IVIC occurs either when a redemption is made; on death of the last annuitant; or, in some cases, on maturity. On disposition, any amounts that have not been taxed (anything over the ACB) will be taxed. Sales charges or redemption charges would reduce the amount of tax as well. The gains on the IVIC will be taxed as capital gains. Partial redemptions will be taxed proportionally, based on the percentage of the fund withdrawn. We will look at an example of a partial surrender (or partial withdrawal, or partial redemption) of a segregated fund. Assume that the investor originally invested $1000 (we will consider this the ACB) and that the market value of the fund has grown to $1200. The investor withdraws $200 and there are no sales charges applicable:

| Percentage of Value Withdrawn | Tax Payable on Total Surrender | Partial Surrender |
|---|---|---|
| $200 | $1200 | $200 (consequences of total surrender) |
| ÷ $1200 | - $1000 | x 16.67 % (Proportion withdrawn) |
| 16.67% | $200 | $33.33 |
| | Taxed as a capital gain | Taxed as a capital gain. |

- **Taxation on Death.** On death of the annuitant or maturity of the contract, the contract owner will be considered to have disposed of the IVIC. The contract owner will have to deal with whatever capital gains or losses have been generated. Note that the contract owner may not be the one to receive the death benefit or annuity payment. For this reason, the agent must be careful when helping the contract owner to determine who the parties involved in the contract will be.

If a death benefit guarantee is required to be paid, this can be quite complicated. This would, of course, only be required if the market value were less than the guarantee value. If this is the case, then we must keep in mind that, throughout the term of the contract there would have been capital losses claimed by the contract owner. As these capital losses were claimed, the ACB of the contract would have been reduced. Therefore, at the time of death, the ACB of the contract would be roughly equal to the market value of the contract.

A death benefit guarantee would, then, be over the ACB of the contract. This would mean that the death benefit guarantee would be taxable. While the Income Tax Act and Canada Revenue Agency are not clear on the tax treatment of this death benefit guarantee, it is usually considered to be a capital gain in the hands of the deceased.

- **Probate**. While probate is not necessarily a tax, it is worth a reminder here that IVICs are not considered part of the estate of the deceased, and will not attract probate fees. Of course, if there is no beneficiary named, or the estate is named as beneficiary, then the IVIC would attract probate.

## LIFETIME INCOME PRODUCTS

A recent innovation in the IVIC market has been the introduction of a guaranteed income component to accompany the death benefit and maturity guarantees already included in IVICs. These products are marketed under a variety of names, including Guaranteed Minimum Withdrawal Benefit (GMWB), Guaranteed Income Funds (GIF), Individual Variable Annuity Contracts (IVAC), Guaranteed Lifetime Withdrawal Benefit (GLWB), and "For Life" products. While there are some differences from product to product, they are similar enough to deal with as one entity here.

Despite the similarities that these products share, they are very complex, and they require due diligence by the agent prior to the agent selling them. Any product requires that the agent know their product prior to selling it, but these products in particular require an eye for detail.

The basic concept here is that the client invests in a segregated fund (IVIC), just as we have seen through the rest of this module. However, at some point, the client chooses to start guaranteed withdrawals out of their segregated fund. All the concepts we have previously seen, such as the guarantees, the parties to the contract, and the taxation of the IVIC, would still apply to this product. The differences and additional features are as follows:

- **Guaranteed Growth.** Normally these products feature a period of guaranteed growth. The guaranteed growth is normally based on simple interest rather than compound interest, and might be in the range of 5%. This means that, during the period when the contract owner has not yet chosen to take income, if the underlying investments perform poorly, there will still be an increase in the value on which the income benefit will be based. So a client who invests $100,000 in a fund with a 5% guarantee over a 15 year period knows that, in the worst case, their income benefit will be based on ($100,000 x 15 x 5% =) $75,000 of growth, for a total value of ($100,000 + $75,000 =) $175,000. The hope is that the value exceeds that, based on the performance of the underlying investments. If that does not happen, though, there is some security in the fact that the income phase will be based on a $175,000 calculation, rather than whatever the actual value of the investments is. Note, however, that this is not growth in the value of the investments. Only the basis for calculating the guaranteed income actually grows at a guaranteed pace. It would be possible for the segregated fund in this example to have a much lower market value than $175,000.

- **Guaranteed Income.** The income guarantee provides that, when the contract owner chooses it, a stream of payments based on the greater of the market value, or the guarantee discussed in the previous section, will begin. Some insurers provide this stream for a minimum of 15 years; some provide it for the life of the annuitant. The income guarantee is normally based on 5% of the higher value. So in the example described in the previous section, if the investments had not done well, then the annuitant would receive an income stream of ($175,000 x 5% =) $8,570 for at least 15 years, and possibly the rest of his life.

Conversely, if the investments had done well, and the market value was, for example, $210,000, then that would provide the basis for calculating the guaranteed income. This would result in ($210,000 x 5% =) $10,500 of annual income. Of course, this income might not necessarily be paid annually. The policy owner may be allowed to opt for monthly payments instead.

Once the segregated fund is in the income phase, it is still theoretically possible for the net value of the fund to continue to increase. The funds are still invested. If the growth in the fund is greater than the combination of the management fees and the withdrawals, then the fund would increase in value. If the fund decreases in value, then the income amount does not change during the guarantee period.

With funds that offer the guaranteed income only for a number of years, rather than for lifetime, it becomes possible for the fund to be depleted after the guarantees expire. This must be considered when deciding at what age to begin the income guaranteed. Contracts do not normally fix this age; they leave it up to the contract owner to decide.

It might seem attractive to opt for this at an early age, such as 55 or 60, but the consequences of doing so can be challenging. There is no inflation protection built into this product, so starting income at an early age will mean inflation can reduce the purchasing power of the income at early age.

When one of these products is held within a registered retirement income fund (RRIF) or life income fund (LIF) the insurer will permit withdrawals according to the required minimum, which is usually greater than 5%. We will discuss these plans in more detail in Module 14.

- **Resets.** The reset feature becomes very useful with these guaranteed income products. During the accumulation phase, the resets allow the contract owner to lock in growth periodically, usually every three years. This resets the maturity and death benefit guarantees as seen earlier in this module. It also resets the basis for the income guarantee.

  Using the earlier example, if $100,000 is invested for three years, we can see that the guaranteed income would be based on a $115,000 value. Using a 5% increase, the income guarantee will continue to grow by $5000 per year. However, if the market value is in excess of $115,000, then a reset can be exercised, and the basis for the guarantees can be increased. So, if the market value is $120,000 when this reset is exercised, then $120,000 becomes the basis for the increases to the guaranteed amounts. From that point on, the basis for the guarantees would be ($120,000 x 5% =) $6000. The guarantee next year would grow by $6000, or if the income phase started, then the income would be $6000 per year, instead of the $5000.

- **Management Fees.** Management fees are an important consideration with these products. As we have already discussed, the management fees for segregated funds result in a management expense ratio that can be as high as 4% per year. The additional management fee for this guaranteed income product is in the range of .5% to 1%, which sometimes brings the management expense ratio into the range of 4 to 4.5%

  While this guaranteed income product can be quite attractive, given its combination of guaranteed income and market growth, the high management fees must be taken into account. This is a classic example of 'you get what you pay for.' This product's combination of income and growth is not seen in other products, and will be very useful for many clients.

- **Liquidity.** These funds are just as liquid as the segregated funds that we have seen earlier in this module. However, there is a factor that must be considered before withdrawals are made. The guaranteed increases to the guaranteed income are calculated assuming that no withdrawals have been made. Depending on the exact nature of the contract, early withdrawals in excess of the guaranteed income usually causes a direct reduction in the basis for the calculation of the guarantees.

  Continuing with our earlier example, if $100,000 is invested in a contract offering a guarantee of 5% per year, and the value grows to $110,000 over the next two years, then a withdrawal of $10,000 would actually result in a reduction of $10,000 to the basis for the guarantees. So, even though there would still be $100,000 in the contract, the basis for the guarantees would now be $90,000.

  For this reason, it is not advisable to have the full amount of a client's investments in funds of this nature. This guaranteed income investment can be very useful in retirement, but some funds should be left in other investments which would not cause losses of this nature if withdrawals are made.

- **Investment Limitations.** Most, but not all, insurers impose some limitations on the types of investments that can be made within the segregated fund. A common type of investment restriction here would be that no more than 70% of the total value invested can be in equities, with the rest being in fixed income or money market investments.

  This restriction varies from insurer to insurer. Because the product is designed to work best based on a combination of growth and income, the restrictive investment choices can reduce its effectiveness. Most people beyond age 50 should probably not have more than 70% of their investments in equity anyways.

This guaranteed income product can be ideal for the segregated fund investor who is looking for guaranteed income, while still being exposed to potential growth in the equity markets. It is generally only available starting at age 50 or later. Some insurers require a minimum period of accumulation prior to starting withdrawals. Many agents describe this product as a self-funded pension plan when they sell it. This is a reasonable approximation; the client puts money away on a regular basis, and will start a guaranteed income phase at some point. Like a pension, it would require regular contributions to build to any kind of meaningful level.

# IVIC REGULATION AND CONSUMER PROTECTION

Several times in this module we have made reference to the Information Folder. While insurers selling segregated funds are regulated by the insurance regulator in the province in which those insurers operate, no regulatory body has passed legislation forcing insurers to create specific disclosure documents. Instead, the Canadian Life and Health Insurance Association has produced guidelines for insurers indicating how an IVIC will be structured and how the structure of the IVIC will be disclosed to the client.

CLHIA guidelines indicate that the client must receive an Information Folder at the time when the IVIC is entered into. In addition, clients must receive a Fund Facts statement with the Information Folder. On an annual basis, the insurer must provide an annual statement that gives the client the opportunity to briefly review the fund's performance and request more specific information, if necessary. Further, all these documents must be made available on the internet. We will examine in more detail what each of the required disclosure documents contains:

- **Information Folder.** The Information Folder is the document that contains most of the technical detail about the structure of the IVIC. Information Folders are generally magazine-size publications of about 100 pages. They can be quite complex. For that reason, it is not sufficient for the agent to simply provide an Information Folder to a client. CLHIA guidelines (and common sense) indicate that the agent must fully explain the IVIC to the client prior to sale. The Information Folder will include:

- **This statement**: "Any amount that is allocated to a segregated fund is invested at the risk of the contract holder and may increase or decrease in value;"
- A description of the guarantees;
- The risks associated with investing in the fund;
- An explanation of how net asset values are calculated;
- Explanations of any fees associated with the fund;
- How often the net asset values are calculated (usually daily, but it can be as rarely as once per month);
- A description of the tax consequences of owning the IVIC, including the taxation of registered plans;
- A promise to notify contract holders of fundamental changes to the fund; and
- An explanation of the Right of Rescission. For IVICs, the Right of Rescission can be as little as two business days.

- **Annual Statement**. The annual statement is intended to keep the investor aware of the performance of, and any changes to, the fund. The annual statement will include the following:

  - A statement as to the current value of the investor's holdings;
  - An explanation of any new allocations;
  - A statement that the contract holder can request audited financial statements for the fund at no cost;
  - A statement indicating that detailed historical performance figures for the fund are available on request; and
  - Information about how to get more information.

- **Fund Facts**. A Fund Facts statement is a short document (3 pages in length) that is designed to give a snapshot of the fund. The Fund Facts statement is to be provided to the client at the same time as the Information Folder, and is available on request. The Fund Facts statement will include a great deal of useful information, including:

  - Net Asset Value per Unit;
  - Management Expense Ratio;
  - Top 10 holdings;
  - Portfolio manager;
  - Portfolio turnover;
  - Historical performance figures;
  - The degree of risk to the investor;
  - A brief explanation of guarantees;
  - Who the target market is;
  - The cost of investing; and
  - An explanation of the Right of Rescission.

All this information is provided in order to allow investors to make an informed decision. The insurance industry does not want investors making ill-informed decisions, as this can cause challenges later on for agents, insurers, and, most of all, the client themselves.

In addition to the protection afforded to clients through the disclosure documents, the insurance industry also provides protection through Assuris, as discussed in Module 3. Assuris protection is quite favourable when compared to the protection afforded other investments:

| Investment Product | Protection Provided by: | What is protected: | Event that will trigger protection: | Upper Limit of Protection |
|---|---|---|---|---|
| Banking Products (GICs, Savings Accounts) | Canada Deposit Insurance Corporation (CDIC) | Up to $100,000 per type of account per institution (Registered accounts, joint accounts, and non-registered accounts are all protected separately.) | Failure of a Chartered Bank | $100,000 per type of account (2 GICs at the same bank would be limited to $100,000) |
| Mutual Funds | Mutual Fund Dealers' Association (MFDA) Investor Protection Corporation (IPC) | Up to $1,000,000 of investments | Failure of an investment dealer | $1,000,000 |
| IVICs | Assuris | 100% protection up to $60,000; 85% protection if the amount protected exceeds $60,000. Protection is based on death benefit or maturity guarantee. | Failure of insurer | None |

# CREDITOR PROTECTION

In addition to all that we have already discussed concerning the IVIC, it is important to remember that the IVIC, as an insurance product, features creditor protection. During the lifetime of the contract holder, if the beneficiary is a parent, spouse, child, grandchild, or is irrevocable, then the value of the contract will be protected from the claims of creditors. On death, the death benefit is paid to the named beneficiary without creditors of the deceased being able to access it, or even knowing about it. If the estate is named as beneficiary then the death benefit attracts probate and can be claimed by creditors. We must exercise some caution when promising creditor protection, because if the courts suspect that a client has deliberately used instruments such as IVICs to hide money from prospective creditors then the courts might overturn the creditor protection. Normally there is no creditor protection in the first year after an investment is made. Within the four years after that, the courts will exercise their own discretion.

# SELLING THE IVIC

Now that we have learned the mechanics of the IVIC, there are a few details to cover concerning sales practices:

- **Net Asset Value**. When selling an IVIC, the agent may, from time to time, be asked what the Net Asset Value Per Unit is. Keep in mind that the Net Asset Value Per Unit (NAVPU) is based on the total value of all holdings of the fund divided by the number of units. Most funds calculate this value daily, at the close of the trading day. The investor will never be allowed to invest at a known price; this is called backward pricing, and it is an illegal practice. Instead, any new amounts invested will be used to purchase units at the next day's reported closing price. While this practice might seem questionable at first glance, it actually works to protect existing investors in the fund from manipulation by new investors. In reality, this is seldom a concern. Most investors are investing for the long term, and are not overly concerned with the day-to-day fluctuations in price that are normal with funds.

- **Past Performance**. Insurers are responsible to disclose past performance of funds. Performance figures will normally reflect 1, 3, 5, and 10 year returns. Recall that these returns will be reported net of MERs, so the figures will show the returns that a client actually would have received. It is vital to recognize that Past Performance is not a Guarantee of Future Results. Just because a fund has attained an average annual return of 8% over the past 10 years, that does not in any way guarantee that the fund will perform as such going forward. As previously discussed, when preparing illustrations, the agent must use a realistic rate of return and a worst-case rate of return.

Armed with a good understanding of the IVIC, you should be able to go out and sell this excellent investment product. Agents sell these to a variety of clients, but some types of clients who might form part of your target market will be:

- **Clients with an Estate Planning Need**. The IVIC is distinct from other assets in that the contract can generate a death benefit that is creditor protected and free from probate. For a client who is putting together a plan for the orderly transition of assets to the next generation, these are very useful features. Imagine a client in British Columbia who has $300,000 sitting in a GIC. On death, that GIC will attract significant probate (1.4% in BC). The client stands to lose ($300,000 x 1.4% =) $4,200 to probate. By moving these assets out of the GIC and into an IVIC (likely a very safe IVIC, such as a money market fund or a bond fund) the agent can help the client to avoid this $4,200 of probate that will otherwise arise on death. In order to make this work properly, the agent must work with the client to name the proper beneficiaries and make sure that the IVIC otherwise fits into the client's overall estate plan. This may require working with the client's lawyer, accountant, or financial planner.

- **The Hard to Insure**. There is no underwriting with IVICs (although some insurers will not allow clients beyond age 70 or 80 to enter into contracts). For a person who has an estate planning need, but cannot acquire insurance, the IVIC can help provide a solution. As in the last scenario, using an IVIC can free the client from having to worry about probate or claims from creditors.

- **Contractors, Business Owners, and Entrepreneurs**. Because these people recognize that they face more risk for claims arising from their business activities than others do, they will often find the creditor protection built into IVICs very attractive. This creditor protection provides a means to invest for their future with a greater degree of certainty.

- **The Risk Averse**. Some clients will seek exposure to investments, but do not want to face the full risks associated with those investments. To help those risk averse clients get into the habit of investing, an IVIC can be a great vehicle. The client can invest with a degree of certainty. This client might even seek an IVIC that offers 100/100 guarantees (100% on maturity or death), but keep in mind that, the higher the guarantee, the greater the cost of investing. Funds with 100/100 guarantees sometimes restrict the client from investing fully in equities, and they normally carry a higher MER than a comparable fund with 75/75 guarantees. Nevertheless, the 75/75 guarantee can still be quite attractive.

- **Selecting the IVIC**. Taking into account all that we have learned in this module, plus Module 4 and 6, we should be able to help clients pick the proper type of fund to meet their objectives. The chart following this module shows the various types of IVICs. (The chart would also apply to Mutual Funds.)

## SUMMARY

You will find that, for exam purposes, many of the technical details concerning IVICs will be tested. You can also count on several questions related to selecting the proper investment for the client. Without a very good understanding of IVICs, it will not be realistic to get through the exam. Having learned IVICs, we can now move on to the other insurance investment we will learn, the annuity.

| Type of Fund | Fund Invests In: | Risk | Volatility | Provides Returns in the Form of: | Time Horizon | Special Considerations | Target Market |
|---|---|---|---|---|---|---|---|
| Money Market* | Treasury Bills; Banker's Acceptances; Commercial Paper | Low | Very Low | Interest | Short | Money Market funds always maintain a NAV of either $1 or $10. Distributions are paid out very regularly. | Looking for stability or liquidity; short-term objectives |
| Mortgage | Residential Mortgages; Commercial Mortgages | Very Low to Low | Very Low | Interest and Return of Capital | Short to Medium | Includes a variety of different types of mortgages (insured, conventional, fixed, variable) with different maturity dates. | Seeking income with low risk |
| Bond* | Corporate Bonds; Debentures; Government Bonds | Low to Medium (riskier bond funds are available) | Low | Interest; Some Capital Gains | Medium | A great variety of bond funds are available to help investors accomplish all sorts of goals. | Seeking income with some risk |
| Income | Corporate Bonds; Government Bonds; Preferred Shares | Medium | Low to Medium | Interest and Dividends; Some Capital Gains | Medium | Will try to maintain a steady NAV and provide regular income to investors. | Seeking tax preferred income |

| Type of Fund | Fund Invests In: | Risk | Volatility | Provides Returns in the Form of: | Time Horizon | Special Considerations | Target Market |
|---|---|---|---|---|---|---|---|
| Balanced* | A fixed (but not equal) proportion of: <br> -Equities <br> -Bonds <br> -Money Market | Medium to High | Medium to High | Interest; Dividends; Capital Gains | Long | Combines all types of investments into one fund. | Seeking a combination of growth and stability |
| Dividend | Preferred Shares; Blue Chip Shares (very large, stable companies) | Medium to High | Medium | Dividends; Some Capital Gains | Medium | Similar to an income fund; slightly more risk because of equity exposure. | Seeking tax preferred income |
| Index | Most index funds are equity funds | High | Medium to High | Capital Gains; Dividends | Long | Uses passive management to select equities that should mirror an index (ie the Standard and Poor's TSX index). Usually has a lower MER than an actively managed fund. | Growth with less volatility than an equity fund |
| Fund of Funds (Portfolio Fund) | Other Investment Funds, usually equity funds | High | Medium to High | Dividends; Capital Gains; Some Interest | Long | Purchases a basket of other funds. This fund is much more diversified than other types. | Investor does not have to choose one fund |

| Type of Fund | Fund Invests In: | Risk | Volatility | Provides Returns in the Form of: | Time Horizon | Special Considerations | Target Market |
|---|---|---|---|---|---|---|---|
| Equity* | Primarily Canadian Equities | High to Very High | High to Very High | Capital Gains; Dividends | Long | The traditional Canadian fund used by most equity investors. | Seeking growth; can handle volatility |
| International Equity | Equities primarily in countries other than US and Canada; mostly invested in developed economies | High to Very High | High to Very High | Capital Gains; Dividends | Long | Exposure to markets outside North America. | Seeking growth; very high volatility; wants to diversify across borders |
| Global Equity | Equities in companies in every country, including Canada and the United States; may have significant holdings in developing economies | Very High to Speculative | Very High | Capital Gains; Some Dividends | Long | Gives exposure to emerging markets. | Seeking growth; can handle volatility; wants to diversify across borders |

| Type of Fund | Fund Invests In: | Risk | Volatility | Provides Returns in the Form of: | Time Horizon | Special Considerations | Target Market |
|---|---|---|---|---|---|---|---|
| Specialty Equity | Equities from one sector only, such as technology, resources, health care, or financial | Very High to Speculative | Very High | Capital Gains; Some Dividends | Long | Removes diversification, one of the key strengths of most funds. | |
| Real Estate | Commercial real estate; Some mortgages | Very High to Speculative (some real estate funds are lower risk) | Medium to High | Capital Gains; Interest; Return of Capital | Long | Not diversified. Invests in an asset which is not always liquid or marketable. | Aggressive growth; diversification away from equities (sometimes provides income) |
| Labour Sponsored | Start-up companies; Unproven technologies | Speculative | Very High | Capital Gains; Dividends; Tax Credits | Long | This is neither a mutual fund nor a segregated fund. Low liquidity. Tax advantages for investors. | Aggressive growth; tax advantages; no need for liquidity |

*These funds are considered "generic" funds for exam purposes.

12-22

# Chapter 13 ANNUITIES

Annuities are not a new concept; we have evidence of annuities dating back to the Roman Empire. An annuity is a fundamental component of retirement planning, but its uses are not limited to retirement. An annuity is, very simply, an income stream. The income stream can be based on several factors, which we will look at in this module. The income stream is usually a fixed amount, but there is some opportunity to vary it. Annuity benefits can be based on either a fixed term, or on the life of one or more annuitants. Insurers are the only entity that can offer life annuities; other annuities are available through insurers, banks, or investment dealers.

The basic structure of an annuity involves the exchange of a lump sum of cash for the fixed income stream. A client who has worked his whole life and built up substantial savings will look to convert those savings into the cash flow to help fund retirement. This is the most common use of an annuity.

In this module, we will first look at the technical details around annuities. We will then look at the target market for the sale of annuity products. It will be useful, prior to reading this module, to go back and review Module 6; you may also find portions of Module 5 necessary for reference.

As with IVICs, annuities can have a contract owner, an annuitant, and a beneficiary. However, these products are far simpler than most IVICs.

## TYPES OF ANNUITIES

There are two basic annuity structures. These are the life annuity and the term certain annuity. Life annuities are designed to provide income until the death of the annuitant, and are almost exclusively used in retirement. Term certain annuities, or term annuities, will pay benefits for a pre-determined amount of time based on the amount of money invested. We will look at these annuities in more detail:

- **Term Certain Annuities**. The decision to purchase a term certain annuity is usually based on a pre-determined need for a number of years. A grandparent might, for example, purchase a 5 year term certain annuity to help fund a grandchild's education. The term certain annuity will provide benefits based on the amount of money invested, the interest rate at which the annuity is purchased, and the number of years for which income is required. Interest rates for annuities are fixed throughout the term of the annuity. Annuity rates are normally similar to government bond yields. A contract owner who purchases an annuity locks in those rates throughout the term of the annuity. A term certain annuity normally has no beneficiary; if the annuitant dies with annuity benefits outstanding, those annuity benefits will pass on to the estate and then to the heirs. Some insurers will have the contract owner name a beneficiary when the annuity is purchased.

- **Structured Settlement Annuities**. This type of annuity is not, strictly speaking, a life insurance product. A structured settlement annuity is a type of term annuity that originates with a settlement from a liability insurance claim, in most cases. The liability insurer will offer the plaintiff a structured settlement instead of a lump sum settlement. This can be attractive for the insurer, because it represents a smaller cash outlay. The annuitant can find this attractive because it is easier to manage a stream of income than a large lump sum.

- **Life Annuities**. As the name implies, the life annuity will pay an income stream throughout the life of the annuitant(s). The amount of the benefit is based on the following factors:

  ○ **Age of the annuitant(s)**. The older the annuitant, the less time the insurer will likely have to pay benefits for. All else being equal, an annuitant who acquires a $200,000 annuity at age 70 will have a greater monthly income than an annuitant who purchases a $200,000 annuity at age 65.

  ○ **Number of annuitants**. If there is only one annuitant, the insurer will only have to pay benefits for as long as that person lives. Once we add a second annuitant, the insurer takes on more risk. (Situations where there are more than two annuitants are incredibly rare.) The insurer's added uncertainty means that the benefit will be reduced. Note also that where there are multiple annuitants, the insurer will base the benefit on the age of the youngest annuitant and then reduce that benefit amount based on the age of the older annuitant. A 60 and an 80 year old entering into a life annuity contract will find their annuity benefit is likely going to be based roughly on what a 55 year old would get if purchasing an annuity alone.

  ○ **Additional features**. We will look at some additional features that can be added to annuities throughout this module. Features such as guarantees, commutable, and indexing all increase the insurer's risk and will cause the insurer to offer a reduced annuity benefit.

  ○ **Gender**. Women tend to live longer than men. Because of this, men will obtain a greater annuity benefit than will women. All else being equal, a man aged 70 purchasing a $200,000 annuity will receive a larger benefit than a woman in the same situation.

  ○ **Poor Health**. There is no underwriting required to purchase an annuity. However, in cases where a potential annuitant's health is failing, the annuitant might apply for an impaired annuity, in which case the benefit will be based on a shortened life expectancy. In order to acquire such an annuity, the annuitant would have to have a doctor's indication that life expectancy is shortened.

  ○ **Interest Rates**. As discussed in the section on term certain annuities, the prevailing interest rate of the day will help to determine how much the annuity benefit will be. All else being equal, an annuitant with a $200,000 annuity and an 8% interest rate will receive a larger benefit than an annuitant with the same amount of money, but a 5% interest rate.

There are several types of life annuities. As an insurance agent, you might sell or deal with any of the following:

- **Life Straight Annuity**. A life straight annuity is an income stream based on only one life. When the annuitant dies, benefits end. Because this annuity covers only one life, it represents the least risk for the insurer. Life straight annuities pay a larger benefit per dollar invested than any other type of life annuity. A life straight annuity is useful for a single person in retirement who has nobody depending on her financially. This type of annuity is also known as a single life annuity.

- **Life Annuity with Guarantees**. With this type of annuity, benefits will be paid for at least as long as the annuitant lives. If the annuitant dies before a certain number of years (5, 10, or 20 are common) has passed, the annuity benefit will continue to be paid to a beneficiary up to the end of the guarantee period. There are two possible scenarios. Let's imagine that we have a 73 year old who has purchased a life annuity with a 10 year guarantee:

  - The annuitant dies during the guarantee period. Our annuitant dies at age 78. The annuity benefit will continue in the hands of the named beneficiary for 5 more years (until the annuitant would have been 83).
  - The annuitant outlives the guarantee period. Our annuitant dies at age 85. The guarantee has expired. There is no benefit for the beneficiary.
  - Life annuities with guarantees are popular for people in retirement who have younger people who are financially dependent on them. This might include a younger spouse, or an adult child who is partially dependent.

- **Joint and Last Survivor Annuity**. The joint and last survivor annuity provides income until the last of two annuitants are dead. It is possible to add guarantees to this annuity as well, just as we did in the last section. Certain joint and last survivor annuities will provide a reduced amount of income (60%, 66.67%, or 75%) to the survivor upon death of the first annuitant. We will see in Module 14 that some retirement plans encourage the purchase of this type of annuity. A joint and last survivor annuity is appropriate for a couple retiring together at about the same age as one another.

- **Variable Annuities**. A variable annuity combines the features of an IVIC with the features of an annuity. This product, properly called an Individual Variable Annuity Contract (IVAC) allows the investor to use funds with variable returns to accumulate value. At the conclusion of the accumulation phase, the insurer provides an income based on either the investment growth, or on a guarantee based on the original amount invested. Once the income phase starts, if the investment returns are strong, the client even has the potential to increase the amount of the retirement income. This product combines the risk and opportunity of investing in the markets with the certainty of an annuity. The variable annuity, as presently available in Canada, was discussed in Module 12 under the Lifetime Income Benefits section.

## ANNUITY FEATURES

Now that we have seen the types of annuities, we will have a look at some of the features that will be built into or added on to annuities.

- **Annuity Timing**. Annuities can be structured to start immediately, or can be deferred:

  ○ **Immediate Annuity**. In an immediate annuity, the contract holder has accumulated some money and wishes to purchase a benefit to start immediately. The payment required to enter into a life annuity is known as a premium, because it is an insurance contract.

  ○ **Deferred (or Accumulation) Annuity**. A deferred annuity is designed to allow the client to use the annuity to accumulate value prior to income starting. Maybe our client has saved up some, but not all, of what they will need for retirement, and they still have 5 or 10 years until they would like to retire. The accumulation annuity can be used to generate the capital needed to purchase the desired retirement benefit. Deferred annuities will sometimes use an IVIC during the accumulation phase, turning the IVIC into an annuity to generate income in retirement. Deferred annuities can also use a GIC type of structure, in which the insurer guarantees a rate of return and the invested principal. As this is an insurance product, it will feature creditor protection of the accumulated values if a proper beneficiary is named. When a deferred annuity is purchased, there will be a term attached to it, like a GIC. If a client determines that the income stream is needed before the end of the term, the insurer will apply a market value adjustment:

    ■ **Market Value Adjustment**. Imagine that when our client acquired an accumulation annuity with a five-year accumulation phase interest rates were 6%. Two years later, the client encounters a problem and decides that he needs to start income payments immediately. The annuity benefit will be recalculated based on the interest rates at that time. If interest rates have fallen, then the annuity benefit will be smaller than expected because there is a shorter compounding period and lower interest rates. If interest rates have risen, then the impact won't be known until the market value adjustment is calculated. It is likely that the payment will be lower just because of the three years of lost compounding, but a higher interest rate could offset some of that lost compounding. The actual calculation of a market value adjustment requires a time value of money calculation and is beyond the scope of this course.

- **Liquidity**. Most annuities do not offer the investor any liquidity. Once the decision is made to purchase the annuity, the premium is lost in exchange for the promise of income. However, there is a feature that can be added to an annuity to allow some liquidity:
  - **Commutable**. A commutable annuity will allow the investor to commute the value built up in the annuity. In exchange for this, the monthly annuity benefit will be less than it would for a non-commutable annuity. If the investor does choose to access the funds in the commutable annuity during the accumulation phase, it could result in a market value adjustment.

- **Indexing**. Insurers allow contract owners to index annuities to inflation. This means the annuity will pay a benefit that will increase over time to keep pace with inflation. The maximum indexed amount allowed within a registered annuity is 4% per year. Of course, this benefit is not free, and the annuitant who collects benefits from an indexed annuity will collect a smaller benefit than the annuitant collecting benefits from a non-indexed annuity.

- **Refunds**. In addition to offering life annuities based on more than one life, and annuities with guarantees, some insurers will also offer the client the opportunity to purchase refunds if the annuitant dies early. These refunds basically take the portion of the invested principal that has not been paid out yet as annuity benefits and refund that principal to a named beneficiary. As an annuity is an insurance product, any amount paid due to the death of a beneficiary is exempt from probate and is creditor protected. A client who chooses a refund has to pay for this; the monthly benefit for a client who chooses a refund will be less than for an annuity with no refunds. The two refund structures available are:
  - **Cash Refund**. With a cash refund, the insurer simply pays out any principal not already used as a one-time lump sum similar to a death benefit from a life insurance policy. Because this is a return of the invested principal (return of capital) it is not taxable.
  - **Instalment Refund**. With an instalment refund, the insurer will pay a beneficiary the unused principal in regular instalments. This turns the benefit into a sort of term certain annuity. The return of principal will not be taxed, but any interest that accumulates during the instalment period will be taxed in the hands of the beneficiary.

# TAXATION OF ANNUITIES

The taxation of non-registered annuities is quite simple. The annuitant earns an income based on a combination of return of capital and interest. The return of capital portion is not taxed. The interest portion is taxed as regular income. Because only the interest is taxed, the annuity ends up producing a large amount of income with relatively little interest to pay. As the annuity pays out its benefits, the amount of principal will decrease because a portion of every annuity payment is return of the invested principal. Over time, then, the annuitant's tax bill will be reduced, because less principal means less interest payments, which means less taxable income. If the amount of principal in a life annuity is reduced to zero, the annuitant is not worried, because the insurer has promised a benefit for life. This structure with a declining tax bill over time is known as an accrued rate annuity.

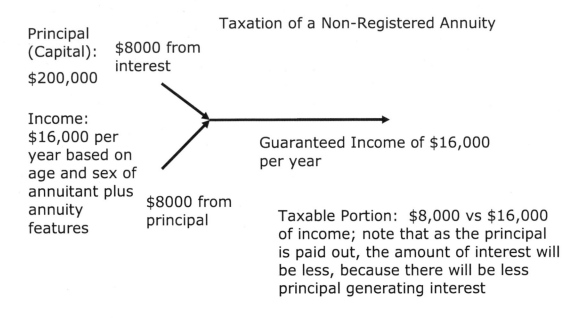

Taxation of a Non-Registered Annuity

Principal (Capital): $200,000

$8000 from interest

Income: $16,000 per year based on age and sex of annuitant plus annuity features

$8000 from principal

Guaranteed Income of $16,000 per year

Taxable Portion: $8,000 vs $16,000 of income; note that as the principal is paid out, the amount of interest will be less, because there will be less principal generating interest

- **Prescribed Annuities**. It is possible to set up an immediate, non-indexed, non-commutable, non-registered annuity in such a way as to level out this tax bill. Instead of a decreasing tax bill as seen in the previous example, a prescribed annuity fixes the tax bill based roughly on the average amount of tax that the investor would pay per year on the annuity income if she lived to age 90. This will mean a smaller tax bill initially, but the tax bill will stay level over time. Prescribed annuities are taking advantage of the time value of money, because it puts more dollars in the annuitant's hands right now.

- **Registered Annuities**. While we have not yet dealt with registered plans, it is worth discussing here that any amounts paid out of a registered annuity will be fully taxed as regular income.

## SELLING ANNUITIES

In many cases, the sale of an annuity is quite straightforward. A client is leaving a pension plan or maturing their Registered Retirement Savings Plan, so they need a source of income. Take some or all of what they have saved and turn it into an annuity. Of course, the annuity must provide enough income to meet the client's retirement objectives. If the annuity alone will not accomplish this, it may be necessary to take a portion of the client's savings and invest it more aggressively elsewhere. Use an annuity to provide a safe minimum amount, and invest elsewhere to try to meet the more elaborate objectives.

There are two sales techniques specifically pertaining to annuities that agents should be familiar with:

- **Leveraged Annuity/Back-to-Back Annuity/Insured Annuity**. This strategy, which goes by any of three names, takes advantage of a combination of annuities and life insurance together. We have previously mentioned that many pensions compel the pensioner to enter into a joint-and-last survivor annuity on retirement. The problem can be that the income provided by the joint-and-last-survivor annuity is not as much as it would be in a life straight annuity. The annuitant wants that higher level of income. One way to accomplish this while minimizing risk is to use an insured annuity. The steps in the insured annuity are:
  - Have the spouse sign a consent form to use a life straight annuity.
  - Acquire the life straight annuity on the pensioner's life.
  - Use the excess annuity benefits to purchase a T100 life insurance policy on the annuitant.
  - On death of pensioner, death benefit is paid to the surviving spouse.
  - The surviving spouse uses the death benefit to purchase a new life straight annuity.

  In truth, we would likely put the T100 policy in force first, because we want to make sure that the annuitant will be insurable for a price that will fit with this strategy. If we fail to put the insurance in place and the annuitant dies early, the surviving spouse will be left with nothing.

- **Annuities vs GICs**. We discussed a similar concept in Module 12. Occasionally you will encounter clients who have very large amounts invested in GICs. This is often done simply because the client has become accustomed to doing all their business at the bank. Let's say we encounter one of these clients, and the client is willing to hear a different concept. By moving the money out of the GIC and into a life annuity, we can generate some advantages. Let's say the client is age 65, earning 4% on a $200,000 GIC at the bank and using that money to fund living expenses. We will use the same rate of return for the life annuity. Let's compare the two:

| | GIC | Annuity | Explanation |
|---|---|---|---|
| Principal Amount | $200,000 | $200,000 | |
| Return | 4% | 4% | |
| Annual Income | $8000 | $15,800 | The GIC pays only interest; The annuity pays a combination of interest and principal. |
| Taxable Amount | $8000 | $8000 | The GIC's interest is all taxable; The annuity's return of principal portion is not taxable. |
| Amount left when client dies | $200,000 | $0 | The GIC will never have its principal impacted; the annuity will be reduced to zero. |

|  | GIC | Annuity | Explanation |
|---|---|---|---|
| Annual life insurance premium | $0 | $5000 | Using the annuity strategy, the client acquires a T100 life insurance policy with a $200,000 death benefit. |
| Liquidity | Partially liquid | Illiquid | The purchase of the annuity, unless a commutable feature is built in (at an additional cost) causes a loss of liquidity. With the GIC, there will be the option to access the funds in the GIC at maturity, which provides greater liquidity than in the annuity option. |
| Tax Payable (assume a 30% tax rate) | $2400 | $2400 | Both generate $8000 in taxable income. We will use a prescribed annuity to keep the tax bill level. |
| Disposable income | $5600 | $8,400 | Using the annuity, the client has $2,800 more disposable income each year. |
| Consumer Protection | $100,000 | Up to $2000 per month | The GIC is protected up to $100,000 by CDIC; the annuity is protected up to $2000 per month by Assuris (and 85% beyond that amount, as discussed in Module 3). |
| Probate Fees | Depends on province of residence; up to $3000 | $0 | The life insurance death benefit will not attract probate. |

## SUMMARY

Even though they have been maligned in recent years because of low interest rates, annuities still provide a cornerstone of retirement income. Insurers offer enough additional features with annuities to allow consumers flexibility. Any time a question about retirement income arises, annuities should be considered as an option. The guaranteed income in retirement offers stability and certainty not found with other products.

# Chapter 14 INVESTMENT PLANS

In Module 6, we learned about our government's use of fiscal policy to accomplish economic objectives.  In that case, we discussed fiscal policy as a broad set of measures designed to encourage manageable levels of growth in the economy.  The government also uses fiscal policy to help Canadians accomplish a variety of aims.  Our government has implemented a number of plans to allow us to save in tax-advantaged ways.  Many of these plans are designed so that we, as individuals, will take responsibility for our own situation, rather than relying on the government to look after us.

In this module, we will look at plans designed to help save for retirement, education, and caring for a disabled person.  It will be useful, prior to reading this module, to review Modules 5 and 6, especially the sections in Module 6 covering taxation of investment income and tax deductions.

For all of the plans we will look at here, there are no particular licensing requirements (except possibly for the Registered Education Savings Plan, which some firms require licensing to provide).  It is the underlying investments that the agent must be licensed to sell, as discussed in Module 6.

## REGISTERED RETIREMENT SAVINGS PLAN

Of all the programs that we will look at in this module, this is the one that Canadians have been exposed to the most.  It is also, likely, the program around which we see the greatest misconceptions.  The RRSP is not an investment, despite what many of us believe.  Instead, the RRSP is a vehicle which holds some investment or investments.

Many, but not all, of the investments we have looked at in this course can be included in an RRSP. While we will cover this in more detail throughout this section, the basic advantages to an RRSP are that the investor receives a tax deduction for contributing to the RRSP, and growth within the investments is tax deferred. The result, though, is that any amounts withdrawn from the RRSP are subject to taxation. Many of the concepts we will learn about with respect to RRSPs apply to other savings plans we will cover through the rest of this module.

- **Deduction Limits**.  Every Canadian who earns an income has the right to contribute to an RRSP.  There is no minimum and no maximum age at which contributions can be made, although many institutions do not allow contributions until age 18.  We will also see later on in this module that it is not possible to have an RRSP in one's own name after the year in which one turns 71.  Tax deductible contributions to RRSPs are limited to 18% of earned income for the tax year in question.  We will examine earned income, along with other provisions relating to RRSP contributions:

  - **Earned Income**.  Earned income for RRSP purposes includes primarily income that can result from employment, or employment type activities.  The following chart indicates what constitutes earned income:

| Items that Increase Earned Income | Items that Reduce Earned Income |
|---|---|
| Employment Income including bonuses, commissions, overtime, employer pension and RRSP contributions, and other taxable benefits minus | Employment expenses |
| Business income minus | Business losses |
| Rental income minus | Rental losses |
| Net research grants | |
| Royalty income | |
| Taxable support payments (spousal support; or child support awarded prior to May 1, 1997) received | Tax deductible support payments paid |
| CPP Disability Benefits | |
| Provincial Disability Benefits | |

The taxpayer would add all these sources of income and multiply by 18%. That figure, up to an annual maximum ($24,270 for 2014, indexed going forward) is how much the taxpayer could contribute to an RRSP for the given year and still earn a tax deduction. You don't need to memorize this figure, but you will be tested on the RRSP maximum deduction allowance calculation. Regardless, everybody employed in financial services in Canada should be aware of the 18% figure. As a quick example, a taxpayer who earned $75,000 of salary, but paid $10,000 in tax deductible support payments, would have earned income of ($75,000 - $10,000 =) $65,000. The RRSP contribution allowance for the next year would be ($65,000 x 18% =)$11,700. Earned income is always used to calculate the next year's contribution allowance.

- **Carry Forward**. Taxpayers who do not use their deduction limit in the contribution year carry it forward. There is no limit to how long, or how much, contribution room can be carried forward. So a taxpayer who never makes an RRSP contribution, but has earned income year after year, may have a massive RRSP deduction limit. Once any contribution is made to an RRSP, the room used in that case is lost forever. There is no opportunity to recover previously used RRSP deductions. (For example, a taxpayer who puts maximum amount into their RRSP for the first 10 years of their working life, then withdraws the whole amount, will have no RRSP deduction room until they again have earned income.)

- **Contribution Year**. The RRSP contribution year is the calendar year plus 60 days into next calendar year. So contributions made in January and February 2015 can be deducted against income for 2014 or 2015.

- **Pension Adjustment**. The government has put the RRSP in place to allow Canadians to put away a reasonable amount (and enjoy a tax deduction for doing so) of money for retirement. Many Canadians already access very similar structures through company-sponsored pension plans (Registered Pension Plans, which we will discuss later in this module). It would not make sense to allow a double benefit. So, for those taxpayers who already have tax deductible contributions to a registered pension plan, the benefit they receive from the pension plan will reduce their RRSP deduction limit. For example, an employee who belongs to a defined contribution pension plan (dealt with later in this module) which generates $10,000 in contributions for 2012 will have the 2013 (the year following the pension contribution) RRSP deduction limit reduced by $10,000. This $10,000 is referred to as the pension adjustment. Note that pension adjustments reduce the next year's RRSP deduction limit. Both employer and employee contributions to the pension plan generate a pension adjustment for the employee.

- **Tax Deduction.** As discussed in Module 5, contributions made to an RRSP result in a tax deduction. A taxpayer who pays tax at a 40% marginal tax rate and contributes $1000 to an RRSP will save (1000 x 40% =) $400 on their taxes. This taxpayer has to earn $1000 in order to be able to contribute $1000 to the RRSP. The same taxpayer would have to earn $1,667 in order to contribute ($1667 - 40% =) $1000 to a non-registered investment. Of course, to realize the full value of the tax deduction, the money saved should be reinvested. Many taxpayers choose not to reinvest their tax savings.

- **Over contributions.** It could occasionally happen that a client is set up on a dollar-cost averaging plan to put regular amounts into an investment held in an RRSP every month. Imagine, though, that the client's income changes unexpectedly. The client might not think to reduce their RRSP contributions, but their RRSP room will be reduced. This could put the client into a situation where they have over contributed to the RRSP. Over contributions normally result in a substantial penalty of 1% per month on the amount over the RRSP contribution limit. There is some forgiveness for over contributions, though. Every taxpayer has a $2000 over contribution allowance. So if a taxpayer over contributes by $1500 in a given year, they would still have $500 of over contribution left. If two years later that person over contributed by $1000, that would put them $500 over what is permitted, and they would end up paying the 1% penalty. The over contribution allowance works like a spring, so if the taxpayer contributed less than their contribution allowance later on, they would actually restore the $2000 over contribution allowance, and it could be used again in the future.

- **Alternative Minimum Tax.** As discussed earlier, it is possible for a taxpayer to build up a huge deduction limit if the taxpayer has earned income year after year but does not contribute to an RRSP. If this taxpayer decided at some point to make a very large RRSP contribution, it would generate a similarly large tax deduction. Even if this tax deduction were large enough to reduce the tax bill to zero, that taxpayer might still be subject to alternative minimum tax (AMT). Alternative minimum tax is a system that ensures that high income earners pay some tax no matter how many tax deductions or tax credits they have. A taxpayer who pays AMT will have that amount refunded over the next 7 years. The actual calculation for AMT is quite complex, and you will not need to calculate it. If you are dealing with a client who earns a high income and has access to huge deductions and credits, it is necessary to consult an accountant.

- ○ **Retiring Allowances**. Sometimes upon leaving an employer, an employee will be given a lump-sum settlement based on long service or other considerations. This lump-sum settlement is not considered earned income for the purpose of calculating RRSP deduction limits. It will be identified as a retiring allowance. Certain amounts of retiring allowances can be used to generate RRSP contribution room. Those amounts are:

  - For each year of service prior to (but not including) 1996, up to $2000 per year; and
  - For years of service before 1989 in which employer pension plan contributions were not vested with employee, up to $1500 per year.

- **Qualifying Investments**. For the purpose of indicating what the qualifying investments within an RRSP are, it is best to look at two investment philosophies. A basic range of investments can be held within a managed RRSP. Managed RRSPs usually have very low, or no annual fees at all. Investors who want more choice with their RRSP investments can deal directly with an investment dealer (a stock broker) to establish a self-directed RRSP. Self-directed RRSPs typically carry an annual fee in the range of $100 per year. Investment choices for RRSPs include:

| Managed RRSP Investments | Self-Directed RRSP Investments | Self-Directed RRSP Investments |
|---|---|---|
| Bank Accounts | Any Managed RRSP Investment | Exchange Traded Funds# |
| IVICs | Canadian Currency | Mortgages# |
| Mutual Funds | Foreign Currency# | Annuities |
| GICs | Government Bonds | Warrants |
| | Corporate Bonds | Rights |
| | Preferred Shares | Options |
| | Common Shares | Limited partnerships*# |
| | Shares in a Small Business*# | Royalty Units*# |
| | Shares in a Venture Capital Corporation*# | Investment grade gold and silver# |

*Under certain conditions (outside the scope of this course)

#Not covered in this course

14-4

The above chart includes almost every investment covered in this course. Some notable exceptions (property which cannot be held in RRSP) include:

- Life insurance policies (although there is technically a way to include the CSV of a whole life policy, this is problematic when the death benefit is paid);
- Real estate (there is a very narrow exception to this when an RRSP holds a mortgage and there is a default in the mortgage); and
- Listed personal property (art, antiques, jewellery, collectables, etc.).
- This is a huge range of qualifying investments. Some clients will be happy to set up a self-directed RRSP and invest on their own. In those cases, the agent must be careful not to advise on investments outside of what she is qualified to comment on. Most clients, though, will choose a managed plan. When this is done, the agent must assist the client with choosing appropriate investments to meet their time horizon, risk tolerance, and desire for liquidity and flexibility. Many clients have the mistaken impression that money invested in an RRSP is safer than money invested outside an RRSP. This is not the case, except for the creditor protection that we will look at later in this section. A client who invests in a Canadian Equity segregated fund within an RRSP faces the same risk as a client who invests in the same fund in a non-registered account.

- **Tax Deferral**. Growth of investments in an RRSP is not subject to any sort of taxation. The RRSP allows the investor to defer taxes. Because of this, there is no need to seek capital gains or dividend-producing investments within the RRSP. There is no advantage to hold these otherwise tax-efficient investments. Foreign investments can also be held in the RRSP and will also benefit from tax deferral (Until 2005, there was a 30% foreign content limit on RRSP investments. Today, there is no limit.) There is also no advantage to capital losses in an RRSP.

- **Withdrawals and Withholding Tax**. Any amount withdrawn from an RRSP during the lifetime of the owner is subject to taxation. Withdrawals from the RRSP are subject to regular income tax. The investor will have to pay tax on any amounts withdrawn, as regular income. Because these withdrawals are taxable, and Canada Revenue Agency generally tries to avoid situations in which taxpayers unexpectedly have to pay large tax bills, a withholding tax will be applied. This is not an extra tax. Instead, much like the tax that is withheld from a paycheque, it is an advance payment on a future tax bill. At tax time, the true amount of tax owing will be calculated. If it is less than the amount withheld, a refund will be generated. If too little tax was withheld, then there will be an amount owing. The amount withheld is determined by the amount withdrawn:

| Amount Withdrawn | Percentage Withheld |
|---|---|
| >$5,000 | 10% |
| $5000 to $15,000 | 20% |
| >$15,000 | 30% |

As with most taxation rules, these amounts are different in Quebec. RRSP providers are supposed to treat a series of withdrawals from the same RRSP as one withdrawal for the purpose of calculating withholding tax. We can see, then, that an investor who withdraws $20,000 from the RRSP will actually only have access to ($20,000 - 30% =) $14,000. At tax time, this taxpayer will have $20,000 added to his taxable income, but will also receive credit for having paid $6,000 in taxes already.

- **Spousal RRSP**. Imagine that we are dealing with a couple. He earns a large income, say $140,000 per year. She stays home and takes care of the household and the kids, and earns no income. He will have a large RRSP deduction limit ($140,000 x 18% = $25,200; however, the 2014 maximum is $24,270, so that will be his deduction limit) and she will have none. If he contributes fully to his RRSP, he will create a large income for himself in retirement, but it will mean no income for her. Thinking back to Module 5, this could mean a large tax bill for just him as opposed to smaller tax bills split between the two of them. Module 7 tells us that it could result in a clawback of his OAS benefits.

  In order to prevent such a situation from arising, couples like this, where there is a significant discrepancy in income, will often use a spousal RRSP. Using the spousal RRSP, the higher income earner contributes to a Spousal RRSP, which is owned by the lower income earning spouse. The contributing spouse will use his own RRSP contribution allowance, which will be reduced accordingly. The contributing spouse will also receive the tax deduction. Withdrawals made in the calendar year of the last Spousal RRSP contribution, or the subsequent two calendar years, will be attributed back to the contributing spouse. Prior to the recipient spouse making any withdrawals, the contributor should go two full calendar years without making any contributions in order to avoid this attribution. As with any RRSP, no contributions can be made after December 31st of the year in which the spouse turns 71. (There actually won't even be an RRSP at that point, as it must have been matured.)

  The end result of a properly employed spousal RRSP will be that both spouses will have roughly similar RRSP balances in retirement, allowing them to each draw roughly equal retirement income. This is preferable over having one spouse with all the income, which creates a much greater tax burden than two moderate levels of income. This concept can be reviewed by examining the marginal tax rates in Module 5. CRA considers the term spouse to mean legally married, common-law, and same-sex couples.

  Interestingly, spousal RRSP contributions can still be made up to 60 days after the death of the contributing spouse. This allows a tax deduction for the contributor's estate.

- **Group RRSP**. The Group RRSP is normally established by an employer. It will normally involve some degree of matching by the employer when the employee contributes to the RRSP. Employee contributions work exactly as described here, including contribution limits. The employer's contributions are a taxable benefit to employee, but that is offset by a tax deduction for the employee for the RRSP contribution. In all other ways, the Group RRSP works the same way as an individual RRSP. Group RRSPs are established where an employer wishes to put in place a plan to help employees retire without the administrative burden of a registered pension plan.

- **Maturity.** The RRSP must be matured by December 31st of the year in which the plan owner turns 71. While it must be matured by that point, there is no requirement to wait until that age. An RRSP owner can cash out or mature their RRSP at any time they wish, as long as it is prior to December 31st of their 71st year. There are three options on maturity:

  ○ **Convert the Plan to a Registered Retirement Income Fund (RRIF).** The RRIF shares many characteristics with the RRSP, but instead of being designed for accumulation, it is designed to provide income. It is still tax-deferred. When this option is chosen, it is generally the case that whatever investments were held in the RRSP are simply rolled over to the RRIF. There is no disposition for income tax purposes, and most financial institutions will allow the transfer without charging any switching fees. We will investigate the RRIF in more detail later in this module. This option is normally chosen when the client wishes to have access to a variety of investments in the income phase.

  ○ **Annuitize the Plan.** The RRSP can be converted to a registered annuity. The annuity options are discussed fully in Module 13. The full range of annuity products can be purchased with the funds in the RRSP. As we go through this module, we will see that annuitization is an option on the maturity of other registered plans as well. This option is normally used by clients who are looking for guaranteed income without risk to help manage the costs of retirement. Studies show that retirees who have a component of guaranteed fixed income as part of their retirement portfolio live longer, happier lives.

  ○ **Cash out the Plan.** The plan owner can simply turn the plan into cash. It will be taxed as described earlier in this module. Failure to elect either of the other two options discussed here will force the RRSP to mature, and the full amount will be taxed in the client's hands. It is rare to see a client deliberately choose this option, but in cases where the client only has a small amount in the RRSP, this might be the most practical scenario.

  The options are not mutually exclusive. An RRSP owner could convert half his RRSP into a RRIF and use the other half to purchase an annuity, for example. This diversification can be useful, because the plan owner will have some growth and flexibility in retirement, while at the same time, there will be a fixed income stream with very little risk attached.

- **Home Buyers' Plan.** The Home Buyers' Plan (HBP) gives home buyers the chance to withdraw up to $25,000 from their RRSP tax-free to assist in the purchase of a new home. The home buyer cannot have owned a home in Canada in the previous five years (four full taxation years). Any amounts used must have been in the RRSP 90 days prior to the start of the year in which the withdrawal is being made. The home cannot have been purchased more than 30 days prior to the withdrawal being made. There must be a written agreement to purchase or build a home before a withdrawal can be made, and the home must be purchased or built by October 1st of the year following the HBP withdrawal. If a couple (married or common-law) are purchasing a home, each of them can borrow up to $25,000 from an RRSP, assuming they both have RRSPs with that much in them. Spousal RRSPs can be used, in which case the recipient spouse is making the withdrawal. Once the withdrawal has been made and the home purchased, the homeowners will have one calendar year (Jan 1 to Dec 31) in which no repayments have to be made. In the year following, though, repayments must start. Repayments are based on a 15 year schedule, during which time the home buyer has to repay 1/15th per year. Failure to repay will result in the borrower being assessed that amount on the tax return for the year, as if the amount had been withdrawn from the RRSP. The Home Buyers' Plan is especially attractive for somebody who wishes to purchase a home, but cannot afford the down payment.

- **Lifelong Learning Plan.** The Lifelong Learning Plan is similar to the Home Buyers' Plan, in that it permits tax-free withdrawals (also sometimes referred to as borrowing) from the RRSP. In this case, though, the money is withdrawn to help provide for the taxpayer's own education. Each of the taxpayer and the spouse can withdraw up to $10,000 per year for up to 4 years, though the overall maximum that can be withdrawn from each plan is $20,000. Upon completion of the program or four years after the first withdrawal is made, repayments must begin. Repayments of 1/10th per year must be made over a 10 year schedule. As with the Home Buyers' Plan, failure to repay the scheduled amount will result in an additional tax burden for the taxpayer. Note that this plan is not designed to help fund a child's education. This plan is designed to help a taxpayer pay, for example, to complete a master's degree, or to finish the schooling for an apprenticeship.

- **Creditor Protection.** Recent legislative changes have made amounts held in RRSPs creditor protected. Amounts held in an RRSP cannot be seized due to the claims of a creditor.

- **Death of an RRSP Owner**. On the death of an RRSP owner, if no beneficiary has been named, the RRSP is considered disposed of. It would be taxed in the hands of the estate just as if the RRSP had been fully cashed in. This can have severe tax consequences. In order to prevent this from happening, the RRSP owner can name certain beneficiaries who can receive the proceeds on a tax-free rollover basis. The plan owner can name the following beneficiaries to gain this tax advantage:

  ○ **Surviving Spouse.** For the purpose of the RRSP, the spouse includes common-law and same-sex partners. If the spouse is named as beneficiary, the amount in the RRSP rolls over tax-free from the deceased plan owner's RRSP to a registered plan (usually the RRSP or RRIF) owned by the surviving spouse. When that spouse dies, though, any amount still remaining in a registered plan will be fully taxed (unless the surviving spouse has a beneficiary who is eligible to receive the tax-free rollover).

- ○ **Dependent Child**. A child includes an adopted child, stepchild, or even a dependent grandchild. In order to receive this rollover, the child must be dependent. The child might be under 18 and therefore dependent by reason of age. If a child under 18 receives a tax-free rollover of the RRSP, the amounts received by the child must be annuitized (meaning the tax will be paid) by time the child reaches age 18. This can be a valuable tax deferral strategy. Say a single parent dies with $200,000 in the RRSP; normally that would result in $200,000 of income being attributed to the estate. However, by leaving the $200,000 to a child, the $200,000 of income could be spread out over all the years until the child turns 18, reducing the tax bill significantly. Children who earn income pay tax in exactly the same manner as do adults who earn income.

  The other scenario in which a child is considered dependent is an adult child who is infirm (that is, unable to care for themselves). An adult infirm child can also receive proceeds of an RRSP on a tax-free rollover basis. In that case, there is no annuitization requirement. We will see later on in this module that it is possible to leave up to $200,000 in the registered disability savings plan (RDSP) of a disabled child (at any age) as a rollover from a deceased parent's RRSP. This is even possible where the deceased parent originally left the funds to their own surviving spouse. The surviving spouse who originally received the funds on a rollover basis can subsequently (within the next full tax year) transfer the funds into the child's RDSP.

- **RRSP Summary**. The RRSP is a valuable investment opportunity for most Canadians. It allows the taxpayer the double tax advantage of tax deductible contributions and tax deferred growth. This must be weighed against the requirement to pay tax on withdrawal, but in most cases the advantages outweigh the disadvantages. For most working Canadians, who will usually be in a higher tax bracket when working than when retired, the RRSP is ideal.

The RRSP does have certain limitations. It is generally best for income earners earning between about $40,000 and $130,000 per year. Outside of that bracket, it starts to lose effectiveness.

Low income earners do not benefit greatly from a tax deduction. If somebody earns only, say $20,000 per year, they likely pay little or no tax. A tax deduction at approximately 22% (roughly the lowest tax bracket in most provinces) is not of great value to this person, and may not even apply. Then, withdrawing funds later on will result in taxable income, which will reduce, for example, the Guaranteed Income Supplement. For this person, the Tax Free Savings Account (which will be discussed later in this module) might be the better alternative.

For a higher income earner, the RRSP may not be ideal. Somebody who earns beyond $130,000 will earn income above the RRSP contribution threshold. They will not be able to use the RRSP to fully meet their retirement savings needs. Of course, they can also use the TFSA, but it will not make a large difference because it only allows $5000 of annual contributions. Universal life is one viable option for retirement savings in such cases. Because universal life insurance contracts base their upper limit for premiums on the face value of the policy, this can be a very effective form of retirement savings for high income earners.

A similar problem arises with business owners. Many business owners take their income only as dividends. (These would be ineligible dividends, as discussed in Module 5.) Dividend income, as with any investment income, does not generate any RRSP contribution room. The business owner who takes only dividend income will not have any RRSP room. Again, Universal life insurance becomes a viable substitute for the RRSP.

Many of the concepts we have discussed when dealing with RRSPs will be revisited as we examine the other investment plans in this module. The RRSP is a must-know for exam purposes and when dealing with clients as an agent in this industry.

## REGISTERED RETIREMENT INCOME FUND

Having learned the RRSP in some detail, we understand how funds will accumulate in a registered plan. However, we have not explored yet how the taxpayer will eventually access those funds. The Registered Retirement Income Fund (RRIF) is the vehicle of choice for many taxpayers who wish to turn their savings (RRSP) into income (RRIF). The RRIF functions in a very similar manner to the RRSP, except that the RRIF does not permit any new contributions. Instead, once a RRIF has been established, the RRIF owner must begin withdrawals starting in the first full year in which the RRIF is held. Like the RRSP, the RRIF is tax-deferred. Growth in the RRIF is not taxable. Also like the RRSP, any withdrawals from the RRIF will be fully taxed as regular income. On death, too, the RRIF is treated exactly as the RRSP is. The qualifying investments within a RRIF are the same as for the RRSP. The RRIF is still creditor protected as well. Unlike the RRSP, there is no provision to take advantage of the Home Buyers' Plan, nor the Lifelong Learning Plan, using a RRIF. Unlike the RRSP, where the focus is on contributions and accumulation, the RRIF is focused on withdrawals:

- **Minimum Withdrawals**. As discussed in the previous section, a RRIF can be set up at any time by electing to transfer the RRSP into a RRIF. This must be done no later, though, than December 31st of the year in which the RRIF owner turns 71. Whichever year the RRIF begins, there will be a minimum withdrawal schedule starting in the year following. The minimum withdrawals are based on the age of the RRIF owner (or their spouse) and the amount in the RRIF. The formula for withdrawals made prior to age 71 is:

RRIF Amount (as of January 1st of the year in question) ÷ (90 - Age (as of January 1st))

It is up to the RRIF owner to choose whether to use their own age or their spouse's.  The younger age can be used if the RRIF owner wants to take small amounts out of the RRIF.  If the RRIF owner plans to make larger withdrawals then the older age should be used.  Starting at age 71, the formula stops being used and a table is used.  (For RRIFs established in 1992 and earlier, other calculations are used.)  The table for the newer RRIFs (also known as non-qualifying RRIFs) is:

| Age on January 1 | Minimum Withdrawal | Withdrawal Assuming a $100,000 RRIF Balance |
|---|---|---|
| 71 | 7.38% | $7380 |
| 72 | 7.48% | $7480 |
| 73 | 7.59% | $7590 |
| 74 | 7.71% | $7710 |
| 75 | 7.85% | $7850 |
| 76 | 7.99% | $7990 |
| 77 | 8.15% | $8150 |
| 78 | 8.33% | $8330 |
| 79 | 8.53% | $8530 |
| 80 | 8.75% | $8750 |
| 94 | 20.00% | $20000 |

The amount increases gradually between 80 and 94, and at age 94, the minimum withdrawal reaches its maximum, at 20%.  The minimum withdrawal stays at 20% until the RRIF has no value left in it, or the RRIF owner dies.  Withdrawals from a spousal RRIF (a RRIF established when a spousal RRSP was converted to a RRIF) are treated the same way.  For exam purposes, it might be useful to know the formula for withdrawals prior to age 71 as well as the age 94 amount.

To use a short example, let's imagine we have an RRSP owner who has $400,000 in her RRSP in the year in which she turns 71.  She is forced by the end of that year to convert her RRSP into a RRIF (or to annuitize it, or to cash it out).  On January 1st of the next year, she has $420,000 in her RRIF, because of good investment performance.  Her husband is 67 years old, and she does not need to take a lot out of her RRIF to meet her living expenses.  Instead of using the chart above, then, she elects to use her husband's age.  Because her husband is not yet 71, she will use the formula to calculate the minimum RRIF withdrawal.  Her minimum withdrawal will be $420,000 ÷ (90 - 67).  (Note that the 90 is just part of the formula; it does not represent anybody's age.)  The minimum amount that she must withdraw by December 31st of the first full year in which she owns the RRIF will be ($420,000 ÷ 23 =) $18,261.  If she determined that she needed more than this, she might use her own age, which would result in a withdrawal of $420,000 x 7.38% (using the table) or $30,996.Once she decides to use either her own age or her spouse's age, that decision cannot be changed for future years.

- **Withdrawals and Withholding Tax**.  As with an RRSP withdrawal, there can be withholding tax on a RRIF withdrawal.  The withholding amount is based on withdrawals above the minimum.  So, if only a minimum withdrawal is made, there will be no withholding tax.  However, the amount withdrawn is still considered income and will be taxed as regular income.  While there is a minimum RRIF withdrawal, there is no maximum.  While all withdrawals are taxable, only the amount above the minimum will attract withholding tax.  RRIF holders who need more income out of their RRIF will typically use the older age of the two spouses when calculating their minimum withdrawal, so as to minimize withholding tax.  This can result in additional tax payable at year's end, but taxpayers at that stage in life have access to the pension income tax credit and the old age credit, both of which can significantly reduce taxes payable.

Using the example above, where our RRIF owner has a minimum withdrawal of $18,261, let's imagine that she instead decides to withdraw $30,000 from the RRIF.  This is ($30,000 - $18,261 =) $11,739 more than the minimum.  This would attract 20% withholding tax, or ($11,739 x 20% =) $2,348 in withholding tax.  The taxpayer would receive credit for this tax paid at tax time, and would have income of $30,000 based on the RRIF withdrawal.

- **Spousal RRIF**.  The spousal RRIF is subject to all the same rules we have seen so far.  We learned in the RRSP section that withdrawals from a spousal RRSP made in the first two years after a contribution were made will result in the income being attributed back to the contributing spouse.  Once the conversion is made to the RRIF, the minimum withdrawal can be made without attribution to the contributor.  Any amount beyond the minimum, though, will be attributed to the contributor.

- **RRIF Summary**.  At retirement, the RRSP owner will have to decide what to do with the RRSP.  The choices, in most cases, are between an annuity, which provides a fixed stream of income, or a RRIF, which provides a minimum stream of income, but still holds investments that can fluctuate.  For the investor still looking for growth or flexibility in retirement, the RRIF is ideal.  Unlike the annuity, which will often leave nothing for beneficiaries, the RRIF will leave its unused amounts to named beneficiaries, or as part of the estate.

Let's look at the case of a single client who establishes a RRIF at age 67.  The RRIF has $246,400 in it at the time of transfer from the RRSP to the RRIF.  Initially, the client is invested in a balanced portfolio with 10% cash; 60% bonds; 30% equity.  All investment growth/ loss figures are fictional, made up by the author.  The client always waits until the last possible day, December 31st, to make the RRIF withdrawal, and always withdraws the minimum amount.

| Year | RRIF Amount at Jan 1 | Client's Age at Jan 1 | Minimum withdrawal | Investment Growth/Loss | Balance at Dec 31, before withdrawal | Balance at Dec 31, after withdrawal | Additional Notes |
|------|------|------|------|------|------|------|------|
| 2011 | $246,400 | 67 | $10,713 | +6% | $261,184 | $250,471 | The gains outweigh the withdrawal |
| 2012 | $250,471 | 68 | $11,385 | -2% | $245,462 | $234,077 | Note the impact of a loss |
| 2013 | $234,077 | 69 | $11,146 | +4% | $243,440 | $234,294 | |
| 2014 | $234,294 | 70 | $11,714 | +5% | $246,009 | $234,295 | |
| 2015 | $234,295 | 71 | $17,291 | +4% | $243,667 | $226,376 | At age 71, use the chart |

We can see that, in the years prior to age 71, the client's RRIF balance stays fairly even. Starting at age 71, though, the client's RRIF balance will start to decline more and more quickly. Also, as the RRIF balance decreases, the client will have less investment returns to offset the impact of withdrawals. Note that waiting until year's end to make the withdrawal allows the client to take full advantage of the year's growth, but also causes the client to fully suffer the consequences of a loss, as in 2012. It is also likely that as the client gets older, the portfolio will be rebalanced to reduce the equity component. This will cause a lower average annual return, but it will also reduce the likelihood of a loss.

## REGISTERED PENSION PLAN

Registered Pension Plans (RPPs) work in a manner very similar to the RRSP. Contributions and accumulation are very similar. The biggest differences between RPPs and RRSPs are that the RPP has a component of employer contributions and that the plan offers the plan holder far less liquidity than is the case with an RRSP. From the employer's perspective, another important difference is that the employer has a fiduciary responsibility to their employees. There are two types of RPPs we will deal with for the purposes of this course:

- **Defined Benefit Plans**. The original RPP is the defined benefit (or DB) plan. DB plans allow an employer to promise to an employee a benefit based on years of service and salary. Employees with higher incomes and longer service would benefit the most from these plans. The basic idea is to provide a life annuity to the employee on retirement. The employer has the obligation to build up enough funds to provide the annuity at retirement, although the employee is often required to contribute to these plans as well. Employee contributions vary, but can range from between 0% up to about 10% of the employee's salary. The employer uses an actuary to figure out how much money needs to be put away to make this promise, and the types of investments that need to be made. The problem with these plans is that the actuarial calculations involve a great number of assumptions (time, employee earnings, salaries, inflation, lifespan, investment returns) so even a very small error can result in the plan being greatly underfunded. The calculation for a defined benefit is based on any of four calculations:

- ○ **Career Average Earnings**. The employer might put into place a plan in which the employee's benefit will be based on the average of all earnings across the employee's career;

- ○ **Final Average Earnings**. The career average might not be attractive, because it will take into account the employee's early years, which are typically lower earnings periods. An employer who recognizes this might offer a final average plan;

- ○ **Best Earnings**. The final average, while more attractive than the career average, will result in the employee being penalized for working reduced hours or reduced responsibilities in their final years of employment, as many people do. To compensate for this, some employers (notably many civil service pensions) offer a best earnings plan. This might pay a benefit based on the best three consecutive years, or the best five years in total;

- ○ **Flat Benefit**. Not all workers who have pensions will earn an annual salary. Trade union members will work on jobs provided for them as those jobs are available. They might work 12 months out of the year, or, in a slow year, they might only work a few months. A pension plan based on average earnings will not work for these people. Instead, unions typically offer defined benefit plans in which the promised retirement benefit grows based on the number of hours, days, or months worked. There might be a flat increase, for instance, of $90 of annual pension for every month spent doing union jobs. This is a flat benefit plan.

Once we know which of these formulas we are going to use, we can calculate the retirement pension. The following formula is used:

| | | Employee Situation | Example |
|---|---|---|---|
| Percentage | Maximum of 2% (up to $2,770 in 2014) of earnings | Our employee earns $82,000 per year and is in pension plan that offers a 1.75% benefit | 1.75% (.0175) |
| x Number of Years Employment | The number of years of pensionable earnings | Our employee has worked here for 26 years | x 26 |
| x Benefit Calculation | Based on career, best earnings, or final average; flat benefit does not use this formula, but instead provides a flat benefit. | Our employee is in a final average plan using the final 5 years; the average is $82,000 | X 82,000 |
| | | The employer has promised the employee an annual retirement benefit of $37,310 | 37,310 |

The employer has an obligation to make sure that the plan is properly funded. Assuming the employer funds the plan properly, this employee can count on an annuity based on $37,310 of annual income. Note that, like the RRSP, there is a maximum contribution with a DB plan. For 2014, this maximum is based on 2% of employee earnings up to $2,770. An employee who earns more than ($2,770 ÷ 2% =) $138,500 will receive the maximum benefit from the DB plan. This is roughly the same as the RRSP maximum, which is $24,270. ($24,270 ÷ 18% = $134,833.) The intent here is to allow those who have pensions to accumulate roughly the same value as those who do not have pensions. (In fact, the RRSP limit always lags one year behind the DB limit. Next year's RRSP limit will be the same as this year's DB limit.)

DB plans were once very common. However, the uncertainty for the employer has lead many employers to stop offering these plans. While most DB plans are relatively stable today, there are some of these plans offered in Canada that suffer from serious funding deficiencies. This puts the employee's retirement income in doubt. DB plan sponsors are required to report the health of their pension plans on a regular basis, but this has not meant that all of these plans have been properly funded. Many civil service and large-scale manufacturing and resources jobs still provide DB plans.

- **Defined Contribution Plans.** Because of the uncertainty and the hard-to-meet funding requirements around DB plans, many employers have switched to the less cumbersome Defined Contribution (DC) plans. These plans are also frequently called Money Purchase plans. A DC plan works more like, say, an RRSP. The employer and employee put money into a plan on a tax deductible basis. The plan grows on a tax-deferred basis, based on the performance of the underlying investments. The investment options normally comprise a range of segregated funds and mutual funds. Some employers offer a very basic set of investment options (low risk, medium risk, high risk) while some offer a large range of funds. The maximum amount that can be put into a DC plan in a given year is called the Money Purchase limit. For 2014, the limit is $24,930. The DC plan, then, allows retirement benefits to accumulate at about the same level as RRSP and DB plans.

  The intent with the DC plan is to grow the investments in the plan during the working years. On retirement, the employee will have access to an annuity based on the accumulated value within the plan. There is a great deal more uncertainty with these plans, as the employer has made no particular promise to the employee, except for the matching of contributions. Contributions to DC plans vary; it is usually between 4% and 7% of employee's salary, with matching contributions from the employer ranging between about $.70 to about $3 for every dollar of employee contributions.

- **Taxation.** With both of these plans, any contributions made by the employee or employer are tax deductible. The growth is tax deferred. Any dollars taken out will be taxed as regular income. This is exactly the same tax treatment as an RRSP. Some employees who have pension plans lament the inability (or reduced ability) to contribute to an RRSP. Recall that contributions to a pension plan generate a pension adjustment, which causes a reduction in the RRSP contribution allowance.  The truth is, though, that this employee receives exactly the same tax benefits as an RRSP contributor.  The difference is that the employee never sees the contributed amounts as salary in the first place, so the deduction is less obvious.  The end result, though, is the same in both cases.  Funds that flow into a pension plan are tax deductible, just as RRSP contributions are.  Note that, unlike a RRIF, withdrawals beyond the schedule annuity benefit are not possible, so there is no concern around withholding tax with pensions.  It is possible that the pension provider will withhold certain amounts, but this is dependent on the client's particular situation.

- **Maturity**.  As with the RRSP, it is not possible to continue to accumulate benefits any later than December 31st of the 71st year.  Many pension plans allow earlier access than that age.  This varies greatly, but is sometimes as young as age 50.  Pensions use a formula to determine normal retirement age, the earliest age at which pension benefits can be accessed.  This formula is based on the number of years of service plus the age of the employee.  Early retirement is often possible, but it will result in a decrease in the amount of the pension benefit.

- **Pension Booklet**.  The specific rules for any particular pension can be gleaned from the pension booklet, which is available from the employee's Human Resources department.  An agent who is helping a client to figure out pension options should acquire a copy of the pension booklet and should put together a list of questions for the client to ask the Human Resources department.  A significant failing of pensions in general is the lack of understanding by employees about their pension options.  Many employees make poorly informed decisions about the handling of their pensions, which can have disastrous effects on retirement planning.  This can be further complicated by the fact that many employers offer different pensions to different employees depending on the start date and nature of employment.  Pensions can be either federally or provincially regulated, depending on the industry.  Pensions in the Territories use federal legislation.  Further complicating this is the fact that there are different rules for different pensions, depending on when the pension was established.  Prior to about 1993, most pensions allowed much more liquidity than is the case today.  In recent years, some of that liquidity was restored.  All these changes mean that an employee can even have different pensions with different rules from the same employer.  Again, the agent dealing with complex pension questions should seek professional advice.

- **Annuitization**.  As discussed in Module 13, the employee will turn the amount accumulated in the pension plan into an annuity.  A life straight annuity will provide the greatest immediate benefit.  If the employee is married, then the employee will be compelled to use a joint-and-last survivor option, which will reduce the benefit, but will guarantee something for the survivor.  Depending on the jurisdiction in which the pension is legislated (a very complex set of rules makes this hard to determine, and expert advice may be necessary) the survivor's benefits will be either 60%,

66.67%, or 75% of the pension. Also as discussed in Module 13, an insured annuity, which requires the spouse's consent, may be a more beneficial arrangement. Where the spouse of a pensioner is terminally ill, it is usually best to waive the survivor's benefits.

- **Eligibility**. Eligibility to join the pension may not come on the first day of employment. An employer can restrict the new employee's eligibility to join the pension until the employee has been employed for as long as two years. Part-time and casual employees also often have no access to the pension. The years of eligible service are used to calculate the pension benefit, but the years of total service are used to calculate the normal retirement age.

- **Vesting**. Vesting is a powerful feature of pension plans. Once an employee has been in the plan for two years, the employer must vest all contributions with the employee. That means that, even if the employee leaves the employer, the amounts contributed by both the employee and employer belong to the employee. The employee might choose, in some cases, to leave the amounts to accumulate in the pension plan until retirement, or the employee might move the funds into a Locked-In Retirement Account (LIRA). The LIRA works in many ways like an RRSP, but lacks the liquidity of an RRSP. If an employee leaves prior to vesting, then the employer takes back their contributions, and the employee gets their contributions returned. The return of contributions to the employee is normally done as a transfer to the RRSP. If it is taken as cash, which is sometimes possible, then it will be fully taxable as regular income. Vesting can be provided after less than two years of pensionable service if the employer wishes.

- **Locking In**. Once the plan is vested, it is also considered locked-in. With the exception of certain unlocking provisions, which we will discuss later in this module, locked-in means that the employee cannot access the funds until retirement age is reached. There are options, such as the LIRA, to allow the employee to manage the investments, but the employee will not be able to take the money out and spend it. Retirement age varies from jurisdiction to jurisdiction, but is normally around age 55.

- **Portability**. Some pension plans permit portability. This is normally done between two similar pension plans in related fields, such as two provincial governments. Where there is portability, an employee leaving one employer can take the funds accumulated in that pension plan and move them to their new employer's pension plan. This allows the employee to treat all their service as if it were with one pension, rather than having to start over. Portability is relatively rare among private sector pensions.

- **Indexing**. Employees receiving benefits through a DB plan will normally have those benefits indexed to inflation. The indexing might be to 100% of inflation, but lesser indexing, such as 60%, is also quite common. This indexing is quite useful in that it allows the employee some certainty around the effects of inflation on their pension plan, reducing inflation risk. Employees receiving benefits through a DC plan do not have automatic indexing, but can choose to purchase indexing as part of their plan. As discussed in Module 13, this will initially reduce the annuity benefit.

- **On Death**. The rules for the death of an employee who is in the accumulation phase of a DC or DB plan are varied and complex. In many cases it will be similar to the rules for the death of an RRSP owner, but this is not a safe assumption. Expert advice must be sought.
- **Leaving the Plan**. An employee who leaves the plan prior to retirement (some plans will not allow this decision after a certain age, such as 50) can take any vested amounts with them. Those amounts will be transferred to a LIRA, or may be subject to unlocking provisions, as discussed later in this module.

## RPP SUMMARY

Registered Pension Plans are declining in use due to the changing nature of employment. With more and more people working on a contract basis and in short-term capacities, employees often do not become eligible for pension benefits. Employers are forced to do more with less, and many employers feel that they cannot afford to offer pension plans. However, this is still a valuable benefit. Everybody needs to save for retirement, and the RPP provides a valuable tool for doing so. An agent who understands RPPs and their benefits will be better able to assist clients in planning for retirement. Some agents make a living helping employers to build these plans, and realizing the benefits that they offer in the form of employee loyalty and retention can set an employer apart in a competitive market.

# LOCKED IN RETIREMENT ACCOUNT

The Locked-In Retirement Account (LIRA) is the same as an RRSP, except for the origin of the funds and the ability to access those funds. The LIRA, as discussed in the previous section, originates when an employee leaves a pension plan and takes the vested amounts with her. The LIRA becomes the vehicle that will hold those investments. It differs from the RRSP, however, in that there is no provision for accessing the funds in the LIRA. There is no Home Buyers Plan, no Lifelong Learning Plan, and no withdrawals or withholding tax. There will also be no further contributions to a LIRA. The only way to add new funds to a LIRA is by leaving a pension plan. Of course, successful investments within the LIRA will increase the value of the LIRA.

The LIRA is similar to the RRSP in that it must be matured by December 31st of the 71st year. It may be able to be matured earlier, depending on the pension legislation in the jurisdiction in question. Usually the earliest age for maturity is about age 55. It offers tax deferred growth. The investment options for a LIRA are the same as for an RRSP (except that income producing annuities cannot be held in a LIRA). Self-directed and managed LIRAs are both possible. On death of the LIRA owner, the LIRA is treated as an RRSP. There are no spousal LIRAs. The LIRA is creditor protected.
On maturity of the LIRA, the owner has the option of annuitizing the LIRA or maturing it into a Life Income Fund (LIF). Two provinces still allow conversion to a Life Retirement Income Fund (LRIF), which is essentially the same as a LIF.

The LIRA is used when an employee leaves a pension plan and wishes to have the ability to manage the funds that accumulated in the pension. It is also useful when the client wishes to ultimately take advantage of unlocking provisions, which we will discuss later in this module.

# LIFE INCOME FUND

The Life Income Fund (LIF) is to the LIRA as the RRIF is to the RRSP. This is the vehicle of choice for holding investments that were held in a LIRA during the working years. Upon maturity of the LIRA, if the client wishes to maintain control over those investments, then the LIRA will be converted into a LIF. If the client is content to receive a stream of income with no flexibility instead, then the client will annuitize the LIRA. The investment options within a LIF are the same as those in the RRSP.

Once the LIF is established, it works like the RRIF. There is a minimum withdrawal every year based on the same formula as for the RRIF. If the client withdraws more than the minimum, then there will be withholding tax. A major difference, though, is the presence of a maximum withdrawal. Unlike the RRIF, a LIF owner cannot clean out the LIF. The funds within are still considered to be locked-In, and this limits the owner's ability to fully access those funds.

On death of the LIF owner, amounts held in the LIF are treated as they would be in an RRSP.

In some jurisdictions, there is a very similar vehicle available called a Life Retirement Income Fund (LRIF). The LRIF and the LIF are nearly identical. The only difference is in the annuitization requirements. In some jurisdictions, annuitization is required at age 80 in the LRIF. In some provinces, it is required at age 80 in the LIF. Most provinces have done away altogether with annuitization requirements. Annuitization just means that the funds in the plan have to be used to buy an annuity.

The LIF is useful when a client wishes to have flexibility to manage their locked-in investments in retirement. It might also be employed while a client wishes to use their locked in funds to purchase an annuity, but is waiting for annuity rates to change.

# PENSION UNLOCKING

Recent legislative changes have increased the ability to access previously locked-in funds. Today, in many jurisdictions, it is possible to access certain portions of a locked-in account (LIRA, LIF, or LRIF) under certain conditions. Unlocking does not mean that the client takes the funds out. Instead, it means a move from a LIRA, LIF, or LRIF, into an RRSP or RRIF. Once the funds are in the RRSP or RRIF then the client could access them normally. Transfers made under unlocking provisions do not require the transferor to have contribution room available. While the actual rules are quite complex, the scenarios that permit unlocking are normally:

- **Small Amounts**. Normally when there is less than 50% of Year's Maximum Pensionable Earnings in a locked-in plan, the plan owner can transfer those amounts to an unlocked plan (RRSP or RRIF).
- **Becoming a Non-Resident**. Cutting residential ties to Canada will allow the plan owner to unlock those amounts.
- **Shortened Life Expectancy**. A plan owner who is not going to live long enough to access the funds at a normal age will be permitted to access them early.
- **Financial Hardship**. A client who can demonstrate financial hardship can unlock these funds.
- **Spousal or Child Maintenance**. In order to access funds to meet a court order for child maintenance or spousal support, these funds can be unlocked.

The previous 5 provisions are in place in most (but not all provinces). They allow unlocking under a very limited set of circumstances. Some provinces and the federal government have recently introduced legislation to allow a one-time unlocking of locked-in funds when the transfer is made from a LIRA to a LIF. So a client who has $200,000 in a LIRA and is transferring to a LIF may be able to move some of that $200,000 into a RRIF instead. Unlocking is available in the following jurisdictions:

- Saskatchewan allows 100% unlocking; and
- Alberta, Manitoba, Ontario, and the federal government allow 50% unlocking.

Unlocking has advantages and disadvantages. The client who chooses to unlock can have easier access to funds, but stands the risk of expending those funds frivolously, hurting their ability to meet their future retirement needs.

## DEFERRED PROFIT SHARING PLANS

A Deferred Profit Sharing Plan (DPSP) is similar to many of the pensions we have already looked at, but is not a Registered Pension Plan. The DPSP is established by an employer who wishes to set up a pension plan for their employees and not have a promise to meet every year. DC and DB plans force the employer to make contributions on a regular basis, and limit the ability of the employer to pick and choose who belongs on the plan. DPSPs give the employer much more flexibility in both the timing of contributions and the selection of pension members.

Once an employer establishes a DPSP, they can make contributions based on profits, if desired. There is no obligation to contribute, unless the employer has some sort of contract with the employees. Employees cannot contribute to a DPSP. Contributions to a DPSP are tax deductible for the employer. Growth in the plan is tax deferred. The employee will receive a Pension Adjustment, which will reduce the employee's RRSP contribution limit for the next year. The limit on contributions is 18% of employee's salary or half of the Money Purchase limit for the current year, whichever is less. (See the section on Defined Contribution plans for more information on Money Purchase limit.)

The investment options for a DPSP are the same as for an RRSP. The employer will sometimes offer a great range of investment options. Benefits must vest within two years. The employee is entitled to receive the benefits when:

- The employee retires or leaves the company; or
- The employee turns 71. Benefits must begin being paid no later than December 31st of the 71st year.

The employee can receive the benefit in one of four ways:

- Lump sum of cash;
- Lump sum of stock in equal value to the employee's share of the DPSP;
- A term certain annuity with a term of no more than ten years; or
- A life annuity with a guarantee period of no more than 15 years.

Whichever option is selected, the amount is taxable in the employee's hands. One way to defer the taxes is to roll the amount in question into an RRSP or RRIF. This can be done even if the employee has no contribution room available, or has already established a RRIF.

Once such a transfer is made, the amounts can be accessed as they normally would from an RRSP or RRIF. DPSPs are attractive for employers who wish to provide a retirement benefit for employees, but do not wish to be forced into making regular contributions. This type of plan can help an employer who is in an uncertain financial position to establish a plan to help retain and attract employees.

## PENSION INCOME SPLITTING

Income splitting refers to spreading income amongst family members in order to pay the least taxes possible, and sometimes to allow the maximum possible access to means-tested benefits such as OAS. There are a number of income splitting strategies that are considered acceptable. We have already looked at two of them in this course. In Module 7, we examined splitting of CPP benefits, and in this module, we looked at the Spousal RRSP. These tools both provide useful methods of income splitting. Couples who take advantage of them may be able to pay less tax and may have increased access to OAS benefits.

Recent legislative changes have opened up the ability to also legally split pension income. Normally, income will be attributed to the taxpayer who earned it, but pension income splitting rules now allow certain types of pension income to be split between spouses. In this case, splitting means that a spouse can attribute up to 50% of the income from a particular source to their spouse. In addition to a decreased tax bill and an increase in OAS benefits, this can also allow both spouses to claim the pension income tax credit.

There are two sets of rules for pension income splitting. The first set of rules applies to people younger than 65. Pensioners under 65 can split income when the source is:

- Income directly from a DB or DC plan (that is, the amount cannot have been transferred to a LIRA, LIF, or LRIF, but must be the annuity directly acquired with the proceeds of that plan); or

- RRIF, DPSP, or RRSP payments received as the result of the death of the spouse or common-law partner. Note that the spouse would have to have remarried in order to be able to split this income!

Starting in the year in which the taxpayer turns 65, a great deal more sources of income can be split:

- The sources discussed in the previous list;
- Income from a RRIF;
- Payments from an annuity held within an RRSP or DPSP;
- Payments from a LIF or LRIF;
- Payments on the termination of a DPSP; or
- The interest portion of a non-registered insurance company annuity.

Note that it is the spouse who is the original recipient of the income who must meet the target age. A taxpayer who is 63 and earns RRIF income could not split that income with a 67 year old spouse. If the 67 year old were earning the RRIF income, though, it could be split with the younger spouse.

Properly done, income splitting can allow a couple to save hundreds or thousands of dollars per year. There are a variety of other income splitting techniques, such as loans between spouses, transfers for fair market value, and employing a family member. Advice from a tax professional is always recommended when using income splitting techniques.

## TAX FREE SAVINGS ACCOUNT

The recently introduced Tax Free Savings Account (TFSA) has some characteristics in common with the RRSP, but is different in many ways as well. This account is designed to offer much more liquidity and flexibility, but also has a smaller contribution limit. We will look at some of the details of the TFSA:

- **Contribution Room.** When initially established, the TFSA had an annual contribution room of $5000 per year. This is not income dependent; there is no calculation. As of 2013, the limit was $5,500 per year. The TFSA will always have a round limit to the nearest $500. So the next increase after $5,500 will happen when the cumulative effects of inflation are enough to increase the contribution allowance to $6000, and then $6,500, and so forth. One must be at least 18 years of age to open a TFSA. Contributions to a TFSA are made with after-tax dollars; there is no deduction or credit for contributing. Over contributions are penalized the same way they are for RRSPs, but with no over contribution allowance. Unlike RRSP over contributions, though, over contributions to the TFSA also result in taxation of the investment returns on the excess contributions.

- **Withdrawals**.  Withdrawals can be made from a TFSA at any time.  There are no tax consequences to withdrawals.  Any amount can be withdrawn at any time without consideration for withholding tax, taxable income, or impact on any means-tested benefits such as OAS.  Unlike the RRSP, withdrawals from a TFSA actually create new contribution room in the next year (but not in the year in which the withdrawal was made).  This makes the account reasonably liquid, but it should still not be used like a daily-use bank account, because there is still only a $5000 annual contribution limit.

- **Carry Forward**.  Unused contribution room is carried forward indefinitely.  To completely understand the contribution room, let's imagine that we have a client who invested $5000 into a TFSA in 2009.  The client's $5000 investment grew to $6000 by 2010.  In 2010, the client would have been granted another $5000 of contribution room, but chose not to contribute.  Instead, the client withdrew $6000 from the TFSA in 2010.  In 2011, the contribution room would be ($5000 of new room for 2011 + $5000 of unused room for 2010 + $6000 based on the withdrawal made in 2010 =) $16,000.  If the client chooses to contribute that year, then some of that $16,000 would be used up.  If no contribution is made, then the contribution room carries forward indefinitely.

- **Taxation**. Contributions made to a TFSA are not tax-deductible.  Growth is completely tax-free. No tax will ever be paid on amounts withdrawn from a TFSA, no matter what the circumstances. Over contributions will be taxed as if they investment had been made in a non-registered account.

- **Eligible Investments**. The eligible investments in a TFSA are roughly the same as in an RRSP, except that a TFSA cannot hold income-producing annuities.

- **TFSA on Death**.  On death, the TFSA would form part of the estate and be tax-free.  Alternately, the spouse could be named as successor owner, which would cause the TFSA of the deceased to be transferred into the spouse's TFSA, tax-free. Any unused TFSA room left at death is lost.

- **TFSA Summary**. The TFSA is a versatile investment vehicle. Its structure is very simple. Contributions up the contribution limit are made, growth is tax-free, and withdrawals can be made at any time. It can be used to accomplish a variety of investment objectives. Selection of investments for the TFSA should take into account the investor's time horizon, risk tolerance, objectives, and desire for liquidity. Because of the relative newness of the TFSA, many of its potential applications have not yet been fully explored. The limited contribution room means that not all investments are appropriate for the TFSA. Certain mutual funds, for example, require a minimum investment of $50,000 or more.

There are differing schools of thought on the ideal investment selection for TFSA. Some advisors recommend putting investments in TFSA that will generate primarily growth and capital gains. Because growth is not taxed, this can result in significant tax savings. However, recall that capital gains outside of TFSA (or RRSP) are only taxed at 50% of the rate that regular income is taxed at.

Alternately, it may be appropriate to include fixed income investments in the TFSA. A savings account held in a TFSA, for example, will allow the interest earned on that savings account to grow tax-free. While there will not be as much growth here, that growth would otherwise be taxed very inefficiently, as regular income.

The choice as to which type of investment to hold within the TFSA should depend on the needs of the client. A good advisor can explain the consequences of each type of investment decision, and help the client to determine what type of investment to hold in the TFSA.

## REGISTERED EDUCATION SAVINGS PLAN

Having looked at some savings plans that will help the investor to save for retirement or other broad objectives, we will now look at two plans that help the investor to save for very specific objectives. The first of these is the Registered Education Savings Plan (RESP). The RESP is designed to help the investor put money aside to fund a future need related to education. We generally think of saving for a child's education, but it is not necessarily the case. In order to understand the RESP, we will look at a few concepts:

- **Plan Subscriber**. The subscriber of an RESP can be anybody, but in some cases, there must be a relationship between the subscriber and the beneficiary. The subscriber is what we would otherwise call plan owner; the one who sets up the plan and owns the underlying investments. Note that anybody can contribute to the RESP; the subscriber and contributor need not be the same person. It is possible for spouses to act as joint subscribers.

- **Beneficiary**. The beneficiary of the plan depends on the type of plan. In certain plans, there must be a relationship between beneficiary and subscriber. There are three plan types:

  - **Family Plan**. A family plan can have multiple beneficiaries. All beneficiaries must be related to the subscriber by blood or adoption (this would include children and grandchildren, and also stepchildren). Beneficiaries can be no more than 31 years of age when named. The family plan generally offers the most flexibility for parents, because if multiple children are named as beneficiaries and one child does not go to school, some or all of the amounts saved on that child's behalf can be easily transferred to another child.

  - **Individual Plan**. An individual plan has only one beneficiary. There does not need to be any relationship between beneficiary and subscriber. This could be set up for a child, a niece or nephew, a favourite neighbour, or even for oneself. If the beneficiary does not go to school, this can cause some tax challenges. This type of RESP is also known as a Non-Family Plan.

  - **Group Plan**. At one time very common, these plans have fallen out of favour because of a perceived lack of flexibility. Group plans essentially function like a series of individual plans.

- **Sponsor.** The plan sponsor is the institution that will provide the investments held within the RESP and take care of the administration, such as registering the plan with the government, applying for grants, and providing any tax documents. It is important to recognize the limitations imposed by the plan sponsor. A Human Resources and Social Development Canada (HRSDC) committee in 2008 published a review criticizing some RESP practices, such as heavy surrender charges and limitations on qualifying education programs.

- **Investment Options.** Investment options for RESPs are technically the same as for RRSPs. Practically, though RESP options are far more limited than they are for RRSPs. Mutual funds, GICs, and bank accounts are widely available. A few insurers offer IVICs as an RESP investment.

- **Taxation.** Contributions to the RESP are not tax deductible. Growth in the plan is tax-deferred. When withdrawals are made, the previously untaxed amounts (grants and growth) will be taxable in the hands of the party making the withdrawal.

- **Contribution Limits.** The lifetime contribution limit to the RESP is $50,000. There is no annual maximum. It should be noted that a lump-sum contribution of $50,000, while possible, will limit access to Canada Education Savings Grants. Contributions can only be made to a plan up until the 31st year after the plan was established.

- **Canada Education Savings Grants.** The CESG is perhaps the most attractive component of the RESP. If the beneficiary of the plan turns 15 years of age or younger when the plan is established, then CESG will provide grant money to match contributions. In the years in which the beneficiary turns 16 and 17, CESG will only pay if there have been previous contributions made. The amount of contribution is based on the beneficiary's family income. Since 2005, the enhanced CESG program allowed for grants as follows:

| Family Income (2014 Amounts) | Grant Matches | Maximum Grant |
|---|---|---|
| $43,561 or less | 40% on first $500; 20% on next $2000 | $600 |
| $43,561 to $87,123 | 30% on first $500; 20% on next $2000 | $550 |
| Over $87,123 | 20% on up to $2500 | $500 |

If a plan is started at some point after the child's first calendar year, CESG will actually allow up to one year of missed grants to be made up at one time.

- **Canada Learning Bond.** Children born after 2003 will also have up to $2000 added to their RESP by the Canada Learning Bond program. The Canada Learning Bond is only available in certain circumstances. It is based on eligibility for the National Child Benefit Supplement, which can be paid to families with net income of less than approximately $110,000, depending on the number of children in the family.

- **Using the Plan.** The plan is designed to be used when the plan beneficiary enters into a qualifying educational program. When this happens, an education assistance payment will be applied for. The initial amount that can be accessed is $5000, based on a program that meets HRSDC's criteria for a qualifying program. Once a program exceeds 13 weeks of full-time education, then all the amounts in the plan can be accessed. Proof of enrolment is required, but the amount does not have to be used to pay tuition. It could be used for books, living expenses, or a spring break holiday, as long as the beneficiary is in a qualifying educational program. The beneficiary will be taxed on any grants and growth taken out, but the original amount contributed will not be taxed when it is withdrawn.

- **Terminating the Plan.** If the plan beneficiary does not end up in qualifying education program by the time she turns 36, or if the beneficiary dies before the plan can be used, then the plan must be collapsed. This results in:

  o The repayment of any grants and bonds received;
  o The return of the contributions to the plan subscriber (this is tax-free, as these were after-tax dollars in the first place); and

  o Any growth that was achieved within the plan will be taxable in the subscriber's hands. This growth will be taxed at the subscriber's marginal tax rate plus a further 20% (ie. a subscriber who would normally be taxed at 32% will instead be taxed at 52%). Where joint subscribers were named, the income can be attributed to either or both subscribers, at the subscriber's discretion. This is not a very attractive proposition, so there is a provision which allows for this amount to be rolled over to the subscribers' RRSP (but not to the beneficiary's RRSP.) In order to take advantage of this provision, the subscriber must have room available. There is a limit of $50,000 of RRSP rollover per subscriber. Remember that it is only the growth that must be rolled over. Contributions and grants will have been returned without tax consequence. Because there is the requirement to have the room available, parents who are nearing the end of the allowable time for a plan to exist should stop making RRSP contributions and ensure that they are named as joint subscribers. (This can be changed at any time.) By so doing, the parents will minimize their tax consequences.

- **RESP Summary.** The RESP, largely because of the free money provided, is a very popular program. Education costs are increasing at a rate beyond inflation, and parents who fail to save for their child's education may be limiting that child's ability to enjoy the benefits of a post-secondary education. Agents must work carefully to ensure that they and their clients fully understand the limitations attached to any RESP being offered.

# REGISTERED DISABILITY SAVINGS PLAN

The Registered Disability Savings Plan (RDSP) was introduced to help create a meaningful amount of savings to assist disabled people to be able to look out for their own financial well-being. The program is a savings plan, and, should be, like the RRSP, primarily regarded as being designed to meet long-term objectives. It is not designed to provide short-term income.

As with the RESP, one of the great advantages of the RDSP is that HRSDC has set up programs to provide free money to RDSP beneficiaries. Let's have a look at the workings of the RDSP:

- **Beneficiary**. The beneficiary of the plan must be a Canadian resident who has qualified for the Disability Tax Credit (DTC). In order to qualify for the DTC, a qualified medical professional must complete a CRA form indicating that the individual is disabled. This can be due to an inability to perform the activities of daily living, or due to blindness, deafness, or reliance on life-supporting therapy. There is only one beneficiary per RDSP. The beneficiary also fills the role of plan owner, unless a minor, in which case a parent or guardian will perform that function. The beneficiary of a new RDSP can be no more than age 59.

- **Contributions.** Anybody can contribute to an RDSP once it is established. The lifetime contribution limit is $200,000 per beneficiary. No more contributions are permitted once the beneficiary is beyond age 59. There is no annual maximum contribution.

- **Sponsor.** The plan sponsor fills the same role in the RDSP as in the RESP.

- **Taxation.** Contributions to the plan are not tax deductible. Growth is tax deferred. Upon withdrawal, untaxed amounts will be taxed in the beneficiary's hands.

- **Investments.** Nearly the same investment options are available here as in the RRSP. However, because the plan is relatively new, there are few plan sponsors. This means that, practically, the range of investment options is somewhat limited. Further, the RDSP cannot have a beneficiary designation attached to it, other than the plan beneficiary (the disabled person). This prevents the use of segregated funds, annuities, or insurance policies within the RDSP.

- **Grants & Bonds.** The most striking feature of the RDSP is the amount of free money available. As with the RESP, HRSDC provides a matching grant when RDSP contributions are made. Grants and bonds are only available up until the year that the beneficiary turns 49. The grant, known as the Canada Disability Savings Grant, works as follows:

| Net Family Income | Grant (matching) | Maximum Grant |
|---|---|---|
| less than $87,123 | 300% on first $500; 200% on next $1000 | $3500 |
| over $87,123 | 100% on first $1000 | $1000 |

There is also a bond that can be paid. Unlike the grant, the bond is not dependent on contributions being made. The bond will be automatically paid into the plan for any beneficiary whose family income is below a certain level. For that reason, even if contributions cannot be made, RDSPs should be set up for eligible beneficiaries with low family incomes.

| Net Family Income | Bond |
|---|---|
| less than $25,356 | $1000 |
| $25,356 to $43,561 | pro-rated up to $1000 |
| over $43,561 | 0 |

This is a substantial amount of free money. For a low income earner, $1500 of contributions will attract $4500 in combined grants and bonds. The lifetime maximum of grants that can be received is $70,000. The lifetime maximum of bonds that can be received is $20,000.

- **Withdrawals.** Withdrawals from the plan can be made by applying at any time prior to age 60. These disability assistance payments are not scheduled, and must be applied for in order to be received. Starting at age 60, the plan moves into a RRIF-type withdrawal schedule known as lifetime disability assistance payments. There is a severe consequence to early withdrawals. Any early withdrawal can automatically trigger a repayment of all grants and bonds received in the previous ten years. Recent legislative changes allow withdrawals without penalty in cases of shortened life expectancy. There is also a different treatment of withdrawals from plans where the principal source of funding for the RDSP is an inheritance from a parent's RRSP. Older grants and bonds are safe, but those received recently must be repaid. Similarly, if the beneficiary dies or gets better (is no longer disabled) then those grants and bonds received in the previous 10 years must be repaid. Further, the beneficiary (or the estate) would receive any untaxed amounts (the growth that happened in the plan) as taxable income at that time. Any time that money flows from the plan into the beneficiary's hands, previously untaxed amounts received will be taxed as regular income.

  Payments out of and assets held within the RDSP will not impact on other federal government benefits. This gives the beneficiary the freedom to take payments as needed without fear about losing other government benefits. All provinces have passed legislation to mirror this provision. This is a very important planning point, as the provinces generally provide means-tested access to free health care and other services for disabled people.

- **RRSP/RRIF Rollover.** When a parent (or grandparent) dies with funds in a RRSP/RRIF/LIF/LIRA, that parent can transfer up to $200,000 into a dependent child's RDSP. Dependent, for this purpose, means the child has income less than about $18,000 for the year. This rollover is tax-free, but it does not attract any grants or bonds. This can also be done if a parent left funds to their spouse.  The spouse can then elect to transfer those funds to the disabled child's RDSP.

- **Terminating the Plan**.  The plan will be terminated on death or improvement of the beneficiary's condition.  As stated above, bonds and grants will be repaid and there will be tax consequences.

- **RDSP Summary**.  For a parent with a disabled child, there are often concerns as to how that child will take care of themselves financially later in life.  The RDSP can help a parent to deal with those concerns.  This could also be a very useful plan for a family who is responsible for caretaking for a disabled adult, such as a brother or sister.  By starting one of these plans, the family can help to improve the quality of life for that person.  The very generous grants and bonds provide an excellent incentive for contributing to these plans.  The liquidity restriction must be kept in mind, though.  Bonds and grants paid in the previous 10 years cannot be accessed, which reinforces the long-term nature of the plan.

# REGISTERED VS NON-REGISTERED INVESTMENTS

Throughout this module, we have looked at a wide variety of investment plans designed to help meet certain objectives.  The government provides tax incentives and, in some cases, free money, to help with these objectives.  However, this comes at a cost.  In most cases, these plans involve building a future tax burden.  There are liquidity restrictions.  Not all investments are available.

For those reasons, some investors prefer to invest in non-registered investments.  Non-registered investments normally do not have all the rules that we have learned in this module.  Liquidity is not restricted by the investment vehicle (although some investments are illiquid by nature).The tax consequences are generally more immediate, but will not create a tax burden to be dealt with later.

When deciding whether or not to use a registered plan, we should consider the tax advantages.  Low income earners tend to get less benefit from these plans than high income earners. At the same time, a few dollars of tax savings can make a big difference to a lower income earner.  High income earners may find themselves penalized later on in life when forced to make very large, taxable withdrawals from their RRIFs.

The agent must be sure that the client is fully aware of any tax consequences and restrictions inherent in these plans.  Our own experience tells us that even though millions of Canadians use RRSPs, Pension Plans, and RESPs, very few actually understand them.

As with all investments, it is usually wise to diversify.  Have some of your client's funds in registered accounts, and some in non-registered.  Use a combination of the RRSP and TFSA.  This will provide the client with the flexibility to access funds when needed, but also with long-term security.  Some amounts will be taxed today, some later, and some not at all.

Finally, do not disregard life insurance when building a retirement plan.  Long-term care insurance can be a powerful tool.  Understanding the RRSP, RRIF, and LIF is necessary for putting the right amount of permanent insurance in place to take care of any tax burden.

## SUMMARY

Having gone through the first 14 modules of this text, you should now be prepared to help families and individuals deal with the three predictable risks.  In the next two modules you will find a selection of case studies and advanced concepts, all of which are useful for reinforcing learning.

# Chapter 15 INSURANCE FOR BUSINESSES

In the previous 14 Modules, we primarily focused on selling and servicing insurance for the individual and family markets. For most insurance agents, this probably represents the bulk of the business they do. There are many insurance agents in Canada who sell insurance primarily to a business market. It is just as important for your success in this course that you understand the business market as the individual market.

In this module, we will look at some very specific applications relevant to the business market. Some of these applications use products that we are already familiar with, but there are a couple of new products we will also look at in this module.

As we go through the products and concepts in this module, we will look at using insurance to protect business owners, the business itself, families of business owners, and the people who work in the business. It is important as part of our risk management to look at what risks the business faces, and how we can use insurance to manage those risks.

For study purposes, much of the material in this module will not directly be tested. The items that will be tested are specifically designated as such. However, in order to understand the topics that will be tested, it is necessary to understand the background information provided in this module.

It may be useful, prior to reading this module, to go back and review Module 5, especially the portion dealing with the taxation of businesses.

## TYPES OF BUSINESSES

This course is not meant to be a course in business administration, but there are some basic concepts that we have to be familiar with in order to understand business insurance. The first concept we will examine here will be types of businesses. While there are many different possible structures of a business, we are going to look here at three of the most common structures. In most cases, you will find that the ideas discussed here would carry over to other sorts of businesses anyways.

- **Sole Proprietorship**. A sole proprietorship is a business in which a person individually owns all the assets of the business. Many businesses start out this way. A person has an idea for a business, and she goes out and buys whatever equipment the business needs to get started. All the income and expenses of the business are attributed directly to the business owner. There is no separation in this case between the business owner and the business. This is the easiest and cheapest type of business to set up. It works fine for an entrepreneur who wishes to run a business on their own with little administrative burden. The chief downside is that there is no protection for the business owner in case of liability in the business, making her personal assets subject to claims by the business' creditors. A further drawback is that it makes the business difficult to sell, should the business owner wish to do so. Sole proprietorships are usually smaller businesses where one person is responsible for most of the revenue and activity of the business.

- **Partnership**. A partnership is essentially two or more sole proprietorships joined together. There are some additional features. In a partnership, there is slightly more formality to the business structure than there is in a sole proprietorship. The partnership needs to file tax returns, and it can own property, although the ownership ultimately resides with the partners. It is possible to use a partnership structure to allow for the orderly sale of a business. There can be limited tax advantages to a partnership, but income and expenses are attributed to the partners. A partnership's chief advantage over a sole proprietorship is that management responsibilities can be shared between two or more owners. Partnerships are relatively cheap and easy to set up. The drawbacks are similar to the drawbacks of a sole proprietorship. Many small and large businesses operate as partnerships.

- **Corporation**. A corporation is a highly formalized business structure. It stands alone as its own legal entity. A corporation can enter into contracts, sue and be sued, and it has rights and obligations under the law. A corporation requires legal and administrative processes in order to start up and stay in existence. The chief advantage of a corporation is that it separates the business assets from the assets of the owners. Another advantage is that ownership of a corporation is broken into shares, and those shares can be bought and sold, meaning that owners can sell their interest in the business more easily than in other structures. There can be tax advantages to the owners of a corporation. Notably, unlike the previous two structures, a corporation is taxed as its own separate entity and it can retain earnings within itself. The disadvantages of the corporation are the cost and administration required. While some small businesses operate as corporations, it is generally more advisable to incorporate once a business has reached a certain size, which would be determined on a case-by-case basis.

## PROTECTING OWNERS

In a business, things can go wrong that will impact directly on the owners and their families. As part of our risk management, we want to put in place measures to ensure that if these things go wrong, the suffering to the owner and family will be minimized.

In the case of a sole proprietorship, the risk management strategies are basically the same as they are for an individual or family. We would put in place whatever A&S policies are required in order to manage the risk. For a corporation or partnership, however, there are additional considerations. A corporation or partnership could be adversely affected if any of the following happened to any of the owners:

- **Death**. On death, ownership of an interest in a business normally rolls to a surviving spouse, if there is one. Ownership would otherwise roll to the estate. The problem that arises is that the ownership interest is probably not any longer in the hands of somebody who is interested in running the business. The challenge, then, becomes finding a way to arrange moving the ownership from the heir to somebody who does want to and should be involved in running the business.

- **Disability**. If a business owner becomes severely disabled, then the business owner will likely look for a way to exchange his interest in the business for cash to help fund the costs of a disability. The challenge will be coming up with the cash, as most businesses do not have ready pools of cash available for such events. (At one time, accounting practice was that businesses would establish a sinking fund of this nature to fund various unplanned obligations.)

- **Retirement**. When it comes time for a business owner to retire, he will likely look for a way to have somebody else buy his interest in the business. The other owners may want to have some input as to who their new partner is, or they may want to buy the interest themselves.

- **Disagreement**. A disagreement between partners can be very messy. One partner may wish to buy the other out, there might be disagreements about a fair price, who takes ownership, timing, or other such issues.

- **Other Situations**. Situations such as divorce of an owner, personal bankruptcy, criminal convictions, and evidence of drug or alcohol use, can all have an impact on the ownership of the business.

- **Buy-sell provisions**. In order to deal with some, or all, of the situations described above, business owners will often use buy-sell agreements. The buy-sell agreement is a legally binding contract entered into during the planning phase of a business. All partners will sign the buy-sell agreement. The intent of the agreement is to avoid complications when any of the situations outlined above arises. So, for example, a buy-sell agreement might include a provision so that, if the partners no longer can get along, they might use a shotgun clause to terminate ownership. In this scenario, each owner makes the other a blind offer for the other's interest in the business, and the owner who has made the lowest offer will be bought out by the other partner. The good thing about buy-sell contracts is that they put everybody in a known situation well in advance of anything going wrong with the business. The challenge with buy-sell agreements is that they are often based on hypotheticals and uncertainties. So, for example, if a business owner does become disabled, the buy-sell agreement might require that the others buy her out. The problem becomes: where do we get the funds to buy out the departing shareholder?

- **Life Insurance**. It is common for businesses to acquire life insurance to help fund the buy-out on death. The actual functioning of a buy-sell agreement can be quite complex, and uses several tax concepts that are beyond the scope of this course. A lawyer and accountant are normally required to structure and execute the buy-sell. In reality, though, it is often an insurance agent who actually initiates the process of a business creating a buy-sell agreement. This is because insurance agents specialize in identifying and dealing with risk. The business owners will acquire insurance on their lives to make sure that, should one of them die, they will have the funds available to buy the shares from the survivor's heirs. This will allow the business to survive and put a fair value for the business in the heir's hands. Sometimes, business owners individually acquire insurance on each other's lives. This is called a criss-cross arrangement. In other situations, the business itself acquires the insurance. Then we have corporately owned insurance. The considerations when selling life insurance to a business are much the same as when selling life insurance to an individual. If the business has a temporary need and not a lot of cash, then term insurance will be used. If the business is flush with cash and has a permanent need (ie. one of the owners is going to stay past the age of 70 or 75) then permanent insurance should be used. Cash value insurance such as whole life or universal life has further advantages in that it provides a tax advantaged investment for the business. Also, in the event of the departure of a partner for other reasons, those cash values can be useful to either help fund a buyout or to help with retirement needs.

- **Disability Buy-Sell**. In the case of a disability for an owner of a company, a disability buy-sell agreement provides the answer. This is not an income replacement disability product like we covered in Module 9. Instead, this policy will provide a lump sum benefit to a disabled business partner in the event of a disability. The underwriting is very similar to the underwriting for traditional disability products, but the structure is different. The business will normally pay the premiums on this policy, which are not tax-deductible. The benefit will be paid tax-free to the business, but when the business pays the amounts out to the departing owner, the amounts would be taxed in that person's hands. In exchange, the departing shareholder's shares in the business would be redeemed, meaning that the cease to exist. The idea being that we would pay out the proper amount from the disability benefit to the disabled shareholder in exchange for them to give up their interest in the business. In order to acquire this policy, the applicant would have to be both an owner and work full-time in the business. These policies usually provide coverage up to age 60, sometimes as late as 65. The benefit will be paid once an elimination period of 12, 18, or 24 months has been met. While this might seem like a long elimination period, the idea is to have an idea as to whether or not the insured actually will end their involvement with the business before any benefit is paid. A disability buy-sell (or disability buyout) policy is an excellent and very clean way to generate the funds to buy out a disabled partner in the business.

## PROTECTING THE BUSINESS

The concepts discussed above are designed to protect the owners of the business. In this section, we will look at some products and concepts designed to protect the business itself.

- **Group Insurance**. Group insurance is very common in Canada. Most Canadians will, at some point during their lives, receive coverage from some sort of group insurance. You might work for an employer who offers group insurance coverage. You might go to a university where the students all have access to group dental coverage or group drug plans. Your bank might provide you with group creditor insurance to make sure that your mortgage will be paid off in the event that you die with that debt outstanding. These are all examples of group insurance. For the purpose of this course, we are primarily concerned with employer sponsored group insurance.

  All of the insurance products we have looked at in Modules 8, 9, and 10, with the exception of medical access insurance, are available as part of a group plan. It is very common to find group plans that include disability benefits, life insurance, accidental death & dismemberment benefits, dental, drug, and extended health. Group policies might also add travel insurance, critical illness insurance, and vision care benefits. It is very rare, though technically possible, for a group plan to include long-term care benefits.

  Group insurance policies are owned by an employer, and provide benefits to the employee. So the question becomes, why would an employer purchase a group insurance plan, which normally commits the employer to pay at least 50% of premiums, if the employees are going to benefit? There are several reasons why employers will provide these plans:

  - Attract and Retain Employees. Especially in a competitive job market, it is vital to the success of a business to be able to count on your staff. In order to ensure that the best staff can be found, and that they will stay once they have been hired, employers put group insurance in place. Because of rules preventing anti-selection, we know that all employees at the group will have the option of belonging to the plan. Group insurance plans become very effective ways to make sure that a company can attract and retain quality people.

  - Tax Advantages. An employer can structure plans to provide tax deductions for the business. An owner of a smaller business might use the group plan specifically to have the business pay the premiums for his family's health care plan, which is a very tax efficient structure for a corporation.

  - Low Cost. Because the coverages are going to be identical or very similar for all members of the plan, and because we spread the risk and administrative costs across the whole group, group insurance is relatively inexpensive. Group insurance plans will allow us to put a good, basic level of benefits in place for a low cost.

- **Business Overhead Expense Insurance**. In a situation where there are one or two people who are fundamental to the operation of the business, a disability to one of those people can be devastating to the business. Let's imagine a dentist's office which might have income and expenses like so:

| Item | Annual Income | Item | Annual Expenses |
|---|---|---|---|
| Work done by Dentist | $400,000 | Staffing Costs | $150,000 |
| Work done by Hygienists | $150,000 | Office Rent | $60,000 |
| Another dentist pays rent for use of the facilities | $100,000 | Equipment Leasing | $80,000 |
| | | Office Overhead | $120,000 |
| Total Income | $650,000 | Total Expenses | $410,000 |

With one dentist responsible for the vast majority of the business' income, the business would probably not survive a disability to that dentist. We can make a few notes from the (simplified) income statement described above. First, we can assume that the dentist who owns the business probably takes a personal income of $240,000 ($650,000 less $410,000 equals $240,000), assuming that he takes all the money out of the business. So, if he were purchasing individual disability insurance, which he probably should, his policy would be based on $240,000 of annual income. Second, the business has $100,000 of passive income, based on the rent paid by another dentist. That income would likely continue even if the dentist who owns the business becomes disabled. The income generated by the hygienists would likely also continue, meaning the business would still have $250,000 of income in the event of a disability. Third, we can see $410,000 of annual expenses. With only $250,000 being generated by the business, it is going to be difficult to meet those expenses. The business is left $160,000 ($410,000 less $250,000 equals $160,000) short of what it actually need to stay in operation. A business overhead expense policy with a benefit of $160,000 per year would help to manage this dentist's risk.

A business overhead expense policy can be used to replace this missing income. The underwriting for an overhead expense policy would be based on a calculation like that done in the previous paragraph. We would also have to underwrite based on the occupation, health, age, sex, avocation, and smoking status of the dentist in question. The waiting period for this policy is normally somewhere between 0 and 14 days for an accident, and 30, 60, or 90 days for an illness. The benefit period is normally 6 months, 12 months, 18 months, or 2 or 3 years. This relatively short benefit period is used to keep the premiums manageable. By time the benefit period ends, we should have an idea as to whether the disabled business owner intends to return to work, sell the business, or terminate the business.

Premiums are tax deductible. Benefits are paid as taxable income to the business. Because they are used to pay tax-deductible expenses, there will usually not be any tax paid on the benefits from this policy, once deductions have been applied against income. ($160,000 of taxable income offset by $160,000 of tax deductible expenses will result in no tax payable.) The benefits can be used to pay for whatever overhead costs the business incurs - the items included in the list above would all be covered. The business will normally have to provide to the insurer receipts proving these expenses. The funds cannot be used for additional items, such as acquisitions of new equipment. If the actual expenses prove less than estimated, the excess amounts can normally be used to extend the benefit period.

Much of what we discussed in Module 9 applies to business overhead expense insurance. These policies will have a specific definition of disability (own occ, regular occ, any occ) built in. They will often offer residual or partial benefits. They normally use a presumptive definition of disability. They are normally only available up to age 65.

Business overhead expense insurance is useful in scenarios such as that described above. If one or two people generate all or most of the business' income, this policy will minimize financial suffering in the event of a disability. It would be nice, as a small business owner, to know for sure that your business will survive your disability. The underwriting and implementation of these policies can be complicated, but it is worth it if something does go wrong.

- **Key Person Insurance.** Businesses will often have people working within them who have expertise or contacts that are unique to them. There may be a technician who has a very particular skill set. A sales representative might be the only person in the business who has relationships with all the clients. A manager in a remote location might be very difficult to replace. In all these cases, a business could choose to minimize its risk by purchasing Key Person disability and/ or Key Person life insurance. Key Person insurance (formerly known as Key Man, and sometimes known as Key Employee) is designed to help a business minimize its losses when a key person becomes disabled. It is not designed to help when a key person is fired, or quits, or gets promoted out of their role.

Underwriting for a key person policy is normally quite complex. It becomes a question of determining exactly what the person in question generates for the business. Key person policies can pay a lump sum benefit, or a regular monthly income benefit. The definition of disability depends on the same factors discussed in Module 9. A simple rule of thumb for key person insurance is that it will pay benefits equal to 2 years of the key person's salary. This will provide a starting point, although actual key person policies might vary.

The premiums for a key person policy are not tax deductible. Any benefit received will be tax-free. The lump sum benefit can be used for whatever is necessary. Normally it will be used to help with the costs of hiring or training a new person, or simply to replace the income that person would have generated.

Key person disability insurance is relatively rare in Canada today. It can be useful in situations where a business has a strong reliance on one or two employees, which can include an owner who is active in the business. Key person life insurance, on the other hand, is a frequently sold product.

# UNDERWRITING CONSIDERATIONS

There are a few additional concepts we have to consider when underwriting business insurance. We will have a look at some of these concepts here. Business owners will usually be familiar with these terms, and if you expect to service this market, you should probably know something about them as well. These documents are sometimes necessary in underwriting, but might again be requested at time of claim.

- **Financial Statements**. Financial statements for a business provide us with an historical record. Financial statements can include:

  o Balance Sheet. The balance sheet shows the current financial position of the company. It shows the value of the company, the debts of the company, and the value of the owners' shares. It is a snapshot in time.

  o Income Statement. The income statement is a history of the company. It describes the business' income and expenses over time. The income statement is useful for determining the financial health of a company.

  o Statement of Retained Earnings. The retained earnings statement describes past successes of the business. This provides an indication of the level to which the owners have reinvested earnings back into the business.

  o Cash Flow Analysis. A cash flow analysis demonstrates whether the business is bringing in more dollars than it is spending. Many analysts consider this the true indicator of a business' health.

  Financial statements are prepared in varying degrees of formality. Sometimes a printout from the company's bookkeeping software will be sufficient. Some companies will have detailed financial statements prepared by an accountant. Some financial statements are simply reviewed by an accountant. Insurers will ask for different components of the financial statement with differing degrees of formality depending on the product being sold, the size of the company, and the expectations of the insurer.

- **Business Plan**. While the financial statements provide a historical record, the business plan is useful for a look ahead. In some cases a business plan is necessary for underwriting purposes, notably to see if the business has a means of dealing with future problems. Underwriters will assess a business plan to make sure that the business will realistically be viable going forward. We don't want to sell insurance in cases where the business might take advantage of it later on and use the insurance to help wind down a business with an uncertain future. This is not a lot different than underwriting for individuals, in that we don't want to insure somebody whose stability or motivation might be questionable.

- **History vs. Predictability.** As with any type of insurance that might be issued, underwriters do not want to take on an unknown or uncertain risk with business insurance.  They want to know that policies will continue to stay in force, and that the likelihood of claims is quite low.  Historical information, such as financial statements and tax returns, is generally the tool that underwriters can best use to assess the risks particular to selling insurance in business applications.  Two years of history is generally enough for most underwriters to make a decision.

Not all businesses necessarily have a history.  Some businesses will just be getting started, and may not be able to provide historical data.  Generally, this is not acceptable for underwriters, who will insist that businesses come back once some history has been established.  However, a well-funded company with a solid business plan might represent a sound risk, and underwriters may allow such a business to enter into insurance contracts.

Contracts of group insurance do not require history; this section refers to coverage such as key person and buy-sell.

- **Other Technical and Legal Documents**.  It might also be necessary to gather other documents, such as:

  o Articles of Incorporation.  This is the 'birth certificate' for a corporation.  It can be obtained from registries offices.  It normally shows who the owners of the business are, where the business is located, and how long it has been in existence for.

  o Buy-Sell Agreement.  The buy-sell agreement is sometimes necessary in order for disability buy-sell insurance to provide its scheduled benefit.

  o Lease, Financing, and Debt Agreements.  A business might be required to provide these documents to demonstrate a need for insurance.

## SUMMARY

The business market is somewhat complex, but provides great opportunities for the agent who understands it.  Not only will the business require insurance for itself, but the owners and employees of the business might also require coverage

# Chapter 16 FAMILY APPLICATIONS

The following case study represents how one typical agent's relationship with a client family might go. The case study is intended to be representative of how any such relationship might work. The recommendations within are this particular agent's recommendations. It is not appropriate to assume that these same recommendations would work in every scenario. This is simply designed to provide you with some concept of how these ideas might work in real life.

Reading this case study, you will see that virtually every concept discussed throughout the text is somehow touched on. Acting as a life insurance agent, there is a large amount of information to be aware of. Even agents who specialize in one field or another will often end up dealing with questions far outside of their comfort zone. As mentioned several times throughout the text, it is appropriate to recognize when outside advice is required.

## CASE STUDY

In your role as a life insurance agent you are referred by a satisfied client to Harvey and Jill McLean. Harvey is a vice-president in a local construction firm. The firm builds residential homes in new developments in a major Canadian city. Harvey has worked for the firm for 15 years and has been promoted into his current role within the past 18 months. Jill, age 37, works as a receptionist/office administrator in a small wholesale distribution company. Harvey, age 40, earns $150,000 per year in his job. They have 3 children, Jonathan 13, Maria 11 and Meghan, 7. His work duties include hiring staff, obtaining building permits, purchasing supplies, dealing with the various suppliers, and dealing with city compliance. Harvey only visits job sites to check on the progress of various projects. He never does any actual construction work. He is careful to never step onto a job site without wearing the proper safety equipment.

You are a 2 year veteran of the Canadian insurance industry with a license to sell insurance in your home province. You have recently applied for a non-resident license to sell insurance and service clients who live in, or have moved to, the neighboring province. You sell insurance for a large, nationally established Managing General Agent. That MGA has contracts to sell the products of several Canadian life insurance companies. You chose this way of doing business as opposed to joining one of the traditional dedicated agency companies where you would only sell the products of that company. Of course making that choice indicates that you may have given up some of the training and support that usually goes with signing on with one of the traditional agency companies. Although you are filling the role of broker, you are still subject to the laws of agency and the legal requirements of an insurance agent. You basically take on the responsibility for your own professional development supported by the training and support offered by the MGA.

You set up a get-acquainted meeting with Harvey at a local coffee house. At that meeting you find out some basic information about Harvey and his situation and you use that opportunity to talk about how you conduct your business. Liking what he sees and your obvious commitment to professionalism, Harvey agrees to your request for an evening appointment with he and Jill at their home the following week. You follow-up with an email to confirm the appointment and a basic outline of what you will talk about during the meeting, asking Harvey if he could possibly have available for the meeting any existing insurance policies that he and Jill already own and also encourage him to have a copy of his employee benefits booklet on hand from his employer sponsored group plan. You also provide Harvey with a copy of your engagement letter, which outlines the services that you provide. It also indicates what Harvey should expect from you and what you expect from your clients.

It is now the following week and you show up at the prospect's home at the appointed time. After a few minutes of basic introductions and getting comfortable you join Harvey and Jill around their kitchen table. You have prepared a proper file for them with any information needed to focus in on the basic needs that Harvey indicated concern about in your previous meeting or in response to your email. Harvey had indicated to you that he had some insurance although was unsure of the amounts and the type of policies that he owned. In order to assist in the education process required to help Harvey and Jill understand what type of insurance that they owned and what each type of insurance is, you obtained a copy of the Canadian Life and Health Insurance Association's *A Guide to Life Insurance* (http://clhia.org/domino/html/clhia/CLHIA_LP4W_LND_Webstation.nsf/resources/Consumer+Brochures/$file/Brochure_Guide_To_Life_ENG.pdf) to go over with them briefly and to leave with them for future reference. With that out of the way you ask about each policy that they currently own and find out why they purchased the insurance in the first place. Your knowledge of the insurance process allows you to gather information in a subtle manner, as you glance through each policy. You can determine the amounts, the effective date, the riders and type from the face page. You can also glean valuable information from the application completed when they bought the insurance policy. That application is attached to the contract and becomes part of the entire contract. Of course, you are gathering this information only with the intent of placing the proper coverage on Harvey and Jill, and you will treat whatever information you gather with the highest standard of confidentiality.

The sales process that you use follows the recognized financial planning process. Your company has provided you with well-thought out legally compliant point-of-sale material that will allow you to follow comfortably through the process and to stay on track. The first part of that process is to find out what their objectives are. It turns out that their basic objectives are to ensure that should one of them die prematurely there will be enough money left behind to allow the family to keep the house and maintain their current life style. They also indicate that they would like your help in establishing a nest egg for their retirement in 25 years. You know that as you work through your planning steps you will likely uncover additional needs and concerns but you now have enough to start the process.

The 2nd part of the planning process involves gathering and analyzing the data. You find out their income by directly asking the question but one could take a slightly less direct approach by reviewing quickly their benefits booklet(s). In the Life Insurance section of their benefits booklet or certificate of insurance it indicates that they have 2 times annual income of life insurance coverage as part of their employee benefits. That would allow you to quickly determine their actual incomes. You might have a computer with software that would establish an insurance amount based on the insurance company's guidelines or you could just use a basic rule of thumb of 10 times annual income for the blue/grey collar workers and 15 to 17 times annual income for the professional/business owner/white collar executive.

Based on Harvey's $150,000 annual income you would start out with a basic assumption of an insurance need of $1,500,000 to 2.2 million worth of insurance. You would then subtract from that any insurance already owned whether that be in their existing policies, with the employee benefits package, or through their mortgage life insurance at the bank. You might even digress at this time to review those existing policies to see if they currently meet the client's needs. If they have renewable term policies, are they nearing a renewal date where the premiums are about to jump significantly? If they have whole life or other forms of permanent insurance, are the cash values significant enough to make the policy something of considerable value going forward? You know from your training that before counseling a client to cancel or replace an existing policy of insurance you must make sure that your recommendation is in the client's best interest.

During the fact finding process you find that the Harvey and Jill have assets and liabilities. The goal is to determine their net worth and to ultimately determine their ability to financially manage the recommendations that you might make to fill any gaps discovered in their financial road map. We will look at both Harvey and Jill and the impact of one of the 3 predictable risks happening to either of them. Remember that their assets represent the things that they own and the liabilities represent what they owe. Their assets and liabilities are as follows:

| Harvey's Financial Snapshot – Assets | |
|---|---|
| Asset Description | Asset Value |
| Principal Residence | $375,000 |
| Savings held in a daily interest savings account (Used as an emergency account/slush fund) | $22,250. |
| Mutual Fund portfolio | $45,000 |
| RRSP – personal | $112,000 |
| Group RRSP | $35,000 |
| Rare hockey card collection –appraised value | $21,750 |
| Personal Auto – 2011 Ford F250 truck Estimated value | $25,000 |
| Total Assets for Harvey | $636,000 |

| Harvey's Financial Snapshot - Liabilities | |
|---|---|
| Liabilities – Description | Liability Amount |
| Mortgage held jointly with Jill | $240,000 |
| Bank Credit Card #1 ($10,000 limit) held in both names | $7,200 |
| Bank Credit Card #2 ($5,000 Limit) held in his name only | $2,000 |
| Bank line of credit ($50,000 Limit) | $28,000 |
| Automobile Loan | $22,000 |
| Investment loan with mutual fund company | $15,000 |
| Total Liabilities | $314,200 |
| Total Assets | $636,000 |
| Net Worth (Total Assets minus Total Liabilities | $321,800 |

You discover after doing your analysis and fact finding that if Harvey dies there is an insurance need of approximately $1,200,000. This will allow Jill to pay all the final expenses associated with Harvey's death, pay off the mortgage and all of Harvey's debts, and have some funds left to invest to make up the shortfall in income needed.

The shortfall arises from the fact that, should Harvey die, Jill may want to take some time to return to work and when she does in about 12 months time, her income alone will not be enough to support the family's ongoing lifestyle. From all of that you determine that Harvey's human life value equals $1,200,000. Your recommendation for an insurance solution has to take into account that Harvey and Jill and the children have active lifestyles and that their discretionary income will not allow them to commit much more than $500 per month to solve this problem.

In your insurance analysis you take a look at the other insurance owned on Harvey's life. Of course they are shocked at the amount you propose and start to throw objections at you. A common objection is that he has adequate group insurance and mortgage insurance at the bank where the mortgage is held. That would mean that based on his $150,000 income and a 2 times annual income benefit amount he would have $300,000 worth of coverage at work. Because the mortgage amount is currently $240,000, that would give him a total of $540,000 worth of coverage. Aside from that he has an old Participating Whole Life policy that he purchased when he was 21, before meeting and marrying Jill. The policy has a face amount of $100,000, a cash value of $42,000 and dividends on deposit of $37,000. You quickly point out that the death benefit on that policy is $137,000 and take a few minutes to explain to Harvey how that policy works and why she doesn't get the cash value on death in addition to the death benefit but rather as part of the death benefit. It is probably now time to educate Harvey and Jill on the other coverages that he has.

Harvey and Jill should recognize that, once the mortgage is paid off, they will have approximately enough income to replace Harvey's salary for three years. While they will no longer have a mortgage to pay for, they still have all the expenses associated with maintaining a household. Jill has indicated that she would like to have a year off work if something happens to Harvey. Their three young children will all have significant expenses, especially as they proceed to post-secondary education, and Jill's income alone is not going to be enough to support this.

A quick review of his employee benefits booklet allows you to discover that even though the benefit amount is 2 times his annual income, it states in the booklet that the maximum on the group life for Harvey's class is $250,000. Harvey hasn't purchased any additional optional coverage because he did not want to go through the hassle of qualifying for that extra coverage. You also take a few minutes to discuss with Harvey his future plans as far as employment is concerned. You discover that even though Harvey enjoys his work and gets along well with his boss, the owner, he realizes that the owner's sons are being groomed to take over the business. He may very well, within the next 10 years, set out on his own and start his own construction business.

This has been a lifelong dream, something that he and Jill have talked about often in the past. This knowledge helps you to point out the problems with the group coverage as it is tied to his current employment. The conversion privilege on the group life is there but has its limitations and may not suffice to meet the ongoing insurance needs. This is especially true as the group conversion will most likely be to term insurance. The older Harvey is when he converts his group insurance to individual insurance, the more costly it will be. Of course, Harvey does not have the opportunity to convert before leaving the group.

As for the bank mortgage insurance, it is relatively easy to point out the deficiencies in that coverage for it is attached to the current mortgage and basically underwritten at the time of claim. That objection of having enough coverage elsewhere is quickly eliminated. You also notice that as you continue without rush to educate Harvey and Jill on the types of insurance that they have and on the various aspects of insurance, that they are actually starting to enjoy the process and are more receptive to your ideas. They are confident of your professionalism and of your commitment to put their interests first.

Along these same lines you compliment Harvey on having the foresight at age 21 to purchase that whole life policy and the discipline over the years to keep paying into it and not strip it of its cash values along the way. You recommend that he keep that policy and thus decrease the insurance needed today to around $1,150,000. Upon looking at the options available to them, you could recommend purely term insurance at a very manageable cost as Harvey is a non-smoker, has no lifestyle habits that pose a risk and his family history reveals no indication of illnesses or diseases that would pose a problem. It looks like a quick solution and a quick easy sale but because you have not yet explained to Harvey and Jill the different types of life insurance you have not yet completed your fiduciary duty.

You explain whole life and how it works, a relatively easy task since Harvey already owns such a policy and can easily see that it works quite well and requires absolutely no decisions by him. The insurer makes all the investment decisions and the only area that might fluctuate is the amount of dividends held on deposit. The insurer might very well adjust its dividend scale thus any long term projections are only projections and cannot be guaranteed. You point out that Canadian insurance companies have a long history of solid investment experience and usually strive to maintain reasonable dividends rates on their participating policies. You might also want to point out that during the recent market downturn (2008 and 2009) the value in Harvey's whole life policy did not go down as other investments might have.

You also know from their net worth analysis that Harvey has some investment experience as he owns some mutual funds and has employed leverage in order to purchase some of those mutual funds. Harvey also has a healthy balance in his RRSP investments. It might be time to talk about those a little to learn a little more about his investment mentality and how he feels about risk. It is quite common for couples to have opposite risk tolerance levels so be careful to include Jill in all of your discussions. You pay particular attention to her body language as well as his. A good question to ask would be how your investments fared over the last couple of years. Their body language and expressions as they share with you that their portfolio suffered a 50% loss in value will be quite telling. Their response to "how do you really feel about that" will help in making the recommendation. You realize that these people recognize that what happened is normal in the markets and that they need to continue to be disciplined in implementing their investment strategies. It doesn't make them feel wonderful about losing money and they are emphatic about being a little more cautious in future decisions.

Now back to assessing the insurance need. You explain the pitfalls of a pure term solution. You discuss a 10 Year Renewable and Convertible Term policy with a premium for the 1st 10 years of around $45 to $50 per month, but when the policy renews in 10 years when Harvey is 50 the premium for the subsequent 10 years would more than double. And further more the policy will expire at age 75.

This could pose a problem because of the fact that he is looking at going into business for himself and they have already alluded to the fact that eventually they will enter the world of self-employment thus potentially building up a significant estate. The tax erosion on death will seriously impact what is left to the next generation. It might be best to look at a permanent solution, but because of the higher cost you might recommend about $500,000 of permanent coverage with a $550,000 term rider ensuring that the term coverage is renewable and convertible.

To further keep the costs in line you might even recommend that Jill's insurance needs be handled with a term rider on Harvey's policy as well. Now, is it whole life or universal life? Because of Harvey's investment expertise, his indication of reasonably high risk tolerance and his demonstrated discipline, you feel comfortable in recommending a universal life solution with a term rider on Harvey and a spousal term rider on Jill. To further cover off one other need you recommend as well a child term rider covering all 3 children. To demonstrate the value of this option point out that the child term rider carries with it the option for each child to convert that coverage to their own personal coverage any time up to their 25<sup>th</sup> birthday. Harvey quickly points out that it was through such an option that he bought his insurance at age 21 based on a plan his father put in place many years prior.

At this point it is time to end the meeting and to schedule a follow-on meeting at which time you will bring back a recommendation. The next meeting is set for 1 week later and you leave but not before pointing out the other areas that you wish to focus on. You advise them that you might also undertake a review of Harvey's disability coverage, recognizing that the employer sponsored group disability has some limitations. You also want to make sure that they are aware of the risks of being diagnosed with a life threatening illness and/or the challenges of growing old with the possibility of experiencing extensive health care costs associated with aging. They substantiate a minor concern in this area based on the experience of having dealt with their own aging parents and other relatives.

In preparation for the next meeting you develop solutions to their problems based on a strategy that meets their needs. You prepare illustrations based on providing the amount of life insurance required. You prepare an illustration using only term insurance, and another using whole life with a term rider. You also create an illustration with universal life, a term rider, a spousal term rider and a child term rider. You plan to propose that Harvey over-funds the policy with an extra $200 per month with returns based on an equity linked mutual fund using 5% long term growth projections. The funds you will recommend are a mix of a balanced fund and a Canadian equity fund. This asset allocation fits nicely with Harvey and Jill's overall asset allocation.

You also determine that their expressed concern about the chances of either one of them being diagnosed or suffering from a critical illness and the financial impact that might have on the family, warrants talking to them about critical illness insurance. In order to keep the premium in line you add a critical illness rider for $200,000 on each of them instead of recommending stand-alone critical illness policies. The critical illness coverage will automatically convert to a long term care policy at age 75 based on the plan design that your company offers.

There is only one more need to pay attention to but to avoid the premium shock you commit to talking to Harvey and Jill about this when you return to implement the plan. That need arose from your assessment of Harvey's disability coverage while reviewing his employee benefits. You discovered that the wording in his group LTD plan said that he had LTD disability coverage for 66.67% of his regular monthly income to maximum of $4,500 per month. That coverage will be based on an own occupation definition of disability for the first 2 years thereafter changing to any occupation. Based on Harvey's job description and future plans you realize that this is inadequate. This would leave him with $54,000 of tax free annual income if he were to suffer a disability. Based on the tax rates in your province, you estimate that this would leave him and Jill missing about $47,000 of annual income.

You now return to meet with Harvey and Jill for the 2<sup>nd</sup> meeting with illustrations and a written plan in hand complete with your recommendations.

You start the meeting by reviewing what you discussed with them initially and restating the need for proper protection. You then present your solution. The total premium commitment is $650 per month giving them $500,000 of Universal Life insurance, a $550,000 10 year renewable and convertible term rider on Harvey, a $500,000 spousal term rider on Jill, a $25,000 Child Term Rider covering all 3 children, and a critical insurance rider for $200,000 on both Harvey and Jill. That still leaves room for $200 per month to invest.

There is initial push-back from them because they did not expect such a significant premium commitment and wonder how they could manage this within their monthly budget. Having already done a thorough assessment of their monthly income and expenditures you can easily see how minor adjustments can free up a few premium dollars. You project that their current RRSP portfolio with a reasonable rate of return and careful management could grow to a significant portfolio of registered funds to draw from in retirement.

Looking forward you can see the use of registered funds alone placing them in an unfortunate tax position in retirement. They have been putting aside $250.00 per month into their personal RRSPs. The contributions are being made by Harvey with $150.00 going to his own RRSP and $100.00 going into a spousal RRSP in Jill's name. Jill has $22,000 in the spousal RRSP and another $17,000 in her personal RRSP. You had also discovered that Harvey has a group RRSP though work and his $150.00 monthly contributions are being matched by his employer. You might advise him to back off on his personal RRSP contributions by $100 per month and remind them that with the new insurance in place they can stop paying for the mortgage life insurance at the bank. That will save them another $60 per month. You have now found a way to allow them to feel better about the $650 per month premium commitment you are asking for. They were already comfortable with $500 and without forcing them to make significant lifestyle sacrifices; you have built a program that will allow them to achieve their goals. At the same time, you obtain a commitment from them that, once their income increases, they will start contributing the $100 per month into savings.

They agree to your recommendations so you proceed with completion of the application. You ask the questions to complete the personal information for each of them. You obtain copies of their birth certificates to confirm their actual age and ask questions pertaining to their employment details and life style activities. You assume that based on what you know that they will likely be standard risks and find out that they are non-smokers with Harvey having quit smoking about 18 months ago and Jill never having smoked. Even though the amount of insurance requires utilizing the services of a paramedical nurse to obtain the medical underwriting information, you complete the long-form application and ask all of the questions yourself as if you were doing a non-medical. This prevents you from getting any surprises and allows you to properly prepare Harvey and Jill for the process that will follow. You discover that Jill sought medical advice for a lump in her breast that she detected 3 years earlier. You find out through further questioning that it was a false alarm and all tests indicated that there was no indication of cancer or ongoing problems. You are able to prepare them well for all this because you recently attended a continuing education seminar in which an expert in the underwriting process talked you through how to best prepare clients.

You advise them that the nurse who comes to do the para-medical will ask the same questions. This nurse, being a qualified medical professional, will likely get more detail and also that the insurer will want to be absolutely sure about the risks so will likely write to Jill's doctor for an attending physician's statement. You have properly prepared the applicants for the process so as not to inconvenience them and to allow them to feel comfortable. You complete the application. Based on your assumption that they should both get standard rates you collect the 1st premium and issue a receipt for temporary insurance being careful to advise them that the amount of insurance that they are covered for under the temporary insurance agreement (TIA) will not exceed $1,000,000 based on your company's TIA limit. You also indicate that there is a time limit on the TIA of 90 days which means that all the underwriting information must be received in a timely manner and that a decision must be made by that time so as not to cause any lapses in insurance coverage. You explain that the TIA stays in effect until the actual insurance policy goes into effect as long as everything happens within those 90 days.

You get all of the appropriate signatures, collect the first premium, and give them the receipt and leave. The next morning you call the para-medical company to order the para-med. A week later you get notice that, as suspected, the insurer's head office underwriters want to get more detail pertaining to Jill's breast lump. The insurer deals directly with her attending physician, including payment to the doctor. You call Jill to advise her about what is happening and ask her to call or see her doctor to speed up the process.

This whole process has now taken you about 8 to 10 hours including the initial get-acquainted meeting with Harvey, the fact finding meeting with both of them and the presentation meeting, each of the latter taking about 2 hours. The balance of the time was what you needed to prepare the proposal and process the application. You still have one more meeting left when the policy is issued for delivery. That should take about 30 minutes. The most important thing to ask at that meeting is whether either of them has experienced anything since completion of the application that would impact the risk or their insurability. If the answer is no, it is okay to leave the policy with them. You now leave with a commitment to communicate with them regularly through your newsletter and to sit down with them at least once per year to review their portfolio and to make any adjustments that ongoing lifestyle changes might require. You should also remind them at this point of their 10 day right of rescission.

At this time it might be proper to schedule another get together to review the disability insurance need that you uncovered for Harvey and also to look at where they have their various investments. Harvey and Jill agree to a meeting in a month's time. To prepare for that meeting you gather all the information you can on where their current investments are held and how they have fared over the last few years. You discover that they are somewhat frustrated with the service they have been getting from a current advisor and from the financial institution where some of the funds are held.  You might even take time to sell them on the idea of having one person provide all of the services for them so as to simplify the planning process and to easily coordinate all aspects of their financial goals and objectives.  They like that idea and once more compliment you on your professionalism and attention to detail.

You now go away with the idea of returning in a month to finish the rest of the plan.  The first thing you do is to attempt to schedule a meeting with Harvey's employer based on gaining an introduction from Harvey.  Your goal here is to get a better understanding of the of the rationale behind the design of the group insurance disability coverage and to see if there is anything else in place to deal with the inadequate amount of disability coverage provided to Harvey.  You also find out that there are 2 other executives with the company who are high income earners quite likely experiencing the same exposure to the risk of having inadequate disability protection.  You make a mental note to call Harvey to perhaps schedule a luncheon meeting with those people, so that he can provide a proper introduction.

You might even ask the employer if there is any willingness on his part to contribute financially to helping these key people obtain proper coverage. If he says yes then you have a way to offset the objection of too much premium cost and you have confirmed the fact that you will get to spend more time with the employer to put these additional plans in place.  Other items that you may want to talk with the employer about are the group RRSP, the employee benefits plan, and his own personal insurance and investment portfolio. The more professionalism you demonstrate the more he will be open to further discussions about his various insurance needs and even his own succession plan as you already learned earlier that his children will be joining him in the business with the eventual goal of taking over.

You also analyze the investment information that you have obtained from Harvey and Jill. Using a spreadsheet, you discover that Harvey's own RRSP will grow to $590,000 at age 65 assuming that he continues contributing $50 per month.  On top of that his employer's matching Group RRSP plan will grow to $270,000 at age 65 based on the current contributions for another 10 years and then leaving the plan in place until aged 65.  In all cases you are assuming a relatively conservative long term return of 6.5%.  Jill will also have total RRSP investments of approximately $275,000 at age 65 as well.  That will give them a total RRSP portfolio of about $1,135,000 at age 65 without increasing their contributions. You recommend to them that most future RRSP contributions for Harvey's tax savings should be made as spousal contributions so as to equal the tax load in retirement.  You note that this would be equivalent to having about $750,000 in today's dollars.  None of this includes the continued build-up of cash surrender value (CSV) and dividends in the whole life policy on Harvey that you counsel him to keep and continue to pay for.  That could provide another couple hundred thousand dollars to use to provide some cushion and possible enhanced retirement income.

The picture looks quite good for their future retirement planning needs so you call them and schedule an appointment.  When meeting with them 1 week later you present the numbers as indicated in your analysis and illustrate to them that they are on the right path and barring any unforeseen financial disasters, they will be in reasonable shape. Be sure to compliment them on their success in building their portfolio. Their hard work and discipline are starting to pay off.

They won't be wealthy but they will be able to enjoy a comfortable retirement assuming that their house will be paid for by that time. Your goal is to become their financial planner as you are starting to better understand the importance of full service financial planning because you have just enrolled in the CERTIFIED FINANCIAL PLANNER[1] designation program with a goal to completing that course and obtaining your designation in about a year and a half. You now present Harvey and Jill with the idea that they should transfer their investments to the companies that you represent. They like what you offer and what you represent and are confident that you represent strong, well structured and financially secure financial institutions. You transfer Harvey's RRSP portfolio into your company's Individual Variable Insurance Contract (segregated fund/IVIC). At a recent meeting of Advocis, of which you are a member (http://advocis.ca/content/member/member.html) you were reminded that it is vital to perform this transaction as a transfer, instead of having Harvey and Jill withdraw the funds. If they simply withdrew the funds, they would be fully taxed on the complete withdrawal and they would not recover the RRSP room that they had previously used to make their contributions.

Based on Harvey's age and investment expertise and the fact that the current market downturn did not sidetrack him from his investment strategies, you put the money into a Canadian Equity IVIC. You also get him to move the money from his non-registered mutual fund into a non-registered IVIC. This time you will recommend a balanced fund. You also set up 2 plans for Jill, one to deposit her personal RRSP funds into and another to use for spousal RRSP purposes. They ask "why not mutual funds?" You outline the benefits of IVICs, especially the death and maturity guarantees, being cautious and emphatic about the fact that those guarantees in the form of insurance come at a cost as reflected in the long term growth of the investments. Further, with Harvey's eventual plan to go into business for himself, the creditor protection offered by IVICs is fantastic. You remind them that they are about to enter that period of their lives when everyday they are getting closer to retirement and that they have to start taking into account the effects of inevitable market downturns. The guarantees built into IVICs help to minimize some of that risk. You must be careful here that you are moving them to IVICs for the correct reasons. The temptation might be to pull them out of their mutual funds portfolio simply because you are not licensed to sell that product. If mutual funds really are better for them, then you should locate a mutual funds representative whom you trust to help them manage those investments.

---

[1] The CERTIFIED FINANCIAL PLANNER designation is a trademark licensed in Canada by the Financial Planning Standards Council.

The next path you wish to follow is Harvey's desire to strike out on his own in about 10 years. Although nothing is definite in that regard you plan as if it is. You talk with Harvey about the risks of being in business and stress that one of the things that you have learned in your time in the business and from your previous business experience is that most new businesses struggle for a variety of reasons. A proper plan and good advice about starting into business will save Harvey a lot of difficulty early.

Harvey and Jill have decent incomes that support a comfortable upper middle class lifestyle. Going into business for himself means that sacrifices will have to be made. You show how the various investments that they have today can be used to offset some of the pressures of financing the new business. The non-registered portion of their portfolio will be worth about $100,000. They could draw from or against that. There will also be about $35,000 in the UL policy account value which could be used as collateral against a bank loan. He could strip out the dividends from the whole life policy. All 3 of these sources would provide significant start-up capital for the new business and help to ensure its success.

You also make note of the fact that there is probably too much money sitting in the daily interest chequing/savings account and upon explaining the relatively new TFSA, you convince them to move their savings accounts into a TFSA. The structure of that account and the rules allow them easy access to their funds but at the same time, allowing for tax deferred growth inside the plan. You also point out that if they need to withdraw money from that account it can be done with no tax implications and withdrawals are added back to future contribution limits.

At this point there isn't much left to deal with except for the fact that Harvey is inadequately covered when it comes to disability insurance. If he were to become disabled through accident or sickness, he would only receive $4,500 per month. That would still be far short of his approximately $8,500 of net monthly income. You point out this deficiency to Harvey and Jill but remind them that the urgency here may not be as great as it was for the other steps but you don't want to leave the need uncovered for very long. It is crucial to document that this discussion took place.

You describe the ideal solution for Harvey would be for him to purchase a personally owned disability plan covering him for the first 2 years for $3,500 per month and then till age 65 for $8,000 per month. If the premium is too prohibitive you might reduce the benefit period to 5 years and use a long elimination period. Both would decrease the cost and Harvey and Jill have adequate resources to self-insure for a considerable time. Keep in mind though that the longer they self-insure the more drain they will put on their future financial accumulation. The reason that you are reluctant to proceed now is that you met with Harvey's employer and brought up the possibility that the employer would help fund the cost of this personal disability coverage for his key employees, the executives like Harvey and the other VPs.

It looks like everything that can be done has been done. You leave making sure that everything is well documented around the entire plan that you have put in place.  Make sure at this time, that if you haven't done so already, you ask Harvey and Jill for the names of anyone they might know who might benefit from this type of service.  Most people initially are reluctant to provide those referrals, but your commitment to serve them and to conduct your business in a professional manner allows them to feel comfortable enough with them to risk providing you with a few names.  You have already diarized following up with Harvey to ask him to set up a luncheon meeting with his 2 fellow VPs and you will be following up with the employer to talk about some key person and life insurance for the executives in the business.

Over the month you meet the other 2 VPs and get enough information to proceed with one of those people to go through the same process as you did with Harvey and Jill.  Keep in mind that one's fiduciary responsibility as a licensed insurance professional is to treat with the utmost confidentiality any information you have on Harvey and Jill and ensure that none of their information gets leaked to the new prospect.  You also managed to meet with Harvey's boss to discuss the disability insurance needs of his key people.  Although reluctant at first, he agrees with your approach and rationale as to why this might be something to look into.  You point out the potential losses to the business if any of these senior executives are unavailable due to death or disability.

The employer knows that he has some of the best people in the area and his competitors would gladly hire away your top people. So you must look for ways that add value to your employees in order to retain them and keep them happy.  Because this is a highly specialized need, you bring in a representative from your disability insurer to help place these policies.  Subsequent discussions involve both the employer and his accountant, and the taxation of premiums and benefits are both major issues.  The end result is that the employer tops up the income of the executives to allow them to purchase their own individual disability insurance.  This expense will be tax deductible to the business and taxable to the executives.  It will also allow the executives, should they become disabled, to receive tax-free disability income.

You now get to place disability coverage on the 3 executives, including Harvey.  What you are doing here is topping up the group coverage.  You now go back to see the employer to discuss the employee benefits plan, the group RRSP and his personal insurance and investment needs.  While coming in and out of his business over the next couple of months  you get to meet and become known quite well amongst the staff of that business and you manage to make a couple of appointments to start other people down the same path.  Life goes on and you get quite busy with all of these people that came from one simple introduction and a quick cup of coffee with Harvey a few months ago.  You have confidence that no matter what happens to Harvey and Jill in way of the 3 predictable risks that they will be okay.  You may have also helped with some life decisions that will need to be made.

Harvey and Jill had thought about going into business for themselves because they considered that as a way to build some wealth for themselves.  Now that you have helped them put their financial road map in place and to get a clear view of where they are headed, it is possible for Harvey to be comfortable starting his company. He will now do it only if the timing, the circumstances and the financials are right.

It has now been 7 months since everything was done and put in place and you get a frantic call from Jill late one evening advising you that on his way home from work early that day, Harvey was in car accident and was rushed to the hospital in fairly serious condition. All she can tell you at this time is that there are numerous broken bones and possible head injuries. He is no longer listed as critical but will likely be in the hospital for an extended period of time. You do what you can to calm her down, indicating that you will ensure that everything is properly handled and that you will assist in obtaining any necessary claim forms and guide them through the process of properly completing those forms. You remind her that Harvey has group insurance coverage and also that the personal disability coverage will also likely come into effect thus ensuring that their income will be roughly the same going forward as it is now.

Jill asks you if Workers Compensation would come into effect. You indicate that it probably would not, as he was not injured on the job. Jill can now relax as the financial worries are taken away, so she can focus on her husband's health and helping him get better.

The next day you contact the plan administrator at Harvey's place of employment to obtain the necessary forms to take to Jill and the appropriate medical professionals. You also ensure that worker's compensation is contacted to determine if there is any possibility of a claim, although you realize that here probably isn't. All of your work thus far has ensured that the employer does not have to worry about the financial consequences of the disability of one of his key employees. You also contact the insurance company where the personal disability plan is in place and obtain the proper claim forms for those benefits. You could very well leave everything now for Harvey and Jill to handle but you understand the need for everything to be handled in a timely fashion. The reality is that it is important to ensure that everything is done accurately and properly. You well understand that having a family member experiencing these serious injuries and going through the recovery process can be a very stressful both emotionally and financially.

Harvey is in the hospital for a period of 3 weeks after which he returns home with the likelihood according to his personal physician of being off work for 8 to 12 months. You understand the uncertainty of disabilities and the fact that reducing stress in Harvey's life will likely allow him to recover faster.

Harvey is collecting, initially, approximately $1,040 per week tax free from his weekly indemnity (short term disability) benefit as part of his group benefit package. He will get this weekly benefit tax free based on having paid the premiums through payroll deduction out of after-tax dollars. The benefit period just happens to be 17 weeks, which you know is the most common benefit period used on these plans. You have also submitted a claim for the personal disability benefit but it has a 90 day elimination period, something you recommended to lower the premium cost. You could have put in place a plan with a 30 day elimination period but the cost would have been prohibitive. You remind Harvey and Jill that the emergency fund that they had already established will need to be used to allow the family to maintain their current lifestyle.

They will only need to draw from this fund until the personal plan starts paying. You walk the claims form through the process, making sure that there are no unnecessary delays, to ensure that at the end of the month starting on the 90th day, the first disability income cheque is received by Harvey. They initially expect a cheque on the 90th day but you explain once again, as you did in the process of selling the policy that DI pays in arrears, meaning at the end of the month.

You learned in your financial planning studies that that this might be referred to as an ordinary annuity, understanding that an annuity is an income contract and any annuity where payments come at the end of the period is known as an ordinary annuity, as opposed to an annuity due where payments are due at the beginning of the period. You might even explain that life insurance contracts and leases are considered an annuity due. This becomes a step in the financial education of Jill and Harvey as you move forward in your relationship with them.

After Harvey has been disabled for a period of about 13 weeks, he receives a letter from the insurance carrier or contact from his group insurance plan administrator asking him to complete the claim for Long Term Disability. Along with that claim form is attached a claim form for the Canada Pension Plan disability benefit. They ask you why they have to bother with the CPP claim form as they have heard negative things about the benefit and dealing with the CPP claims process. You remind them that it is written into the group carrier's master contract that employees must apply for this benefit and furthermore when the benefit is received, it will offset what he gets from his long term group disability benefit. You should also explain that CPP disability will likely take several months to approve and start paying and that when the claim is approved and benefits start to be paid, the group LTD benefit would be reduced by whatever CPP is paying. You are sure to make note of the fact that if CPP approves the claim they will not only pay going forward until the end of disability or age 65 but will also back-date to the 120th day of disability. However, you believe that it is unlikely that CPP will pay, because Harvey's disability is temporary. Any retroactive CPP benefits received must be returned to the insurer to satisfy the offset requirements.

It is now 11 months into Harvey's disability and he returns to work. You find that this is an appropriate time to sit with Jill and Harvey to do a plan review. They thank you for your assistance through the process and offer to pay you for your services. You remind them that would not be appropriate because you were paid well by the insurers that you placed the coverage with and that you continue to get paid through renewals and on the investment business they are doing with you. At this time they realize that the period of disability hardly put a dent in their long term financial plans and no adjustments are required. In response to the query about you getting paid, you also remind them that their current plan will need adjustments based on their changing needs and circumstances.  Thus every 5 or 6 years you may need to revisit their insurance portfolio and offer them new products to fit their needs at that time.

What you have achieved to this point is educating Harvey and Jill on the process of planning to offset the impact of the occurrence of the 3 predictable risks. They now understand the process and see the value of having a professional advisor look after their needs. You move forward visiting annually as promised and making adjustments where necessary.  You realize from your studies that there are many outside influences that could impact their ongoing plans and you commit to staying abreast of market influences that may impact them.

# Chapter 17 EXAM PREP AND STUDY STRATEGIES

Many students writing these exams find significant challenges. We hope that we have provided material that is logical and easy-to-read. This will put you in a position to go forward confidently and pass your exams.

Having read and understood the material, there are a few items that it will be worth your time to consider going forward.

## MATH

While this is not a math exam, some students do struggle with the math in this course. It is critical that you have a good understanding of simple math, and that you are able to use a basic calculator. Financial calculators are neither permitted, nor useful, in the exam process. If you find that the math is causing you troubles, there is a good chance that it is actually not the math that you need to study more. Instead, go back and focus on the concept to which the math relates.

## CASE STUDIES

The exam requires you to read and understand lengthy case studies. These case studies are meant to replicate real-life dealings with clients. Your ability to identify what is appropriate and correct for the client will be tested. In some cases, students identify that they find the questions 'subjective' or 'relative'. In reality, a student with a good understanding of the material will be able to pick out exactly what it is about a product or solution that should appeal to a client based on the information provided in the case study.

Answering case study questions can be somewhat tricky. We recommend first reading the question (not the whole case study, but just the question at or near the end). Then read the solutions provided, making a brief note about each. Finally, read the actual case study. Now you should be prepared to answer the question.

## MEMORIZATION

While there are likely many new and unfamiliar concepts in this text, it is not intended that you memorize everything. It is comprehension and application that will be tested. You will have encountered some lists of items as you read this material. Those lists are there for you to better understand the material, not so that you will memorize list after list.

# STUDYING

Many of us have been out of school for some time, and our study skills may be lacking. There are a few things you can do to make studying easier:

- **Study Schedule**. Many students take months or even years to get through this course. While this is possible, it is a very challenging way to approach this material. In our experience, a student who sets an aggressive study schedule and sticks with it has the best chance of passing this course. It is possible to get through this course in less than a month, and many people do it in less than two weeks.

- **Time Management**. When setting your study schedule, block aside study time when you know you can be fresh and free from distractions. Early in the morning is often the best time for somebody to absorb information.

- **Treat this like a Job**. If you read in bed in the evenings or on the bus on your way to work, it is likely that you will not retain much information. You wouldn't do your regular work at that time. Sit down at your desk and work like you would if somebody were paying you.

- **Use a Variety of Techniques**. It helps to know what kind of learner you are. If you don't, then you will have to figure it out. Do you learn best by simply reading? Do the videos available online help you? What about reading the material out loud? We see many people who show up to class with books very thoroughly marked up, highlighted, with sticky flags and notes in the margins. This does not necessarily lead to comprehension. Make sure you try out whatever study technique you are using by going through the Modular exams that are available online.

# ABBREVIATIONS

While there are many new and unfamiliar terms in this course, you will have noticed very few abbreviations. It is not necessary to memorize any abbreviations. Every exam you will write will spell out fully whatever terms you come across.

# FRUSTRATION

Students sometimes report frustration at the difficulty and scope of this material. It is true that there is a lot to learn, and that the exams are especially challenging. You are not alone in this process. Whoever hired you will want you to succeed. Tutoring and support are available from Business Career College. There are a variety of support structures available. Take advantage of the available support.

## PRACTICAL APPLICATION

Think of this exam like a practical. Instead of seeing yourself at an exam sitting trying to guess the right answer, imagine yourself sitting across from a client as the client explains to you, for example, what she does for a living. What disability product will she need? Does she already have disability insurance? Will her family be looked after? Will her business suffer? What do you need to present to her in order to make sure that her needs are met? If you can take yourself out of the exam, and see yourself in the shoes of an agent dealing with a real-life problem, it will help you significantly in achieving success in this course.

# Chapter 18 MOCK EXAM

1. A participating policy is known as such because it:

   a. Offers dividends.
   b. Offers non-forfeiture options.
   c. Offers stock dividends.
   d. Is more expensive than a non-participating policy.

2. Johnny, a new agent, has collected an individual life insurance application form and a cheque for the first premium. He issued a Temporary Insurance Agreement to this new client, his brother-in-law. His Errors and Omissions insurance will likely not cover:

   a. Recommending that a client purchase shares in an oil and gas company.
   b. Beneficiaries claiming the client was undersold.
   c. The client claiming he was oversold.
   d. Losing his briefcase (containing the application form and cheque) in a bar.

3. Julie and Wilhelm are approaching retirement. Julie has a pension that she is going to have to start drawing income from in the near future. She and Wilhelm are both in good health, and they expect to live a long time in retirement, as all four of their parents are still alive at this point. They would like to know for certain that they will have resources to last them as long as they live. Which of the following would give them the best combination of guaranteed lifetime income and future flexibility?

   a. Purchase a life straight annuity on Julie and a life insurance policy on her life at the same time.
   b. Purchase a cash refund annuity with Julie as the annuitant and Wilhelm as the beneficiary.
   c. Move the commuted value of the annuity into a Locked-In Retirement Account, purchase a portfolio of mutual funds, and transfer it to a Life Income Fund and start drawing income.
   d. Purchase a joint-and-last-survivor annuity.

4. Six months after a policy is delivered and a receipt is collected, which of the following could be true, not necessarily simultaneously:

   i. Temporary Insurance Agreement is valid
   ii. Grace period has started
   iii. Policy has lapsed
   iv. Incontestability period is in force
   v. Fraudulent acts could void the coverage

   a. ii, iii, v
   b. ii, iii
   c. i, ii, iii, iv, v
   d. i, iii, iv, v

5. Which of the following statements about key person life insurance is true?

   a. The company owns the insurance on the key person and is also the beneficiary
   b. The beneficiary should be the estate of the key person
   c. The employee contributes toward payment of premiums
   d. Executives of a company are not normally covered by key person insurance

6. Billy and Bobby recently got married, a second marriage for both. Bobby has one child, Beth, who is 24.
   Billy has no children. Both are carrying a heavy debt load. They are each purchasing new individual life insurance policies on their own lives and would like to make each other their beneficiaries, with Beth being the contingent beneficiary for both. They are unsure whether to make each other irrevocable beneficiaries. Which statement is true?

   a. An irrevocable beneficiary cannot have a contingent beneficiary
   b. If both Billy and Bobby were to die at the same time, then Beth's estate would receive the death benefits
   c. A contingent clause would remove the creditor protection given when an irrevocable beneficiary is named
   d. If they divorced later, it might be possible to restructure the irrevocable beneficiaries

7. You have a new 25-year-old client named Mandy. She has recently moved out of her parents' house into a condominium she has purchased with a 30% down payment. It is located near her parents, in a community called Westwood, quite near downtown and should rise in price rapidly. The best example of "Know Your Client" rules is:
   a. The name of her dog
   b. Her debt/asset ratio
   c. The amount of the inheritance she will get from her parents
   d. The value of an average home in Westwood

8. Sarah works for a life insurance broker as an unlicensed administrative assistant. She should be careful to avoid:

    a. Helping to complete a life insurance application
    b. Witnessing a client signature on a life insurance application
    c. Pre-positioning a need via a broadcast mailout
    d. A&B

9. Which of the following are reasons to insure the lives of children:

    i. Future insurance needs in case of future uninsurability.
    ii. Children are in a lower tax bracket.
    iii. Mortality rates will increase with age.
    iv. Children have a greater risk of death in an auto accident.
    v. Investments accumulate tax-deferred.
    vi. Wealth transfer via absolute assignment.

    a. i, ii, v
    b. i, iii, v, vi
    c. i, iii, v
    d. iii, iv, v, vi

10. Jamie has a Renewable & Convertible $300,000 Ten-year Term policy purchased Jan. 25, 2008 as a 32- year-old non-smoker. She wants to convert it on June 25, 2010. She could convert to:

    a. Five-year Term which will be cheaper
    b. Whole Life, age 33 non-smoker, $350,000
    c. Universal Life for $250,000
    d. Whole Life, age 32 non-smoker, after a paramedical exam

11. The three personal financial risks are:
    a. disability, premature death, old age
    b. accident, sickness, premature death
    c. paycheque deductions, annual taxation, estate taxation
    d. investment returns, taxation, & inflation

12. Which is true?

    a. Inflation is always at a steady rate each year so insurance software will factor this in to any illustration
    b. If a concert ticket cost $250 today and inflation is 5% this year and 4% next year, it will cost $267.50 in 2 years
    c. I would need $3.88 this year to buy a dozen bananas if they will cost $4 next year and inflation is at 3% during this coming year
    d. Inflation does not need to be factored into retirement planning since wages will go up as well as consumer goods. All that matters is the rate of return.

13. Kevin, an insurance agent, assisted his client, Brad, in the completion of an individual life insurance application form. The paper application was in Kevin's handwriting. He made six mistakes including age and smoking history and had Brad initial next to each correction. Brad wrote a cheque for the first premium. Later, the insurance company found the cheque to be uncashable because the written figures and numbers did not match each other. Which is true?

    a. Brad is guilty of coercion. Kevin is guilty of forgery
    b. Kevin is guilty of fraud. Brad is guilty of using apparent authority
    c. Both are guilty of misrepresentation.
    d. Neither is at fault

14. Julian Brassard is a wealthy 47-year-old dentist. He has no living relatives except for an adopted son, Radisson, age 8. Julian has maximized his Registered Retirement Savings Plan (RRSP) contributions and has very few other ways to ease his tax burden. He is approaching retirement and considering an Individual Pension Plan (IPP) through his professional corporation. He might also want to set up a Universal Life policy on Radisson's life now because:

    a. The Cash Surrender Value (CSV) will have a lower tax bracket if Radisson is the life insured when the policy is set up.
    b. Julian can make use of the tax-free rollover provision when Radisson is of legal age
    c. Julian can invest into a dividend fund within the Universal Life policy which will give him a tax break each year the policy is in force
    d. Julian and Radisson can take advantage of income-splitting provisions in the Tax Act each year until Radisson is 18, increasing the rate of growth of the Cash Surrender Value during the next 10 years.

15. Your client, Saddiq, would like to lower his tax bill. He is in the top tax bracket as a result of his income as an orthopaedic surgeon. His regular accountant suffered a heart attack in August so his corporate taxes were filed at the fiscal year end (September) by a newly-hired junior member of the accounting firm. He did not sit down with the accountant after the return was filed but does have a copy of the return. He is interested in using life insurance to improve tax efficiency in his corporation which has active income as well as a stock portfolio, and has issued him non-eligible dividends for the past 3 years. What should you do?

a. Examine his tax returns for the past 3 years to see what his real rate of return is on his investments. Then you can compare it to some insurance illustrations.
b. Advise him to seek professional legal advice even though his investments are down and he doesn't think he can afford it.
c. Tell him his accountant should analyse things better or he should find a new one. A fee may be involved.
d. Sit down with the accountant and lawyer in privacy so you can develop a plan of action to present to Saddiq.

16. Ruth Lesset has made her fortune producing and selling skin abrasion products. Her corporation runs a production plant consisting of 10 recent immigrants working in a warehouse in an area with cheap rent. You have just completed application forms for business overhead insurance, key person insurance on herself, and a group package for her employees. Her corporation's gross income was $867,000 last year, of which she spent $130,000 on new bottling equipment. The warehouse rent is $4,000 per month. The employees make an average of $14 per hour. Which of the following is most correct?

a. The higher the occupation class, the more per month Ruth's corporation will be paying from their pocket for disability coverage. So it is in her interest to convince you that all ten employees do manual labour and none, except herself, fulfill a management role.
b. The employees must be in Canada a minimum of one year, either as permanent residents or as citizens, before they can be covered. This means that only 4 of the 10 can be covered so that would violate the principle of 'non-discriminatory benefits'. Ruth will have to wait to set up the group benefits plan, but she can certainly set up the business overhead insurance and key person coverage.
c. In order to apply for business overhead insurance, Ruth will have to submit financial statements prepared by an independent accountant.
d. Since skin abrasion products are not common, the underwriters would likely have many questions for the agent and will be phoning Ruth's lawyers for additional information. Also, this is considered a 'small group' and would have more stringent underwriting than usual. They would cover Ruth up to 65% of her taxable income as shown on her last year's tax return.

18-5

17. Sheldon Brass, age 32, got trapped in the pinsetter of a bowling alley and permanently lost use of his left arm. He has an individual disability policy with a 60-day wait, 2 years of benefits, presumptive benefits, and a zero-day qualification period. He also has a $250,000 life policy with AD&D and owner's waiver of premium. It is now six years after the accident and he has not worked since. Which statement is true?

a. Sheldon would receive ongoing benefits from CPP disability & Accidental Death benefits. He would also have received one-time compensation from his presumptive clause and his waiver. Workers compensation, if paid, could either be a lump sum or a monthly benefit.
b. Sheldon would receive ongoing benefits from CPP disability, & employment insurance. He would also have received compensation from his presumptive clause, his AD&D policy, and his waiver. Workers compensation, if paid, could either be a lump sum or a monthly benefit.
c. Sheldon would receive ongoing benefits from CPP disability only. He could also have received one- time compensation from his disability policy and his AD&D policy. His life insurance premium would be paid by the insurance company. Workers compensation, if paid, could either be a lump sum or a monthly benefit.
d. Sheldon would receive ongoing benefits from CPP disability and his individual disability policy (under the recurrence clause). He would also have received compensation from his presumptive clause and his AD&D policy. His life insurance premium would be paid by the insurance company. Workers compensation, if paid, could either be a lump sum or a monthly benefit.

18. Bob & Mary have current assets worth $18,000. Final expenses (funeral, etc) are $180,000. Mary will have an annual income of $50,000 if Bob dies. She will need $67,000 per year to maintain her style of living. She could make 4% in GICs, she figures. Using the capital needs approach, how much life insurance is required by Bob?

a. $875,000
b. $425,000
c. $623,000
d. $587,000

19. Ben and Jerry are 32-year-old, male, non-smoking twins who do most things in a similar way but with small differences. Both bought the same whole life policy from the same company for the same face value but Ben's policy is par and Jerry's is non-par. They recently purchased the same sports car in two differing colors, street raced each other while high on ecstasy, and both were killed. Which could be true?

    a. Ben's death benefit could be higher than Jerry's due to the flexibility offered at time of purchase.
    b. Jerry's death benefit could be higher than Ben's since non-par is a lower cost per thousand.
    c. Street racing would be considered a standard exclusion on most life policies.
    d. Both death benefits must be the same amount since whole life always has a level death benefit.

20. Corey Doren owns a janitorial company as a sole proprietor and purchased individual disability insurance from you. His policy is guaranteed renewable to age 65. It is a "B' occupation class and has an elimination period of 90 days and both partial and residual benefits. His premium is $230 per month, including waiver of premium, and is due on the first of each month. His basic monthly benefit is $2,900. He slipped and twisted his knee while supervising a staff member who was polishing an aisle floor in a commercial building on Sept 12, 2008. He filed his claim on October 1, 2008. Which statement is most correct?

    a. He would have to file a claim within two years but it may take that long for him to complete physiotherapy. He would have to make premium payments in the meantime or the policy would be terminated.
    b. Given that he owns the company, he should have been sold a non-cancellable guaranteed renewable policy with an own occupation definition of disability.
    c. The residual definition of disability could help him to manage a return to work.
    d. Corey will not have to pay any premiums.

21. Paul wants to save $172,000 for retirement. He has 22 years to save the money. Extremely risk adverse, he plans to keep it in a savings account paying almost no interest. Assuming no growth, what percent of his $97,000 annual salary must he save each year?

    a. 5%
    b. 8%
    c. 10%
    d. 18%

$ 7.818

22. Duncan's wife Marta committed suicide in 2008 unexpectedly after losing their son, Brian, in a car accident at age 17. She was 56. Both Duncan and Marta had 20-pay non-participating whole life policies purchased in 1993, naming each other as beneficiaries. If Marta's policy had a renewable 10-year term rider for $100,000, how much would Duncan receive upon her death beyond the face amount?

a. Cash value plus term rider
b. Face amount only since term rider would have expired when the policy was paid up
c. Term rider
d. Suicide is not covered so Duncan receives nothing

23. Duncan's wife Marta committed suicide in 2008 unexpectedly after losing their son, Brian, in a car accident at age 17. She was 56. Both Duncan and Marta had 20-pay non-participating whole life policies purchased in 1993, naming each other as beneficiaries. If Duncan's policy had a spousal rider for $100,000 and owners' waiver of premium, what would happen to his policy upon her death?

a. Spousal rider pays out and his waiver of premium benefit begins.
b. Spousal rider pays out and his policy remains in force.
c. Spousal rider pays out and his policy remains in force. His premium will drop by the cost of the spousal rider.
d. Spousal rider would not pay out since they did not die within 30 days of each other. If he remarries later, he can convert this rider to the new partner.

24. Duncan's wife Marta committed suicide in 2008 unexpectedly after losing their son, Brian, in a car accident at age 17. She was 56. Both Duncan and Marta had 20-pay non-participating whole life policies purchased in 1993, naming each other as beneficiaries. Which statement pertains to Duncan's situation?

a. Duncan would have to pay tax on any rider payouts since this policy was purchased in 1983 or later.
b. Participating whole life policies often pay additional benefits on the death of a spouse or child
c. If Duncan had a child rider on his policy, he would have received something upon Brian's death without surrendering his policy
d. None of the above

25. Fred and Wilma have disposable assets of $666,000 and liabilities of $297,000. Wilma is a homemaker with 5 children. If Fred dies, Wilma will need $4000 each month. Interest rates are running at 5%. How much
life insurance does Fred need, using the capital retention approach?

a. $742,000
b. $1,329,000
c. $591,000
d. $3,000

26. Which is not considered to be a generic fund because it invests in a very specific set of investments?

a. Labour-Sponsored Venture Capital Funds
b. Equity Funds
c. Balanced Funds
d. Income Funds

27. Daphne Hamilton purchased a Universal Life policy on her own life with the intention of having some savings for retirement. Her premium was $133 per month and she chose to deposit $120 more and place it
in very aggressive equity funds. She reallocated conscientiously, always selecting other aggressive funds. She had a good income working downtown as an office manager for a large instrumentation company. After seven years, she had only $9,465 of cash surrender value due to declining markets. She also changed careers and had a temporary cash flow problem. The insurance company paid her premiums out of her cash
value for several months plus she took out a policy loan to tide her over. During this time, she moved to a
cheaper apartment, still in the downtown area, and did not notify the insurance company of her new address. Which statement is false?

a. Daphne can send in a cheque for the annual premium and cease the monthly pre-authorized chequing at any time
b. If the account value increases due to market recovery, and Daphne repays the loan, it is possible that the premium payment arrangements may continue indefinitely
c. Daphne will have 30 days to make her premium payment after the cash value is depleted, or else the policy will lapse
d. Daphne's beneficiary, her mother, will be sent notification of required premium payment when the post office returns the letters that the insurance company had sent to Daphne as "undeliverable"

28. Gerald Ramsay is a 55-year-old quality control inspector at a large manufacturing plant, making $87,000
per year. He is divorced with few expenses and no debt. His house has equity of $346,000 with a small remaining mortgage and he has a bond portfolio of $665,000. He has no RRSPs. He wants to provide vacations for his 25-year-old daughter, her husband, and their 2 small children each year for the next 5 years only. The two-week vacation packages, to a particular resort in the Caribbean, currently cost $12,000 and are rising at a rate of 6% each year. He is thinking of making a donation to a program in Africa of
$80,000 this year. Ignoring his current income and the effect on his taxes, what total assets would he have left after making this donation and after reserving enough future funding for the vacations?

a. $915,850
b. $943,355
c. $863,355
d. $743,445

29. Gerald Ramsay is a 55-year-old quality control inspector at a large manufacturing plant, making $87,000
per year. He is divorced with few expenses and no debt. His house has equity of $346,000 with a small remaining mortgage and he has a bond portfolio of $665,000. He has no RRSPs. He wants to provide vacations for his 25-year-old daughter, her husband, and their 2 small children each year for the next 5 years only. The two-week vacation packages, to a particular resort in the Caribbean, currently cost $12,000 and are rising at a rate of 6% each year. He is thinking of making a donation to a program in Africa of
$80,000 this year. Gerald wants to retire at age 60. He will stay in his house. He figures he will need
$46,000 per year to maintain his standard of living in retirement, and he expects to make a 4.5% rate of return in his bond portfolio. Without factoring in inflation, taxes, vacations, donations, or government benefits, how much more will he have to build up his bond portfolio in the next 5 years, in order to have a nest egg that will meet his retirement needs?

a. $1,022,222
b. It would not be possible for him to retire at 60 without government support
c. $667,070
d. $357,222

30. Gerald Ramsay is a 55-year-old quality control inspector at a large manufacturing plant, making $87,000 per year. He is divorced with few expenses and no debt. His house has equity of $346,000 with a small remaining mortgage and he has a bond portfolio of $665,000. He has no RRSPs. He wants to provide vacations for his 25-year-old daughter, her husband, and their 2 small children each year for the next 5 years only. The two-week vacation packages, to a particular resort in the Caribbean, currently cost $12,000 and are rising at a rate of 6% each year. He is thinking of making a donation to a program in Africa of $80,000 this year. Gerald wants to retire at age 60. He will stay in his house. He figures he will need $46,000 per year to maintain his standard of living in retirement, and he expects to make a 4.5% rate of return in his bond portfolio. If the Consumer Price Index (CPI) were to rise by 2.7% each year, how many years would it take for him to need $57,000 per year? Do not factor in taxes and round off to the nearest $1000 increment.

a. He will need $57,000 eight years after retiring
b. He will need $57,000 five years after retiring
c. He will need $57,000 twelve years after retiring
d. He will need $57,000 four years after retiring

31. Vanessa Hebert purchased an individual renewable and convertible 10-year term policy in 1995 in order to be able to leave a clear title house to her elderly father, should she die before the mortgage was paid off, even though her bank did not require her to do so. The beneficiary is her father. The death benefit was level. She doubled up some mortgage payments and also made some additional principal payments, She developed cancer 12 years after policy issue and passed away within a short time, with only one more monthly mortgage payment owing. Which statements are false?

i. There is no death benefit payable since death did not occur in the first 10 years
ii. The death benefit will be equal to the face value minus the original mortgage value
iii. The death benefit would be less than face value due to increased premiums in the 2nd decade
iv. The death benefit will be equal to the face value minus the mortgage payment
v. The total premiums paid in the first decade will exceed the total paid by Vanessa in the 2nd decade
vi. Her father could continue premium payments until age 75 in order to build account value

a. i, ii, iii, v
b. i, ii, iii, iv, vi
c. ii, iii, vi
d. ii, iii, v, vi

32. Your client, Richard, age 28, is debating which type of universal life insurance to purchase: level cost of insurance or yearly renewable term (YRT). He has moderate risk tolerance, smokes, and rides a motorcycle daily. Which is false?

    a. If he chooses YRT, he is taking more risk than with level cost of insurance.
    b. YRT would be more appropriate if he is looking to invest heavily in the policy right now.
    c. The YRT cost of insurance would be calculated each year and Richard would find out his premium for that year in a statement that the insurer would send to him.
    d. Choosing a YRT cost of insurance is generally appropriate for somebody at a younger age.

33. Martha is a new lawyer who recently started earning $200,000 per year. Stewart is a sculptor currently
    without an income. They have no assets and will need $40,000 for funeral costs if Stewart dies plus Martha figures she would need a year off work to recover. Interest rates are 6% and they intend to start large catch- up Registered Retirement Savings Plans before December 31st. How much life insurance does Stewart need?

    a. $240,000
    b. $573,333
    c. There is no need for insurance
    d. $40,000

34. Mohammed (age 34, non-smoker) and Anna Rahal (age 30, non-smoker) have two children age 4 & 5. He
    has a contract to drive a courier truck and currently makes $65,000 per year. She works part-time in a convenience store and makes $26,000 per year. They have no insurance and have asked you to recommend a product that fits their needs and abilities. You have calculated that Mohammed currently needs coverage of $550,000 and Anna needs $375,000. They have high hopes that the children will attend university and get medical degrees. Mohammed's wealthy grandfather left him a trust, but the funds from the trust will not be available for ten years. The trust represents enough wealth that Mohammed and Anna figure that they will never have to work again. As a broker, you present several products from several companies. Given that they can afford about $60 per month in premiums currently, which would be the most suitable product for them?

    a. Joint-and-first-to-die ten-year renewable and convertible term.
    b. Twenty-year renewable and convertible term on each of them.
    c. Ten-year renewable and convertible term on each of them.
    d. One-year renewable and convertible term on each of them.

35. Carrie Anne needs some individual disability insurance. She is currently an auctioneer but may become a draftsperson. You present her two illustrations with occupation classes of 2A and 3A. She notes that the premiums differ due to which of the following factors:

a. The longer the elimination period the smaller the premium , the longer the benefit period the larger the premium, the higher the occ class the lower the percent of income covered by benefits
b. The longer the elimination period the larger the premium , the longer the benefit period the smaller the premium, the higher the occ class the lower the percent of income covered by benefits
c. The longer the elimination period the smaller the premium , the longer the benefit period the larger the premium, the higher the occ class the fewer the exclusions
d. The longer the elimination period the smaller the premium , the longer the benefit period the larger the premium, occ class will affect premium rate per thousand

36. Jeffrey and Jill are a young couple with limited disposable income. You have previously done business with Jill's parents, and they have referred you to this young couple. They have just taken out a mortgage and did not choose to acquire the bank's mortgage life insurance product. Which type of policy should they acquire?

a. Term to 100 joint and first to die
b. Renewable and convertible joint and first to die 20 year term
c. Renewable and convertible joint and first to die 10 year term
d. Renewable and convertible joint and first to die yearly renewable term

37. Jan is a heating and air conditioning estimator making $50,000 per year. He purchased an individual disability policy since his employer provided nothing except worker's compensation. His policy was a non- cancellable, guaranteed renewable policy with an "own occ" rider. It has a 5-year benefit period and 90-day elimination period with 70% total disability benefits. His monthly premiums are $190. He was in a car accident which left him unable to use his right arm and shoulder. He had six months of severe neck pain. His feet lost all sensation at the time but with physiotherapy he was walking again by the 8th month. What is likely the case?

a. During his 6 months of total disability, worker's compensation may have given him taxable benefits as first payor. His individual disability will only "top up" beyond that to the maximum CPP allows
b. He will receive CPP disability benefits during the months of total disability as well as $35,000 in individual disability benefits
c. His individual disability benefits are a qualifying medical expense on his tax return for the year of his injury
d. Any individual disability benefits he receives are not taxed even though he began doing in-house sales for a plumbing company and had a tax bracket of 32% the following year

38. Bridget was a baker in a large bread factory. She purchased an individual disability policy. Shortly after, she severely burned both her arms while on the job. She received disability benefits and returned to work 3 months later. She found herself unable to face the ovens and quit to take a job as a barista in a coffee shop. Which would be the result, upon taking the new job?

a. If Bridget had purchased a non-cancellable and guaranteed renewable policy, her benefits would remain unchanged
b. If Bridget had purchased guaranteed renewable policy, her premiums and benefits would remain unchanged
c. If Bridget had purchased a cancellable policy, her coverage would cease
d. None of the above

39. Marvin, age 35, is looking to buy some life insurance because he just got engaged. His mother died at his birth. His father died when Marvin was a teenager and left him a steady income from a trust fund as well as some cash. This allows Marvin to pay for rent and food but little else. Marvin has opened a wicker furniture import business which is slowly providing good but seasonal income. Marvin's insurance agent has determined that Marvin is extremely risk averse due some exposure to gambling addictions among his friends. Which universal life insurance investment is most appropriate?

a. Guaranteed investment accounts.
b. A mix of equity and money market investments.
c. A bond fund.
d. Since universal life investments must be equities, the best choice is a balanced fund.

40. Sonia Burke is 75 years old and was widowed 3 years ago, when her husband Antonio suffered a heart
attack at age 76. Antonio had been taking care of their two managed accounts: the registered assets are in index funds now worth $350,000, and the non-registered assets are in balanced funds worth $475,000. Both accounts have done well and are currently giving a good rate of return. The economy is generally good and interest rates are up. She has met with her financial advisor since her husband's death but did not really follow what he was saying. She is also finding it hard to keep up with the maintenance on their 50-year-old bungalow and her eyesight is worsening. She has looked at several assisted living facilities and will move into one within a year. What option would be most suitable for her?

a. Move the registered assets into a bond fund; move the non-registered assets into an annuity.
b. Move the registered assets into a money market fund; move the non-registered assets into a bond fund.
c. Move the majority of the registered assets into a bond fund, some into a money market fund, and move the non-registered assets into an annuity.
d. Move the registered funds into an annuity; move the non-registered funds into a bond fund.

41. Hubert is aged 64. He contributes the maximum possible amount to his RRSP each year and would like to find additional opportunities for tax deferred investment growth. His RRSP investments are currently in bonds, GICs, and high-quality preferred shares, which perfectly matches his risk tolerance. He requires an
insurance policy to take care of potential taxes due on his death, which he anticipates will be at least twenty to thirty years away. He has a well-developed estate plan, so he knows today roughly how much those taxes will be. Which type of insurance policy should he acquire?

a. Universal Life.
b. Non-par Whole Life.
c. Par Whole Life.
d. Term to 100.

42. Tyler Booth, 29, is a blues singer who has had some minor success in his home town. His taxable income was $12,000 last year. His wife, Angelica, 36, works as a human resources manager for a large paper company, and earns $87,000 per year. She has worked her way up through this company and has
expectations of remaining there indefinitely with increasing success. She has a very nice executive level group benefits package with an employee assistance program. She is happy to support both of them. They own a loft condominium worth $575,000 with a mortgage of $400,000 at a rate of 5%, due to Angelica's excellent credit rating. Angelica incurred credit card debt of $37,000 last year when they redecorated, which she is paying off gradually. The interest rate is 18%. They are unsure whether to start an RRSP soon or wait until the mortgage is paid off. They are not planning on having any children but would like to pay for their two nephews' university educations. The nephews are twins, currently 2 years old. Tyler and Angelica do not have any individual insurance nor do they have any investments. They are considering purchasing investment products next month to meet their goals. They have heard that a life insurance policy can be used to fund a child's education. Which of the following would not be true about life insurance policies they might consider purchasing for the twins?

a. Angelica and Tyler would be able to assign the policies to either twin when they reach the age of majority in their province. If they do so after that then there would be tax consequences.
b. If their objective is to invest the maximum possible amount into the policies, Angelica and Tyler should choose a yearly renewable term cost of insurance.
c. They would not be able to purchase these policies without the consent of the twins' parents.
d. Angelica and Tyler would choose the beneficiaries for these policies.

43. Claudia makes $48,000 per year and has never contributed to an RRSP. Her husband, Oliver makes $78,000
and has always put in maximum contributions. He has more than enough to make a contribution this year. What is the best way for them to reduce their total tax burden?

a. He makes a spousal contribution to her RRSP
b. He contributes to his own RRSP
c. She contributes to her own RRSP using his money
d. She makes a spousal contribution to his RRSP

44. Mitchell runs a carpet cleaning business which he recently incorporated. He is drawing an irregular
director's bonus, depending upon the company profits which fluctuate seasonally. He understands the value of tax-sheltered growth and has maximized his RRSPs each year. He has a moderate risk tolerance and puts in long hours at work. His townhouse is paid off and he has little debt but he may want to expand his business soon and will need capital. Which is most appropriate?

a. A whole life policy since he could use the non-forfeiture options to pay his premiums if his income declined
b. A universal life policy since he could use the cash surrender value to fund his premiums if his income declined
c. A term insurance policy since he has no time to monitor his investments and is already experiencing tax deferral in his RRSPs
d. Either of A or B

45. Sasha and Jimmy Booker are considering purchasing whole life insurance policies since they like the idea of guaranteed cash values. They consider themselves to be conservative investors and are amused by their
friends that "play the markets" even when they are successful. Since Sasha and Jimmy always consider the
pros and cons of every decision they make, they have asked you about the negatives of whole life insurance. Which statement below is not valid?

a. Whole life insurance, even if participating, will never pay out more than the face value
b. If equity markets take off, the cash surrender value will not reflect any increases even if the prime rate rises dramatically
c. If Sasha and Jimmy find themselves in a financial pinch, the use of the cash surrender value to pay the premiums will have some constraints
d. If they want to increase their use of this tax-effective investment, they will be unable to do so without underwriting considerations

46. Sasha and Jimmy Booker are considering purchasing whole life insurance policies since they like the idea of guaranteed cash values. They consider themselves to be conservative investors and are amused by their
friends that "play the markets" even when they are successful. Since Sasha and Jimmy always base their decisions on comparison with other products, they have asked you about the advantages of universal life insurance. Which statement below is not valid?

a. Universal life policies that pay out the face value at death will cost less than those that include the cash surrender value
b. There is a wide variety of investment funds that can be chosen, including guaranteed products
c. A universal life policy could be "paid up" in the same time frame as a whole life policy
d. The choice of investments does not allow for comparison of fees at the time of purchase

47. Nina has purchased a whole life policy on her baby daughter, Maria, with a Guaranteed Insurability Benefit
(GIB). The premiums, including all riders, total $48 per month. The GIB is $4 per month and is connected to the policy anniversary nearest to age 21 and 30. Which of the following is incorrect?

a. The premium will drop to $44 per month only when both opportunities for increase have passed and have not been exercised
b. The premiums will remain the same if the GIB opportunities are exercised
c. If Nina develops diabetes, the death benefit cannot increase
d. B&C

48. Travis recently divorced. During his separation period, he lapsed his whole life policy. In order to reinstate:

i. The insurer determines Travis' current financial situation and health
ii. Outstanding premiums and interest will be payable
iii. He will forfeit his non-forfeiture options
iv. A beneficiary change, to remove his ex-wife, is required
v. The contestable period will start again from the date of the missed premium
vi. There may be a deemed disposition triggering taxes

a. i, ii, vi
b. i, ii, v, vi
c. i, ii, iv, v
d. ii, iv, v, vi

49. Randy owns a universal life policy on his daughter's life, purchased when she was a baby. She took over the task of paying premiums when she got married at age 23 and Randy transferred ownership to her. The policy has been more than minimally funded. Mandy is now age 26, single and healthy, with a small child, and struggling to make ends meet. Randy is reluctant to pay the premiums since he trying to save for his impending retirement. What is the best choice?

    a. Policy Loan
    b. Reduced paid up insurance
    c. Absolute assignment to Randy
    d. Full surrender

50. Susan was 84 years old, living on her own since her husband passed away 8 years ago. Her son, William,
    purchased a long term care policy on his mother 10 years ago and has paid the premiums since then. Susan recently had a fall that left her needing hands-on assistance in her home. Fortunately, Susan responded well to physiotherapy and is able to regain her independence after six months. Unfortunately, she suffered a stroke at age 85. With the help of her son, and the right caregiving support, she is able to stay at home for the next two years, and then moves to an assisted living facility before her death at age 88. Which could be true?

    a. Susan could have received benefits after the fall, after the stroke, and in the nursing home
    b. The benefits would not start until she is in a nursing home
    c. The benefits would typically be paid to William and would be taxed since the premiums are a qualifying medical expense
    d. The policy would have terminated at maximum issue age of 80 so no benefits would be paid

51. Ella Vetora is your client. She owns and operates a company as a vertical transportation specialist. You
    have prepared several illustrations for her and just spent 45 minutes explaining your disability products. Ella makes the following statements, paraphrasing your presentation, in order to confirm with you that she understands it all correctly. Which one of the following could not be true?

    a. Waiver of Premium means that, if I fell down a shaft or something, the $158 a month payments you showed me would be paid by the insurance company.
    b. The Future Purchase Option means that as long as I can prove my income has increased, the insurance company will keep my benefit at 65% of whatever I make. I won't need to see a doctor to do this.
    c. The Cost of Living rider is suitable for me due to my age. If I got disabled for the rest of my life, I could still have the same purchasing power even decades from now.
    The Cost of Living rider means my coverage will automatically increase every year to keep pace with inflation.

52. Marla, age 53, was a securities analyst until she decided to quit in order to care for her aging parents. She is single, never had children, and will receive a small inheritance at her parents' death. She has not worked in 5 years and is living off her savings. Her days are filled with care giving plus she also manages a 20-suite apartment building she purchased a while ago. She will sell it soon. Her parents are not expected to live much longer. She belongs to a paintball club and coaches a children's baseball team. Which insurance product is most appropriate for her?

a. Universal life with an aggressive investment choice, to match her risk tolerant profile
b. R&C Term to age 75, due to her commitments
c. Par whole life with paid up additions to combat inflation on her death benefit, since her parents may live for years more
d. Term-to-100 since that will allow her to "invest the difference"

53. You have entered the client's home in order to present a recommendation for life insurance. It is your second visit after doing a needs analysis last week. As you walk up the driveway, you notice scuba diving equipment in the back of their pickup truck. As you enter the home, you notice a reminder postcard on the hallway table from their doctor for an annual check up. You complete the individual life insurance application. You are able to issue a Temporary Insurance Agreement. The client is buying Term to 100 with waiver of premium and a term rider. The paper illustration you have brought with you is for T100 with no riders. You estimate the amount of extra premium and collect a cheque for the higher amount. Which is true?

a. You have used apparent authority in calculating the premium. The client is not covered for the term rider amount.
b. You have acted within your actual authority according to the law of agency
c. A temporary insurance agreement can bind the insurer for the face amount plus the term rider.
d. B&C

54. You have entered the client's home in order to present a recommendation for life insurance. It is your
second visit after doing a needs analysis last week. As you walk up the driveway, you notice scuba diving equipment in the back of their pickup truck. As you enter the home, you notice a reminder postcard on the hallway table from their doctor for an annual check up. You complete the individual life insurance application. You are able to issue a Temporary Insurance Agreement. The client is buying Term to 100 with waiver of premium and a term rider. The paper illustration you have brought with you is for T100 with no riders. You estimate the amount of extra premium and collect a cheque for the higher amount. Which is true?

a. You should note the scuba diving equipment on the Advisor Report
b. You should ask the client about their scuba diving habits and perhaps do a questionnaire
c. You should ignore the equipment as it might belong to a friend. If the client chooses to tell you about their hobbies, that is "constructive notice".
d. They are uninsurable if they scuba dive

55. Katie Downey is interested in investing in a segregated fund. She is concerned about losing money. Her
agent tells her the following. Which is false?

a. The CLHIA regulates the amount of assets required by an insurer that sells segregated funds.
Provincial regulators approve the information folder without CLHIA involvement.
b. The CLHIA monitors the "holding out" of segregated funds. Assuris provides consumer protection that, while voluntary for the insurer to join, has membership of most large insurers
c. The CLHIA, a self-regulating organization, enforces regulation of delinquent insurers on a needs basis with the federal regulator's assistance
d. All of the above

56. You have entered the client's home in order to present a recommendation for life insurance. It is your second visit after doing a needs analysis last week. As you walk up the driveway, you notice scuba diving equipment in the back of their pickup truck. As you enter the home, you notice a reminder postcard on the hallway table from their doctor for an annual check up. You complete the individual life insurance application. You are able to issue a Temporary Insurance Agreement. The client is buying Term to 100 with waiver of premium and a term rider. The paper illustration you have brought with you is for T100 with no riders. You estimate the amount of extra premium and collect a cheque for the higher amount. You ask about the scuba equipment and they state it belongs to a friend and they just storing it for them. They appear embarrassed and you suspect they are lying. You should:

a. Leave the home without placing a policy
b. Explain to them the consequences of fraudulent misrepresentation and how sports are underwritten
c. If they do not admit to using the equipment, note it on the Underwriting Report
d. Counsel them that they should be careful while diving since they could go to jail if caught

57. You have entered the client's home in order to present a recommendation for life insurance. It is your second visit after doing a needs analysis last week. As you walk up the driveway, you notice scuba diving equipment in the back of their pickup truck. As you enter the home, you notice a reminder postcard on the hallway table from their doctor for an annual check up. You complete the individual life insurance application. You are able to issue a Temporary Insurance Agreement. The client is buying T100 with waiver of premium and a term rider. The paper illustration you have brought with you is for T100 with no riders. You estimate the amount of extra premium and collect a cheque for the higher amount. You ask about the scuba equipment and they state it belongs to a friend and they just storing it for them. Which is true?

a. The TIA will cover scuba diving accidents, if the sport is disclosed on the application.
b. The TIA will include the waiver of premium rider.
c. The TIA will be in force for 90 days in all circumstances.
d. All of the above.

58. Keith is an insurance agent who has almost completed a buy/sell agreement for Tri Hard Plumbing Ltd.
There are 3 owners involved, two of which are in New York on vacation. The 3rd owner has signed the agreement and the life insurance application on behalf of the corporation and provided medical information
on all 3shareholder/owners. The accounts payable department has issued a cheque for the first premium.
Keith would like to get the insurance started since the need is apparent. Which is true?

a. Keith must leave the application and return to pick it up when the other two owners have signed.
b. Keith must witness the other two owners signatures.
c. Keith could issue Temporary Insurance Agreements without signatures.
d. The lawyer who prepared the agreement can waive the need for signatures.

59. Adele is a dentist in a small town. She has never had a spouse or children. She is contemplating retiring in
the same small town this year at age 58. She has $1,300,000 in non-registered assets. She would like a regular income stream to pay her home expenses, food, and other basic costs which currently total $2500 per month. Which would be the best choice to purchase with all or part of her funds?

a. A registered annuity since there will not be a withholding tax applied
b. A series of non-redeemable GIC's since the interest will grow in a tax-sheltered environment until maturity
c. An indexed non-prescribed annuity that provides for her current expenses
d. A prescribed annuity with a cash refund in case she changes her mind.

60. Taylor is considering an individual accident and sickness policy. He is a 33-year-old in good health, working as a mechanic. Which of the following is true?

a. These premiums could be only tax advantaged if he is self-employed since they will then be a business deduction
b. Extended health benefits will never cover services of a Chiropractor, Chiropodist, Osteopath, Naturopath, or Podiatrist.
c. The premium charged and/or benefits offered could be subject to adjustment or modification of coverage based on family medical background
d. Individual A&S products are not affected by province of residency due to consumer standardization laws.

61. Ethan is a 24-year-old oil rig worker who has been saving to go to university for the past few years. Tuition
for the first year is due next week and will be $18,000 including books. If tuition experiences 6% inflation, how much will Ethan need to have in his bank account now, to be able to pay for a four year degree?

a. $78,743
b. $77,582
c. $76,320
d. $83,468

62. Hailey's husband, Jack, worked many years for an insurance company. He committed suicide last week
when the company entered preliminary bankruptcy proceedings. He had held a $956,000 life insurance policy for many years with this same company. Hailey is the beneficiary. Hailey phones you, her agent, a few days after the death, very worried that the policy will not be able to be paid out since she saw a news story that the insurer is in liquidation. You should advise her:

a. Assuris will pay $60,000 and she may get more from the liquidators
b. Assuris will pay $812,600
c. She will have to wait until the maturity date to get anything
d. Because of capital requirements put in place by the federal government, it is impossible for an insurer to go bankrupt.

63. Logan is manager of a sporting goods store and makes $69,000 per year. He often helps lift heavy items onto the shelves. His mother is becoming forgetful and can no longer take the bus to go shopping but remains at home. She has had arthritis for several decades and has a nurse comes in three times a day to assist her. Logan is engaged to be married to Nikola, a self-employed tailor working from her home, and he carries a heavy credit card debt which he does not want his future wife to inherit, should he die prematurely. Logan's employer offers no group benefits and Nikola has had several expensive treatments on her teeth, paid for by Logan. He would like to finish getting crowns on her teeth but is not sure when he will be able to afford it. He has a life insurance policy with a face value of $250,000 which he thinks is sufficient. His family has no history of hereditary diseases and Logan is currently completely healthy. Logan ends up purchasing a cancellable individual disability policy with an any occupation definition of disability and presumptive benefits as well as a waiver of premium rider. Which of the following circumstances might cause his policy to be modified in some way?

a. Logan falls off a ladder and fractures his hip. He is disabled for several months but then returns to work full-time.
b. Logan feels depressed about his work. His doctor advises him to take some time off. Logan submits a disability claim which is denied by his insurer because depression is excluded from his policy.
c. Logan leaves the sporting goods industry and goes to work in a meat-packing plant. He ends up doing a physically demanding job around heavy machinery.
d. Logan misses a premium payment but upon receiving notification of this from the insurer two weeks after it happens quickly makes up the missed premium.

64. Marta is a young aggressive investor. She is looking for a segregated fund that has the potential to make her a lot of growth. Since she will not make any withdrawals until maturity, volatility is not a concern to her. Which is the best fund for her?

a. A Canadian mortgage fund
b. An index fund that tracks global emerging markets.
c. A U.S. balanced fund
d. A Canadian balanced fund

65. Sophie invested $145,000 into an Individual Variable Insurance Contract (IVIC) on June 27, 2009. She chose a balanced fund with a 3% MER, a 75% maturity and death benefit guarantee, and two reset options per year. According to her statement, the fund increased for a while reaching $178,000 then dropped to $135,000 as of March 13, 2015. If she had exercised a reset option when the fund was at its peak and held it to maturity, what would she have gained beyond the original guarantee?

a. The difference between 75% of $178,000 and $135,000
b. The difference between 75% of $145,000 and 75% of $178,000, less 3%
c. The difference between 75% of $178,000 and 75% of $145,000
d. 25% of $178,000

66. Jade Chew has a group plan at her workplace, where she has been employed for four years. She develops severe migraines due to job stress and has some time off with disability benefits. She decides to quit and open up a pottery studio. As soon as she makes this decision, her migraines ease off and she returns to work full-time. After researching her new endeavour for a few months, she quits and moves to the Yukon where she opens up the studio. How many days does she have to convert her group plan to individual coverage?

a. She cannot convert because she has submitted a claim within the past 12 months.
b. 31 days
c. She cannot convert because she has only been with this employer for four years.
d. 61 days

67. Georgette is looking to buy an annuity and has asked her agent to explain the various types to her. Her husband has predeceased her and she has no children or grandchildren alive. Which types of annuities do not have a named beneficiary?

a. Life straight annuity, and joint & last survivor annuity
b. Life certain annuity and commutable annuity
c. Variable annuity, life straight annuity, and joint & last survivor annuity
d. Fixed term annuity and prescribed annuity

68. Tristan was disabled in a workplace accident. His condition enables him to get CPP disability benefits. He is a single parent with three children: Shelby is 22 and has a severe mental disability; she lives in a care facility. Dustin is 23 and attending school full-time at a local college, renting a nearby apartment. Lydia is 26 and living with Tristan while she completes her master's degree in kinesiology. Who will receive CPP benefits besides Tristan?

    a. Dustin only.
    b. Dustin and Lydia
    c. Shelby and Lydia
    d. None of the above

69. An Individual Variable Insurance Contract's (IVIC) information folder provides details on:

    i. Fees
    ii. Reset options
    iii. Method to determine the new guarantee after withdrawal
    iv. Statement of client's notional units
    v. How an IVIC would work within a Registered Retirement Savings Plan (RRSP)

    a. All of the above
    b. i, ii, iii, v
    c. i, ii, iii
    d. i, iv

70. Mark has $200,000 in group life insurance. He will have $45,000 in a GIC available at his death but will need $233,000 in order to leave his house mortgage-free to his wife, Joan. Joan will need $3500 per month for her and her children's needs. She will earn $68,000 as a claims adjuster. Using a 3% rate of return, how much insurance does Mark need?

    a. $854,667
    b. $128,667
    c. There is no need for insurance
    d. $38,000

71. Audrey, a 36-year-old journalist for a city newspaper, developed severe tonsil cancer and required chemotherapy and various medicines. She spent $2000 per month on a condo in Windsor while she received treatment across the border in Detroit, $1,000 per month for her rent in her own city, and lost $36,000 in income, during her 5 months of treatment. Her treatment was successful and she returned to work shortly after. In retrospect, what would have been the best types of individual policies for Audrey to have purchased?

a. Long term care, A&S
b. Critical illness, A&S
c. Disability, critical illness
d. Living benefit all sources

72. Ivan is looking to purchase a non-registered Individual Variable Insurance Contract. He is considering one insurer's contract which offers 75% guarantees, a Deferred Sales Charge over the first 6 years, and a 2.2% Management Fee. What should he also inquire about, with regard to features of this product?

a. A back end load
b. Availability of resets
c. Underwriting requirements
d. A temporary insurance agreement

73. Bart is the owner of a convenience store and has obtained a life insurance license to use in his off hours. He has told his staff members that he will give them a raise of $1 per hour if they buy a universal life insurance policy from him for $160 per month (the number of hours they work in a month). If they refuse, he will not give them the preferred shifts. In order to keep Bart happy, three of the employees comply and accept the raise. Which of the following is true?

a. Bart has committed a misrepresentation.
b. Bart coerced the employees into purchasing these contracts; if one of the employees suffers a loss that would normally be covered, no benefit will be paid.
c. Bart has committed fraud.
d. Bart has committed coercion.

74. Jacob is a computer consultant making $65,000. His employer provides him with group disability benefits that offered 60% total disability benefits with a regular occupation definition of disability and 5 years of benefits. When he developed a corneal ulcer, he had several eye surgeries and was unable to work for 3 years. Jacob's grandparents left him a trust account that pays him $300 per month, indexed to inflation, until the funds run out. How much will his monthly benefit be during the sixth month of his disability?

   a. $3250
   b. $2950
   c. $3550
   d. $5417

75. Leanne is an extreme sports enthusiast. She works as a mechanical engineer and enjoys good group benefits including Accidental Death & Dismemberment that is three times her salary. Which of the following accidents would be covered under most AD&D policies?

   i. She had a spinal injury while bungee jumping which later required surgery
   ii. She lost an arm after hitting a tree while flying an ultralight plane she had built
   iii. She was arrested for climbing an office building wall without a permit and suffered loss of use of her right hand due to overly tight handcuffs
   iv. She drowned while canoeing in the Amazon
   v. She died from poisonous gases she breathed in while climbing the chimney of a plastics factory that she had broken into
   vi. She was electrocuted by lightning while chasing a storm in a hot air balloon and passed away after 5 days in the hospital

   a. iv only
   b. ii
   c. None of the above
   d. iii, iv, v

76. Cathy is covered by a critical illness policy, a life insurance policy, and a disability policy. Her disability policy has a 30 day waiting period. Tragically, Cathy is diagnosed with cancer and dies two weeks after diagnosis, leaving behind shocked loved ones and friends. Which of her policies would pay a benefit?

   a. All three of them would pay a benefit.
   b. None of them would pay a benefit.
   c. The life insurance policy and critical illness policy would, but the disability policy would not.
   d. The life insurance policy only.

77. Which statement would be most useful in explaining to a client how mutual funds and segregated funds function?

a. Both segregated funds and mutual funds work on the pool concept. Professional fund managers monitor all investments closely.
b. The provincial government provides regulation for both.
c. Mutual funds and segregated funds are very similar, but segregated funds carry additional costs based on the mortality of the contract owner.
d. Segregated funds are individual variable insurance contracts that are regulated under the Life Insurance Act. Mutual funds, although regulated differently, can also offer some guarantees based on past performance.

78. Lisa, a lawyer, has applied for $1.5 million of life insurance with Inconceivable Insurance Co. Matthew, her agent, issued a Temporary Insurance Agreement (TIA) with a limit of $1,000,000. The insurer became insolvent a few days later, before the underwriting was complete. Lisa was killed in a skiing accident the next day. Assuris will pay out:

a. $425,000
b. $1,275,000
c. $850,000
d. $60,000

79. Theo and Amanda are both 38 and have been married 6 years. They both work for the same employer, a Schedule I bank. They have excellent group benefits through the same insurer for 8 years and have a good understanding of the coverages. They have asked you to present individual insurance products to them so they can compare. Which statement is not correct?

a. Group insurance often will have insufficient life coverage but may have adequate A&S and disability coverage
b. If Amanda goes on maternity leave, she could convert the group insurance to individual as long as she has worked there five years
c. The bank can deduct the full premium from income tax as long as they provide coverage to all employees
d. Theo and Amanda will have the same master contract even though they hold different jobs within the bank

80. Theo and Amanda are both 38 and have been married 6 years. They both work for the same employer, a Schedule I bank. They have excellent group benefits through the same insurer for 8 years and have a good understanding of the coverages. Theo has recently had some dental work done and made a claim through the bank for reimbursement. Which is incorrect?

a. Theo must claim as primary first before making a dependant/spousal claim even if he has already made a claim this year
b. Theo's own cost will be a combination of a co-pay amount plus a deductible amount but could be zero
c. After the co-insurance factor is calculated, the deductible is subtracted and Theo will pay the difference
d. Theo's payment to the dentist was made with after-tax dollars

81. Theo and Amanda are both 38 and have been married 6 years. They both work for the same employer, a Schedule I bank employing several thousand employees. They have excellent group benefits through the same insurer for 8 years and have a good understanding of the coverages. They have asked you to explain how their premiums are calculated. Which is true?

a. Since the bank has been in existence for 88 years, an experience rating was used
b. Since the bank has only 46,000 employees (less than 100,000) there is little credibility
c. Since the bank merged with another bank 10 years ago (under 15 years), a blended rating must be used
d. The insurer would not use a manual rating for such a large employer

82. Theo and Amanda are both 38 and have been married 6 years. They both work for the same employer, a Schedule I bank. They have excellent group benefits through the same insurer for 8 years and have a good understanding of the coverages. Which is a true statement?

a. A large, national bank would typically use a refund method of accounting since that gives the most reimbursement to the employees
b. Self-insuring is a technique used by corporations, individuals, and governments
c. The bank could use stop-loss insurance to protect their Retention Reserve
d. An Administrative Services Only contract is only available to very small companies who would not know how to process claims

83. Julie earns $140,000 each year as a chiropractor. She would reduce her hours of work if her husband,
Verne, were to die, dropping her income by $70,000 per year. They have paid off their house and currently spend just $62,000 per year, including maximizing their RRSP contributions. Verne's needs at death would be $417,000 to pay off his credit card debt and mortgages on his rental properties which currently show no profit. He has a "face plus" life insurance policy for $100,000 face value plus $67,432 in cash surrender value. Current interest rates are 3%. How much should Verne's life be covered for?

a. $517,000
b. $2,320,000
c. There is no need for life insurance on Verne
d. $250,000

84. Emily Dorval (born Feb 1, 1979) and Emile Dodwell (born Feb 2, 1979) are a common-law couple both
employed as engineers. She works for Santori Ltd. and is covered by a group plan that has $50 single deductible and a $100 family deductible. The co-pay factor is 90/10. Emile works for EME Engineering Ltd. and his plan is through a different insurer. It has a $75 single deductible and $200 family deductible, with 90/10 co-pay. Their son, Aiden, is two years old and has chronic ear infections. They made a claim for him on January 1 of this year for $358 of antibiotics, through both insurers using coordination of benefits. What is the result?

a. Emile's plan would reimburse $215.80 and Emily's plan would reimburse $142.20
b. Emily's plan would reimburse $232.20 and Emile's plan would reimburse $142.20
c. Emily's plan would reimburse $277.20 and Emile's plan would reimburse $80.80
d. Emily's plan would reimburse $186.40 and Emile's plan would reimburse $171.60

85. Hector married late in life, at age 47. He is an aggressive investor and has played the market for years,
mostly with penny stocks. His new wife, Mariana, is 38 years old and has 2 young daughters. Hector realizes he must be more conservative with his non-registered funds and is about to start an RRSP. Which choice is likely to give Hector the least risk with the most potential return?

a. Put half his RRSP contribution into a money market mutual fund and half into small cap stocks
b. Put his RRSP contribution into an Individual Variable Insurance Contract with investments in a variety of specialty equity funds
c. Put all of his assets into Guaranteed Investment Certificates, at various banks due to CDIC limits
d. Put his half of his non-registered assets and half of his registered assets into a deferred annuity, since rates are the highest they have been in the last 5 years

86. Hector married late in life, at age 47. He is an aggressive investor and has played the market for years,
mostly with penny stocks. His new wife, Mariana, is 38 years old and has 2 young daughters. Hector realizes he must be more conservative with his non-registered funds. He purchases a deferred annuity with his wife as annuitant. He also invests into a $65,000 Individual Variable Insurance Contract with 100% guarantees and names himself as annuitant and his wife as beneficiary. When Hector dies of a heart attack four years later, the IVIC has dropped to $45,000. What will his beneficiary receive from the IVIC?

a. $45,000
b. $65,000
c. $48,750
d. Nothing since Mariana did not die

87. Hector married late in life, at age 47. He is an aggressive investor and has played the market for years, mostly with penny stocks. His new wife, Mariana, is 38 years old and has 2 young daughters. Hector realizes he must be more conservative with his non-registered funds. He purchases a deferred annuity with his wife as annuitant. He also invests into a $65,000 Individual Variable Insurance Contract with 100% guarantees and names himself as annuitant and his wife as beneficiary. When Hector dies of a heart attack four years later, the IVIC has dropped to $45,000. Mariana is startled to learn of the large drop in market
value since Hector had told her it was invested in a bond fund. She calls her life insurance agent and
pledges to start a law suit against him for improper sales practices. The agent should immediately contact:

   a. His lawyer
   b. His errors and omission provider
   c. The executor of Hector's estate
   d. His license sponsor

88. Daniela, age 58, has multiple sclerosis which is worsening daily. It is not affecting her life expectancy. She
is seeking alternative treatments overseas since medications are not working. CPP benefits:

   a. Will be paid to Daniela as early as age 60
   b. Are available to her once she is unable to function on a normal basis
   c. Are only for accidents in the workplace
   d. Will reimburse her for the alternative medication and travel expenses

89. Lena is covered under an individual disability policy which specifically excludes disabilities caused by a
normal pregnancy; war; duty in any Armed Forces; and donation of organs to another. Six years after purchasing the policy she stays late at the bar one night, drinks several cocktails, and attempts to drive home. In the course of her drive home, she drives into a tree and becomes disabled. Which of the following is true as it concerns the claim that she submits?

   a. It would be denied based on the fact that she was driving while intoxicated.
   b. It would be accepted and she would receive disability benefits.
   c. It would be denied only if she were criminally charged with impaired driving.
   d. It would be denied if she were pregnant at the time of the accident.

90. Mitchell is looking over some life insurance product brochures. He is considering whole life and wants to know what will cause his cash surrender value to increase. You explain about adjusted cost basis and how
taxation of a cash surrender value is calculated when monies are withdrawn. He asks you what will cause adjusted cost basis to reduce. Which of the following is most complete?

    a. All policies issued after 1982, partial surrender, policy loans
    b. All policies issued before 1982, partial surrender, dividends received
    c. All policies issued after 1982, dividends received, proceeds of disposition
    d. All policies issued before 1982, partial surrender, dividends received, policy loans

91. You are a new agent just learning the business. Your prospect, Jenna, is a 33-year-old, non-smoking
warehouse manager. She makes a modest income, is currently single, and has two young children from a prior relationship. She is asking you to replace a policy she was sold two years ago by another agent. Which statement is false?

    a. Replacement can be a good idea if the existing policy's premiums are higher than an equivalent product (with the same level of protection) offered by your company
    b. Replacement is not an option since the other agent will be already receiving renewal commissions based upon Jenna's continuation
    c. Since Jenna is now two years older, the premiums may be higher and she may have started smoking, so replacement could be a poor idea
    d. If Jenna waits until next year, mortality rates may change

92. Ronaldo, age 54, and his wife, Judy, age 53 are doing some estate planning. They want to leave as much as
possible to their children. They are concerned with inflation eroding the death benefit and with taxes being siphoned off. Of the following, which is the best choice?

    a. Joint-Last-to-Die par whole life with paid up additions
    b. Term-to-100
    c. Joint-First-to-Die with guaranteed insurability option.
    d. Universal Life, depositing the level cost of insurance

93. How does the insurance industry insure that group long-term disability claims do not become profitable to
the injured employee, thus reducing false claims?

    a. Non-discriminatory benefits schedule
    b. Issue limits
    c. Through the use of deductibles and co-insurance
    d. All sources maximum

94. Amber had made premium payments of $120 per month and deposits of $185 per month for 12 years to her
   universal life policy, which has a level death benefit plus total account value. Her account value now stands at $48,800, which is $18,500 above the Adjusted Cost Basis. She withdrew $5,500 to use towards her RRSP this year. What is her taxable gain on the withdrawal?

   a. $1,042
   b. $5,500
   c. $2,085
   d. $0

95. Amber had made premium payments of $120 per month and deposits of $185 per month for 12 years to her
   universal life policy, which has a level death benefit plus total account value. Her account value now stands at $48,800, which is $18,500 above the ACB. She withdrew $5,500 to use towards her RRSP this year. What will the consequences of this withdrawal be towards her future death benefit?

   a. A direct reduction.
   b. No impact.
   c. Reduced by the amount of the withdrawal plus a reasonable rate of interest charged by the insurer.
   d. Reduced by the amount of the withdrawal plus any future potential growth on that amount.

96. Amber had made premium payments of $120 per month and deposits of $185 per month for 12 years to her
   universal life policy, which has a level death benefit plus total account value. Her account value now stands at $48,800, which is $18,500 above the ACB. She withdrew $5,500 to use towards her RRSP this year. If her taxable income is $78,000 including the withdrawal, what is the effect on her taxes as a result of her RRSP contribution – ignore any tax consequences related to her life insurance policy – if she is in a 32% tax bracket?

   a. $1,760 tax saved
   b. $5,500 tax saved
   c. $1,375 tax saved
   d. $1,760 tax due

97. Bailey Madison is a 62-year-old president of a manufacturing company. She is retiring soon and wants to
provide a perk to her best executive-level employees that does not involve giving them ownership in the company. What would be the best choice?

a. Key person insurance
b. Deferred profit sharing plan
c. Employee assistance program
d. Disability buy-out insurance

98. Group insurance is attractive as compared to individual insurance for all of the following reasons except:

a. There is little or no underwriting.
b. Disability benefits tend to pay sooner.
c. It covers health and dental expenditures not covered in individual health and dental plans.
d. Riders attached to group policies are more generous.

99. Phil Rupert worked in a gas station for many years. When he developed crippling arthritis at the age of 56,
he became wheelchair-bound and qualified for CPP disability benefits. The amount of disability was based upon his CPP entitlement, plus a flat rate of $414.08/month. If his retirement benefits are to be $504.00/month at age 60, what advice would you give him?

a. Take both CPP disability and CPP retirement at age 60.
b. Stop CPP disability and start taking CPP retirement as soon as possible at age 60.
c. Stop CPP disability and start taking CPP retirement at age 65.
d. Take CPP disability as long as possible.

100.     You sit down with a client of yours, Vince. Vince is the owner and president of an educational services
company, Can-U-Learn. Vince would like to acquire group benefits for his employees. You obtain quotes from several insurance companies. You and Vince carefully review the quotes. Vince likes the group life insurance plan offered by Great Canadian Life and he likes the disability plan offered by Trans-Union Life. He believes that he can structure a benefit plan for dental benefits for his employees that will be more cost-effective than either of the plans offered by Great Canadian or Trans-Union. How should you structure Vince's group plan?

a. Put the whole plan with Trans-Union.
b. Put the whole plan with Great Canadian.
c. Put the life portion with Great Canadian and the disability portion with Trans-Union. Self-insure the dental portion.
d. Put the life portion with Great Canadian and the disability portion with Trans-Union. Use an Administrative Services Only contract for the dental.

101. Harry is putting together a benefits plan for his employees. He would like to make sure that, should one of
his employees become disabled, that the employee will receive their disability benefit tax-free. Which of the following structures would not accomplish Harry's aim?

a. Harry increases his employees' salaries and has them purchase individual disability policies.
b. Harry pays the premiums for a group disability plan and passes the amount of the premium on to the employees as a taxable benefit.
c. Harry has the employees pay the premiums for the disability portion of a group plan.
d. Harry pays less than 50% of the amount of the premium for the disability portion of a group plan.

102. Nicholas and Ruby are in their mid-30's with a five-year-old child. Due to having to declare bankruptcy 10 years ago over some poor investments, they are now extremely risk adverse. They would like to buy some
insurance for estate planning needs. Nicholas' elderly parents own a house in an area of town that is
undergoing a decline and they are unable to sell it, even though it was intended to fund their nursing home fees. They can no longer manage the stairs in the home. They may become dependent upon Nicholas and he is fixing up his basement for them to live in. Which are the most appropriate life insurance products for  them to purchase?

a. Universal life on Nicholas and Ruby, five-year term insurance on the child
b. Whole life on Nicholas, Ruby, and the child
c. Joint-last-to-die T100 on Nicholas' parents, T100 on the child
d. Universal life on the parents (in guaranteed investments), term insurance on Nicholas and Ruby

103. Nicholas, age 36, buys a $500,000 T100 policy naming his 82-year-old parents as the primary beneficiaries.
His parents will soon need an assisted living facility. Nicholas is killed in a farming accident shortly after policy issue. Which settlement option is most appropriate?

a. The life annuity option so that the parents cannot outlive their income
b. The instalment option so that the parents have a higher monthly income than the life annuity option
c. The interest option since the parents are not educated enough to manage a large portfolio
d. The lump sum option since the parents will want to leave some to their grandchild

104.     Nicholas is now 49 and divorced. He worked long and hard at a pharmaceutical company and has many
employee benefits. He has managed to save a substantial amount on his own. He wants to retire this year and will have more than enough money to do so. Of the choices below, which is the only source of funding he will be able to use for his daily needs during this early retirement?

a. RRSP
b. LIF
c. LIRA
d. CPP

105.     Nancy has been a notary for many years. She recently became legally blind from water-borne parasites
within 4 months of returning from Africa where she had been volunteering during a vacation. She submits a claim under her disability policy. The portion of the plan that will provide her with an income benefit will be:

a. Partial Benefits
b. Residual Benefits
c. Presumptive Benefits
d. Rehabilitation Benefits

106.     Laura is 63 years old and ready to retire in 3 years. She has $500,000 in non-registered assets due to the downsizing of her home. She has an RRSP of $350,000 and an employer's pension of $3,500 per month
(indexed). Current interest rates are 3.75%. She is single with an adult son, Jordan, living independently
from her. She would like to use the non-registered funds to supplement her pension on a monthly basis. She has looked at buying a GIC from her bank as well as a deferred annuity from an insurance company. What reason(s) might she have to choose the deferred annuity over the GIC?

a. The deferred annuity will offer greater liquidity than the GIC will.
b. The deferred annuity will allow her to bypass probate processes on death.
c. Annuity rates will always be higher than GIC rates because insurers offer better rates than banks do.
d. Consumer protection in the event of insolvency will be better with the deferred annuity.

107.     Sandra is 63 years of age. She is currently living on a pension from her previous employer of $22,000 per year and no other income. The pension is indexed and will increase by 60% of inflation each year going forward. She has $350,000 in an RRSP, but she has managed to not withdraw funds from the RRSP to this point. Her RRSP is growing at a rate of 5.5% per year, based on investments in income mutual funds. She is also due to receive a Canada Pension Plan benefit of $900 per month starting at age 65, and an Old Age Security benefit of $520 per month at age 65. Since she retired 3 years ago, she has accumulated $33,000 debt on her line of credit, which is charging her 3% interest. Which of the following options would allow her to stop accumulating debt and meet her living expenses?

a. Start her CPP now and make RRSP withdrawals as required to meet her living expenses.
b. Start her CPP now and mature her RRSP into a RRIF. Use the RRIF withdrawals to meet living expenses.
c. Start her CPP now and leave the RRSP untouched.
d. Mature her RRSP into a RRIF and use those withdrawals to meet living expenses.

108.     Laura is 64 years old and ready to retire in 2 years. She has $500,000 in non-registered assets due to the recent downsizing of her home. She has an RRSP of $350,000 and an employer's pension of $3,500 per month (indexed). She is single with an adult son, Jordan, living independently from her. She purchased a $500,000 non-registered deferred annuity exactly one year ago. Since then interest rates have fluctuated severely. She has now decided that she would like to buy a condo in Arizona for $200,000. She makes a withdrawal from the annuity. There will be a market value adjustment that is based on:

a. Fees and penalties outlined in the contract
b. Current interest rates compared to those at time of purchase
c. The amount of economic hardship she can prove
d. A&B

109. Ryan has purchased a par whole life policy and chosen paid up additions as his dividend option. This will have an impact on which of the following:

i. His death benefit
ii. The amount he can borrow if he uses the cash value as collateral at a bank
iii. The amount of policy loan the insurer will allow
iv. The riders available to him
v. His cost per thousand compared to other dividend options

a. i, iii, v
b. ii, iii
c. i, ii, iii
d. i, ii, v

110. Seth is 68 and set up a RRIF two years ago on advice of his accountant. The current balance is $453,287.
Which could be true?

a. His minimum withdrawal this year is $20,604
b. Setting up a RRIF early is recommended when regular withdrawals are required
c. There is withholding tax on amounts above 1/22nd of his balance
d. All of the above

111. Sabrina's husband was killed when he drove his car into a tractor trailer. He had purchased an individual life insurance policy, so she contacted her agent. The agent provided her with claims paperwork and the paperwork was submitted to the insurer. The claim was subsequently denied. Which of the following could not be a reason for the denial of the claim?

a. He was drunk at the time of the accident.
b. He failed to disclose in his application for insurance that he had previously been in treatment for alcohol abuse.
c. His policy had lapsed for non-payment of premiums.
d. He had failed to sign the application.

112. Nancy has died unexpectedly of a sudden stroke. She named her husband, who is now deceased, as her primary beneficiary for her life insurance policy, and her two young children as contingent beneficiaries. At the time of her death, the death benefit on her policy is $100,000. The youngest of her children, Erin, is 16. The older child, Harry, is 19. What will happen to Nancy's death benefit?

a. The full $100,000 will be paid to Harry.
b. $50,000 will be paid to Harry and $50,000 will be paid to Erin.
c. $50,000 will be paid to Harry and $50,000 will be held in trust by the insurer.
d. $50,000 will be paid to Harry and $50,000 will be paid to Nancy's estate.

113. Yolanda is covered under a group insurance policy. She also has an individual disability policy. She works as a bus driver for the City of Calgary. One day while helping a passenger on to her bus, she is hit by a cyclist and suffers a disability. Which of the following benefits would be the first payor during her subsequent disability?

a. Employment Insurance.
b. Worker's Compensation.
c. Her group disability coverage.
d. Her individual disability coverage.

114. Which of the following premiums would not be at least partially tax deductible?

a. Premiums for a group disability policy paid by an employer.
b. Premiums for an extended health care policy paid by an employer.
c. Premiums for a key person disability policy paid by an employer.
d. Premiums for a business overhead expense policy.

115. Darryl has an individual disability policy with a waiver of premium. The policy has a 120 day waiting period. He applies for and receives Employment Insurance sickness benefits during the waiting period for his disability policy. Which of the following benefits can he count on receiving after he has been disabled for 90 days?

a. Employment Insurance only.
b. Employment Insurance and his waiver of premium benefit.
c. Partial benefits from his disability policy plus his waiver of premium benefit.
d. He will receive no benefits from any disability plan after 90 days.

116.    Vern and Peta have been married for 3 years. Vern has asked about making a spousal RRSP contribution on Peta's behalf for 2010. Vern earned $68,000 in 2009. Peta earned $31,000. How much could Vern contribute to her RRSP, and what would the tax consequences be?

a. $12,240, and Vern would deduct that amount from his income.
b. $12,240, and Peta would deduct that amount from her income.
c. $5,580, and Vern would deduct that amount from his income.
d. $5,580, and Peta would deduct that amount from her income.

117.    Julianna and Ken are a couple, both aged 55. They have been fortunate enough to save enough money that they have decided to retire. They intend to acquire an annuity in order to provide some guaranteed income for as long as they need it. Which annuity should they purchase?

a. A life straight annuity on Ken's life with a 20 year guarantee.
b. A life straight annuity on Julianna's life with a 20 year guarantee.
c. A joint and last survivor annuity with a 20 year guarantee.
d. A joint and last survivor annuity, indexed.

118.    You have recommended to your clients, Kip and Sandy, that they should acquire travel insurance for their planned year-long vacation around the world. They decide to take you up on your recommendation. Which risk management technique have they employed?

a. Risk transfer.
b. Risk segregation.
c. Risk reduction.
d. Risk retention.

119.    Marina and Steve are a young couple, each earning more than $200,000/a. They have no children yet, but they plan to. They have always maximized their contributions to their RRSPs, and neither has any RRSP carry forward. Because of their high incomes, they pay a lot of income tax. They are looking for a plan which will allow them to invest a significant amount on a tax deferred basis to an extent that it will reduce the tax burden that they would face if they were to invest elsewhere. Which of the following would you recommend?

a. Universal life insurance.
b. Tax free savings account.
c. Registered disability savings plan.
d. Individual variable insurance contract.

120. Hector is a business owner. His company has 250 employees and generates $22,000,000 in annual revenue.
He finds that his group insurance premiums have been fluctuating unpredictably over the past few years, and he is looking for a way to add some predictability to his premiums. Which method would you recommend for him?

a. Establish an Administrative Services Only plan.
b. Have his insurer convert his policy to a five-year term.
c. Remove the coverage that is being used excessively from the master contract.
d. Have his insurer establish a Claims Fluctuation Reserve.

121. Which of the following investments presents the investor with the least risk?

a. Bonds.
b. Individual Variable Insurance Contracts.
c. Treasury Bills.
d. Guaranteed Investment Certificates.

122. Irving recently married Giselle, a much younger woman whom he met on vacation in Brazil. Not longer after their wedding, Irving dies. On Irving's death, he owns $400,000 worth of shares in a small business, for which he paid $50,000. He also owns a cottage worth $300,000, which cost him $150,000. He has a Registered Retirement Income Fund worth $200,000. His marginal tax rate is 40%. He leaves everything to Giselle. How much tax will be paid, and by whom?

a. Neither will have any tax to pay.
b. Irving's estate will have to pay $180,000 in tax; Giselle will have no tax to pay.
c. Irving's estate will have to pay $280,000 in tax; Giselle will have no tax to pay.
d. Irving's estate will have no tax to pay; Giselle will have a tax bill of $180,000.

123. Marvin entered into an Individual Variable Insurance Contract in 2006 with an investment of $10,000. The
IVIC is held in his Registered Retirement Savings Plan. The contract features guarantees of 75% on death or maturity. Today, the contract is worth $7,800. The Deferred Sales Charge schedule calls for a 2% sales charge to be paid on any withdrawals made this year. Marvin's marginal tax rate is 32%. If Marvin were to die, what would his beneficiary receive after all taxes and fees are paid?

a. $7,800.
b. $7,644.
c. $5,304.
d. $5,198.

124.    Jeffrey owns a life insurance policy with a $300,000 death benefit, a $100,000 cash surrender value (CSV), and a $60,000 adjusted cost basis. If he were to take out a policy loan of $80,000, what would the tax consequences be?

a. The policy loan would be tax-free.
b. Jeffrey would have to report $20,000 of income.
c. Jeffrey would have to report $48,000 of income.
d. Jeffrey would have to report $20,000 of capital gains.

125.    Meredith is 53 years old. She is concerned about her ability to care for herself in old age, as her husband, Stanley, who is just 64, is already in a nursing home. She wants to know whether a long-term care policy would be a good product for her. Specifically, she is concerned about whether the policy would pay a benefit when she feels that she needs it. The following is true about the benefit paid from a long-term care policy:

a. It is paid on diagnosis of conditions associated with aging, such as alzheimer's disease or amyotrophic lateral sclerosis.
b. It is paid at the time when the insured checks into a nursing home or similar acility.
c. It is paid when the insured is unable to perform certain activities of daily living.
d. It is paid when the insured is under the care of a medical professional.

126.    Meredith is 53 years old. She is concerned about her ability to care for herself in old age, as her husband, Stanley, who is just 64, is already in a nursing home. She wants to know whether a long-term care policy would be a good product for her. Specifically, she is concerned about whether the policy will provide enough funds for her to afford the costs of health care. Long-term care benefits can be paid in any of the following ways except:

a. As monthly income.
b. As daily income.
c. As a lump sum.
d. As needed on a reimbursement basis.

127. Desmond is the life insured on a life insurance policy owned by his father, Roger. Desmond wishes to make his new wife, Christina, the beneficiary of the policy. Which of the following steps would help to accomplish Desmond's aim?

a. Roger could absolutely assign the policy to Desmond.
b. Roger could collaterally assign the policy to Desmond.
c. Desmond could change the beneficiary designation by writing a letter to the insurer.
d. Desmond could write in his will that Christina will be the beneficiary of the life insurance policy.

128. Kelly is a self-employed accountant. He specializes in valuation of incorporated businesses, earning $112,000 per year over the past three years. He is taxed at a rate of 38%. He has purchased an individual disability policy with an own occupation definition of disability, residual benefits, a future purchase option, and a cost of living adjustment. The policy provides a benefit based on 60% of his income. The benefit period is to age 65, and the elimination period is 120 days. Kelly suffers a minor stroke, which leaves him totally disabled for a period of 6 months. In the seventh month, he is mostly recovered, and returns to work. However, his disability sees his income reduced, and he is only able to earn $4500 of income in that month. How much total income will he have available, taking taxes into account, in the seventh month of his disability?

a. $2790
b. $2912
c. $4595
d. $5702

129.    Kelly is a self-employed accountant. He specializes in valuation of incorporated businesses, earning $112,000 per year over the past three years. He is taxed at a rate of 38%. He has purchased an individual disability policy with an own occupation definition of disability, residual benefits, a future purchase option, and a cost of living adjustment. The policy provides a benefit based on 60% of his income. The benefit period is to age 65, and the elimination period is 120 days. Kelly suffers a minor stroke, which leaves him totally disabled for a period of 6 months. In the seventh month, he is mostly recovered, and returns to work. However, after three more months, the return to work is causing him too much difficulty, and he finds it is not manageable. His physician agrees, telling Kelly that his body needs a proper chance to recover. How will his insurance policy react?

a. This will be treated as a recurring disability and total benefits will resume with no elimination period.
b. His insurer will treat this as a new disability claim and he will have to meet his elimination period again.
c. Any further claims will consider this a pre-existing condition and no further benefits will be paid.
d. He will be allowed to continue receiving residual disability benefits.

130.    Kelly is a self-employed accountant. He specializes in valuation of incorporated businesses, earning $112,000 per year over the past three years. He is taxed at a rate of 38%. He has purchased an individual disability policy with an own occupation definition of disability, residual benefits, a future purchase option, and a cost of living adjustment. The policy provides a benefit based on 60% of his income. The benefit period is to age 65, and the elimination period is 120 days. Kelly suffers a minor stroke, but the effects are more severe than originally expected, and Kelly ends up spending 6 years collecting disability benefits. During those 6 years, inflation is 3% per year. How much disability income will Kelly collect in the first month after the sixth year of his disability?

a. $5600
b. $6440
c. $6492
d. $6687

131. Rhonda and Homer, a husband and wife, each have group benefits through their employers. Both offer coverage for prescription drugs. Rhonda was born in May of 1968 and her plan features 80% co-insurance with a $50 deductible. Homer's plan features 70% co-insurance and a $60 deductible, and he was born in November of 1967. Their son Nathan has a prescription that will cost $210 to fill. How will Rhonda's and Homer's plans react?

a. Homer's plan will pay $105; Rhonda's plan will pay the remaining $105.
b. Homer's plan will pay $105; Rhonda's plan will pay $78.
c. Homer's plan will pay $82; Rhonda's plan will pay $128.
d. Homer's plan will pay $32; Rhonda's plan will pay $128.

132. Glenn has, sadly, died while pursuing his favourite hobby, snowmobiling. He has left behind Samantha, his widow, and their two young children, ages 6 and 10. Both Glenn and Samantha have worked in Canada their whole adult lives. Which of the following government benefits would Samantha and the children receive?

a. Samantha would receive an income from Canada Pension Plan.
b. Samantha and the children would receive an income from Canada Pension Plan.
c. Samantha would receive an income from Worker's Compensation.
d. Samantha and the children would receive an income from Canada Pension Plan and education and retraining benefits from Worker's Compensation.

133. A life insurance agent located in the province of Manitoba is introduced to a new client. Upon reviewing the client's personal financial information, it becomes obvious that the client's previous insurance agent was personally spending the client's money. What action should the new agent take?

a. Report this action to the police.
b. Report this action to the provincial insurance regulator.
c. Send the offending agent a letter detailing the concerns.
d. Report this action to the offending agent's compliance department.

134.     Gurpreet and Imelda are in their mid 40s. They have started thinking seriously about retirement. To this point, they have saved a little bit. Gurpreet is a member of a defined benefit pension plan that provides nearly the maximum allowed level of contributions, and he has always assumed that the pension plan would take care of him later in life. A friend of his, however, works for a company that recently experienced a bankruptcy, leaving his friend's pension in doubt. As a result, Gurpreet would like to pursue an aggressive retirement plan that will allow him to take some risks and, ideally, build some wealth outside of his   pension. Imelda is not so sure about this, and she does not like the idea of exposing their investments to risks. Imelda has a modest amount of savings, mostly in Guaranteed Investment Certificates (GICs).   Which investment strategy would you recommend for them?

a. A leveraged investment using equity segregated funds for Gurpreet; Imelda should start a pre- authorized contribution plan using balanced mutual funds.
b. A pre-authorized contribution plan using equity segregated funds for Gurpreet; Imelda should start investing in a Registered Retirement Savings Plan (RRSP) using GICs.
c. An RRSP using equity mutual funds for Gurpreet; Imelda should continue investing in non-registered GICs.
d. A leveraged investment using equity segregated funds for Gurpreet; Imelda should start investing in a RRSP using GICs.

135.     Superfriendly Inc. has purchased a universal life policy on the life of one of its shareholders and managers, Tim. The policy has a $250,000 death benefit; $80,000 in cash value; and an adjusted cost basis of $35,000. Superfriendly is both the owner and beneficiary of the policy. Which of the following is not a reason why Superfriendly might have purchased this policy?

a. To help buy Tim's shares in the event of his premature death.
b. To generate a tax deduction for premiums paid.
c. To provide a retirement benefit for Tim.
d. To generate tax-deferred investment growth for the corporation.

136.     Eric owns a life insurance policy on the life of his nephew, . Jared has turned 30 this year, and Eric plans to assign ownership of the policy to Eric.  The policy has a $100,000 face value, a cash surrender value of $18,000, and an adjusted cost basis of $9,800.  What are the tax consequences of this assignment?

a. Neither Eric nor Jared will have any income to report.
b. Eric will have to report $8,200 of income; Jared will have no income to report.
c. Eric will have no income to report; Jared will have to report $8,200 of income.
d. Eric will have to report a capital gain of $8,200; Jared will have to report $18,000 of income.

137. Fernanda is purchasing an individual disability policy. She discloses in the application that she broke her pelvis when she was hit by a car three years ago, and that she is still on medication to treat her pain. Which of the following would not represent a way that the disability underwriter might deal with this policy?

a. Issue the policy with an increased premium.
b. Issue the policy with an exclusion for car accidents.
c. Issue the policy with a benefit period less than what Fernanda has applied for.
d. Issue the policy with a benefit period that will be shorter in the even that Fernanda's disability is related to her hip.

138. Veronica plans to leave a substantial charitable bequest. She is currently 47 years of age. You have discussed with her the idea of funding her charitable bequest with life insurance, and she thinks it is a good idea. She would like to leave a death benefit that will grow to keep pace with inflation, and she would like to be certain that the policy will not lapse if she fails to pay premiums after she retires in her late 60s. Which policy should she acquire?

a. A term to 100 policy.
b. A universal life policy with a level death benefit, indexed.
c. A participating 20 pay whole life policy with paid up additions.
d. A non-participating 20 pay whole life policy.

139. Veronica has died at the age of 71. As part of her last wishes, she left a $1,430,000 death benefit from a life insurance policy to her favourite charities. What are the tax consequences of this death benefit?

a. Her estate will receive a tax deduction for $1,430,000; this can be used to offset any income.
b. Her estate will receive a tax credit for $1,430,000; this can be used to offset any income.
c. Her estate will receive a tax deduction for $1,430,000; this can be used to offset capital gains taxes owing on her death.
d. Her estate will receive a tax credit for $1,430,000; this can be used to offset capital gains taxes owing on her death.

140.     Urban works for an employer who offers a pension plan. Urban has never been able to contribute to the pension plan. Contributions made by his employer reduce his ability to contribute to his Registered Retirement Savings Plan (RRSP). Urban knows a few people who have recently left the plan, and been given either shares in the company or a lump sum of cash on departure. Urban describes this plan to you, and asks you what type of pension plan it is:

a. Deferred profit sharing plan.
b. Defined contribution pension plan.
c. Group registered retirement savings plan.
d. Employee stock options plan.

# End of Exam

Use this sheet to record your mock exam answers.

| | | | | | | | | |
|---|---|---|---|---|---|---|---|
| 1 | | 40 | | 79 | | 118 | |
| 2 | | 41 | | 80 | | 119 | |
| 3 | | 42 | | 81 | | 120 | |
| 4 | | 43 | | 82 | | 121 | |
| 5 | | 44 | | 83 | | 122 | |
| 6 | | 45 | | 84 | | 123 | |
| 7 | | 46 | | 85 | | 124 | |
| 8 | | 47 | | 86 | | 125 | |
| 9 | | 48 | | 87 | | 126 | |
| 10 | | 49 | | 88 | | 127 | |
| 11 | | 50 | | 89 | | 128 | |
| 12 | | 51 | | 90 | | 129 | |
| 13 | | 52 | | 91 | | 130 | |
| 14 | | 53 | | 92 | | 131 | |
| 15 | | 54 | | 93 | | 132 | |
| 16 | | 55 | | 94 | | 133 | |
| 17 | | 56 | | 95 | | 134 | |
| 18 | | 57 | | 96 | | 135 | |
| 19 | | 58 | | 97 | | 136 | |
| 20 | | 59 | | 98 | | 137 | |
| 21 | | 60 | | 99 | | 138 | |
| 22 | | 61 | | 100 | | 139 | |
| 23 | | 62 | | 101 | | 140 | |
| 24 | | 63 | | 102 | | | |
| 25 | | 64 | | 103 | | | |
| 26 | | 65 | | 104 | | | |
| 27 | | 66 | | 105 | | | |
| 28 | | 67 | | 106 | | | |
| 29 | | 68 | | 107 | | | |
| 30 | | 69 | | 108 | | | |
| 31 | | 70 | | 109 | | | |
| 32 | | 71 | | 110 | | | |
| 33 | | 72 | | 111 | | | |
| 34 | | 73 | | 112 | | | |
| 35 | | 74 | | 113 | | | |
| 36 | | 75 | | 114 | | | |
| 37 | | 76 | | 115 | | | |
| 38 | | 77 | | 116 | | | |
| 39 | | 78 | | 117 | | | |

# Chapter 19 Mock Exam Solution

Complete solutions, including rationales for right and wrong answers, are available at

www.moodle.businesscareercollege.com.

**There are many additional questions to be found there**

| | | | | | | | |
|---|---|---|---|---|---|---|---|
| 1 | A | 40 | C | 79 | B | 118 | A |
| 2 | A | 41 | B | 80 | C | 119 | A |
| 3 | A | 42 | A | 81 | D | 120 | D |
| 4 | A | 43 | A | 82 | B | 121 | C |
| 5 | A | 44 | D | 83 | D | 122 | A |
| 6 | D | 45 | A | 84 | C | 123 | C |
| 7 | B | 46 | D | 85 | B | 124 | B |
| 8 | D | 47 | D | 86 | B | 125 | C |
| 9 | B | 48 | A | 87 | B | 126 | C |
| 10 | C | 49 | A | 88 | B | 127 | A |
| 11 | A | 50 | A | 89 | B | 128 | D |
| 12 | C | 51 | D | 90 | C | 129 | A |
| 13 | D | 52 | B | 91 | B | 130 | C |
| 14 | B | 53 | D | 92 | A | 131 | C |
| 15 | C | 54 | B | 93 | D | 132 | B |
| 16 | C | 55 | D | 94 | C | 133 | A |
| 17 | C | 56 | B | 95 | D | 134 | D |
| 18 | D | 57 | A | 96 | A | 135 | B |
| 19 | A | 58 | B | 97 | B | 136 | B |
| 20 | C | 59 | C | 98 | D | 137 | B |
| 21 | B | 60 | C | 99 | C | 138 | C |
| 22 | C | 61 | A | 100 | D | 139 | B |
| 23 | C | 62 | B | 101 | D | 140 | A |
| 24 | C | 63 | C | 102 | B | | |
| 25 | C | 64 | B | 103 | A | | |
| 26 | A | 65 | C | 104 | A | | |
| 27 | D | 66 | B | 105 | C | | |
| 28 | C | 67 | A | 106 | B | | |
| 29 | D | 68 | D | 107 | A | | |
| 30 | A | 69 | B | 108 | B | | |
| 31 | B | 70 | C | 109 | C | | |
| 32 | C | 71 | C | 110 | D | | |
| 33 | A | 72 | B | 111 | A | | |
| 34 | C | 73 | D | 112 | C | | |
| 35 | D | 74 | A | 113 | B | | |
| 36 | B | 75 | A | 114 | C | | |
| 37 | D | 76 | D | 115 | B | | |
| 38 | A | 77 | A | 116 | A | | |
| 39 | A | 78 | C | 117 | D | | |

# Chapter 20 INDEX